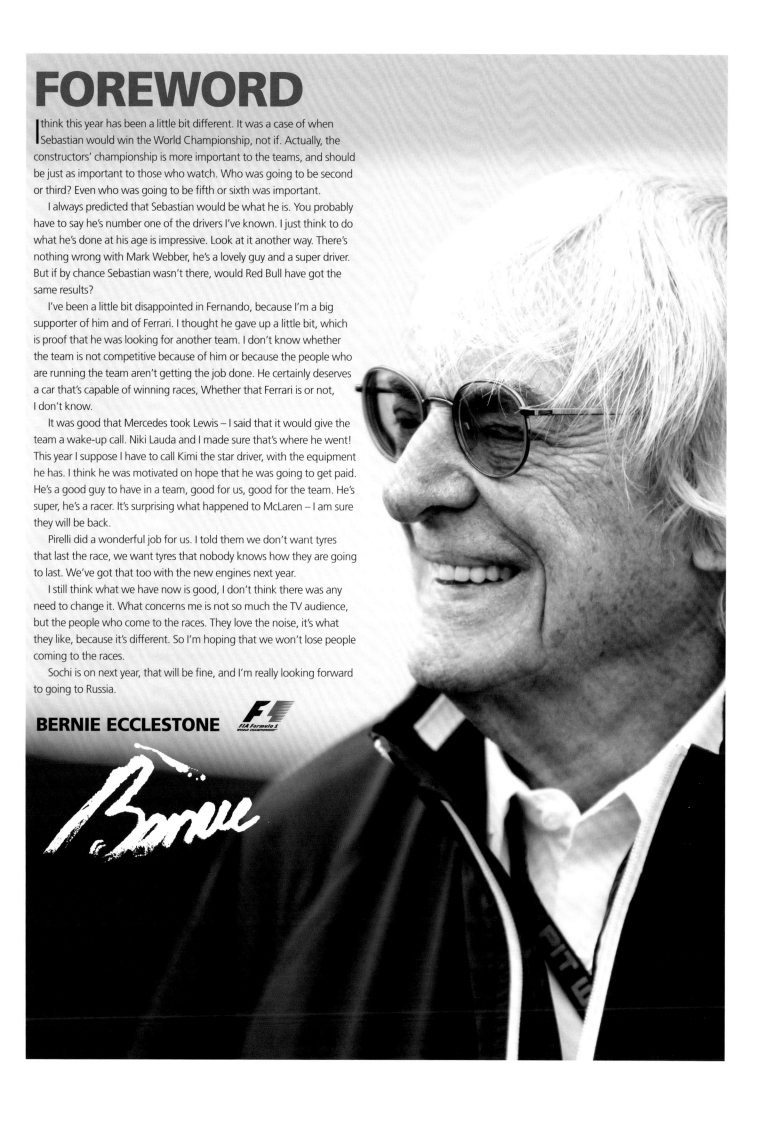

FOREWORD

I think this year has been a little bit different. It was a case of when Sebastian would win the World Championship, not if. Actually, the constructors' championship is more important to the teams, and should be just as important to those who watch. Who was going to be second or third? Even who was going to be fifth or sixth was important.

I always predicted that Sebastian would be what he is. You probably have to say he's number one of the drivers I've known. I just think to do what he's done at his age is impressive. Look at it another way. There's nothing wrong with Mark Webber, he's a lovely guy and a super driver. But if by chance Sebastian wasn't there, would Red Bull have got the same results?

I've been a little bit disappointed in Fernando, because I'm a big supporter of him and of Ferrari. I thought he gave up a little bit, which is proof that he was looking for another team. I don't know whether the team is not competitive because of him or because the people who are running the team aren't getting the job done. He certainly deserves a car that's capable of winning races, Whether that Ferrari is or not, I don't know.

It was good that Mercedes took Lewis – I said that it would give the team a wake-up call. Niki Lauda and I made sure that's where he went! This year I suppose I have to call Kimi the star driver, with the equipment he has. I think he was motivated on hope that he was going to get paid. He's a good guy to have in a team, good for us, good for the team. He's super, he's a racer. It's surprising what happened to McLaren – I am sure they will be back.

Pirelli did a wonderful job for us. I told them we don't want tyres that last the race, we want tyres that nobody knows how they are going to last. We've got that too with the new engines next year.

I still think what we have now is good, I don't think there was any need to change it. What concerns me is not so much the TV audience, but the people who come to the races. They love the noise, it's what they like, because it's different. So I'm hoping that we won't lose people coming to the races.

Sochi is on next year, that will be fine, and I'm really looking forward to going to Russia.

BERNIE ECCLESTONE

CONTENTS

It will come to be remembered as a season of two halves: 2013 – the year when Räikkönen, Hamilton, Alonso and Rosberg all rose to challenge the Vettel-Red Bull stranglehold of the FIA Formula One World Championship™, only to be effortlessly slapped down post-summer break. After the Belgian GP, round 11, Seb and his Red Bull flying machine were so dominant that they all-but-obliterated the memory of Lewis's brilliant win at a frying-pan-hot Hungaroring late in July.

At that point, with Mercedes seemingly having licked the rear tyre wear issues that had blighted their early season form (if not their outright speed), it seemed that Hamilton and Mercedes might mount a credible title challenge. Everyone, though, had underestimated how beneficial to Red Bull would be the 'new-old' tyre constructions introduced by Pirelli for the German GP, following the failure problems at Silverstone.

Free, on tougher rubber, to exploit the massive downforce advantage enjoyed by the RB9, Vettel spent the second half of 2013 simply driving away from the field to a fourth straight title. It was as dominant and immaculate a performance as the sport has ever witnessed, elevating Vettel to the league of all-time greats at the age of just 26. He didn't do it alone, of course: a car built by an Adrian Newey-led design team confers a clear competitive advantage; meanwhile Red Bull's generous funding of the race team and Renault's standard-setting V8 engines were also vital to that smooth-oiled winning groove.

But, boy, did he take full advantage of what he had. When the dust settles, it'll be hard to recall much else about 2013 besides a smiling blond kid winning out front in a Red Bull rocket.

ANTHONY ROWLINSON
EDITOR, *F1 RACING* MAGAZINE

Published in December 2013

A catalogue record for this book is available
from the British Library

ISBN 978 0 957 532 0-3-8

Editor F1 Racing magazine Anthony Rowlinson
Editor F1 Custom Steve Bidmead
Editor Bruce Jones
Managing Editors Jon Crampin, John Lilley
Design Richard Parsons, Torben Krog, Ewan Buck
Contributors Adam Cooper, Tony Dodgins,
Bruce Jones
Photographs All by LAT (Steven Tee,
Andrew Ferraro, Glenn Dunbar, Charles Coates,
Alastair Staley, Steve Etherington, Andy Hone,
Jed Leicester, Sam Bloxham).
All imagery © LAT photographic
Operations Manager LAT Tim Clarke
Illustrations Alan Eldridge
Director F1 Racing Group Ian Burrows
Account director Emma Shortt
Publishing manager Sunita Davies

F1 Racing Magazine
Haymarket Media Group,
Teddington Studios,
Broom Road, Teddington,
Middlesex TW11 9BE, UK

Tel: +44 (0)208 267 5000
Website: www.haymarket.com
Printed by: Butler Tanner & Dennis,
Frome, Somerset
Reprographic Haymarket Pre-press

£35

REFLECTING ON THE 2013
FORMULA ONE SEASON

THE 2013 SEASON

With Lotus, Ferrari and Mercedes all challenging in the first half of the season, 2013 looked like being a close fight for the championship, before Red Bull and Sebastian Vettel shot off into the distance

We've been spoiled in recent years by some tight championship battles. The 2006, 2007, 2008, 2010 and 2012 seasons all concluded with memorable finales, which in most cases kept us on our toes until the final lap.

The 2013 season wasn't quite like that, and a quick look at Sebastian Vettel's margin of victory – along with his extraordinary run of wins in the second half of the year – shows what a contrast we had with the recent past. Until the summer break, the championship still seemed to be fairly open, with Fernando Alonso and Kimi Räikkönen very much in the mix. Then, when Lewis Hamilton won in Hungary, it appeared that the momentum was with Mercedes and that he had a genuine shot at the title.

However, when action resumed at Spa-Francorchamps at the end of August, Vettel and Red Bull Racing appeared to have found an extra gear and they never looked back. Instead of a tight battle, we watched in awe as Vettel continued his assault on the record books.

Two unusual factors played a big role in how the season unfolded. One was the build-up to the 2014 season and the comprehensive package of

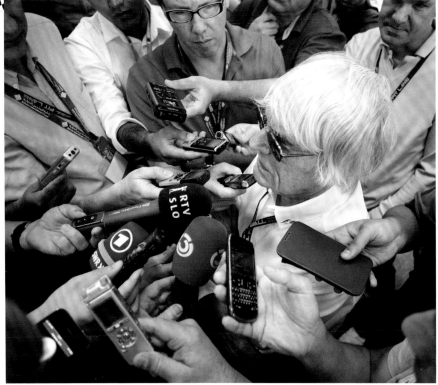

rules changes that could turn the sport on its head. Teams had barely got their 2013 cars out of the door before they began the process of switching their R&D focus to the new era. The point at which that focus approached 100 per cent was a topic of conversation all year, and there was a huge impact as one by one teams cut off the usual flow of new parts as they in effect wrote-off the rest of 2013.

Secondly, there was the change of Pirelli tyre specification, a direct result of the debacle of the blow-outs at the British GP. It was clear in the first half of the season that some cars were more suited than others to the 2013 spec tyres. Red Bull was clearly not one of them, and Christian Horner made his displeasure known at every opportunity. Quite simply, the team felt it had the best car and yet was not dominating, and tyres appeared to be the key. Silverstone provided a handy opportunity for the FIA to mandate a change back to 2012's constructions, and after the summer break we saw just how much that helped Red Bull.

There was more to it than that, of course. Adrian Newey fine-tuned a package that has been the one to beat for the past four or five years, and he continued to find useful benefits from the flow of exhaust gases, while pursuing little gains in every area. Then there was Vettel, who barely put a foot wrong all year. A Silverstone gearbox failure aside, he rarely had any bad luck, but did a brilliant job of managing his races. Despite his infamous propensity for logging fastest laps, it often seemed that he went as fast as he had to, and had plenty in hand.

The Malaysian GP 'Multi 21' saga cost him a lot of goodwill however, and in the light of Mark Webber's decision to move to sportscar racing, a win for the Australian in that race would have been a fine sign-off. As it is, Webber endured a tough year that was spoiled by the odd reliability issue and

sheer bad luck. He proved that he could still get the job done by taking pole positions, but things rarely went his way on Sundays.

For Alonso and Ferrari, it was another year of frustration. The Spaniard won in China and Spain, and typically feisty drives kept him in the title hunt until the summer. However, he was always flattering a car that was rarely good enough to qualify higher than fifth or sixth. From there he could get to the podium, but wins remained out of his grasp. There was a wobble in the middle of the year when it appeared that his relationship with the team was under serious strain, but he kept the faith. Felipe Massa continued to operate in Alonso's shadow, and then seemed to find his speed of old after being told he was not staying on for a ninth season.

Hamilton's decision to join Mercedes was vindicated when the team made a big step forward. Watching races from his living room, the retired Michael Schumacher could be forgiven for feeling frustrated by the timing of the upturn. The W04 logged a string of poles, with Hamilton and Nico Rosberg contributing until Vettel found another gear at the end of the season.

The weakness was in races, as more than once the silver cars slipped back down the order. Rosberg scored a superb victory in Monaco, and another at Silverstone, albeit after Vettel retired. Hamilton was awesome in Hungary, but was often disappointed in his own performance, perhaps a little harshly at times. The consensus is that Mercedes will have a good package in 2014, so it will be fascinating to see what happens.

Räikkönen and Lotus got off to a flying start at the season opener in Australia, and for a while the Finn looked like a genuine title contender as he consistently logged points. He lost momentum with a run of mid-season misfortune, and the change

of tyres badly hampered him in qualifying as he struggled for front end bite. Meanwhile, he became embroiled in a dispute over pay, which ultimately led him to rejoin Ferrari for 2014. An operation on an ongoing back problem was a handy reason to walk away from the team with two races to go.

Romain Grosjean was undoubtedly one of the stars of the season for Lotus, and in the latter half he often got the better of team-mate Räikkönen, with an impressive series of podium finishes. As with everyone else, wins remained out of reach thanks to Vettel's pace. However, Grosjean firmly established himself as a top-line driver and put the previous year's troubles behind him.

For McLaren, 2013 proved to be a total nightmare. Not for the first time, one of the best-resourced outfits on the grid produced a car that wasn't great out of the box. Unlike previous years, though, there was no dramatic revival as months went by. Jenson Button and Sergio Perez could on occasion creep into Q3 and score points, but they were never even close to troubling the frontrunners.

The poor form was a huge disappointment for Button, in his first year as clear team leader after Hamilton's departure, and well aware that he is rather closer to the end of his career than the beginning. It proved even more catastrophic for Perez, who found himself booted out at the end of the year. The Mexican showed flair and aggression – overstepping the mark on occasion – but for some reason his face didn't fit, and the lure of the raw talent of Kevin Magnussen proved so strong that the management decided to fast-track the Dane into a 2014 race seat.

The upside for McLaren was that the team was able to write-off the season and switch its R&D efforts towards its 2014 car rather earlier than rivals who still had an eye on the title battles, and that

ABOVE So often in the season, the Red Bulls led the pack, with Ferrari, Mercedes and Lotus their nearest challengers

OPPOSITE PAGE Kimi Räikkönen got off to a flying start at the season opener in Australia and, for a while, looked like a title contender

ABOVE So often in the season, the Red Bulls led the pack, with Ferrari, Mercedes and Lotus their nearest challengers

OPPOSITE PAGE Kimi Räikkönen got off to a flying start at the season opener in Australia and, for a while, looked like a title contender

could pay dividends. Looking further ahead, the return of Honda in 2015 is a tantalising prospect that will give the team a huge boost, in financial terms as well as performance.

Force India's season got off to a bang in Australia when Adrian Sutil signalled his return after a year off by leading the race. A bold strategy got him there and he dropped back after a pit stop, but nevertheless it was an impressive effort from a man who had spent a season on the sidelines, wondering if he would race again.

It was no fluke. The team had put extra emphasis on designing a car to work with the original 2013 tyres, and it paid off. In Bahrain, Paul di Resta challenged for a podium before finishing fourth, while a puncture forced Sutil into a first lap pit stop before he completed the remaining laps faster than race winner Vettel. The team's season took an abrupt downturn after the change of tyre specification, and several races were wasted before the drivers became regular points contenders once more. They were evenly matched and both had good days, but di Resta proved less adept at keeping the team on his side.

It was all change for Sauber in 2013 as Nico

Hulkenberg and Esteban Gutierrez replaced Perez and Kamui Kobayashi. Eyeing the Swiss team's run of podiums the previous year, the German had jumped ship from perennial constructors' championship rivals Force India, and he was in for a rude shock in Australia when his replacement Sutil starred while he endured a difficult weekend.

In the first half of the season, the grey and white cars rarely scored points, but aero updates – and the change of tyres – led to an impressive turnaround in the second half of the year. Hulkenberg qualified third at Monza and became a regular top-six contender, confirming that he is a great talent, despite the lack of faith shown by the top teams. With little in the way of preparation, Gutierrez struggled to make an impression, although there were occasional glimpses of talent later on.

From early in the year, it seemed likely that Scuderia Toro Rosso team-mates Daniel Ricciardo and Jean-Eric Vergne would be auditioning for the Red Bull seat, and that became a reality when Webber's decision was announced at Silverstone. The timing proved to be perfect for Ricciardo, who put in some stunning qualifying performances throughout the year, and deserved his promotion.

Vergne had some good races but missing out on the promotion was a blow to the Frenchman, although he did enough to retain his seat for 2014.

After winning the Spanish GP the previous year, Pastor Maldonado could be forgiven for thinking that Williams would once again be at least challenging for podium finishes, but the car proved to be hopelessly uncompetitive. Usually Maldonado and rookie team-mate Valtteri Bottas were stuck in 17th and 18th, just ahead of the 'new' teams, and sometimes even under threat from Marussia and Caterham in the races.

A minor miracle occurred at the end of the year when the team finally dumped its Coanda exhaust and bolted on a conventional set-up, and the car was instantly more competitive. Bottas, who had shown a hint of his talent with an opportunistic third on the grid at a damp Montreal, delivered a fabulous race in Austin, taking eighth place, ahead of Rosberg's Mercedes. By then, Maldonado had burned his bridges, and for team and driver the end couldn't come soon enough.

With HRT consigned to the history books, Caterham and Marussia spent the year battling for last place. They could occasionally give Williams a hard time in races, at least in the early laps, but in essence they were once again battling in a class of their own. Timo Glock and Heikki Kovalainen were gazumped by paying drivers, and thus both teams had inexperienced line-ups.

Ferrari protege Jules Bianchi was a late nomination for Marussia and, with little to lose and experience to gain, he did a good job. Little was expected from team-mate Max Chilton, but the British rookie quietly impressed alongside the more in-vogue French driver. Chilton enjoyed an astonishing finishing record and showed an ability to stay out of trouble. At Caterham, Giedo van der Garde often had the better of team-mate Charles Pic, who had given Glock a run for his money at Marussia in 2012.

There were no new events on the calendar in 2013 and, with Valencia dumped, the schedule dropped from 20 to 19 events. Next year's schedule looks a little different, with India and Korea replaced by Russia and Austria. The big change of course involves the rules and, until the cars hit the track, no one really knows what to expect. It will be fascinating to see how the technology and the pecking order evolve.

ROUND TABLE

Our panel of paddock insiders review a 2013 season dominated by Sebastian Vettel, tyres, driver politics and colourful radio language. They also debate the 2014 regulations and reveal how they'd spend a $50m investment

Sebastian's four titles – how much of that is the RB5-RB9 family and how much is Seb?

Horner It has to be a combination of the two. For any driver to have achieved four successive titles is outstanding. Sebastian has continued to improve each year since his first championship and this year has driven better than ever.

Wolff It's always a combination of the two, but you need a good car if you're going to attract an outstanding driver who can win a championship, and it's always the same guy in the Red Bull winning the world titles. It's not a big margin, but Sebastian certainly makes the difference.

Hughes He's had the best car and he's made outstanding use of it. When you watch trackside and see how Seb has adapted to some of the exhaust-blown technology, he's very special. Quite often you see Seb pull off something in races that's right on the edge, and he's delivered it.

Edwards He's got a great team-mate in Mark Webber, who hasn't finished runner-up to him in any of the championships, and that's an indication of the difference Seb makes. One question on that for you Christian, how much has the car developed because of Seb's mental approach to it. How well do they go together in that respect?

Horner Sebastian and Mark contributed equally to the development of the car. I just think that Sebastian seems to have the ability to adapt very quickly, whether that's going from no fuelling to refuelling, Bridgestones to Pirellis, blown diffusers to double diffusers. That's one of his greatest strengths. You see it again with his poles, his ability to sense and feel the grip. The more pressure you put on him, the better he delivers.

Wolff The first time I met Sebastian was on a flight from Shanghai, three years ago. There were a lot of drivers on that plane but he was the only one writing in his notebook. For the first three or four hours, he was on it. Everyone else was chilling out, but not him.

Adrian Newey says there wasn't one magic bullet, but how much of it was optimising the exhaust-blowing via cylinder cutting? Was more made of that than was the reality?

Horner In reality, probably yes. It's a lot of detail, and just working in the attention to detail areas that we did, we managed to achieve a balance with the car. We could see from pre-season testing that RB9 was a successor to RB8, which had been a difficult car on occasion. The RB9 had tidied up some of the weaknesses of RB8 and the development programme that we had, the way that the design team managed to react with the development parts has been massively impressive. It's been a season dominated by tyres. I said at the start of the year that we felt the tyres were too marginal. We were still achieving wins, but we felt they were too marginal, as we saw at Silverstone.

"IT'S UNIMAGINABLE FOR FERRARI TO BE WITHOUT A LEAD DRIVER, SO THEY SIGNED KIMI AND DECIDED TO TAKE WHATEVER FLAK MIGHT COME"

Mark, you watch out on the track a lot. Did you notice a big change from the beginning of the year?

Hughes Just that the tougher the tyre the more a high downforce car can show. You can see that even on a marginal tyre on a one-off lap, such as India where we went to a tyre that was really too soft. The RB9 was still able to put in a stunning qualifying lap, but it destroyed the tyre very quickly. As soon as you put the tougher tyre on, its superiority carried through in the race. That paints a picture nicely of what happened pre-Silverstone and post-Silverstone.

Christian, how close a call was the Daniel Ricciardo decision for 2014?

Horner We took a long time considering the options. Adrian and I deliberated about who was available in terms of experience and Kimi was a very appealing option. When we broke it down and considered who was better, not just for Melbourne next year but also the medium and longer term, having seen the progress Daniel has made over the past two years and the performances he's put in with our car, we thought it was right to give him the opportunity. From a Red Bull perspective, it made a great deal of sense as he is a product of the Toro Rosso junior team. Otherwise we have to ask a question about what the purpose of Toro Rosso is. Daniel has earned that seat on merit and we're optimistic about how he's going to perform.

Hughes It gets stale when you've got the same people in the top cars all the time, so you want to see what one of the young guys can do. It's easy to look like you might be able to do it, but you don't know until you get the opportunity. I find Daniel a much more exciting choice than if they'd put Kimi in.

Wolff Kimi would have been a better solution for next year's Australian GP maybe, but you never know. Ricciardo has proved to be really good in the junior formulae.

Horner He's very quick. Only time will tell how strong he is under the spotlight and with the pressure of being Sebastian's team-mate. It's not a task to be underestimated; it's the toughest seat in the pit lane at the moment.

Do you see Australian/German relations being repaired, or will it be just as niggly if Daniel's quick?

Hughes No, I think Daniel's a different character from Mark. He's at a different stage of his career and is excited about being an F1 driver. He's quick, he's optimistic and he's got a broad pair of shoulders. The great thing about Daniel is that no matter how badly his day's going, he's still smiling!

Is Räikkönen's return to Ferrari a risk for them? Does it reflect uncertainty over Alonso's commitment? What do you expect of him versus Alonso?

Wolff Maybe they went for the safer bet, putting someone in who will get them results rather than maybe Christian's situation with Daniel. I was surprised actually, because there were some other choices that would have been maybe a bit more risky, but good.

Horner Their relationship with Fernando in the summer wasn't great. They didn't know whether they were going to keep him or not, so it was logical to sign Kimi. I'd have done the same if I didn't know whether my lead driver was going to be there or not. It's unimaginable for Ferrari to be without a lead driver, so they signed Kimi and decided to take whatever flak might come from the other driver. It's going to be fascinating, and exciting for Stefano Domenicali, for sure!

Hughes There will be days when Kimi is quicker and it becomes a drama for the team. I don't think that overall he'll have the upper hand. It'll still be Alonso. The reason his relationship hit problems is partly to do with Red Bull's domination. That's put a big strain on everyone and among the top teams, Ferrari is the most susceptible to fracture.

(From l to r) Horner, Hughes, Edwards and Wolff debate the key issues of the season

Edwards Taking Kimi is the low-risk strategy and going into 2014 with the new rules you have a very solid power base in terms of scoring points. If you get poor reliability with next year's power units, you have to think Alonso and Räikkönen will deliver points consistently. Massa, though quick over one lap, hasn't shown that ability.

Kimi's radio comments were a feature of 2012 – being short with his engineer. But in India in 2013, with Alan Permane and his "get out of the effing way" instruction, the boot was on the other foot. Where did your sympathies lie?

Wolff Not fully appreciating the relationship, you can only give an opinion based on the radio message. Mine is that neither was right. Either you are disciplined, polite and respectful or not. I think Kimi was too harsh on the radio last year, as you don't undermine your race engineer, who is doing everything he can to help you. On the other side, maybe they shouldn't have chosen the words they did in India. I tend to be more sympathetic to the team, but maybe that's not right!

Hughes It's emotion, isn't it? A team looking at a constructors' championship position is different from the interests of a driver, being in a situation like that and being annoyed by a message and letting his opinion be felt in terms of how he'd been spoken to. Christian,

have you ever been in a situation like that?
Horner Errr, yes!
Edwards It does show the power shift there [at Lotus]. We've talked about Kimi moving to Ferrari and he was no longer the golden boy that they're putting all their efforts into. We're seeing Romain Grosjean as the guy for the future, and you can see how that developed. They needed Grosjean to come through.

Alan wasn't swearing at Kimi, it was just the situation, wasn't it?
Hughes Yes, quite. You're battling with Ferrari for third in the constructors' championship, the Ferrari's bearing down on you, one guy's 3s off because of his tyres and the other guy's got an air pressure problem so, yes, it's going to get fraught. And while Alan was just caught in the moment, the background for Kimi, the lack of respect, is probably founded on his well-documented payment problems.

Tyres were a dominant topic for the second consecutive season.

Do you have sympathy for Pirelli's predicament at the British GP?
Horner It's difficult to have sympathy. They've come up with a product that hasn't been up to the job in many respects. The one positive is that it's produced entertaining races. Whether that's through design or accident, who knows? Although there have been some exciting grands prix, it hasn't been acceptable to see large chunks of rubber coming off tyres, and we've been lucky that nobody got hurt. The key thing is that Pirelli learns from that for 2014.
Wolff What was asked of Pirelli was to provide tyres that gave more exciting racing. But, as Christian says, safety is of the utmost importance. You can't have bits of tyres flying around missing drivers by small margins. That's not acceptable. But we must have sympathy with Pirelli. They're our tyre supplier and partner and we must support them in any way possible. That's crucial for them. Give them time and miles to test in order to have the best possible tyre next year that provides good and safe racing, we need to accommodate them.

"THE BACKGROUND FOR KIMI AT LOTUS, THE LACK OF RESPECT, IS PROBABLY FOUNDED ON HIS WELL-DOCUMENTED PAYMENT PROBLEMS"

Are you confident that Pirelli can achieve that?

Hughes If you listen to their motorsport director, Paul Hembery, they're totally confident they can…

Edwards It was a difficult situation. I'm not sure they handled it particularly well at the beginning of the year. There were clearly problems early on and ultimately nothing was changed until we got to the British GP, which was obviously very embarrassing for them. But that's not entirely Pirelli's fault. The teams were pushing in different directions and some wanted to stay on the tyre and were happy with what they had.

Hughes I'm not a fan of using the tyre to manipulate the competitive order, but I do think that once the problems became apparent, their hands were tied in terms of the solution. They wanted to test more and were told they couldn't. They needed unanimous agreement and that didn't happen, and so the outcome was the tyres exploding at Silverstone, which was obviously unacceptable.

After the Hungarian GP, Mercedes looked set for a strong challenge in the second half of the year. Why didn't that materialise?

Wolff I think that somehow after the summer break we took the wrong turning. The tyres were new in Hungary, we'd been struggling with them and we tried to adapt to the fact that we were killing the rears. Then, post-break, Red Bull got it right and we got it wrong. Ferrari didn't get it right either.

Edwards There were a few operational errors at Mercedes too. An unsafe release from the pits and a nose collapse in Korea, niggly things that, when you're going for a championship, you can't let happen.

Wolff It started at Spa. We just had the car wrong from the first session and didn't recover. We were looking at gear ratios as we were struggling out of Eau Rouge, which you could see on lap 1 when Sebastian just went around the outside of Lewis. The assessment of those issues dragged in further complications and then, as you say, you add in some operational wobbles, like the unsafe

release, which was a procedural mistake, not the mistake of a single individual. When you're doing things right, the way Red Bull did, it just rolls. When you're not getting it right, these kind of hiccups happen.

Lewis Hamilton and Nico Rosberg proved to be very evenly matched. Was that a surprise to you, Toto?

Wolff Maybe it wasn't entirely expected, but then looking at the way they operate it's no surprise anymore. They are totally different as drivers and their set of skills is totally different, but they kind of come out on the same level and pushed each other all the way through the year in every single session. That's to the benefit of the team.

When you say the skill sets are different, can you elaborate?

Wolff I must be careful! Lewis has a huge talent and is an extremely gifted, natural driver. It comes from his feeling. Nico's approach comes more from assessment and analysis. He looks at data an awful lot and tries to understand why things are happening they way they do. I'm not saying that one approach is better than the other, and they both end up with similar lap times.

Hughes I've been really impressed by Nico this year. I think he's raised his game. For sure Lewis is a fantastically gifted driver, but

"SOMEHOW, AFTER THE SUMMER BREAK, RED BULL GOT IT RIGHT AND WE GOT IT WRONG. FERRARI DIDN'T GET IT RIGHT EITHER"

"2014 MAY BE CONFUSING, BUT I'M LOOKING FORWARD TO IT. ANY CHANGE OF RULES GIVES YOU SOMETHING ELSE TO THINK ABOUT"

Nico has actually done a super job. He's won two races to Lewis's one and seems to have brought the best out of himself this year. It's certainly a very strong driver pairing.

Edwards Even with Alonso and Räikkönen, the Mercedes driver pairing is the strongest at the moment. In theory, the mental approach will be better with the new rules, but you still need instinct because you're going to have to react quickly to any change.

With 2014's rule changes, what will be the gap from pole position to the back of the mid-grid next year?

Wolff The amount of work we have to do over the winter to just get it right, is unbelievable. There are big changes to the aero and chassis regulations as well as the whole new powertrain concept. It's just so different to get it into the car and package it in the right way and cool it. Reliability is going to be an issue. I'm not sure that we're going to see a lot of cars driving at Jerez for the first test in January. Is it going to be a powertrain dominated year? I don't know. I was in Maranello two months ago and have seen the engine plant there, and it doesn't look to me like this is the Italian red wine attitude – easy-going and laissez-faire. There are some good guys there pushing hard and so, honestly, at the moment, it's going to be like looking into a crystal ball.

Hughes The gaps are going to be as big as ever. When there was a significant chassis change in 2009, the gaps between teams were significant. And we've not only got a reasonable chassis change but a massively significant powertrain change and a different style of racing next year dictated by fuel economy. It's going to be very different.

Do you think it risks alienating and confusing the fans?

Horner I think there is a risk if it isn't covered properly. If we get into fuel-saving mode and so forth, then I think the commentators need the tools to be able to understand and read the race. They will also need to understand what's going on with the strategy of the teams and the drivers, otherwise it is potentially confusing.

Edwards It is going to be confusing, but I'm looking forward to it. I think any change of rules gives you something else to think about, not just for the teams but for the viewer as well. And never underestimate the F1 viewer. They're a clever bunch and they'll

get on top of it. It will be a learning process for all of us. I think there's a risk that we may lose some value as you may get one team that dominates and that will take away some interest. At the end of the day, people want to see different winners and there is a danger going into 2014 that one team will be well on top and we'll end up with a 1988 situation where McLaren won all but one race.

Hughes While there is potentially a big gap between engines, you do have some fascinating combinations. If, for example, the Mercedes engine is two seconds faster than the Ferrari engine, where's the Force India going to be relative to the Ferrari? There are always upsides.

You've got a notional $50 million to invest in a driver. You can take a driver with up to a year's experience of F1 but no more. Who would you take and where would you put him?

Hughes I'd take the $50m and do something else!

Wolff That would have been my answer too. It has massively changed over the past few years. You can see that starting

from karting onwards. You can spend €100,000 on karting, do a national series, and something goes wrong. If you look at the GP2 field today, it's costing €1.3 million and more. So, are we seeing the best talent coming up? Probably not. If you have $50 million to invest in a driver, can you ever recover that? If you look, there aren't even a handful of drivers earning really good money. I'd probably put the money in a bank account and look at the market again in 12 months.

Horner What we'd do is look at a talented 19-year-old Russian who looks like he's got a whole bunch of natural ability and put him in a Toro Rosso. And, hang on a minute… I think that's what we've done!

Edwards The best rookie this year has been Valtteri Bottas, but he's not had the chance to show that as the Williams has not been up to it. So maybe you could invest the money into making the car a bit faster.

Wolff So you want to buy a share?

Edwards I wish I had the money, Toto!

Wolff It actually reminds me a bit of Alonso in the Minardi where you saw some outstanding performances. Valtteri qualified third in the wet at Montreal and has done well against his team-mate Pastor Maldonado who is known to be quick on a single lap. Jules Bianchi looks good and both the Toro Rosso drivers look quick, so maybe there is another generation of drivers coming up who are just not able to show it yet.

NEW ENGINE REGULATIONS FOR 2014 WILL CHANGE F1

IN WITH THE NEW

Next season will see the biggest technical regulation change ever to hit F1 – the return of turbo-powered engines. It has the potential to turn the sport upside down

This season may have had a familiar ending, with Sebastian Vettel and Red Bull wrapping up a fourth consecutive clean sweep of drivers' and constructors' championships, but things could be about to change. From next season, new engine regulations and the return of turbo power threaten to turn the established order of Formula 1 on its head.

Turbo engines were last seen in F1 in 1988, eventually being outlawed after an 11-year period in which they changed the face of the sport. Renault first introduced its 'blown' 1.5-litre V6 turbo-powered engine in 1977, and over the following 12 seasons, peak power outputs doubled from around 700bhp to the one-lap qualifying engines – nicknamed 'grenades' – capable of around 1,400bhp. Turbo power had turned the cars into brutal monsters: immensely powerful and thrilling to watch, but incredibly aggressive. Even in F1, such excess couldn't last forever.

A greener, cleaner sport

The FIA attempted to curtail the rise in turbo power, introducing measures such as reducing the volume of fuel allowed in each car. But with the technology

used to monitor fuel consumption still in its infancy, the result was a succession of drivers running out of fuel within sight of the flag. Turbo engines were outlawed in 1989, and since then, normally-aspirated (non-turbo) engines have remained the only way to power an F1 car.

Until now. From next season, turbo-charged engines are back, along with a number of other power-enhancing devices. But unlike their previous incarnation, the 2014-spec F1 engines have efficiency as their mantra rather than pure power, in keeping with a more frugal age. With these units incorporating sophisticated technology including two electric motors and an energy recovery system as well as the 'base' single-turbocharged V6 engine, manufacturers believe it's no longer appropriate to refer to them simply as 'engines', preferring the label 'power units' instead.

However, this shake-up in regulations goes beyond mere technical change and will have a profound effect on F1, not least in the philosophical shift of becoming a greener, cleaner sport. From 2014 onwards, 'efficiency' will be the key word.

Exciting news for fans

It has always been that way, of course. In the previous turbopowered era, Honda engines dominated not because they were the most powerful, but because they had the best balance of power, fuel efficiency and reliability. This still holds true in 2014. "Any big rule change brings a period when people are not at the same level of reliability," says Rob White, Renault F1 deputy managing director (technical). "Then there's a period of convergence and life follows its course. We are inevitably in one of those periods. Testing and development has been very intense."

The most obvious change could be to the on-track pecking order in F1 next season. The overall level of motive force will be similar, but the 2014 cars are unlikely to be as sweetly controllable as the V8s, and the current correlation between throttle input and engine response is likely to evaporate. Minimizing this turbo 'lag' has been a priority. "There will definitely be lag if we haven't sorted it out," says Rob White. "This is a big turbo with a big old electrical motor, and that gives the potential for completely unacceptable turbo lag... of many, many seconds."

For F1 fans, that's potentially exciting news, since drivers will have to contend with power units delivering huge amounts of power, very suddenly, which equals lots of opposite-lock oversteer. A headache for them, but great for those who think F1 has become a bit too predictable this year.

But of even greater concern to the engine developers is the packaging and cooling requirements of the 2014 units. A current V8 weighs 120kg with all ancillary components (such as radiators) included. However, next year's powerplants will weigh 200kg all-in, thanks to the 145kg engine, a 35kg battery, then a further 20kg for the intercooler and other radiators.

The extra cooling capacity demanded by the electric motors and turbo not only adds weight; it means a bigger overall package to accommodate within the car's skin and also requires more voluminous air intakes. Chassis and aero teams will be dealing with dramatically different sets of numbers to those they've been used to, and inevitably, a few will get their sums wrong. Engine failures, so rare in modern F1, may return – caused either by overheating or 'under cooling' (the result of a desire to minimize disruption to airflow).

TECH TALK

HERE IS THE TECHNOLOGY EVERYONE WILL BE TALKING ABOUT IN 2014:

MGU Motor generator unit. Converts electrical energy to mechanical and mechanical energy to electrical. There are two MGUs: MGU-H and MGU-K

MGU-H Connected to the turbo. It absorbs power from the turbine shaft to recover heat energy from the exhaust gases, which can either be directedto the MGU-K or stored in the battery.

MGU-K Connected to the crankshaft of the V6. Under braking, it recovers kinetic energy and converts it into electricity. Under acceleration, it acts as a motor to propel the car.

ERS (Energy recovery system) Electronically controlled, ERS uses the MGU-H and MGU-K plus an energy store (battery). Stored energy can be used to propel the car or accelerate the turbo, and will be twice as powerful as the kinetic version used in 2013.

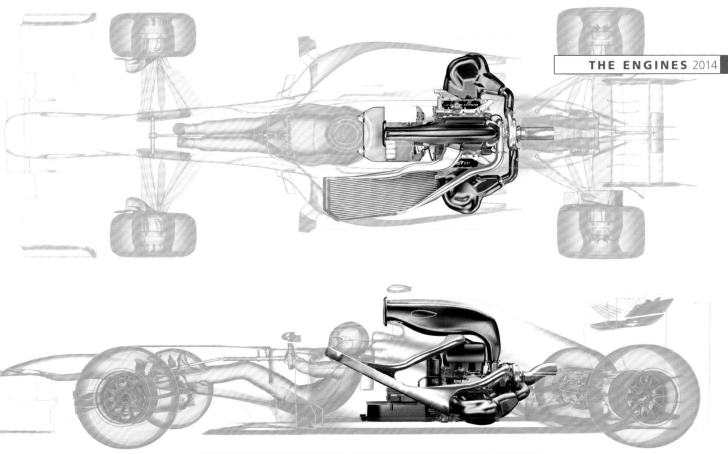

OPPOSITE PAGE Engine developers have spent hours working on the new packaging and cooling requirements

ABOVE AND LEFT The shake-up in regulations will have a profound effect on Formula 1. From 2014, 'efficiency' will be the key word

Step into the unknown

With potential reliability issues on the horizon and a lingering uncertainty over whether teams have got their sums right, Formula 1 could look very different next season. Red Bull Racing team principal Christian Horner believes the first few races of 2014 will be a step into the unknown: "Only when you get to the first race will you see what the new pecking order is," he says. "Strategy will become an even more important element and we'll be learning how to plot our way through a grand prix with a different set of parameters. The races themselves might take a completely different strategic shape and grands prix that are already marginal on fuel consumption, will be extremely tough."

The reassuring certainties of the past few years in F1 are soon to become history. The cosy familiarities of incremental year-on-year design are firmly in the past. The rulebook has been torn up, the race card scrapped. Formula 1 is about to take a big, bold leap into a higher-tech future.

STATS 2013 (V8) vs 2014 (V6)

ENGINE	2013	2014
Displacement	2.4l	1.6l
Max revs	18,000	15,000
Pressure charging	n/a	single turbo 3.5bar
Fuel flow	unlimited	100kg/hr (-40%)
Fuel permitted	unlimited	100kg (-35%)
Configuration	90deg V8	90deg V6
Cylinders	8	6
Bore	max 98mm	80mm
Stroke	unregulated	53mm
Crank height	Min 58mm	90mm
Valves	4 per cylinder	4 per cylinder
Exhausts	twin outlets one per bank	single outlet from turbine on center line
Fuel	Indir Fuel Inj	Dir Fuel Inj
Units per driver pa	8	5

THE DRIVERS

Twenty-three drivers competed in the 2013 FIA Formula One World Championship™, but one man consistently came out on top. After a season full of highs and lows, it was Red Bull's Sebastian Vettel who had the last laugh

SEBASTIAN VETTEL
RED BULL RACING

"THE HIGHLIGHT OF THE YEAR WAS THE IN-LAP AFTER THE GERMAN GP, THE FEELING I HAD WHEN I CROSSED THE LINE"

"When I was child it was always my dream, just a dream to race in F1. To be as successful as I have been, of course I'll take it and it makes me very, very proud. Equally, every race is a new challenge and every year is a new challenge, so I'm not lacking motivation, because I know how hard it is every single time to deliver inside the car, to get everything right.

"The freshest example is Abu Dhabi. I was second in qualifying, I tried a little bit too hard and Mark Webber did a better job than me. After qualifying I wasn't that happy. Now, you could argue 'Calm down, you won the championship', but it's part of me. I'm ambitious, I want to win and, if there's a chance to do so, then I want it. Fortunately, I had a very good start on the Sunday and a very good race after that!

"People tend to call it domination. I don't like the word domination, because it makes things sound easy and if we look back to every single individual race it was very, very hard work, and we put everything into it. We got great results as well as the wins, great results to finish on the podium on days when probably we shouldn't have. It's a long season, and you always want to get to your 100 per cent. If you're completely honest, you can't do that all the time, but you can get very close. That feels good when you look back.

"Obviously, when you look back at the races we had, if you look at the scoreboard, it was a great position to be in, and then of course people miss the excitement a bit. But you don't, because you know how much work you put in. I think the whole factory, everybody, knew how hard it was to get the car where it is now and to score all the points that we did.

"The highlight of the year was the in-lap after the German GP, the feeling I had when I crossed the line and to see so many people standing up cheering, It was a very special moment. I tried many times in the past couple of years to win in Germany and finally succeeded. We weren't the quickest on that day, Lotus was quicker. There was a lot of pressure from behind, yet we managed to stay in front. We got the strategy right, even though it was difficult to predict on the day how long you can go on the tyres, and I didn't do a mistake. In that regard, I got it right.

"As team-mates for the past five years, Mark and I have got to know each other very, very well, meaning that I know his strengths and not his weaknesses, but maybe the corners where I have a little bit of an advantage and vice versa. It has always been extremely close, maybe closer than how people remember, so I appreciate that and therefore have enormous respect for him.

"You have to be honest as well. We probably didn't have the best relationship on a personal level if you look back but, at the end of the day, I think we

were very successful for the team as well, winning four constructors' titles in a row. We made sure that together we scored enough points for the team.

"Next year, Daniel Ricciardo is coming in. It's difficult to judge right now, but I'm sure he will do a good job, and he will try very hard to give me a hard time. Equally, you could look back and say if you look at the line-up in 2009, Mark was part of the team and a strong element of the team, and if you want to have a successful future why would you sign up a young driver? Sign up somebody else, spend some more money, and maybe you have success. But I think this wasn't the approach back then, which is why I'm still sitting here, and it's good to see that the approach hasn't changed to make use of the drivers that Red Bull has in its driver programme."

NATIONALITY
German

DATE OF BIRTH
3/7/87

PLACE OF BIRTH
Heppenheim, Germany

HONOURS
2010, 2011, 2012 and 2013 F1 World Champion, 2004 German Formula BMW champion, 2001 European junior kart champion

and three times finished second, which is sad in a way because you are close to fighting for the title and winning. On the other hand, I'm extremely proud, as I've had the best form and the best races of my life in these years, so when I go to bed I'm extremely proud.

"When I signed for Ferrari, it was a dream come true, I came to this fantastic team. I had been fighting to get past the second qualifying session in 2009, but when I joined Ferrari in 2010 I knew that I would have the possibility to fight for the world title and maybe get it, maybe not, because this is a sport and anything can happen. Three times I fought for the World Championship, so it's more or less as I expected.

"If I didn't get it, there was one team and one driver better than us in each of these four years. They deserved it and we congratulate them. Each year, we need to raise our game and do better. Next year, we start again in that position with hopes to keep improving and to do better in 2014.

"I just need to trust the team, as I keep saying only good things about them, and for next year it will be the same. Anything can happen. Ferrari has the possibility to start this new set of rules well, as we have the facilities, the motivation and the determination to do it. There are some new names in which we have a lot of trust, like James Allison, and some others who have joined us recently, and that is our biggest motivation: the new names and the new philosophy that the team can have next year. They have real confidence that things will come back to normal next year, but it's only a hope, so we need to really push very hard, because we want to stop the Red Bull Racing domination, and next year is the time to do it.

"When he arrived this year, James had a look in terms of how the car works, and what philosophies the team has followed in the past two years, especially with the blown exhaust. Some things he agreed with and some things he probably didn't agree with, but we have a lot of changes in the team's structure and in the organisation of the aerodynamic side as well for next year. He has been more focused on that than the parts on the car for next year.

"The motivation is always high. Obviously, we are fighting for the world championship which is an extra boost, but if not the motivation is still always there, even if I do a race in karts with my friends, because, if I lose, I don't like it! So imagine in an F1 Grand Prix, the motivation is always 100 per cent.

"I have a lot of expectations of me at every race I attend, to see what I can do different or what I can do to improve the result that we should be getting. I know that I need to always push harder, and that's my motivation, because people expect a little bit extra from me, and I try to do it."

2 FERNANDO ALONSO
FERRARI

NATIONALITY
Spanish

DATE OF BIRTH
29/7/81

PLACE OF BIRTH
Oviedo, Spain

HONOURS
2005 and 2006 F1 World Champion, 1999 Formula Nissan champion, 1997 Italian and Spanish kart champion, 1996 World kart champion

"Obviously, we would have liked to have been more competitive, but we know that at some tracks we historically struggle a bit more, and we confirmed that this year in a way. We were not very competitive at the end of the season, but then again we were not competitive in July, not competitive in August and also not competitive in September, but we still collected five podiums, including three consecutive second places in the Belgian, Italian and Singapore GPs. These results masked the problems that we were having a little bit, and later we came back to reality.

"Of course I would like to win, and I am still only 32, so it's not the last year of my career. I am sure that I will have further opportunities and of course I would like to win more championships. In these past four years, I fought for three World Championships,

"I'VE BEEN VERY FORTUNATE TO HAVE A LONG CAREER IN F1. NEXT YEAR WILL BE A NEW CHAPTER FOR ME WITH PORSCHE"

"You use all the energy you can to lift and perform, work hard with the guys. Even when you've got a handy car, you've still got to put the work in to be at the front and challenging week in, week out. I've pushed Seb, I pushed Fernando over the line at Monza, which was a great battle between the pair of us. In Singapore, I was challenging at the end, closing Kimi down for a podium when the engine went.

"The German GP was a good battle for Seb and I, the out-lap was going to be tight for him, I was going to be close to jumping him, but we lost the tyre in the pit lane and so I lost a lot of points there.

"I feel as though I've been driving really, really well. It's been nice in a way because I made the decision that I wanted, but I wanted to be able to show some results, and that's the more frustrating thing as a lot of results have slipped through my fingers for absolutely no fault of mine. For whatever reason, that's what happened. There's nothing like that smell of champagne, which I've experienced a lot obviously, but this year has been quite bizarre really in terms of the technical failures.

"I don't know why we had so many problems this year. The guys do what they can on the cars to get them as well prepared as possible, but we seemed to be having a lot of issues, which was disappointing for all of us in the team, and not just me.

"Seb has had an incredible run. Some of the championships have been tight, some less so. Obviously, 2011 and this year have been pretty much a non-event, but 2010 and 2012 went up to the last race. I think he's done an incredible job. He has been very strong on the Pirellis. It was a little bit tighter between us on the Bridgestones, but on Pirellis he's certainly been very strong and shown no real weaknesses on those tyres. He has been super consistent, and that's what's made him strong, as well as getting the most out of the package. The car's been quick and he's capitalised on a lot of venues. He's won with a dominant car, but he has also won with a car at some races when it hasn't been so. Seb has certainly won some races over these past four years that he probably shouldn't have won.

"I've been a bit less fired up for the past few years, let's say, and the decision to leave F1 was getting close around Christmas 2012. I've been very fortunate to have a long career in F1. Next year will be a new chapter for me with Porsche. Obviously, a lot of people are interested in Le Mans and Porsche's return. I accepted that I couldn't be in F1 forever, and you'll see many of the other guys also stopping in the next one or two years as this generation is coming to an end. I did what I could in F1, of which I'm proud, and now I'm heading on to the next chapter.

3 MARK WEBBER
RED BULL RACING

"I want to have good motivation for Porsche as there's no point in getting there when you are completely empty, so I'll be in good shape for them. We have a good association with them for the future, both with the racing cars and the incredible road cars they have. I'm looking forward to good times ahead.

"I'll miss a lot of races, like Melbourne, Monaco, Monza, the British GP and Suzuka. Bizarrely, the only track where I haven't been on the podium is Melbourne, so I was pretty disappointed not to manage that. I know that, apart from Le Mans, I'm not going to get that type of atmosphere again.

"I hope Daniel Ricciardo does well, and I hope he does a lot of winning and can fly the flag. I took the championship to the last race in 2010, so he has to try to go one better and win it… That's his job."

NATIONALITY
Australian

DATE OF BIRTH
27/8/76

PLACE OF BIRTH
Queanbeyan, Australia

HONOURS
1996 Formula Ford
Festival winner

"It's been above expectations this year in terms of the team's performance and how I've got along with the team, which is great. From my side of things, I'm not 100 per cent happy with my performance during the year. I can't pinpoint exactly why.

"Qualifying has been strong, which is nothing new for me, I've generally been a good qualifier, really. I would say more so my race performances haven't been so good this year. We would have loved to have won more races, as it would have been cool to have been able to convert poles into wins. We generally had a quicker car in qualifying than we did in the races.

"I'd been at McLaren for a long time, and every year I'd pretty much had the car built for me, around me, and I was more comfortable in the car. The car was at a point where I could put it where I wanted to put it, as we'd tuned it for a long, long time. This year, I've really struggled with the car, so inevitably I've not been able to reach my real potential.

"There have been some good races. The times when the car was really good, like Monaco for example, when I should have been on the top of it, but I really struggled with it. I've been struggling mostly with the car and the electronics and everything.

"I didn't want fewer controls on the steering wheel, I'm always looking to make the steering wheel lighter, and they have a lot more buttons and things on the steering wheel, lots more options than I had at McLaren. I didn't need a lot of them, as some things you just don't need. I don't need a radio reset button, as you can have that on a multi-function switch if you need to reset it for example, so that's one less switch. So, it's things like this that I tried to do and for next year you'll see I will have fewer switches.

"The Hungarian GP win and the podiums we had were highlights, and the pole positions were pretty cool. Again, all the pole position laps apart from the one at Silverstone, weren't even that special laps. Just imagine if I was happy in the car, it would have been a lot different. I'm not a long, long way off, but it's not 100 per cent, that's for sure. I have a lot more input into next year's car, so I won't be driving Michael Schumacher's car next year, I'll be driving my car.

"We're very fortunate that we have a very stable platform. Nico Rosberg has been here for some time, so we're the only team that's not having to work with a driver change really. So hopefully that will have a positive effect next year.

"This year hasn't been perfect for me, and I'm always trying to learn and improve. There are lots of areas that can always be improved on, from myself and from the team, and we're just working on those because we don't want to carry the negatives of anything we have into next year.

4 LEWIS HAMILTON
MERCEDES

"Red Bull Racing have done an incredible job for some time now, so they've raised the bar and everyone just needs to work harder. We're working as hard as we can as a team to put the energy into next year and hope that we can compete with them. That's what I'd love to do and ultimately what the team desires too. That's what the dream is. There's a long steep curve for us to climb for next year, but it's more of a level starting field for everyone, and you can either get it right or wrong. Hopefully we're on the right side.

"It would have been nice to be fighting with Seb in those years. I was very, very fortunate when I came into the sport, as not many people get to come in and be in a top team and have a chance to fight for the World Championship in the first year, and I was very, very fortunate to do that."

NATIONALITY
British

DATE OF BIRTH
7/1/85

PLACE OF BIRTH
Stevenage, England

HONOURS
2008 F1 World Champion, 2006 GP2 champion, 2005 European F3 champion, 2003 British Formula Renault champion, 2000 European Formula A kart champion

5 KIMI RÄIKKÖNEN
LOTUS

NATIONALITY
Finnish

DATE OF BIRTH
17/10/79

PLACE OF BIRTH
Espoo, Finland

HONOURS
2007 F1 World Champion,
2000 British Formula
Renault champion,
1998 Finnish and
Nordic kart champion

"We didn't have very good qualifying in the second half of the season, but we were still up there in the races, and that's what counts in the end. Since we changed the tyres mid-season, it was more like it was in 2012, and for me it was definitely better in qualifying with the other tyres as they were a bit more sharp at the front. We had to find a way to get it back where we wanted to be, and it hit us quite hard in qualifying.

"The limits on the cambers and pressures add up to a lot. There aren't many things you can do, and unfortunately we were a bit stuck. If we were free to do what we want with the cambers, it would be a much easier thing. For one lap, it was an issue, but in the race it's not so much as you don't push as much in certain places.

"WE HAD TO FIND A WAY TO GET IT BACK WHERE WE WANTED TO BE, AND IT HIT US QUITE HARD IN QUALIFYING"

"I like to race and that's the only reason why I'm here. It doesn't matter which team it is and obviously the reason why I left Lotus is purely on the money side. They haven't got my salary, so it's an unfortunate thing. As for Ferrari, I just have to say things change a lot in F1. I never had a bad feeling with them, really. I still have a lot friends and good memories from there. I knew that my contract will end at the end of this year, so I had to make some kind of decision what to do for 2013.

"I know the team and I know the people. Obviously, there are some new people and some have left since I was there, but most are the same. I don't think it will be too difficult to go there and do well. The car will obviously be different, so I think that will be the most difficult thing, to get the cars right and get them running reliably. Whoever makes the best car will probably make the best out of it.

"I don't see the reason why it wouldn't work with Fernando. We're old enough to know what we're doing, and the team is working for the right things to make sure. If there is something, I'm sure we can talk it through. It's not like we are 20-year-old guys any more. I might be wrong, but time will tell. I'm pretty sure everything will be good. For sure, though, there will be hard fights on the race circuits.

"You always learn from different team-mates. Everyone does different things. Maybe they do something better than you, but often there are a lot of things that only suit one guy, and it doesn't work if you try to do the same thing for yourself. I know the team, I know the people. Like I said, I have no worries about going there and have something that won't work. I don't really worry about it. I've never worked with Fernando. Of course, I know him from racing but I'm sure it will be fine.

"Obviously, there are new rules so it will be more challenging for all the teams, but I have no worries about those things. Ferrari built very good cars and engines in the past, they've won a lot of championships as a team, but you have to look at teams like Red Bull or Lotus with Renault, who have done very well. It's very hard to say which way it's going to go with 2014's new rules, and who's going to have the best package.

"There are a lot of stories about certain engines that will be much stronger than others, but there are so many different things that you have to look at and go through and make sure that it works that I have no idea which team will be strongest and which team will come out on top. We have to wait and see, really, for the first few tests. I don't see any reason at all why we shouldn't be able to produce a very good car for next year and keep improving it."

6 NICO ROSBERG
MERCEDES

"I've really enjoyed this season, because it's the first time in my career that I've really had a car that on numerous occasions I can win with. To come to a grand prix knowing I can put it on pole and win the race is a really great feeling.

"Monaco will remain the highlight for many, many years. It's the most prestigious race to win, the most difficult race to win, the most historic race to win, and it's my home town where I grew up. It was really amazing.

"The low was Nürburgring qualifying, my home race, where I had a shot at pole, and qualified 11th. The other frustrating one was Korea, where my front wing dropped off just as I was set for a podium finish. Then there were all those poles where I just dropped back in the race, like in Bahrain and Spain. I led the whole first stint in Barcelona and, even at that point, I was still thinking I could pull this off all the way to the end. To then just get swallowed up is not a nice feeling…

"It was a completely different experience with Lewis this year compared to Michael. The challenge is similar as both are very tough competitors, but just everything is different, from the way to work with the other person, the strengths and weaknesses. There are a lot of differences. For us, though, it's working well. We push each other and this means that through a weekend we step up our game and learn from each other, so it's working well.

"The target is to be the best, we have to win next year. The regulation changes are a great opportunity for us. Of course, it won't be easy and nobody knows, so it's so difficult to expect anything for next year. The main difference is obviously the engine, and not having the Coanda exhaust, so you will have all that torque but less grip on the exits.

"The tyres might prove to be another aspect. It could be like when traction control was dropped and we were all panicking. Then, actually, it was very straightforward, so I'm not very concerned. There will be a lot of work going into fuel consumption and managing your race, and things like that. I don't think it's going to be boring for the fans, but it will be something we have to work on."

NATIONALITY German
DATE OF BIRTH 27/6/85
PLACE OF BIRTH Wiesbaden, Germany
HONOURS 2005 GP2 champion, 2002 German Formula BMW champion

7 ROMAIN GROSJEAN
LOTUS

"I wish I could have produced some better races early on, but I had a very slow start. Staying out of trouble was clearly one of the objectives. Also, we had a KERS map that wasn't suiting me and I couldn't get any feeling from the car. However, things began to get a little bit better as we sorted out the engine map and made it back to the podium at the Bahrain GP.

"It came together in the German GP, and that was a good race. We then had a run of podiums at the end of the season. I made a small mistake in Korea, when Kimi got past, and I advanced from there, working out what had happened, what I had done wrong. That's what keeps me moving forward. The Japanese GP was a very good race, and India was a good one too. If you told me after qualifying in India that I'd be on the podium, I'd have said you're crazy!

"In the second stint in Japan, we had hard tyres, but they were already five laps old. With a different qualifying strategy, maybe with new tyres, we could have just about opened a gap. You never know, as you need to get everything perfect to win races. It didn't work very well in qualifying in India, because we wanted to keep as many sets of options for Q3 as we could, but sometimes you need to take risks to get to the next level.

"Monaco was the biggest disappointment. The car was good and we were back to a super quick level. It was a good weekend, but I crashed in the race and got a ten-place grid penalty for the next one, and it wasn't a good memory. I wanted to go too quick, dancing quicker than the music, so I learned from that to just do things step-by-step.

"We missed the low downforce package for some reason, but the car we had since Singapore was working very well, being very consistent at every single track we went to. Qualifying was getting better and the races were getting better too. We developed a very good baseline set-up that allows us to get more time and try new things when we wanted to. If they didn't work, we just put them to one side."

NATIONALITY French
DATE OF BIRTH 17/4/86
PLACE OF BIRTH Geneva, Switzerland
HONOURS 2011 GP2 champion, 2010 Auto GP champion, 2007 European F3 champion, 2005 French Formula Renault champion, 2003 Swiss Formula Renault 1600 champion

8 FELIPE MASSA
FERRARI

"It's not been the best season for me, I can do much better than what I did this year, and over the last couple of years. I think what is important to know is that I have the speed, I know how to win, I know how to be competitive, and we just need to try to put things together. This season we had some very good races, but we had some very difficult races.

"I'm very honoured to finish a very long time with Ferrari. I had incredible moments in this team, very happy moments and so many victories. I was a long time in Ferrari. I've had a contract with them since 2001, so I was with the team even longer than Michael Schumacher, and I think that's really an honour to finish this moment in a very happy way for both me and for Ferrari. Ferrari will always part of my history, I'll always be close to this team.

"However, I'm very enthusiastic and very happy to sign a contract with Williams for next year. I'm really looking forward to this challenge in my career, and I'm very

motivated. I'm sure I have a lot to give to Williams, there's a lot of work to try to get away from this difficult moment that Williams has been passing through.

"I think it's a very big team. I was really surprised for what I see inside the company. I think they have all the possibilities to have all the infrastructure to do a good job. It's always important to put the pieces together, and what I'm very happy about is that so many pieces are changing inside the team to help and to try put together a change for the future, to try to bring back Williams to what they were for a long time: a competitive team, a competitive car and part of the history of F1. They are going to have the Mercedes engine, which I'm pretty happy about, because people are talking optimisitically about Mercedes for next year.

"For sure, big teams always have more possibilities to build a good car, but it's a big change for everybody, and maybe you will see teams that didn't have a good year in 2013 being in good shape for 2014."

NATIONALITY Brazilian
DATE OF BIRTH 25/4/81
PLACE OF BIRTH Sao Paulo, Brazil
HONOURS 2001 Euro F3000 champion, 2000 European Formula Renault champion

9 JENSON BUTTON
McLAREN

"The season wasn't what we expected at the end of last year, after winning the final two races. When we got to the first race this year, we realised there was a problem, and we changed a lot on the car through the year.

"The aim of catching up with the top teams was always going to be impossible, because they're not hanging around either. We have improved our car over 1s compared with last year, but the problem is that other cars were 2s up the road, like the Red Bull. I think we've done a good job in terms of development, but we started from such a low place that it was always going to be tricky.

"We still thought that we could catch up but, looking at it now, it was never going to happen. I think we were just excited at the start of the year. You hope that you can get back to the front, because it's what I've been used to with this team since I've been here. I think we realised when we got to Canada that we weren't going to win a grand prix.

"The Belgian GP was a good turning point, and we felt we had turned a corner and

improved the car, and we had, but we didn't really improve from then. We finished sixth at Spa, which was a good race, but still behind the top teams. Then we didn't make progress after that. What threw us more was that the Saubers were quick once they had sorted out their issues.

"The car was good in India, but I didn't get the result that I wanted as I crashed with Fernando at Turn 4 and that gave me a puncture so it destroyed the race. Checo did really well, though, to get a fifth place. It would have been nice if we could both have been up there. The car didn't feel bad in the last few races but, as we were a full second faster than last year's car, it shouldn't feel bad. The other cars were just even quicker. I can't imagine what it's like to drive a Red Bull!

"It was a tough year, but I think a good learning year in terms of when you're not fighting for a championship you try everything. You try every set-up that you possibly can, and we've definitely done that this year, so we've learned a lot."

NATIONALITY British
DATE OF BIRTH 19/1/80
PLACE OF BIRTH Frome, England
HONOURS 2009 F1 World Champion, 1998 Formula Ford Festival winner, 1997 European Super A kart champion

10 NICO HULKENBERG
SAUBER

"The first half of the year was disappointing, especially if you look at somewhere like Barcelona, where I did a stunning lap in qualifying. It couldn't have been better, it was the perfect lap for me, yet I ended up 15th!

"That was pretty frustrating, because you do a move to another team and obviously you always want to go forward, and then it turns out to be not so good. On the other hand, you can't be thinking about that all the time, you just need to give your best. At least when I achieve 100 per cent that gives me a certain satisfaction, which I can live with.

"In Malaysia, I scored some points in my second race with Sauber, after a difficult race spent fighting the Lotuses off, including Kimi Räikkönen who had won the first race, so it wasn't too bad. Then I led for a while in China, but even though I wasn't the true leader – I was in front because of a running different strategy compared to the frontrunners – it was a bit of a highlight.

"After that, though, it wasn't looking so good. In the first half of the year we clearly didn't have the performance, we didn't have the speed to challenge for Q3 or for the points. Our problem was that the Sauber C32 suffered from a lack of grip that stopped us going around the circuit quicker. Of course we put on some updates, with a big one in Budapest and then some small bits and bobs. I think the tyres did the rest.

"Going to the Italian GP, I wasn't really sure that we'd be that good, and going away from Monza having had the good results I wasn't sure what to expect for the next couple of races, because it's a unique circuit.

"What we did in Korea was outstanding. I'm really happy and proud of that, but we probably punched above our weight and outperformed a few cars that we shouldn't. There was an opportunity and we grabbed it.

"Our understanding of how we set up the car and how we operate it was very different to the beginning of the year when we weren't competitive. We learned how to get around some of the weaknesses of the car and that was pretty powerful."

NATIONALITY German

DATE OF BIRTH 19/8/87

PLACE OF BIRTH Emmerich, Germany

HONOURS 2009 GP2 champion, 2008 European F3 champion, 2006/07 A1GP champion, 2005 German Formula BMW champion, 2003 German kart champion

11 SERGIO PEREZ
McLAREN

"It has been a shocking year, and I'm disappointed and frustrated, not only for myself but for McLaren. I joined a team that had been pretty much on top in recent years as well as throughout its whole history. This is F1, though, and things change quickly.

"We thought we could improve during the season. It was my first season with McLaren, and all I knew was the history, that they had had to recover from bad cars. We did very big steps, but the issue was that we started so far behind and other teams improved as well. Then we had to stop development on the car to focus on 2014. We did that sooner than other teams, so it's been a very painful year, and that's no secret. We got it wrong, basic parts of the car were wrong and to recover from that was very difficult.

"As much as it has been painful for me, it has been painful for every single guy that works back at base and at the track, coming here knowing that we'd be fighting just to get into Q3, fighting the midfield teams. This isn't McLaren and it's not where we wanted to be.

"McLaren works in a very different way to other teams I've worked with, so it took time to adapt myself to the team, the philosophy and the way we set up the cars. Also, it didn't help with the car being so difficult, but it helped my learning, and my learning with the team was pretty strong. The results probably don't show the progress we made as a team.

"We had some bad luck in the races. If you look at Monaco, it was great until I retired. If you look at Silverstone, it was great until the tyre exploded. If you look at Korea, it was going to P7 without the tyre exploding. If you look at Japan, without the many issues we had I'd have got P7 or P6. It reflects that when you're fighting just to get into Q3, you're out of the points if the race doesn't go perfectly and nobody looks at the performance. When you're fighting for ninth and 10th, or 12th and 13th, nobody looks at you at or at your potential, but this is F1.

"I'm sure I'm a better driver than I was last year, and I'm just becoming stronger."

NATIONALITY Mexican

DATE OF BIRTH 26/1/90

PLACE OF BIRTH Guadalajara, Mexico

HONOURS 2007 British F3 national class champion

12 PAUL DI RESTA
FORCE INDIA

"The work for 2013 actually started on Friday morning in Brazil last year when we got the new tyres to test. I think the team was quite clever in how we approached it, and what we came away thinking. I know it was different to what other teams thought. And, yes, that car was designed around the tyre. Unfortunately, that changed due to unforeseen circumstances after the British GP.

"Looking at the results tells the story of how our season's been as a team since Silverstone. We were hampered because of the tyre change, but it was encouraging how we got it together again. There was a point when we wondered as a team whether we were going to get back on track. And we did it.

"Credit to everyone, credit to the whole team. I think every single person had the faith. It's been a joy to drive the last few races and actually feel like the car was back on song. It was looking like we weren't going to get it back, but if you have the feedback, those are the results you can get. That's the consistency you need. It's something this team is very good at. After finishing sixth in Abu Dhabi, we were probably happier than the guys who won.

"We've been close to podiums and had qualifying results that stand out like Silverstone. To qualify fifth around probably one of the hardest tracks on the calendar, when the pressure's on with it being a British team and everybody's home grand prix, there was a lot to take from it. Some of the race strategies stand out, and one that really does is Canada. We had a difficult qualifying, started at the back, and did a one-stop to seventh place. It was crazy.

"Sometimes we were racing the guys that qualified on pole. In Barcelona, my DRS broke and I finished seventh racing against Rosberg. Had the DRS worked, I'd have finished sixth, and that was against the car that was on pole. We haven't been able to replicate that too much, but we have put ourselves in the mix.

"Fortunately, in that run of retirements I had there was only really one chance to score points, and that was Singapore. That was quite a big chance to score eight points, but in the other ones I don't think we were up to speed."

NATIONALITY British
DATE OF BIRTH 16/4/86
PLACE OF BIRTH Uphall, Scotland
HONOURS 2010 DTM champion, 2006 European F3 champion, 2001 British Super 1 kart champion

---

13 ADRIAN SUTIL
FORCE INDIA

"It was nice to be back in the sport, and it was nice to have a very good car at the beginning of the season. I had one year off to think, to reset everything, to consider what you want in your life, are you still happy in the sport or not?

"In Australia, I chose a different strategy, and also the car was very fast. It was my first race with only a few test days before, so it wasn't the best preparation, but still I found it quite easy to step back in the car, and I didn't forget how to drive an F1 car. It was nice to lead the race for such a long time. I think I showed what I'm able to do, that I'm also fine to race in the front. If the car is fast enough, I can do it, and I think that it was a good message out to the world.

"We gave away four great races, though. We had a pit stop problem in Malaysia, when a strong finish was definitely possible, and also in China, where I was hit by Esteban Gutierrez. In Bahrain, we had a chance almost to win the race. I had a puncture on the first lap there. I got it from Massa and then I had the fastest race pace in the whole field – even faster than Vettel. It just shows that was the chance of the year. Then we went to Spain and we had another problem with the pitstop when I was on the way to fifth position.

"Putting this all together, if we had just scored half of the points that we were able to get we would be looking really, really good. So, on the one hand, it was nice to be back, but we missed a few good opportunities. Then Monaco was great, where finally we finished fifth in the race.

"We had a little down after Silverstone with the change of the tyres. It happened quickly and suddenly we had no chance any more and you could really see that it was going backwards, and we didn't really know how to improve. Also knowing that we weren't developing the car any more wasn't helping. So it was really, really difficult to handle the situation, but we worked hard then got back in the points and had some good races."

NATIONALITY German
DATE OF BIRTH 11/1/83
PLACE OF BIRTH Starnberg, Germany
HONOURS 2006 Japanese F3 champion

14 DANIEL RICCIARDO
TORO ROSSO

"A big goal of mine was if the Red Bull seat became available this year to get it, and I've achieved that. I don't think anyone has had the perfect year – apart from maybe Seb! A lot of other guys will always say they could have done better, but generally speaking my runs in Q3 have been good.

"I think the qualifying definitely helped. For sure Red Bull want to see speed, and Vettel's got the speed and racecraft. I think you can get quicker, but it's something that you have or you don't. Racecraft is a bit easier to learn. That's the thing I had going for me in 2012. My Sundays were improving this year, not all of them, though I converted more of those races when I reached Q3 into points, and that was good.

"It didn't really show in the first two races, as Australia and Malaysia weren't good for us, but come China we really put our foot down and got the result I knew we had in us. It was nice to get that quite early.

"When Mark Webber announced his retirement, the focus was on me and Jean-Eric Vergne in particular, although there was Kimi Räikkönen as well. They were seeing how we went under pressure, and that's when I had a really good run of qualifying and races. In terms of qualifying, my Silverstone lap was excellent, Germany and Hungary were really good ones too – particularly the Q2 laps there to get me into Q3, I was really impressed with those.

"The team has worked better as a unit. There was a bit of change going on in 2012, and during the season these things aren't ideal. This year we came in and there was a bit more stability, so that helped the guys build a better car. I think that I was driving better, too, so it all worked hand-in-hand.

"James Key has been good. Obviously, no disrespect to Giorgio Ascanelli, as I got on with him well. James had a pretty big task ahead of him, but I think he's coped really well and they have produced a better car this year. It's never as good as they want, and that's motorsport, but I think that they have done a good job."

NATIONALITY Australian
DATE OF BIRTH 1/7/89
PLACE OF BIRTH Perth, Australia
HONOURS 2009 British F3 champion, 2008 WEC Formula Renault champion

15 JEAN-ERIC VERGNE
TORO ROSSO

"It's been a frustrating season. When you look on paper it looks quite bad, with many DNFs and many bad results, but the fact that I'm staying for next season means something, and it means that the team has the tools and they know exactly what's going on at every race. They know my performances. The problem is that so many things went wrong this year, bad luck, problems, mistakes from me, from the team, so I think it's been really down.

"I improved a lot after Bahrain, so from the Spanish GP onwards. I had a good race there, and then I had a tyre explosion. In Monaco finally the work I was putting in paid off, and I finished in a good position. Then Canada was an absolutely normal weekend, no problems, no luck, nobody in front of me crashed or whatever, and I finished sixth.

"At Silverstone, we had a really good car, I was heading for Q3 and I got stuck on my flying lap and went off. So I was in Q2 while Daniel went into Q3. Then I was doing a really good race and I had my tyre explosion. After the safety car, I had less downforce because the car was too damaged, so I came in. I was quicker than Massa for the whole weekend. I was two cars in front of him at the restart of the race after the safety car, and he was one of the only drivers to have new options at the end like me. And he finished fourth...

"Then we had the announcement of Daniel driving for Red Bull at the Silverstone rookie test, so I was feeling a bit down after that, as I knew it was him and not me for 2014. After that, I just had problems and bad luck. It's been a bit tough! Something broke on the floor in qualifying at Monza, and in the race the driveshaft broke. It was brakes in Korea then a brake fire in Japan. It's been like this for the whole season. Every time there's been something, whether I finished the race in bad position or don't finish the race at all.

"I feel really comfortable in the team, I really like the team and I like working with the great people working here. Obviously James Key arrived and made his input into the team, which has been great – and we'll really see the results with next year's car."

NATIONALITY French
DATE OF BIRTH 25/4/90
PLACE OF BIRTH Pontoise, France
HONOURS 2010 British F3 champion, 2008 French Formula Renault champion, 2007 French Formula Campus champion

16 ESTEBAN GUTIERREZ
SAUBER

"There were a lot of things happening through the year, to be honest, things that probably made my rookie experience a bit more unstable than it could have been. The team's situation wasn't an easy one, with all these rumours and drama happening in the middle of the year. At the same time, we were struggling a lot at the beginning. We don't have a simulator where I could train, and testing wasn't allowed. On three of the six days of testing I did in the winter it was raining, so there were a lot of things to be considered.

"From starting my first grand prix in Melbourne to my feeling now, there has been a huge difference. It took me a little time as a driver to understand all the things on the technical side, from the engineering point of view. But once I really managed to understand the whole picture, and to adapt completely to it, I became very confident about every decision I made with the engineers. At the same time, I got the confidence to push in certain directions and take more risks, as I did in Singapore.

"My range of knowledge is very wide thanks to everything I've been learning. I've been experimenting as well, and sometimes experimenting means you take risks. You have to take them and sometimes you make mistakes, and then you learn from them.

"The main thing was that the difference to my team-mate, Nico Hulkenberg, at the beginning of the year was quite big, and I was closing that gap in the last few races. Not only was I doing this in qualifying, but also in the races. At the end of the day, my focus was on my job. The team knew very well how the situation was and, considering that, how my development has been. Also, you need to gain experience in your rookie season, you need to learn through the difficult things, you need to experience that. It's the same for every rookie.

"In terms of the races, I'd say Japan and India were the best. Seventh place in Japan was a great result. Unfortunately, I had a drive-through penalty for a jumped start in India, which affected me a lot. However, if you see the performance during the race, the fights and everything, it was very good."

NATIONALITY Mexican

DATE OF BIRTH 5/8/91

PLACE OF BIRTH Monterrey, Mexico

HONOURS 2010 GP3 champion, 2008 European Formula BMW champion, 2005 Mexican Rotax Max kart champion

17 VALTTERI BOTTAS
WILLIAMS

"It's been tough, and I've learned a lot, that's for sure… I think, being such a demanding season, 2013 has also made me stronger as a driver. The most difficult thing has been finding out that when you give everything and think you've had a good race, the result still isn't there.

"I've learned, though, that once you come to the race weekend and tune the set-up and do everything you can, then after that the car is what it is, and the main thing for you is always to make the most of it. I think that's been a very important lesson, and definitely this year's experience will help me next year.

"I always think I'm never going to give up, I'm always going to give everything to the car we can find. It's just tough. We really tried to develop it and improve it, and tried many things at the beginning of the season and the mid-season. But a lot of things didn't seem to work. There were bigger problems with the car that were masking some of them. It has been a good decision to really focus on next year.

"In Austin, though, we did a perfect race – with the strategy, pit stops, and perfect communication about the tyres from the pit wall, all race long. Better late in the season than not at all! It was good fun, I really enjoyed it, especially the pass on Esteban Gutierrez. The team told me that I needed to save the tyres, but I decided that for one lap I'm going to go for it, and see if I can catch him and go. We did, and after that it was just about tyre management. It's all about choosing when to push, when to manage.

"I think I was as well prepared as it's possible to be nowadays, with the Fridays and young driver tests and all that stuff. I felt ready, but I know that if I could go again now to Melbourne I would do better. It's up to us to make a better car for next year and that way get a better result. I'm definitely looking forward to 2014, because with the new rules there's a chance for us to catch up with the others.

"I'm just really looking forward to working with the team next year and with the new car. We're going in the right direction, I feel very good in the team, and for me it's like a family. I'm just really looking forward to the future."

NATIONALITY Finnish

DATE OF BIRTH 28/8/89

PLACE OF BIRTH Nastola, Finland

HONOURS 2011 GP3 champion, 2009 and 2010 F3 Masters winner, 2008 European and Northern European Formula Renault champion

18 PASTOR MALDONADO
WILLIAMS

NATIONALITY Venezuelan
DATE OF BIRTH 9/3/85
PLACE OF BIRTH Maracay, Venezuela
HONOURS 2010 GP2 champion, 2004 Italian Formula Renault champion, 2003 Italian Formula Renault winter champion

"It has been a very tough season for Williams and for me – the worst in the team's history, which has been hard to accept. We worked well and the team did a great job, but maybe we weren't 100 per cent together in accepting the problem. The main thing was the wind tunnel and aero issues. We went back to last year's style of exhaust, and the car was quicker, so we lost a year because we had something better at home. Not that we'd win races, but potentially we'd be in the points.

"The performance was the same all year, which was most disappointing. I think we needed to be honest with ourselves and accept that we'd made big mistakes, especially in building the car. We made the wrong decisions for this year, and we paid for it, all together.

"It's very tough, because I was always in the top five in Formula Renault, World Series, GP2 and karts. I was always fighting for victories, for podiums, so it's hard to accept you're only competing with your team-mate.

"I'm not leaving the team only because the car was slow. It's a personal decision, the best I could make, for the team and for myself. I wish them all the best with Felipe Massa. He's a good guy, a good driver and my friend. For sure Williams can improve. They have all the facilities to do quite well, as we've seen in the past.

"We had a fantastic year in 2012, and a victory. Yet I've been doing an even better job this year. I had solid races, a good pace, even fighting for positions when the car wasn't meant to fight around those places."

19 JULES BIANCHI
MARUSSIA

NATIONALITY French
DATE OF BIRTH 3/8/89
PLACE OF BIRTH Nice, France
HONOURS 2009 European F3 champion, 2008 F3 Masters F3 winner, 2007 French Formula Renault champion

"This year has given me a really positive feeling. The team helped a lot, because they really taught me how to get on a good pace straight away with a good way of driving. So I was really confident at the first test in Barcelona, even if we didn't do many laps.

"The first races were pretty good for us. Compared to the team we were fighting, Caterham, the car was good, so we were in front. We had a great result in the second race in Malaysia when I finished 13th. After that, it became more difficult, but again the team were very good, always trying to improve. This was the positive thing and I learned a lot.

"I never thought it would be bad for me to join a team at the back of the grid. Obviously, we weren't

in a position to fight for points or podiums because our target was different: we wanted to finish in front of the Caterhams. When we did, it was like a victory. Qualifying was the same, you pushed to the maximum, tried to take the maximum out of the car and be in front of them.

"What I try to do is focus on myself, try to improve all the time, try to set the car up as well as possible. And, again, being in front of the Caterhams was a victory, so I just focused on that every weekend. It's really good that we had at least one team that was close to us because if you're alone, fighting with no one but your team-mate, it's a bit less exciting. But this year we had a really good fight with Caterham."

20 CHARLES PIC
CATERHAM

NATIONALITY French
DATE OF BIRTH 15/2/90
PLACE OF BIRTH Montelimar, France
HONOURS None

"For sure, you are stronger in your second year, because you have one year's experience. So I was stronger than in 2012. I saw the problems quicker and my feedback was better. However, the second year wasn't easier than the first. It was different, but not easier. You have one year's experience so you have to improve, and everybody expects you to do the job, as you're not a rookie any more. You have to do everything right; you're not allowed to get it wrong.

"But when you know that if you do everything right you will get 19th and no better, it isn't easy! But that's the way it works and you have to find a way to keep your motivation upper-most and fight for the team every weekend, and also find your target.

"Of course, we were fighting with Marussia and wanted to be in front. We started in Melbourne with the 2012 car. We didn't have the new car, but Marussia built one, so there was a reason why they started in front of us. They had an advantage of 0.4 to 0.5s.

"Then Caterham made a good job of closing this gap with new aero, front wing, rear wing, floor… stuff like that. We caught them up and had a strong point during the season from Barcelona to Monza, where we had an advantage. Silverstone was a good race as we fought with Williams until the last few laps, and we were close to them in terms of race pace, having made a great job of optimising the car. After Monza it's true that Marussia caught us a bit, especially over one lap."

21 GIEDO VAN DER GARDE
CATERHAM

NATIONALITY Dutch
DATE OF BIRTH 25/4/85
PLACE OF BIRTH Rhenen, Holland
HONOURS 2008 Formula Renault 3.5 champion

"To be honest, a first year for a rookie isn't easy, to come into the big game where everything is happening. Even though I had four years of GP2 experience, F1 is still a different game. You go from a team with 15 people to a team with 200-plus and, even at the track, you're with 60 people.

"So you have to get used to it, you have to work yourself in. Some people get used to things more quickly than others – I think I'm a little late in everything in my life! In the end, I hope I've proved that I belong here in F1 and that I showed good potential.

"I think the team didn't expect too much this year, to be honest, with 2014 coming. In the beginning, they didn't do a lot of development and the car was very

hard to drive and had a lot of issues. It wasn't really balanced and I was struggling a lot with the tyres. Once we came back to Europe we had a big update, and from there it started to get better and better as we developed the car quite well. It wasn't easy in the beginning. In the middle of the year, we showed good potential, then Spa was our last update.

"My team-mate had a big gap to me to start with. We were always very close in qualifying, but in the races he was much stronger. The biggest thing that helped me a lot was the tyres changing. After Budapest, I beat him almost every race, although sometimes I had bad luck or some things didn't go right, but more or less I was always quicker than him in the races."

22 MAX CHILTON
MARUSSIA

NATIONALITY British
DATE OF BIRTH 21/4/91
PLACE OF BIRTH Reigate, England
HONOURS None

"I'm pretty happy with my season, and I've been a lot happier since the Hungarian GP, just before the summer break. You've always got your team-mate to compare yourself with, and I've learned a lot from Jules this season. From the August break, it's been a lot closer. I've beaten him in qualifying and races, so that's been good for my confidence, and it's good to learn from someone who is so highly rated. I'd rather have had someone like him in the car than someone who's seen as an 'all right' driver. If I beat him it was good, and it was good for the team.

"In the last few races, we caught up with Caterham again, and could actually have a bit of a race. It was like that at the start of the year, but at Silverstone they kind

of pulled away a bit, so there were quite a few races where it was quite hard. You were going around and around and didn't really have anyone to challenge.

"Spa qualifying was very good. I wouldn't say it was the best lap I've ever done, it was more to do with the choice we made. Monaco was good for me. What happened with Maldonado in the race was a shame, but the pace was good, so I was happy with that. I had my best qualifying of the year at Suzuka. I'd never been there before and to outqualify my team-mate and both Caterhams was a really good moment. The finishing record was a nice thing to have, but you don't want to go out in a race and have that as your main focus, because you're not going to get the most out of it."

23 HEIKKI KOVALAINEN
LOTUS

NATIONALITY Finnish
DATE OF BIRTH 19/10/81
PLACE OF BIRTH Suomussalmi, Finland
HONOURS World Series by Nissan Champion 2004

"The fact that I was driving for Caterham in some first practice sessions definitely helped me get the Lotus drive.

"It was good to be back in Austin. It was a really good weekend – up until Sunday. Then, in the race, I began to lose some front grip straight after the pit stop, so had to stop for a new front wing. As soon as we changed the wing it was better, then the KERS went.

"I didn't know what to expect, but I thought I could do the job and it was just a matter of how soon I could get up to speed. It's good to see that things worked out slightly better than perhaps I was anticipating.

"I was pleasantly surprised to see a lot of familiar faces at the factory and also around the race team. People know me well and they were very welcoming,

and I think they enjoyed having me back as well.

"There were many elements that I recognised straight away from my Renault days, including some of the procedures and how we ran the race weekend. Also I could see some improvements the team had done since I was there last. There were differences, but some routines that I was used to, so that helped a bit.

"Having Mark Slade as my engineer was a significant factor. It was relatively easy to start working with him because I knew him from my McLaren days. He knows what I need too. If I got lost, he made suggestions just by looking at the telemetry, so it was helpful. I had a good time at McLaren with him and he's worked with some really good drivers and is clearly a top engineer."

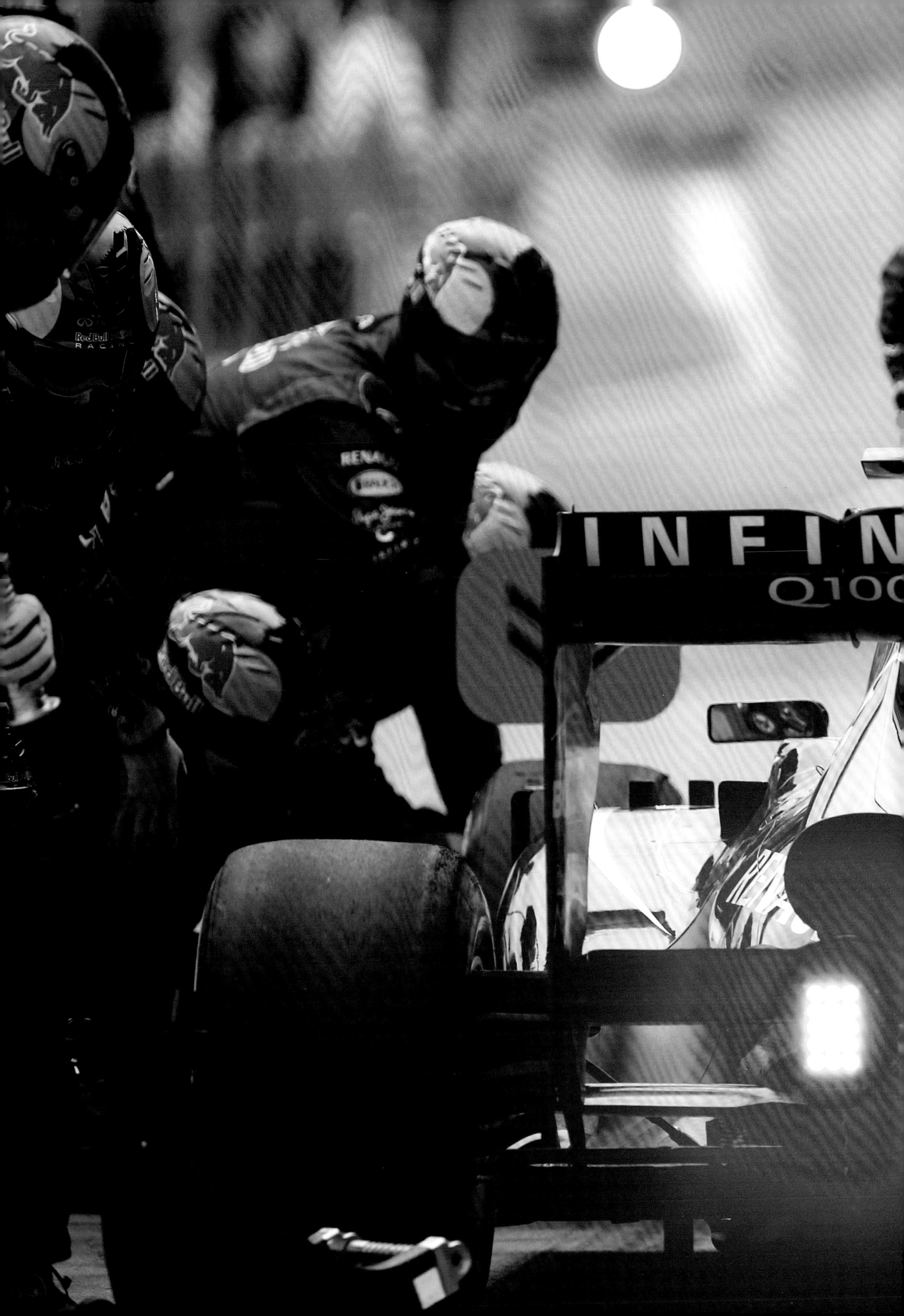
INFIN
Q10

PHOTOS OF THE YEAR

The LAT photo agency captures 2013 track time and down time, chosen by LAT's Managing Director, Steven Tee

From 11th to the podium: Romain Grosjean in Bahrain

It's a long-horn story at the US GP, Austin, Texas

"Pie in your eye" – Webber and Vettel mug Horner after their US GP win

Williams's Bottas has his own entry technique

"Is that me up there?" Perez on media duty

Red Bull's Horner and Newey can't stop smiling

Kimi and Lotus boss Boullier win in Melbourne

Great colour, bad vibe: Alonso crashes, Malaysia

Another race, another win: more congrats for Vettel from Newey

Van der Garde and Rosberg check the net in New Delhi

Alonso escapes the misery at Sepang

Vettel: it's fitness with a winning smile

Hamilton and Rosberg take to calmer waters

Looking good,
looking cool:
Button in Monaco

Keeping warm
and grippy: Toro
Rosso rear tyres

In a galaxy as
close as Canada,
George Lucas
checks out F1

Daniel Ricciardo
finished a happy
11th in Austin

Yep, Giedo, no
F1 car has a
cornering limit
this good

Button hoping for a chance at Q3 qualifying

Kovalainen subs for Räikkönen at Lotus in Austin

Grosjean was impressive for Lotus in 2013

Action stations for McLaren in Bahrain

The Caterham pit prepares for qualifying

Prep for Lotus's
podium boy in
Spain: Räikkönen

Vettel's
team are as
meticulous
as he is

No race today:
Caterham's back-up
boy, Kovalainen

Bottas was
pleased
with 12th in
Monaco

Red Bull in India
– a win for Vettel
but retirement
for Webber

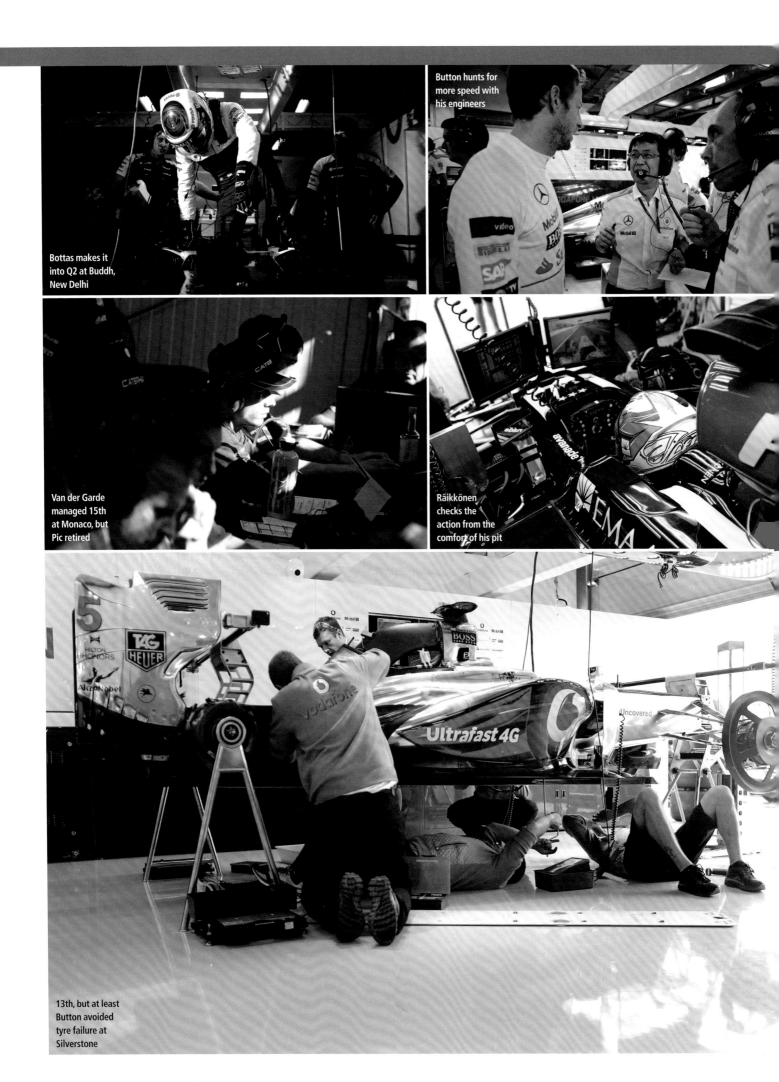

Bottas makes it into Q2 at Buddh, New Delhi

Button hunts for more speed with his engineers

Van der Garde managed 15th at Monaco, but Pic retired

Räikkönen checks the action from the comfort of his pit

13th, but at least Button avoided tyre failure at Silverstone

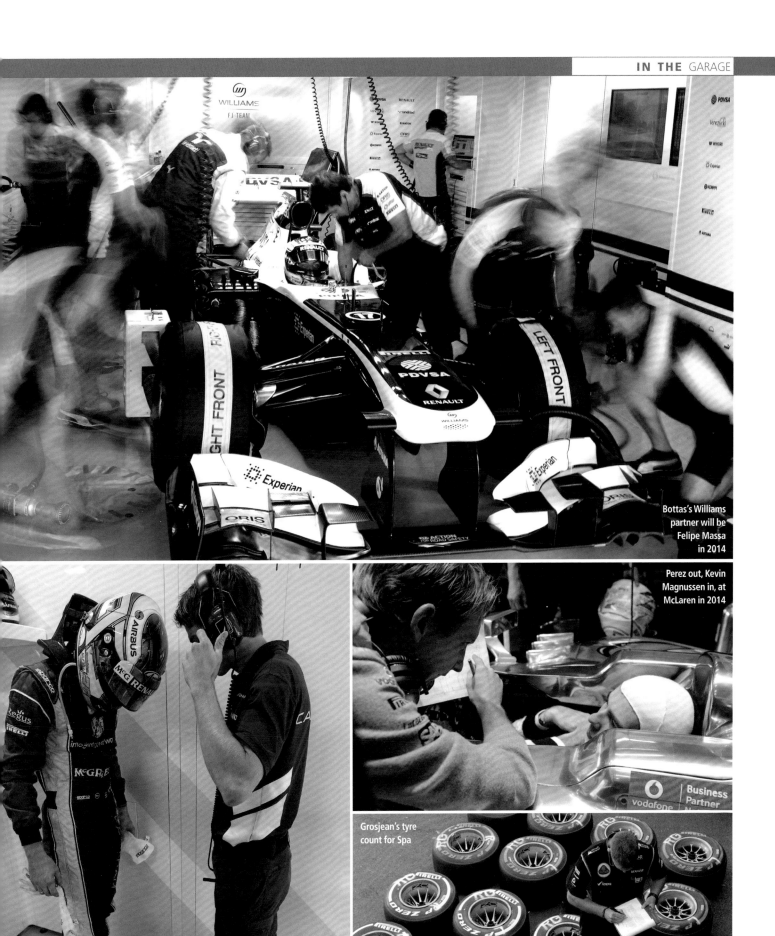

Bottas's Williams partner will be Felipe Massa in 2014

Perez out, Kevin Magnussen in, at McLaren in 2014

Grosjean's tyre count for Spa

He ain't heavy, he's Charles Pic

Rosberg savours a 1955 300 SLR Mercedes at the Nürburgring

Guess where? That's right, Vettel wins in Canada

Perez signs up with Chinese fans in Shanghai

Vettel gets friendly down under in Oz

Van der Garde on autograph duty, Malaysia

Tamara Ecclestone gets the lowdown in Abu Dhabi

James McAvoy checks Caterham in Montreal

Matt LeBlanc looks for Friends in the Texas pit

Michael Fassbender meets his Red Bull twin

Gordon Ramsey talks turkey at the Circuit of the Americas

Silverstone pulls in Marvin Humes of LJS and Rupert Grint

DC and EJ talk F1 in Singapore with Bob Geldof

David Beckham gets a winning line from Red Bull's Horner

A McLaren fan? Cameron Diaz checks out the Monaco garage

Rowan Atkinson enjoys a little Monza sunshine

Bottas with girlfriend and Olympic swimmer Emila Pikkarainen

Silverstone pit lane walk for celebrity chef James Martin

2013
TEAMS

The stories of the 11 teams, from their senior technical staff, as they battled for the 2013 constructors title, coped with tyre issues and kept one eye on developing their cars for next season

RED BULL

INFINITI RED BULL RACING

PERSONNEL
CHAIRMAN Dietrich Mateschitz
TEAM PRINCIPAL Christian Horner
CHIEF TECHNICAL OFFICER Adrian Newey
HEAD OF AERODYNAMICS Peter Prodromou
CHIEF DESIGNER Rob Marshall
HEAD OF CAR ENGINEERING Paul Monaghan
HEAD OF ELECTRONICS Paul Everington
CHIEF ENGINEER, PERFORMANCE ENGINEERING
Pierre Wache
CHIEF ENGINEER, VEHICLE DYNAMICS Mark Ellis
TECHNICAL DIRECTOR, RENAULT ENGINES Rob White
TEAM MANAGER Jonathan Wheatley
DRIVERS Sebastian Vettel, Mark Webber
RACE ENGINEER (VETTEL) Guillaume Rocquelin
RACE ENGINEER (WEBBER) Simon Rennie
CHIEF MECHANIC Kenny Handkammer
TEST/THIRD DRIVER Sebastien Buemi
TOTAL NUMBER OF EMPLOYEES 550
NUMBER IN RACE TEAM 60
TEAM BASE Milton Keynes, England
TELEPHONE +44 (0)1908 279700
WEBSITE www.infiniti-redbullracing.com

TEAM STATS
IN F1 SINCE 1997 as Stewart Grand Prix, then as Jaguar
Racing from 2000-04 **FIRST GRAND PRIX** Australia 1997
CONSTRUCTORS' TITLES 4 **DRIVERS' TITLES** 4

SPONSORS
Red Bull, Infiniti, Total, Renault, Rauch, Geox, Pepe Jeans, Casio,
Singha Beer, AT&T, Joraku, Sonax, Alpinestars, Pirelli, Siemens

1 SEBASTIAN VETTEL   **2 MARK WEBBER**

"THERE WAS NO SINGLE MAGIC BULLET"

BY ADRIAN NEWEY
CHIEF TECHNICAL OFFICER

"It was a season of continual development with a car that was a close relation to the 2012 RB8, both visually and under the skin.

"The 2013 tyres were an unexpected difficulty. Those teams who claim that they understood them as a result of a test in first free practice at the 2012 Brazilian GP, with a track temperature of around 50 degrees, are clearly much cleverer than we are.

"I just don't believe that you could have got any real understanding from that. For some teams, the characteristics of their car lucked in and, for others, they didn't. For me, it was luck. There was no skill involved.

"The change back to 2012 tyres midway through the season certainly helped us quite a lot. We were starting to get on top of the 2013 tyres, but the characteristics of the 2012 tyres definitely suited our car better. The 2013 versions were very sensitive to high load conditions. So, basically, you couldn't go through high-speed corners, certainly in race conditions, without destroying them. The 2012s were a little better in that respect. Given that our car was good in high-speed corners, going back to 2012 tyres worked in our favour.

"The truth is that the car was always going to be inherently better suited to the 2012 rubber. But, at the same time, developing the car through the season, those developments would probably have helped regardless. Overall, the combination of development and the return to 2012 tyres was a powerful help.

"The steps we made before that were partly down to the amount of practice the drivers had on Pirellis and developing the car to suit the tyres. There are still things you can do even with a tyre that's very easily overloaded – a combination of aero and mechanical work – and the real trick is getting those two aspects to work together.

"We went with a full Coanda exhaust effect again rather than the coke bottle and, to be honest, I didn't look at the other alternatives as I just didn't like the idea. I just couldn't get my head around the whole principle of trying to blow gas contrary to the natural direction of the coke bottle flow if you've got an open system. I'd much rather have something more defined, where the gas had half a chance of knowing where it was meant to be going.

"Even though Sebastian Vettel was good at dealing with any instability on corner entry, I wouldn't say that he drove the direction of our exhaust blown development. It was basically driven by both CFD research and the wind tunnel. Between Sebastian and Mark Webber there haven't been comments that led us to go in one direction rather than the other. Mark, in fact, in terms of comments, was the driver who would normally pick up on small aerodynamic changes with a greater degree of sensitivity than Sebastian.

"Some suggested that the alternative layout may be better in the off-throttle situation and that ours was more of a compromise in that regard. Well, if we had no exhaust at all we wouldn't make the sidepod that shape, so there must be some level of compensation, but I think it was quite small. We adopted it so long ago now and haven't bothered going back to check it, so I don't have a definitive answer.

"The exhaust blowing became quite topical again after our strong performance at the Singapore GP, when Giancarlo Minardi heard the car on the circuit and said that he thought we were doing something different. I'm not being elusive, but it's difficult for me to comment because we were just doing our job, and don't know what the others were doing.

"The engine mapping obviously plays a role and, in terms of driveability and power delivery, the exhaust is a factor. Was our engine different from others?

TECHNICAL SPECIFICATIONS

ENGINE
MAKE/MODEL
Renault RS27-2013
CONFIGURATION
2400cc V8 (90 degree)
SPARK PLUGS Not disclosed
ECU FIA standard issue
FUEL Total
OIL Total
BATTERY Not disclosed

TRANSMISSION
GEARBOX Red Bull Racing
FORWARD GEARS Seven
CLUTCH AP Racing

CHASSIS
CHASSIS MODEL Red Bull RB9
FRONT SUSPENSION LAYOUT
Double wishbones with torsion
springs and anti-roll bars

REAR SUSPENSION LAYOUT
Double wishbones with torsion
springs and anti-roll bars
DAMPERS Multimatic
TYRES Pirelli
WHEELS OZ Racing
BRAKE DISCS Brembo
BRAKE PADS Brembo
BRAKE CALIPERS Brembo
FUEL TANK Not disclosed
INSTRUMENTS Not disclosed

DIMENSIONS
LENGTH Not disclosed
WIDTH Not disclosed
HEIGHT Not disclosed
WHEELBASE Not disclosed
TRACK, FRONT Not disclosed
TRACK, REAR Not disclosed
WEIGHT 640kg (including
driver and camera)

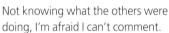

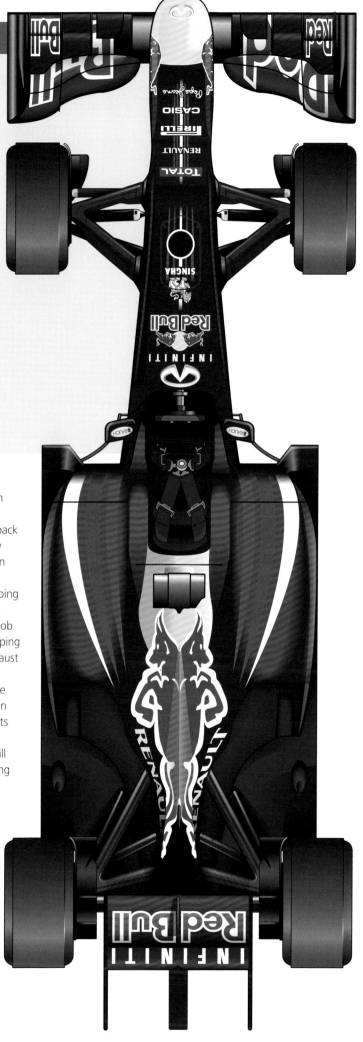

Not knowing what the others were doing, I'm afraid I can't comment.

"I think that a bit of our advantage in the second half of the year was the nature of the circuits. We had been competitive in Bahrain and Montreal with medium downforce, but weren't fully on top of high downforce front-limited tracks like China. That was certainly true earlier in the season. We struggled at Barcelona too. Having said that, Korea, which is probably the most front-limited track of them all, seemed to be alright. As we developed, we managed to overcome some of the problems. Spa-Francorchamps and Monza suited us and by the time we got to Singapore we were more on top of the high downforce.

"We'd made some decent steps and introduced quite a few parts to the car, some for the Hungarian GP, and really that was a race that got away from us – a weekend when we didn't manage to deliver the full potential of the car and Sebastian also got stuck behind Jenson Button. That perhaps masked where we'd got to, but there was no single magic bullet or component to the upturn in form. We had a couple of races when we should have done better: Silverstone was an easy win, but for input shaft failure.

"We certainly never expected the second half of the year that we had. It was quite like 2011 where Ferrari had started well and, mid-season, McLaren were strong and we were worrying that their development rate was higher than ours. It was the same with Mercedes this time. We were worrying that we'd be on the back foot, so kept pushing, arguably with 20/20 hindsight more than we needed to in view of 2014.

"The new regulations are going to be challenging for everyone. We've probably done a better job than our competitors in developing the best use of the current exhaust restriction, so we stand to lose the most again. Next year, there will be a single pipe exit position and the turbo will take away lots of the energy.

"A big problem next year will be the narrow front wing. Taking 100mm off the wing doesn't sound much, but it's actually a big change because it puts the endplate right in the middle of the front tyre. I think that on the straight aerodynamic side, trying to recover from that is going to be a big issue.

Then there's the whole challenge of packaging the power unit, which is a very complicated beast. It will be a two- or three-fold jump in complication compared to installing a V8."

MERCEDES

MERCEDES AMG PETRONAS F1 TEAM

PERSONNEL
NON-EXECUTIVE CHAIRMAN Niki Lauda
EXECUTIVE DIRECTOR, BUSINESS Toto Wolff
TEAM PRINCIPAL Ross Brawn
EXECUTIVE DIRECTOR, TECHNICAL Paddy Lowe
TECHNICAL DIRECTOR Bob Bell
TECHNOLOGY DIRECTOR Geoff Willis
ENGINEERING DIRECTOR Aldo Costa
HEAD OF AERODYNAMICS Mike Elliott
CHIEF DESIGNER John Owen
CHIEF ENGINEER Russell Cooley
DRIVERS Lewis Hamilton, Nico Rosberg
SPORTING DIRECTOR Ron Meadows
CHIEF RACE ENGINEER Andrew Shovlin
CHIEF TRACK ENGINEER Simon Cole
SENIOR RACE ENGINEER (HAMILTON) Peter Bonnington
SENIOR RACE ENGINEER (ROSBERG) Tony Ross
CHIEF MECHANIC Matthew Deane
DEVELOPMENT DRIVER Sam Bird
TOTAL NUMBER OF EMPLOYEES 600
NUMBER IN RACE TEAM 60
TEAM BASE Brackley, England
TELEPHONE +44 (0)1280 844000
WEBSITE www.mercedes-amg-f1.com

TEAM STATS
IN F1 SINCE 1999 as BAR then as Honda Racing 2006-08 and as Brawn GP 2009 **FIRST GRAND PRIX** Australia 1999
CONSTRUCTORS' TITLES 1 **DRIVERS' TITLES** 1

SPONSORS
Petronas, BlackBerry, MIG Bank, UBS, Allianz, Isofoton, IWC Schaffhausen, Monster Energy, Pirelli, Puma, spg, Lincoln Electric, Solace Systems

9 NICO ROSBERG   **10 LEWIS HAMILTON**

"2013 WAS CORE DEVELOPMENT, NOT INNOVATION"

BY ROSS BRAWN
TEAM PRINCIPAL

"We had a much more competitive year in 2013 and that's down to the investment and changes that were made for 2012. We strengthened the aero group with Mike Elliott and it wasn't just about the headline guys – it all fed through.

"We had the fifth biggest budget in 2011 and finished fifth in 2012. There have been teams with huge budgets that failed and teams with small budgets, like Brawn GP, that won a championship. However, Brawn was not a sustainable model and teams failing with huge budgets were just doing a very bad job. We've increased our resource quality and it's come through this year.

"We also reaped the benefit of going from a 50 to 60 per cent wind tunnel model, which was a big interruption last year. It's a massive project. It's not just making 60 per cent models, it's going through all the correlation. With the 50 per cent model we couldn't fit any more instrumentation on, but with 60 per cent you can, and then you can measure things more effectively. It's more involved, though. An example of this is that we had to buy a bigger mill because the one we had wasn't large enough to make 60 per cent wings. We bit the bullet and did it. Lotus – Mike Elliott's previous team – did it a year before us and saw the benefits.

"We'd also fallen behind in understanding the principles and subtleties of the Coanda exhaust. Over the winter, we put a huge effort into understanding the nuances. That involved a lot of dyno work and we decided we couldn't investigate both the ramp and coke bottle approaches. Doing one really well was more important.

"The route we took was the one we understood and, with the engine mapping we had at the time, the preferred route. Maybe at the end of the year, though, the conclusion was that we could have been better off taking the other approach. It may be that we saw some subtleties of engine mapping develop that suggested stronger benefits in that second approach. Our method produced, for sure, a better car off-throttle, when the exhaust was not blowing. I don't think it was too bad overall.

"The front-rear interconnected suspension was not hugely different from what we introduced in 2011, it just gets enhanced and tuned each year. Indeed, the low front ride heights that teams are running these days wouldn't be possible without it.

"I was pleased with the gearbox technology, with a double skin casing allowing different suspension mounting points. It definitely gave us more adaptability. Aldo Costa and I have talked about it for years but shelved it for cost reasons.

"Early in the season, we had to try to understand what was generating stress and strain on the rear tyres. We tried swapping the rear tyres and didn't get that good a result. We tried it occasionally in practice, but then we started to understand what the behaviour of the tyres was in those situations and that became quite significant. Just as we were thinking we were getting on top of it, the British GP came along with its blow-outs and the whole tyre situation changed.

"Frankly, we didn't understand the very sensitive nature of certain aspects of the tyre. Things that we didn't think were so significant turned out to be very much so in terms of how you run the car, suspension settings and so on. We started to understand that these tyres were much more sensitive to certain chassis settings that over the years have never been particularly critical. The procedure of swapping the tyres around helped us to understand those sensitivities.

"As last year, we saw driver specific differences. The challenge was to find how close you could get to the edge without falling over, because if you're too far away you're not getting all the performance from the tyre. So you can have one driver who

TECHNICAL SPECIFICATIONS

ENGINE

MAKE/MODEL
Mercedes-Benz FO108F
CONFIGURATION
2400cc V8 (90 degree)
SPARK PLUGS Not disclosed
ECU FIA standard issue
FUEL Petronas
OIL Petronas
BATTERY Not disclosed

TRANSMISSION

GEARBOX Mercedes AMG Petronas
FORWARD GEARS Seven
CLUTCH Not disclosed

CHASSIS

CHASSIS MODEL
Mercedes F1 W04
FRONT SUSPENSION LAYOUT
Wishbones and pushrod-activated
torsion springs and rockers

REAR SUSPENSION LAYOUT

Wishbones and pullrod-activated
torsion springs and rockers
DAMPERS Penske
TYRES Pirelli
WHEELS OZ
BRAKE DISCS Not disclosed
BRAKE PADS Not disclosed
BRAKE CALIPERS Brembo
FUEL TANK Not disclosed
INSTRUMENTS Not disclosed

DIMENSIONS

LENGTH 4800mm
WIDTH 1800mm
HEIGHT 950mm
WHEELBASE Not disclosed
TRACK, FRONT Not disclosed
TRACK, REAR Not disclosed
WEIGHT 640kg (including
driver and camera)

MERCEDES AMG PETRONAS
FORMULA ONE™ TEAM

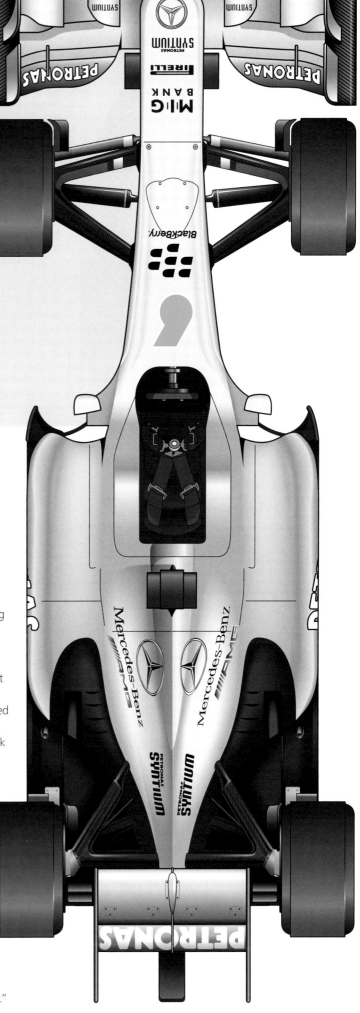

cruises around all day and says the tyres are fine, but you've still got 10 or 20 per cent of the tyre that he hasn't used because he hasn't dared get near the edge.

"The other driver tries to get near the edge and falls over. Then you're sad as well. That's what we were seeing. Some managed to keep it right on the critical point, some fell over it and some never got near it. It wasn't the same problem every weekend, either. Some weeks it was front graining, other weeks it was rear degradation. It was a juggling act with loads of balls in the air.

"Lewis Hamilton had some brake issues too, but we made progress. I think that we've had a few years with neither of the drivers challenging the reference and then a new driver came in and said, 'Actually this isn't very good'.

"When Lewis joined us, he said that the actual retardation was all right but the feel on the brake was poor. As a consequence, we started to focus more on that and when you do that you sometimes also help the driver who thought previously they were alright. It was really to do with thermal management of the brake: how much you cool the surface, how much the core. So we added some options in terms of how we distributed cooling. We've had to improve our sophistication.

"We looked at thermal treatment of the wheel rims too. When you have a tyre problem, you start to explore every nuance. You see areas you can get a bit more out of

that other people don't bother with. We looked at everything: the air plume over the wheel, the treatment and finish of the wheel.

"There was a lot going on that wasn't so visible. We had the ambition of trying to add a tenth of a second of performance per lap every race and we weren't far off achieving that. It was stronger consistent development. There was no real new innovation, just core development. We did quite a lot of it. We had several different floors, the front wing was altered quite a bit and the brake ducts received a huge amount of work for two reasons: performance and temperature management of the tyres. We also tried suspension geometry changes, several exhaust systems and rear wing detailing.

"The Monaco GP was a good step up for us, and produced a win, and there were very few races where we didn't have upgrades. As well as that, of course, we had to concentrate on 2014, when the changes will be huge."

FERRARI

SCUDERIA FERRARI

PERSONNEL
PRESIDENT Luca di Montezemolo
CHIEF EXECUTIVE OFFICER Amadeo Felisa
TEAM PRINCIPAL Stefano Domenicali
TECHNICAL DIRECTOR James Allison
ENGINEERING DIRECTOR Pat Fry
PRODUCTION DIRECTOR Corrado Lanzone
ENGINE AND ELECTRONICS DIRECTOR Luca Marmorini
CHIEF DESIGNER Nikolas Tombazis
DEPUTY CHIEF DESIGNER Simone Resta
HEAD OF AERODYNAMICS Loic Bigois
DRIVERS Fernando Alonso, Felipe Massa
SPORTING DIRECTOR Massimo Rivola
CHIEF RACE ENGINEER Steve Clark
RACE ENGINEER (ALONSO) Andrea Stella
RACE ENGINEER (MASSA) Rob Smedley
CHIEF MECHANIC Francesco Uguzzoni
TEST/THIRD DRIVERS Pedro de la Rosa & Marc Gene
TOTAL NUMBER OF EMPLOYEES Over 600
NUMBER IN RACE TEAM Approx 70
TEAM BASE Maranello, Italy
TELEPHONE +39 0536 949450
WEBSITE www.ferrari.com

TEAM STATS
IN F1 SINCE 1950 **FIRST GRAND PRIX** Britain 1950
CONSTRUCTORS' TITLES 16 **DRIVERS' TITLES** 15

SPONSORS
Philip Morris International, FIAT, Santander, Shell, Kaspersky lab, Weichai Power, UPS, Hublot, TNT Energy Drink

3 FERNANDO ALONSO   **4 FELIPE MASSA**

"WE WERE SIX-TENTHS OFF THE ULTIMATE PACE"

BY PAT FRY
ENGINEERING DIRECTOR

"Throughout the winter of 2012-2013 we had a reasonable development period and a sensible development gradient. The first race upgrade package worked quite well, and some bits proved better than we were expecting.

"Then, midway through the season, we took a different top body to the Canadian GP and we were a bit unsure about it. That gave us a few issues as we tried to understand it and that's where our development started to roll over. If you've got one thing that's not 100 per cent, what do you do with it? Because, by that time, the wind tunnel model has progressed, and when you try to back out of something it gives you a whole load of problems.

"Set-up wise, it's true that Red Bull runs quite high rake and Mercedes seemed to go in that direction as well. We actually worked in the wind tunnel over a much higher ride height range than we ran at the track, always to check where the performance was. We were running less rear ride height than them, but that was the range in which our car was working.

"People commented that our long run tyre durability was an initial strength and that traction was a weakness, but in reality I think we moved the problems around.

"If you look at the season as a whole, we never had the quickest car in qualifying. We were at least six-tenths off the ultimate pace. At the start of the year, though, we were obviously much easier on the tyres, so our race performance was better because of it.

"To some degree, it was similar to what happened in 2012, when the compounds were harder and we struggled a bit more. If anything, we were struggling with warming the tyres, whereas other teams had the opposite problem and so were struggling with overheating them. Across the season, we didn't really improve the qualifying situation, which was a problem from race one.

"At the Chinese and Spanish GPs, which Fernando Alonso won, our race pace was pretty good but, as compounds and constructions changed, that put us in an area where we struggled more.

"I think I'm firmly in the camp that believes that you'd have been very clever if you took a set of tyre data from the test run we all had at the 2012 Brazilian GP and managed to iterate around that. I think we did only about seven laps on those tyres! The reality in some cases was that the tyres just played to the historic strengths of cars of the past couple of years.

"I don't think reverting to the 2012 tyres midway through this season had a huge impact on us relative to the opposition. The shape of the tyre did change a bit and, if anything, we did actually gain a small amount of downforce from that. However, when you look at where we were in qualifying, the position was pretty similar.

"With the Coanda exhaust, Sauber made a big improvement when they went from the McLaren-style arrangement to the Red Bull type. We tested it quite a few times in the wind tunnel but, with the rest of our car, it was never close to being worth making from the numbers that we saw. Eventually, we decided to stick with the concept we had. Whether that was the right decision in the end, we will never know.

"We brought quite a lot of aero updates throughout the year that were quite visible. Mechanically, though, we didn't change any suspension geometries but were constantly working on different suspension mechanisms.

"Red Bull's race pace improved significantly mid-season, but if you plot the qualifying gap it was between 0.6s and 1s pretty consistently for most of the year. I knew what was in the development

TECHNICAL SPECIFICATIONS

ENGINE

MAKE/MODEL
Ferrari 056
CONFIGURATION
2398cc V8 (90 degree)
SPARK PLUGS Not disclosed
ECU FIA standard issue
FUEL Shell V-Power
OIL Shell Helix Ultra
BATTERY Not disclosed

TRANSMISSION

GEARBOX Ferrari
FORWARD GEARS Seven
CLUTCH Not disclosed

CHASSIS

CHASSIS MODEL
Ferrari F138
FRONT SUSPENSION LAYOUT
Independent pullrod-activated
torsion springs
REAR SUSPENSION LAYOUT
Independent pullrod-activated
torsion springs
DAMPERS Not disclosed
TYRES Pirelli
WHEELS OZ Racing
BRAKE DISCS Brembo
BRAKE PADS Not disclosed
BRAKE CALIPERS Not disclosed
FUEL TANK Not disclosed
INSTRUMENTS
Ferrari/Magneti Marelli

DIMENSIONS

LENGTH Not disclosed
WIDTH Not disclosed
HEIGHT Not disclosed
WHEELBASE Not disclosed
TRACK, FRONT Not disclosed
TRACK, REAR Not disclosed
WEIGHT 640kg (including
driver and camera)

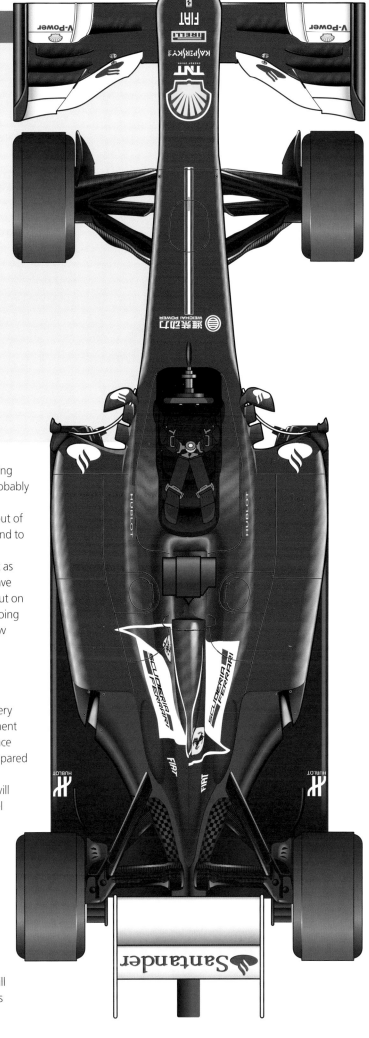

pipeline for Ferrari and it was always going to be hard to close a 1s gap. Red Bull were only ever going to pull away in the championship. You had to keep on trying, but if you were realistic you knew where you stood.

"On the personnel side, James Allison arrived from Lotus and it's great having him at Ferrari. There's a huge amount of work to do to move forward, attacking every area from updating the wind tunnel to improving our simulation facilities. It's good to have the load shared, particularly heading into next year with the major technical changes that this will entail. The more bright brains you have thinking about things, the better we should do. It's a fairly easy and simple split between us as we're both sensible, and it works very well.

"You do need a few good brains. Whether you need five or not, I don't know… But, as F1 gets more and more complicated, the devil does end up being in the detail.

"Next year, as everyone realises, is a big challenge. We've dedicated wind tunnel time to it and obviously a lot of work was going on optimising the engine installation, which has been going on for a couple of years now. We did set up a separate team in the design office just to look through that, with some input from Rory Byrne as well.

"The opportunities for getting it wrong in 2014 are really quite massive. We hope that we've got our sums right, but there will

be a lot of people left scratching their heads. And there will probably be more interim cars because you've got to get a package out of the door initially to do miles and to get the powertrain running.

"Aerodynamics will be just as important for 2014 as they have been for the past ten years, but on the engine side, reliability is going to be the issue, which will slow things down. It's a hugely challenging project.

"In terms of performance, I expect that in the end it will gravitate to everyone being very similar, but the fuel management side will be important. The pace you can run in qualifying compared to the pace in the race will be dramatically different and it will all be down to how much fuel you can save and how much energy you can store.

"That side will be a bigger factor, but how it will play out in the end, nobody knows. You could have a car that's 1s a lap quicker but runs out of fuel ten laps before the end. The engine rules are quite complex, let's say, so there will undoubtedly be opportunities for the FIA to get involved…"

LOTUS

LOTUS F1 TEAM

PERSONNEL

CHAIRMAN Gerard Lopez
CHIEF EXECUTIVE OFFICER Patrick Louis
CHIEF OPERATING OFFICER Thomas Mayer
TEAM PRINCIPAL Eric Boullier
TECHNICAL DIRECTOR Nick Chester
TRACKSIDE OPERATIONS DIRECTOR Alan Permane
CHIEF DESIGNER Martin Tolliday
HEAD OF AERODYNAMICS Nicolas Hennel de Beaupreau
RENAULT SPORT F1 TEAM SUPPORT Ricardo Penteado
DRIVERS Romain Grosjean, Kimi Räikkönen
TEAM MANAGER Paul Seaby
CHIEF RACE ENGINEER Ciaron Pilbeam
SENIOR RACE ENGINEER (GROSJEAN) Ayao Komatsu
SENIOR RACE ENGINEER (RÄIKKÖNEN) Mark Slade
CHIEF MECHANIC Greg Baker
TEST/THIRD DRIVER Davide Valsecchi
TOTAL NUMBER OF EMPLOYEES 550
NUMBER IN RACE TEAM Around 50
TEAM BASE Enstone, England
TELEPHONE +44 (0)1608 678000
WEBSITE www.lotusf1team.com

TEAM STATS

IN F1 SINCE 1981 as Toleman, then as Benetton
1986-2001 and as Renault 2002-11
FIRST GRAND PRIX San Marino 1981
CONSTRUCTORS' TITLES 3 **DRIVERS' TITLES** 4

SPONSORS

Lotus, Renault, Total, Rexona, Clear, Pirelli, Japan Rags, Genii
Business Exchange, Peace One Day, Microsoft Dynamics, AGT,
Avanade, Burn, Richard Mille, Emaar Properties

 7 KIMI RAIKKONEN   **7 HEIKKI KOVALAINEN**   **8 ROMAIN GROSJEAN**

"OUR SO-CALLED DOUBLE DRS DEVICE ISN'T DEAD"

BY ALAN PERMANE
TRACKSIDE OPERATIONS DIRECTOR

"The E21, the second car from Martin Tolliday, was a development of the E20 and further refined into a tidier package.

"We struggled a bit on the harder tyres at the Barcelona test and watching Red Bull and Mercedes switch them on over one lap was a bit worrying, but we were up and running on longer runs.

"Then we had the wonder of the Australian GP. We didn't have an easy qualifying on a cold, half-wet track, but then had a comfortable race win on the supersoft and medium tyres.

"With Romain Grosjean we got on top of the qualifying, not at Vettel's level but pretty much there with the rest. Romain was better at switching the tyres on. Kimi Räikkönen is very sensitive to tyre pressure and struggles to get the fronts working, which is why he has traditionally had problems in places like Monaco where there's very little tyre input. However, he does have a feel for exactly how hard he can push them in the race.

"Romain is now better able to set the car up how he wants it and some of that is down to experience. He's quite sensitive to braking and we initially spent a lot of time with the KERS mapping and brake harvesting. However, he ended up better able to get the best out of the car and in Korea was 0.3-0.5s quicker than Kimi pretty much all the time.

"Romain has changed this year. He started very much as he finished last year, to be honest. Monaco was just awful, giving us real flashbacks as he crashed in almost every session… He was very quick, but kept putting it in the wall and then just drove into the back of Ricciardo in the race, desperate to overtake him.

"From around Nürburgring time though, his attitude changed. His wife had a baby and whether that took his focus off enough

to relax him a bit, I don't know, but since then he's been on a steady upward slope.

"Before, there'd be a problem with the car, as there always is, and that would be his entire focus. But now, if Romain has a problem he puts it to one side and gets on with the rest of it. Out of the car, he's very different: calm and rational and no longer comes on the radio screaming that he's got no grip. He used to get quite animated, which is a novice driver's thing, as there's nothing we can do in a race. It's not as if we can change the grip button! He's grown up and did a great job.

"Kimi was leaving us and that obviously shifted our focus to Romain a bit more and you could see him blossoming. Qualifying in Korea was a fantastic example. We put huge pressure on him. We wanted to take two sets of supersofts through to Q3 and that meant running a scrubbed set of supersofts in Q2 or a set of Primes in Q1, which we thought was the better route. When you do that, you've got to run them towards the end of the session because of the track evolution, and that means you get one shot and can't screw up. Okay, you put fuel in for three laps because the tyres can do that, but you've got to deliver, and he did, in Singapore and Korea even if it did backfire on us in India. But he still salvaged a podium there.

"I think we can be pretty satisfied. While Red Bull were quick everywhere they went, we lost a bit at Spa and Monza, probably with our low downforce package. That wasn't really proven, but we definitely felt more comfortable when using high downforce levels.

"We also had a bit of a mid-season lull when Mercedes's form really took off and they took a load of points out of us. And Fernando did as well.

"Our longer wheelbase car came out of the vehicle dynamics group two or three months before summer. We got

TECHNICAL SPECIFICATIONS

ENGINE
MAKE/MODEL
Renault RS27 2013
CONFIGURATION
2400cc V8 (90 degree)
SPARK PLUGS Not disclosed
ECU FIA standard issue
FUEL Total
OIL Total
BATTERY Not disclosed

TRANSMISSION
GEARBOX Lotus F1 team/Xtrac
FORWARD GEARS Seven
CLUTCH Not disclosed

CHASSIS
CHASSIS MODEL Lotus E21
FRONT SUSPENSION LAYOUT
Carbon-fibre top and bottom
wishbones with pushrod-operated
torsion bar and inboard dampers

REAR SUSPENSION LAYOUT
Carbon-fibre top and bottom
wishbones with pullrod-operated
torsion springs and transverse-
mounted dampers
DAMPERS Not disclosed
TYRES Pirelli
WHEELS OZ Racing
BRAKE DISCS Not disclosed
BRAKE PADS Not disclosed
BRAKE CALIPERS AP Racing
FUEL TANK ATL
INSTRUMENTS McLaren
Electronic Systems

DIMENSIONS
LENGTH 5088mm
WIDTH 1800mm
HEIGHT 950mm
WHEELBASE Not disclosed
TRACK, FRONT 1450mm
TRACK, REAR 1400mm
WEIGHT 642kg (including
driver and camera)

it so that it was aero efficient, but it was done primarily for mechanical stability.

"We ran some simulator sessions and Romain, Davide and Nicolas Prost said it was a little quicker, nicer and more stable. So we took it to Monza with Kimi and ran it on the Friday. The odd thing was that both drivers did the same lap time, but Kimi said he couldn't really feel any difference with it, so we went back to standard and had a normal race.

"With Singapore requiring a higher downforce set-up, I decided not to take the long wheelbase. Logistically it's a bit of a nightmare because it's a different floor and it's incredibly expensive to ship large things like that around the world as they don't fit in standard freight. We decided that when we moved on to the more flowing tracks like Yeongam and Suzuka we'd commit to it again. Then Kimi wanted the short wheelbase car for Abu Dhabi.

"Our so-called double DRS 'device' isn't dead. The concept worked but there were down sides: it lifts the centre of gravity a bit, hurts the cooling a tiny amount and wasn't giving us enough of an advantage. We raced it at Silverstone and it was okay, but with no testing it's very difficult. You tend to spend all your Friday doing aero runs and don't have enough time to get the rest of the car dialled in.

"It's honestly difficult to say how the return to 2012 tyres impacted on us. It helped Red Bull, although I suspect they had some pretty major updates on their car, and it seemed to help Mercedes as they weren't disappearing off the planet when the race started.

"On the personnel side, it was disappointing to lose some top guys. Dirk de Beer only left late in the year and it's early days, but James Allison is an impossible guy to replace as he's a unique character and great at getting the best out of people. This isn't to take anything away from Nick Chester, who stepped into his shoes and is doing a great job.

"I don't get involved in the financial side, but it's very clear we don't have the same money as Mercedes, Ferrari and Red Bull. No way. So, to say we can compete in a development race isn't true, but we built a nice racing car and developed it all year.

"We do have to pick and choose what we do with an eye on money, but there never came a point where there was no point trying anything new in the wind tunnel as we couldn't make it."

McLAREN

VODAFONE McLAREN MERCEDES

PERSONNEL
TEAM PRINCIPAL Martin Whitmarsh
MANAGING DIRECTOR Jonathan Neale
TECHNICAL DIRECTOR Tim Goss
SPORTING DIRECTOR Sam Michael
OPERATIONS DIRECTOR Simon Roberts
ENGINEERING DIRECTOR Matt Morris
**DIRECTOR OF DESIGN AND DEVELOPMENT
PROGRAMMES** Neil Oatley
CHIEF ENGINEER Doug McKiernan
HEAD OF AERODYNAMICS Martin Budkowski
COMMERCIAL AND FINANCIAL DIRECTOR John Cooper
TEAM MANAGER David Redding
DRIVERS Jenson Button, Sergio Perez
PRINCIPAL RACE ENGINEER Phil Prew
RACE ENGINEER (BUTTON) Dave Robson
RACE ENGINEER (PEREZ) Mark Temple
CHIEF MECHANIC Paul James
TEST AND DEVELOPMENT DRIVERS
Gary Paffett, Oliver Turvey
TOTAL NUMBER OF EMPLOYEES 550 (McLaren Racing)
NUMBER IN RACE TEAM Not disclosed
TEAM BASE Woking, England
TELEPHONE +44 (0)1483 261000
WEBSITE www.mclaren.com

TEAM STATS
IN F1 SINCE 1966 **FIRST GRAND PRIX** Monaco 1966
CONSTRUCTORS' TITLES 8 **DRIVERS' TITLES** 12

SPONSORS
Vodafone, Mercedes-Benz, Mobil 1, SAP, Pirelli, Johnnie Walker, Santander, TAG Heuer, Hugo Boss, Claro Video, Akzo Nobel, Hilton HHonors, Aon, Sun Lites

5 JENSON BUTTON   **6 SERGIO PEREZ**

IN SEARCH OF EXHAUST-BLOWN PERFORMANCE

BY TIM GOSS
TECHNICAL DIRECTOR

"When we were working on the MP4-28 concept in 2012, we were winning races but slipping behind in the championship, so had to go a step further to take it from a race-winning car to a championship-winning car.

"The front wing was an evolution of the MP4-27's but moving back down the car we changed pretty much everything aerodynamically. The chassis was raised for aerodynamic reasons and it went hand-in-hand with the pullrod front suspension. We couldn't do that without raising the chassis.

"Moving back down the car, we changed our approach on the sidepod entry and what we call the lower lip, which is, in effect, the floor just below the intakes. We worked on a different side impact arrangement and went to a shortened twin tube arrangement because it allowed us to give the floor below the sidepods a different treatment. It's actually a part of the car that very few people see, so they might not realise there was any difference.

"We worked on several things with the bodywork. The top deck was flatter and lower and we were aiming just to squeeze the engine cover in, drop the top deck and get greater downwash and quality of flow to the rear of the car. We did that by rethinking the way the exhaust was packaged, which allowed us to drop the top deck. In doing that, we had to make a few compromises to the coke bottle line but, again, it went hand-in-hand with another feature, which was to try to get more exhaust blown energy into the rear corner. That was aimed at driving the rear corner and flow structures that you generate from the exhaust blowing much harder.

"We changed the rear suspension, going to the raised rear lower wishbone and shrouded driveshaft for aero reasons to reduce losses and, again, to ensure greater quality flow both to the rear corner and the main upper diffuser ramp.

"The rear wing concept was an evolution, but in 2012 our DRS performance was probably the class of the field. We developed the wing to be nicely on the edge, so when you deployed DRS you could stall quite a lot of the wing and get quite a big drag reduction. Coming into 2013, the rules changed, so that advantage in terms of qualifying performance was lost owing to the reduced DRS activity.

"The final significant conceptual change was to the front and rear brake ducts as we went to a scoopless duct. There are pros and cons, but it was aimed at reducing losses and giving more scope to play with flow structures.

"The rear wheelbase of the MP4-28 was a bit shorter. We just needed to adjust the weight distribution to take a little weight out of the car to spend on other features because our rear suspension and pullrod front suspension costs a bit of weight.

"We pushed the internal aerodynamics harder as well, so that the chassis was narrower where the cooling flow goes up and over it.

"Each of the projects was well researched, but you tend to do it in isolation, so when we pulled all of that together and ran that version in the wind tunnel for the first time, it just didn't click. It took us until December to get the performance back up to a reasonable level.

"We did do that, but ended up with quite a peaky characteristic. We extracted some reasonable performance in the Barcelona test, but by the time we got to the much bumpier track in Melbourne we had to run the car away from its peak performance and really suffered.

"We decided it was probably still possible to get some exhaust-blown performance, so everything we ran in the tunnel was what we at McLaren call a slope and slide – a

TECHNICAL SPECIFICATIONS

ENGINE
MAKE/MODEL
Mercedes-Benz FO 108F
CONFIGURATION
2400cc V8 (90 degree)
SPARK PLUGS NGK
ECU FIA standard issue
FUEL Mobil
OIL Mobil 1
BATTERY GS Yuasa

TRANSMISSION
GEARBOX McLaren
FORWARD GEARS Seven
CLUTCH Not disclosed

CHASSIS
CHASSIS MODEL McLaren MP4-28
FRONT SUSPENSION LAYOUT
Inboard torsion bar/damper system
operated by pullrod and bellcrank
with a double-wishbone arrangement

REAR SUSPENSION LAYOUT
Inboard torsion bar/damper
system operated by pullrod
and bellcrank with a double-
wishbone arrangement
DAMPERS Not disclosed
TYRES Pirelli
WHEELS Enkei
BRAKE DISCS Not disclosed
BRAKE PADS Not disclosed
BRAKE CALIPERS Akebono
FUEL TANK Not disclosed
INSTRUMENTS McLaren
Electronic Systems

DIMENSIONS
LENGTH Not disclosed
WIDTH Not disclosed
HEIGHT Not disclosed
WHEELBASE Not disclosed
TRACK, FRONT Not disclosed
TRACK, REAR Not disclosed
WEIGHT 640kg (including
driver and camera)

VODAFONE McLAREN MERCEDES

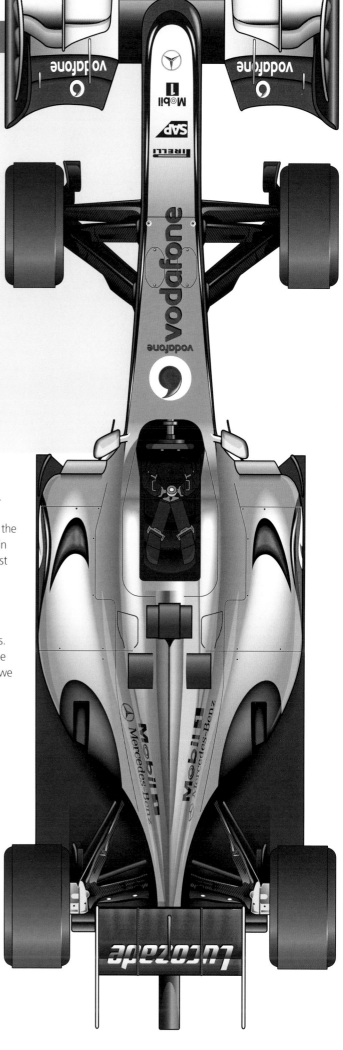

sloping top deck that looks very similar to the Red Bull approach.

"The issue was that in having the big ramp run down to the corner, your unblown losses – in other words the performance of the car without the exhaust blowing – were significantly disrupted. Because you'd got a lot of blockage there with the inwash that you were trying to get into the upper diffuser surface and the starter hole.

"We ran it for a while in the wind tunnel and CFD, and were making good progress and proving that we could get the exhaust to turn, but the ultimate step was to be able to retain the original coke line while still getting the exhaust blown performance. That's when we came up with what we called a slide or exhaust liner, where, in effect, you get the exhaust plume to jump the gap.

"There had also been a clamp-down on how much you could use engine mapping. I think at the start of 2012 the only two teams that got exhaust blowing right were ourselves and Sauber.

"To make the car more driveable for the Malaysian and Chinese GPs, we tried to broaden the operating envelope, which we did successfully as soon as Malaysia. In doing that, we lost a bit of peak performance but it was easier for the drivers to drive and engineers to set up.

"The bodywork change came in time for the Chinese GP, and we went back to the MP4-27 exhaust exit. A bit of a bulge appeared around the engine cover because the exhaust bundle had gone from being low to being pushed up high.

"We ran a significant bodywork change in Spain when we changed the coke line. We compromised it a bit in the launch version to get the exhaust bundle low, and realised we were pulling off some unwanted losses that were tracking down the car.

"The front wing was evolving too, but they were the big packages. The next big phase came around the German and Hungarian GPs when we went back to a low exhaust bundle but packaged things more tightly.

"It wasn't a season to be proud of in terms of performance or championship position, but we're proud of the way we stuck together. We do a lot to measure aero performance and can see that we've put a significant amount of performance on the car, but the top four made similar progress.

"We were about six months behind and, in performance, that's about where we were too. The desire to win is why we tried to take a much bigger step. It took us a while to understand how some subtle interactions can drag down the car's performance, but I'm sure we'll come back stronger as a consequence."

FORCE INDIA

SAHARA FORCE INDIA
F1 TEAM

PERSONNEL

TEAM PRINCIPAL AND MANAGING DIRECTOR
Vijay Mallya
CHAIRMAN Subrata Roy Sahara
CO-OWNER Sahara India Pariwar
SHAREHOLDER Mol family
DEPUTY TEAM PRINCIPAL Robert Fernley
CHIEF OPERATING OFFICER Otmar Szafnauer
TECHNICAL DIRECTOR Andrew Green
PRODUCTION DIRECTOR Bob Halliwell
CHIEF DESIGNERS Akio Haga, Ian Hall
AERODYNAMICS DIRECTOR Simon Phillips
DRIVERS Paul di Resta, Adrian Sutil
SPORTING DIRECTOR Andy Stevenson
CHIEF RACE ENGINEER Jakob Andreasen
RACE ENGINEER (DI RESTA) Gianpiero Lambiase
RACE ENGINEER (SUTIL) Bradley Joyce
RESERVE DRIVER James Calado
RACE TEAM OPERATIONS MANAGER Mark Gray
NO 1 MECHANICS Nicholas Howe, Greg Borrill
TOTAL NUMBER OF EMPLOYEES 335
NUMBER IN RACE TEAM 70
TEAM BASE Silverstone, England
TELEPHONE +44 (0)1327 850800
WEBSITE www.saharaforceindiaf1.com

TEAM STATS

IN F1 SINCE 1991 as Jordan, then as Midland
2005-06 as Spyker 2007 **FIRST GRAND PRIX** USA 1991
CONSTRUCTORS' TITLES 0 **DRIVERS' TITLES** 0

SPONSORS

Vladivar, Kingfisher, Whyte & Mackay, UB Group, Royal Challenge,
Fly Kingfisher, Pirelli, Internap, Alpinestars, Chatham Marine

14 PAUL
DI RESTA

15 ADRIAN
SUTIL

"2012-SPEC TYRES BLEW OUR SEASON APART"

BY ANDREW GREEN
TECHNICAL DIRECTOR

"Our 2013 car was a progression, taking into account the tyre information we had and the modelling we did. There was no wheelbase change, but the aero balance and suspension balance were altered to suit the tyres.

"We understood that we had some stability issues at high speed and worked at improving that while keeping the things that were good: low speed traction and braking stability.

"As in 2012, we put a huge effort into the tyres and it backfired on us completely. To move back to the 2012 tyres again after the 2013 programme wasn't the work of a moment, particularly with the radically different 2014 car dominating the horizon. With our level of resource, we simply couldn't back-pedal without compromising next year.

"We looked at the front and rear tyre characteristics and put that into all the simulations, which drove us in a direction to optimise the set-up, not just mechanically but aerodynamically as well. The more simulations we did, the better and better the car got, and so we based the whole car around that.

"We also understood the added benefit of swapping the tyres left to right straight from winter testing. We saw it as soon as we got the data through at the end of last year. Pirelli had got them around the wrong way as far as we were concerned and we couldn't understand why they would ever want to run them like that, so we instantly swapped them the other way around for the second run in winter testing. For us it was clear – not on one lap performance, but over a run the gain was huge: 10-20 per cent less tyre wear. You'd take that every day…

"Obviously, a few people then started catching on to what was going on – whether they completely understood the reasons we don't know – but by the time we got to Silverstone most people were doing it. Then we had the British GP problems, reverted to the 2012 tyres, and that was it. It blew our season apart.

"Prior to that, we had sometimes been making one fewer pit stops in the races and the Bahrain GP was a prime example of how we managed the tyres, but unfortunately Adrian Sutil was caught in a collision on the first lap, had to pit, came out in front of Vettel, the race leader, and gapped him for the whole race. That's where we were at that stage. So to say it was disappointing later on is a bit of an understatement!

"When we knew that the tyres were reverting to 2012 spec we suspected that we could be in trouble, but funnily enough at the Silverstone test the problems weren't too apparent and we started to wonder whether we'd got away with it. However, it just happened to be a lovely, hot day with 45 degree track temperature and lots of fast, flowing corners.

"So, it didn't become apparent immediately that we needed to put a lot more energy into the tyres. And so the German GP was a big problem, but Spa not so much because there's a lot more energy to play with there. Then it came back again at Monza and in Singapore. We knew we were going to be in trouble on a street circuit, especially with Pirelli's conservative compound choice. The more conservative they went, the worse it was for us and the better for teams like Red Bull.

"We hoped that we could engineer our way out of it, but that took longer than we thought. Trying to experiment at a race meeting is incredibly difficult. You get a handful of runs in FP1 and then you're into race mode, with long run stints in FP2 ready for Sunday. Then Saturday morning is preparation for qualifying. It takes three or four grands prix to do what you could do in a single day of testing at Barcelona.

"We couldn't generate heat anymore

TECHNICAL SPECIFICATIONS

ENGINE
MAKE/MODEL
Mercedes-Benz FO 108F
CONFIGURATION
2400cc V8 (90 degree)
SPARK PLUGS NGK
ECU FIA standard issue
FUEL Mobil
OIL Mobil 1
BATTERY Sahara Force India

TRANSMISSION
GEARBOX McLaren
FORWARD GEARS Seven
CLUTCH AP Racing

CHASSIS
CHASSIS MODEL Force India VJM06
FRONT SUSPENSION LAYOUT
Aluminium uprights with carbon-fibre
composite, trackrod and pushrod.
Inboard chassis-mounted torsion
springs, dampers and anti-roll bar

REAR SUSPENSION LAYOUT
Aluminium uprights with carbon-fibre
composite, trackrod and pullrod.
Inboard chassis-mounted torsion
springs, dampers and anti-roll bar
DAMPERS Penske
TYRES Pirelli
WHEELS BBS
BRAKE DISCS Brembo
BRAKE PADS Brembo
BRAKE CALIPERS AP Racing
FUEL TANK ATL
INSTRUMENTS McLaren
Electronic Systems

DIMENSIONS
LENGTH 5100mm
WIDTH 1800mm
HEIGHT 950mm
WHEELBASE Not disclosed
TRACK, FRONT Not disclosed
TRACK, REAR Not disclosed
WEIGHT 642kg (including
driver and camera)

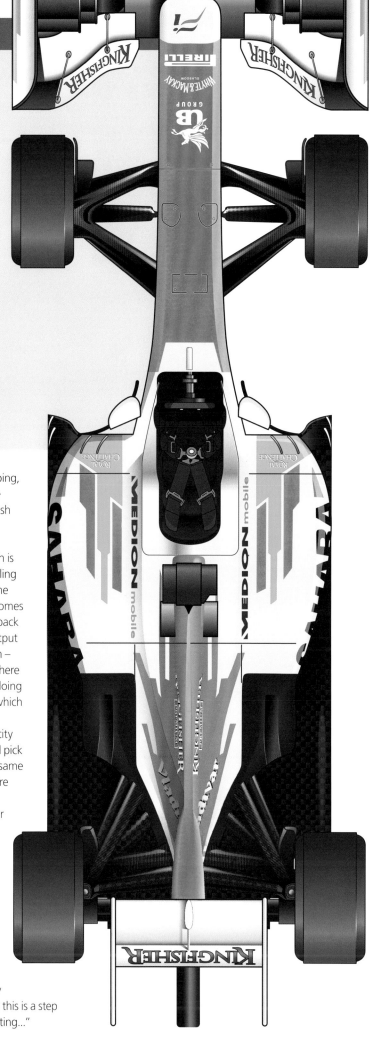

and the tyres were running cold. We weren't getting any payback in the race either because we were too far back, stuck in traffic, with tyres running cold, sliding around and wearing out. It was a lose-lose situation. We also suspected that it may hurt Paul di Resta a bit more than it hurt Adrian in qualifying because Adrian is a bit more aggressive.

"We hadn't been able to simulate the Coanda exhaust effects in 2012 due to dynamometer resource and so did a lot of on-track testing, using rakes to measure where the plume was going and what it was doing. Then, once we got it sitting in the right place, we left it.

"We were far from optimal operationally for the first half of the 2013 season. We had a huge pace advantage that we didn't maximise through too many errors. We had the pit stop error and a mechanical issue in Malaysia, which should have been a huge point score, when the wheel nuts jammed. In Bahrain, we had the issue with Adrian getting tagged on the first lap. We ran underweight at Silverstone and had problems in Monaco and Canada when we should have been way up the points table. That was all disappointing. At the time, we thought it would come to us, but then it was taken further away.

"It was nice to beat big outfits like McLaren with their huge resources, but we knew that it would be difficult to keep them behind us because they'd just

keep developing and developing, which they did, almost to the point of a new car at the British GP. We can't do that.

"We'd had to start concentrating on 2014, which is a huge challenge. The modelling has all changed because of the thermal aspects. The car becomes a giant radiator and the ERS pack – with a magnitude more output than the current KERS system – needs to be cooled as well. There are lots of different ways of doing it and it's about finding out which one's the most efficient.

"We don't have the capacity to do all the experiments and pick out the optimum. We're the same size as we were last year, we're limited and we have to work harder and think a bit smarter while making sure that we don't fall over and make a huge mistake. That's the danger, that you misread all the data and are out of the operating window.

"Whereas in recent years you've had the previous year's car to go back to and compare the new car with – and your new car is always an iteration. But this is a step change. It will be very interesting…"

SAUBER

SAUBER F1 TEAM

PERSONNEL

TEAM PRINCIPAL AND CHIEF EXECUTIVE OFFICER
Monisha Kaltenborn
OPERATIONS DIRECTOR Axel Kruse
CHIEF DESIGNER Matt Morris, then Eric Gandelin
HEAD OF AERODYNAMICS Willem Toet
HEAD OF VEHICLE PERFORMANCE Ben Waterhouse
TEAM MANAGER Beat Zehnder
HEAD OF TRACK ENGINEERING Tom McCullough
DRIVERS Esteban Gutierrez, Nico Hulkenberg
SENIOR STRATEGIST Giampaolo Dall'ara
RACE ENGINEER (GUTIERREZ) Francesco Nenci
RACE ENGINEER (HULKENBERG) Marco Schupbach
HEAD OF TRACK OPERATIONS Otmar Bartsch
CHIEF MECHANIC Reto Camenzind
TEST/THIRD DRIVER Robin Frijns (until September)
TOTAL NUMBER OF EMPLOYEES 300
NUMBER IN RACE TEAM 65
TEAM BASE Hinwil, Switzerland
TELEPHONE +41 44 937 9000
WEBSITE www.sauberf1team.com

TEAM STATS

IN F1 SINCE 1993 then as BMW Sauber 2006-10
FIRST GRAND PRIX South Africa 1993
CONSTRUCTORS' TITLES 0 **DRIVERS' TITLES** 0

SPONSORS

Claro, Telmex, NEC, Oerlikon, Chelsea Football Club, Cuervo Tequila, Interproteccion, Certina, Emil Frey AG

11 NICO HULKENBERG

12 ESTEBAN GUTIERREZ

MID-SEASON UPDATE BOOSTS PERFORMANCE

BY TOM McCULLOUGH
HEAD OF TRACK ENGINEERING

"In the past year at Sauber, we've had quite a few changes on the personnel side. Pierre Wache, head of vehicle performance left, and was replaced by his number two, Ben Waterhouse. Similarly, Matt Morris, who had been chief designer, moved on to McLaren and so Eric Gandelin, who was the head of composite design, stepped up. Eric was working mainly on next year's car at the same time as getting involved with a few projects on this year's C32. Willem Toet continued as head of aerodynamics, and I joined as head of track engineering.

"We operated as a four-man technical committee and made all the decisions as a team. We don't have a technical director as such and operate a very flat system, unlike most other teams. I was a bit sceptical when I joined, but have been quite impressed with it. We're quite lucky that there are no big egos, no one person looking to take the credit for things. We're all very humble and self-critical, and that's the most important thing. If one of you will never admit to making a mistake, then you're scuppered.

"Even though the C32 looked quite different from last year's car, there was quite a lot of carry-over in the packaging as the engine and gearbox were the same.

"The chassis was changed to accommodate different sidepods and cooler arrangements. There were two additional top coolers above the engine: one each for the water and the gearbox. That reduced the space for the radiators, so we needed a different packaging exercise there.

"We changed the exhaust concept on the C32 at the start of the year. That and the sidepods all related to the flow to the back of the car and how close the exhaust Coanda was to the tyre seal/diffuser area. We ran a similar concept at some stages last year, but we'd taken a more aggressive approach at the start of the year.

"The peak performance was pretty high but, for usability and stability at the back of the car in cornering, we ended up going back to an exhaust system a bit like the Red Bull Racing style. This put the exhaust back down nearer the area we needed it, but with the idea of the undercut flow under the side of the car.

"We brought the update package to the Silverstone Young Driver test at the end of July and ran it for the first time at the Hungaroring. You're getting the best of both worlds: you're still getting the very good flow down to the back of the car for the cornering and you're also still directing the exhaust plume much closer to where you want it.

"At lower speeds especially, it meant that we had a bigger operating window and a lot more stability at the rear, which is something you're always chasing with the Pirelli tyres. With the mechanical set-up, that meant we didn't have to be as protective as we'd been, which, overall, improved the car's harmony as well as the balance from corner entry through to mid-corner and exit, in low, medium and high-speed corners.

"At the start of the year, we were underperforming massively, but we could see that, even when the car wasn't working we still weren't too far away in lap-time terms. Because the midfield was so tight, though, we just weren't scoring points. So it was fundamental to doing a good car next year to sort out the C32 aerodynamically.

"I looked upon it as though we had messed up. Fifth or sixth overall is where we see ourselves. We don't have the budget of teams like Red Bull, Ferrari and Mercedes, but we were disappointed that we weren't at our natural level at the start of the season.

"For Esteban Gutierrez, in his rookie season, it was pretty brutal. When the car was two- or three-tenths slower than it should have been, that could make the difference between tenth and 18th place

ENGINE
MAKE/MODEL
Ferrari 056
CONFIGURATION
2398cc V8 (90 degree)
SPARK PLUGS Not disclosed
ECU FIA standard issue
FUEL Not disclosed
OIL Not disclosed
BATTERY Sauber

TRANSMISSION
GEARBOX Ferrari
FORWARD GEARS Seven
CLUTCH Sauber

CHASSIS
CHASSIS MODEL Sauber C32
FRONT SUSPENSION LAYOUT
Upper and lower wishbones,
inboard springs and dampers
actuated by pushrods

REAR SUSPENSION LAYOUT
Upper and lower wishbones,
inboard springs and dampers
actuated by pullrods
DAMPERS Sachs Race
Engineering, Penske
TYRES Pirelli
WHEELS OZ
BRAKE DISCS Brembo
BRAKE PADS Brembo
BRAKE CALIPERS Brembo
FUEL TANK ATL
INSTRUMENTS Sauber

DIMENSIONS
LENGTH 5240mm
WIDTH 1800mm
HEIGHT 1000mm
WHEELBASE Not disclosed
TRACK, FRONT 1495mm
TRACK, REAR 1410mm
WEIGHT 642kg (including
driver and camera)

Sauber F1® Team

and put him out in first qualifying. Those technical committee meetings at the start of the year forced us to have conversations that weren't nice to have…

"The front and rear wing designs were all evolutions from last year. We started off actually running with ones from 2012 and developed them through the year.

"Initially, we spent time focusing on rear wing performance, introducing the main pod/exhaust update at the Hungarian GP, and then we had normal developments, subtle things such as reshaped sidepod deflectors, small front wings, the vanes underneath the front of the chassis, the front and rear brake ducts and the diffuser. There were lots of small changes.

"Sauber has had the front-rear inter-connected suspension for two or three years, which is all about maximising the aero map. When you bolt it onto a car, yes, it's better if you can dynamically run your ride height lower. However, it's also a bigger picture thing in that we could adjust the weightings in the wind tunnel to maximise the car – a lot of work that had been done by Pierre and the guys before me.

"Having had that system for two or three years, the aero development has been focused around that. So once the car was all working, the system was pretty important to the dynamic ride heights that we run.

"As a company, we had good tyre understanding because of personal history within the team – Wache was ex-Michelin – and I was impressed with that side of things when I turned up. Aerodynamically, the generation of tyres that we had at the start of this season required you to run the car with a 3-4mm higher front ride height and most F1 aero maps benefit from lowering the front of the car. Plus, the deflection of the tyres was different, so we had to tune it and change it back a lot to suit those tyres, but they definitely didn't hurt us.

"The second half of the year was obviously vastly better and Nico Hulkenberg drove some great races, notably at the Italian and Korean GPs, where he came fifth and fourth respectively. We had a strong race to get our cars home in sixth and seventh places in Japan as well, where Esteban scored his first points.

"Work on next year's car started early on the conceptual side. It progressed well and we hope to be fighting as we were at the end of this season. But let's see how the powertrain side works out."

TORO ROSSO

SCUDERIA TORO ROSSO

PERSONNEL
TEAM OWNER Dietrich Mateschitz
TEAM PRINCIPAL Franz Tost
TECHNICAL DIRECTOR James Key
CHIEF DESIGNER Luca Furbatto
HEAD OF AERODYNAMICS Brendan Gilhome
HEAD OF VEHICLE PERFORMANCE Laurent Mekies
SPORTING DIRECTOR Steve Nielsen
DRIVERS Daniel Ricciardo, Jean-Eric Vergne
TECHNICAL CO-ORDINATOR Sandro Parrini
LOGISTICS MANAGER Domenico Sangiorgi
RACE ENGINEER (RICCIARDO) Marco Matassa
RACE ENGINEER (VERGNE) Phil Charles
CHIEF MECHANIC Corrado Cardinali
TOTAL NUMBER OF EMPLOYEES Around 300
NUMBER IN RACE TEAM Not disclosed
TEAM BASE Faenza, Italy
TELEPHONE +39 (0)546 696111
WEBSITE www.scuderiatororosso.com

TEAM STATS
IN F1 SINCE 1985 as Minardi until 2005
FIRST GRAND PRIX Brazil 1985
CONSTRUCTORS' TITLES 0 **DRIVERS' TITLES** 0

SPONSORS
Red Bull, CEPSA, Falcon Private Bank, Nova Chemicals, Red Bull Mobile, App Tech, CD Adapco, Del Conca, Duravit, HANGAR-7, Hansgrohe, OMP, Pirelli, Siemens, USAG, Volkswagen

18 JEAN-ERIC VERGNE   **19** DANIEL RICCIARDO

BUILDING UP THE AERO TEAM FOR 2014'S CAR

BY JAMES KEY
TECHNICAL DIRECTOR

"There were three things to do this year, and it was a complex mix. The first was better performance. I arrived in September 2012 when a lot of the STR8 was already defined, but it was heading in a good direction. We were trying to make that happen off the back of a situation in which we were ranked ninth out of 11 teams.

"Our second aim was to grow the team, which doesn't happen overnight. It takes a good few months to attract the right people to the team and wait for their notice periods to be served. That is still happening now.

"Then we had to try to prepare for the major rule changes for 2014 as well. It's been completely the wrong time for a regulation change for us. A frustration is that we've had to do it all very quickly, without having enough time to settle and get a clear direction, nail it, move on to the next bit, get that to fall in line with what you'd already done, and then turn this blueprint in your head into reality.

"We knew that as a result of all that we'd be on the back foot to begin with. The launch car was almost an interim step to what would be a European season car. We did an aero update for that, which was a good step on some chassis work we did at the Chinese GP that immediately showed good results as Daniel Ricciardo both qualified and finished seventh.

"Come the Spanish GP, we refined the chassis updates and brought a large aero package with us that we'd worked on since November, and reaching the third qualifying session and scoring points was beginning to come.

"Last year I said that we could do with an extra dozen guys in the aero department and we've now gone beyond that. The team is really well supported by its owners and we've recruited a lot of people and primarily they are the people arriving now.

"We've restructured as well, and that's beginning to show some promise, but putting better structures in place throughout the team is still a work in progress. We attacked the performance areas that were still growing, but have had to deal with 2013 and 2104 car programmes simultaneously. We've had no choice in that.

"We looked at both exhaust-blowing approaches. We launched with the McLaren-style slot in the top and bigger coke bottle. That's what our 2012 car had. We didn't concentrate massively on that area because we wanted to change the philosophy of the sidepods, as we'd had those very big undercut pods for a couple of years. It looked like that was stalling the development at the back of the car and it was clear we had to pursue a similar philosophy to others. As a result, that approach really didn't help us develop much.

"We got to a sort of hybrid of the Sauber 2012 ramp and what Lotus/Red Bull had. We ended up with that after quite a bit of work. When we saw that Red Bull had retained it and that Lotus had adapted it, we thought, okay, it's probably got some legs.

"It's also about the front wing interaction with the rear of the car, brake duct philosophy and the bigger picture. With the engine mapping, we were free to work with Ferrari on any ideas, and they were very accommodating, but it's extremely tightly restricted.

"We didn't have the front-rear interlinked hydraulic suspension to begin with, but played with it as the season went on. It's a pitch/stiffness damping-type device and we sometimes raced with it, but it wasn't fully established with us.

"On the tyre front, we were much better on the original 2013 tyres. That's what we designed the car around, both for the race and for qualifying. Tyre degradation was never a big issue for us and we liked the 2013 tyre.

TECHNICAL SPECIFICATIONS

ENGINE
MAKE/MODEL
Ferrari 056
CONFIGURATION
2400cc V8 (90 degree)
SPARK PLUGS Not disclosed
ECU FIA standard issue
FUEL Not disclosed
OIL Not disclosed
BATTERY Not disclosed

TRANSMISSION
GEARBOX Not disclosed
FORWARD GEARS Seven
CLUTCH Sachs

CHASSIS
CHASSIS MODEL Toro Rosso STR8
FRONT SUSPENSION LAYOUT
Upper and lower wishbones, torsion
bar springs and anti-roll bars

REAR SUSPENSION LAYOUT
Upper and lower wishbones,
torsion bar springs and anti-roll bars
DAMPERS Multimatic
TYRES Pirelli
WHEELS Apptech
BRAKE DISCS Brembo
BRAKE PADS Brembo
BRAKE CALIPERS Brembo
FUEL TANK ATL
INSTRUMENTS
Scuderia Toro Rosso

DIMENSIONS
LENGTH Not disclosed
WIDTH Not disclosed
HEIGHT Not disclosed
WHEELBASE Not disclosed
TRACK, FRONT Not disclosed
TRACK, REAR Not disclosed
WEIGHT 642kg (including
driver and camera)

SCUDERIA Toro Rosso

"No matter what some say, you do design around the tyres and they are a significant part of vehicle dynamics. You might find that a car has a naturally sharper or lazier turn in, and there are things you can do with the suspension to try to improve that. If you have a lazy front tyre and then, mid-season, you swap it for a sharper one after you've spent all season up to that point trying to sharpen the car… there are all sorts of vehicle and aerodynamically related things too. It was a game changer for us and we didn't quite get it back.

"On the driving side, there was a noticeable maturity and confidence change. When we've had a strong weekend with the car, both the drivers and the rest of us expect to get through to the third qualifying session and then go on to score points. When we were in that position, we were generally able to do it. Our belief and confidence were more apparent than they'd been in 2012.

"The drivers' feedback definitely improved too. Jean-Eric was much more technical than in his first year. The carrot of the Red Bull Racing seat didn't actually change anything and they worked as well as any driver pairing I've seen. Both were team players and shared their feelings about the car. Of course, there was competition too, but it wasn't tense.

"Daniel's single lap pace was strong and reliable. Jean-Eric can be strong too, but freely admits that getting everything together on one lap is his weakness. And, if you're going to get your tyres to last through to the third qualifying session, you have to do it. He's not quite as strong at that as Daniel but, as a racer, he's really good. Give him some free air and Jean-Eric will just nail it.

"It's frustrating to lose Daniel to Red Bull Racing. You always want to hang onto your drivers if they're doing a good job for you, but it shows that the Red Bull process works.

"The pattern of our season seemed to be a little out of phase with Force India and Sauber, our two closest rivals. From a resource level, we were competitive with them, but two things are missing. One is the history. Sauber was a race-winning team with BMW, whereas Toro Rosso is still building. We're a much younger team than the other two. Toro Rosso is built from the remnants of Minardi but it has only been a constructor for the same time as Caterham and Marussia.

And, second, Toro Rosso is based in an isolated community in Faenza, with different ways of doing things, and a different history and legacy."

WILLIAMS

WILLIAMS F1 TEAM

PERSONNEL

TEAM PRINCIPAL Sir Frank Williams
CO-FOUNDER Patrick Head
DEPUTY TEAM PRINCIPAL Claire Williams
CHIEF EXECUTIVE OFFICER Mike O'Driscoll
CHIEF TECHNICAL OFFICER Pat Symonds
TECHNICAL DIRECTOR Mike Coughlan (until July 2013)
CHIEF DESIGNER Ed Wood
HEAD OF AERODYNAMICS Jason Somerville
HEAD OF VEHICLE DYNAMICS Rob Gearing
RENAULT SPORT F1 TEAM SUPPORT Laurent Debout
DRIVERS Valtteri Bottas, Pastor Maldonado
TEAM MANAGER Dickie Stanford
CHIEF RACE ENGINEER Xevi Pujolar
RACE ENGINEER (BOTTAS) Jonathan Eddolls
RACE ENGINEER (MALDONADO) Andrew Murdoch
CHIEF MECHANIC Carl Gaden
DEVELOPMENT DRIVER Susie Wolff
TOTAL NUMBER OF EMPLOYEES 650 (Williams F1)
NUMBER IN RACE TEAM 80 (47 operational, 33 ancillary)
TEAM BASE Grove, England
TELEPHONE +44 (0)1235 777700
WEBSITE www.williamsf1.com

TEAM STATS

IN F1 SINCE 1973 **FIRST GRAND PRIX** Argentina 1973
CONSTRUCTORS' TITLES 9 **DRIVERS' TITLES** 7

SPONSORS

PDVSA, Renault, Venezuela Tourism, Randstad, Wihuri, Hatch, Astana, Experian, ORIS, Kemppi, Thomson Reuters, Pirelli, Shoretel, Michael Johnson Performance, Puma, McGregor, Man, Dom Reilly, Rays, PPg, Michael Caines, Ingenie

16 PASTOR MALDONADO

17 VALTTERI BOTTAS

"OUR PROBLEMS WERE BIGGER THAN THE TYRES"

BY XEVI PUJOLAR
CHIEF RACE ENGINEER

"The FW35 was an evolution of the FW34 which worked well in 2012. We had some areas that we were struggling with on the previous car, however, and the target for 2013 was to improve those areas. But it didn't work out like that and we affected other aspects of the car.

"With last year's FW34, we didn't have the Coanda exhaust because the car was working reasonably well without it but, towards the end of the year, we could see that everyone was going in that direction. We did some tests and could see the potential of the Coanda exhaust, so decided to start with that for 2013. However, we were behind relative to other teams. We used the Coanda from the start of 2013, but were not at the level of the others and that's one of the reasons we were behind in performance. In Abu Dhabi, in fact, we took the Coanda exhaust off the cars and Valtteri Bottas reported no loss of performance and a more stable car.

"Key areas that needed improvement were the aerodynamics forward of the driver, but what technical director Mike Coughlan and aero chief Jason Somerville decided to attack didn't work as expected. We had lost overall performance at the beginning of the season and the downforce numbers were worse. It was more than one thing, though – a case of a few things not integrating as they should have done. And it wasn't just a case of then being able simply to revert to what we had before. The whole thing was extremely complex.

"We also had to contend with senior figures leaving the team. Mark Gillan left the post of chief operations engineer last winter and then Mike Coughlan left during the season. The main problem with people coming and going is the lack of stability and structure that this triggers. Nobody is irreplaceable; it's just that you lose time,

then need to reorganise. And now, with so many races and the season finishing so late in the year, it's quite difficult.

"Mechanically, the FW35 was an evolution and was working with no problems. The issues were aerodynamic and both drivers were struggling with that. Valtteri hadn't had so much mileage and experience with the FW34 and was perhaps not so sensitive, but Pastor Maldonado really liked the FW34 and, in combination with the tyres and what was happening with FW35, he was really struggling to feel it and to get 100 per cent of the performance.

"Pastor was complaining quite a lot, so we made some changes that improved the situation a little, but never managed to really catch up. Initially, you could say that Pastor was struggling compared to Valtteri, sometimes because he couldn't really feel the car. While we made a little bit of progress with that element, the performance was still poor.

"The set-up and the direction in which they pushed was very similar, as both guys run near exactly the same cars, but Pastor needs to feel the front more. The way he turns in to a corner, he's reading a lot of what is happening on the front axle and using that to judge how much speed to carry into the apex. So, if he doesn't get the right information, the performance won't be strong, and that's complex to solve.

"You need to understand where the feel is. If you have understeer, you can change the aero balance mechanically, but then you change it all the way around the corner. Also, the feeling may be an initial one and then a bit later a different one, then mid-corner another one, at which point you're losing the information and the feel for what is happening.

"Even though a lot of people struggled to get their cars right at the beginning of the 2012 season when we had seven

TECHNICAL SPECIFICATIONS

ENGINE
MAKE/MODEL
Renault RS27 2013
CONFIGURATION
2400cc V8 (90 degree)
SPARK PLUGS Not disclosed
ECU FIA standard issue
FUEL Total
OIL Total
BATTERY Not disclosed

TRANSMISSION
GEARBOX WilliamsF1
FORWARD GEARS Seven
CLUTCH Not disclosed

CHASSIS
CHASSIS MODEL Williams FW35
FRONT SUSPENSION LAYOUT
Double wishbones with pushrod-
activated springs and anti-roll bar

REAR SUSPENSION LAYOUT
Double wishbones with pullrod-
activated springs and anti-roll bar
DAMPERS WilliamsF1
TYRES Pirelli
WHEELS RAYS
BRAKE DISCS Not disclosed
BRAKE PADS Not disclosed
BRAKE CALIPERS AP Racing
FUEL TANK ATL
INSTRUMENTS McLaren
Electronic Systems

DIMENSIONS
LENGTH 5000mm
WIDTH 1800mm
HEIGHT 950mm
WHEELBASE FIA maximum
TRACK, FRONT 1450mm
TRACK, REAR 1400mm
WEIGHT 640kg (including
driver and camera)

WILLIAMS
F1 TEAM

different winners in as many grands prix, we didn't think that our problems were tyre-related. We knew the tyres were a bit different, but our problems were much bigger. The rubber didn't help, but it wasn't the reason.

"Last year I'd say we were quite good on the tyres. You can have a car that might be strong in the race, but you struggle a bit with warm-up on one lap. The FW34 was good in qualifying and we could manage the tyres with the performance we had in the races.

"This year, when we dropped so much performance that we struggled more in the race with the tyres as we didn't have any margin to look after them. That has been one of the problems. It's not that our degradation was really bad, but sometimes, when we were on the edge of a two- or three-stop, racing three or four guys around us, needing to push, there was a limitation. The Pirelli changes midway through the season had little impact on us. We hadn't had any tyre issues anyway, as we probably weren't stressing them hard enough!

"The year was all about solving problems and trying to catch up, but we didn't achieve what we wanted. We didn't have big upgrades; we tried to improve by adding things: floor, front wings, rear wing. We also did a lot of changes in the floor area, trying to catch up with all the Coanda work.

"It was frustrating because we knew the limitations and it was about solving

them, but we managed only small improvements so that the drivers could push a bit harder.

"I think it's a shame that the car wasn't strong enough because Valtteri had a very strong rookie season. That was often masked by the car, but he showed that he has real talent, in particular in Canada where he qualified third in the wet conditions. He was always right there in qualifying, pushing Pastor very hard, and in the races he made very few mistakes. He wasn't racing like a rookie, but like a driver with years of experience.

"On top of our trials and tribulations, we also had to contend with the tight deadlines for the major rule changes in 2014, which wasn't ideal. We were actually working on this year's car trying to find solutions until quite late, but we also started the 2014 programme quite early, and with Pat Symonds on board from August there was still time to change, if maybe not for race one, then for races four or five. We've got to hope that 2014 will be better!"

CATERHAM

CATERHAM F1 TEAM

PERSONNEL
OWNERS Tony Fernandes, Dato-Kamarudin Meranun
TEAM PRINCIPAL AND CHIEF EXECUTIVE OFFICER Cyril Abiteboul
TECHNICAL DIRECTOR Mark Smith
DEPUTY TECHNICAL DIRECTOR Jody Egginton
PERFORMANCE DIRECTOR John Iley
CHIEF ENGINEER Lewis Butler
HEAD OF AERODYNAMICS Hari Roberts
HEAD OF VEHICLE DYNAMICS AND R&D Eliot Dason-Barber
HEAD OF PRODUCTION Graham Saunders
DRIVERS Charles Pic, Giedo van der Garde
TEAM MANAGER Graham Watson
CHIEF RACE ENGINEER Gianluca Pisanello
RACE ENGINEER (PIC) Juan Pablo Ramirez
RACE ENGINEER (VAN DER GARDE) Tim Wright
CHIEF MECHANIC Stuart Cramp
RESERVE DRIVERS Heikki Kovalainen, Alexander Rossi
TOTAL NUMBER OF EMPLOYEES 320
NUMBER IN TEAM 78 (48 operational, 30 ancillary)
TEAM BASE Leafield, England & Kuala Lumpur, Malaysia
TELEPHONE +44 (0)1953 851411
WEBSITE www.caterhamf1.com

TEAM STATS
IN F1 SINCE 2010 as Lotus Racing then Team Lotus until 2011
FIRST GRAND PRIX Bahrain 2010
CONSTRUCTORS' TITLES 0 **DRIVERS' TITLES** 0

SPONSORS
GE, EADS/Airbus, Safran, McGregor, Regus, Beelen.nl, Dell/Intel, CNN, Renault, Caterham, Naza, Tune Group, Truphone

20 CHARLES PIC   **21** GIEDO VAN DER GARDE

BALANCING THIS YEAR'S GAINS AGAINST 2014'S

BY MARK SMITH
TECHNICAL DIRECTOR

"It's my opinion that we followed the wrong strategy regarding exhaust blowing in the second half of 2012. We went fairly late into the season, clinging onto the hope that 'maybe we're nearly there, nearly there'. Then it didn't really happen. That hurt our early development of the 2013 car.

"We took the view that rather than push things onto the car for race one that hadn't really have been properly developed in the wind tunnel, we'd do a bit of an interim step so that the monocoque itself was a carry-over.

"There were lots of reasons for that, not least that we were moving from Norfolk to Oxfordshire and the least pain we could give ourselves with homologation and manufacturing, the better.

"We decided to do a fairly limited amount of new stuff for race one on the basis that we'd keep iterating front, middle, rear development in the tunnel up until the Spanish GP. Really, the car we took to Barcelona was what we regarded as our 2013 car. We managed to get probably half of the gains onto Charles Pic's car in Bahrain and that looked quite promising.

"We then wanted to make a massive switch in emphasis to 2014, but when Marussia came out as close to us or even slightly ahead of us as they did, all of that was rather turned on its head. This was a great shame because, rather than switch over to the 2014 model in the wind tunnel – because primarily we'd gone over to 2014 after we'd finished the Barcelona update – there was a lot of agonising about the overall strategy (trying to finish in the top 10 in the constructors' championship) and so then we had to switch back out.

"The problem with that is that by the time you get the parts on the model in the tunnel there have been many weeks of creative thinking, model design, making components, finishing them and getting them to the tunnel and, because we flipped back out, we lost some of that.

"The target we set ourselves was to put roughly another half second on the car, but the gradient at which we were able to develop in the tunnel wasn't as good as we'd done up to Barcelona, simply because we'd wrong-footed ourselves. We'd have been better keeping going longer on 2013 in the first place, and it obviously wasn't ideal for 2014 either.

"We clearly went to a much less experienced driver line-up in 2013 and, if I'm honest, I think we suffered because of that. Which is not to criticise Charles and Giedo van de Garde. It's just that the tyres were different and finding the confidence to believe that we were going in the right direction was a little bit difficult. When Heikki Kovalainen came in and did the first free practice in Bahrain, that was quite useful because it did give us the confidence we wanted in some of the things we were looking at.

"The good thing is that it's all moved in a positive manner, particularly in respect to Giedo. By the second half of the season there wasn't a great deal between them, but initially both drivers were using their tyres completely differently. There was very little common ground and, in terms of trying to find a development direction for the car, it's not the easiest thing if you haven't got the continuity of at least one driver. Charles was very capable of managing the tyres and Giedo was very aggressive with them, so they were massively different from each other. After the tyre construction changed following the British GP, though, that difference seemed to almost disappear. Earlier in the season, it was night and day.

"Getting back to the Coanda, at the end of 2011, I said to our technical guys

TECHNICAL SPECIFICATIONS

ENGINE

MAKE/MODEL
Renault RS27-2013
CONFIGURATION
2400cc V8 (90 degree)
SPARK PLUGS Not disclosed
ECU FIA standard issue
FUEL Total
OIL Various
BATTERY Caterham F1 Team

TRANSMISSION

GEARBOX Red Bull Technology
FORWARD GEARS Seven
CLUTCH AP Racing

CHASSIS

CHASSIS MODEL Caterham CT03
FRONT SUSPENSION LAYOUT
Twin non-parallel wishbone,
pushrod actuated

REAR SUSPENSION LAYOUT
Twin non-parallel wishbone,
pullrod actuated
DAMPERS Caterham F1 Team,
Penske & Multimatic
TYRES Pirelli
WHEELS BBS
BRAKE DISCS Various
BRAKE PADS Various
BRAKE CALIPERS AP Racing
FUEL TANK Caterham F1 Team & ATL
INSTRUMENTS Various

DIMENSIONS

LENGTH More than 5000mm
WIDTH Not disclosed
HEIGHT 950mm
WHEELBASE More than 3000mm
TRACK, FRONT Not disclosed
TRACK, REAR Not disclosed
WEIGHT 640kg (including
driver and camera)

CATERHAM F1® TEAM

that we weren't going to pursue exhaust blowing in 2012. We were well aware of our limitations, the first being that we weren't able to model it properly in the wind tunnel. We didn't have the flow capacity for it to be representative.

"Then John Iley joined us from McLaren, who were making extremely good use of it, and so it was logical that we took another look at it. The thing that hadn't changed was our ability to model it. Then the first race that we ran it was Silverstone 2012. All right, the weather was rubbish but I think the writing was on the wall that we weren't getting what some people expected us to get from it.

"By the time we got to Hungary my frustrations were significantly higher and I remember asking for a back-to-back because we'd got the kit to be able to run the previous spec car effectively. We did that and there was nothing between them.

"I would have abandoned it but we didn't for a whole host of reasons, and unfortunately it drained a load of resources. Because we were doing it, one of the things I pushed quite hard on, not in isolation, was an upgrade to the tunnel we were using at Williams, so that by mid-November we then did have the ability to at least have a reasonably representative model of the exhaust blowing on the car, and in 2013 we pursued it as best we could.

"What pulled us a little away from Marussia, though, was development across the whole car. The front wing was definitely a good step. The Barcelona update was a lot of new stuff – the front wing was part of that package along with rear development around the exhaust blowing. We did an aero test in advance and the correlation was almost 100 per cent at the front.

At the rear, low speed was pretty good, but as we went up the speed range it wasn't just that we didn't get the gains we were looking for, but also that we were losing relative to the previous package. We worked on trying to pull some of those gains out and succeeded to a decent extent. In the end we had something that was reasonably well-balanced.

"The other thing we did was the hydraulic axle linking which allowed us to drag out a bit more performance. We went to the Young Driver test and it worked well straight out of the box. By then, we had to accept that we had what we had. There were more gains to be had at the factory working on our car for 2014."

MARUSSIA

THE TEAM

PERSONNEL
TEAM PRINCIPAL John Booth
CHIEF EXECUTIVE OFFICER Andy Webb
PRESIDENT AND SPORTING DIRECTOR
Graeme Lowdon
CHIEF DESIGNER John McQuilliam
DEPUTY DESIGN CHIEF Rob Taylor
HEAD OF AERODYNAMICS Richard Taylor
HEAD OF RESEARCH AND DEVELOPMENT
Richard Connell
HEAD OF MANUFACTURING Christian Silk
CHIEF ENGINEER Dave Greenwood
TEAM MANAGER Dave O'Neill
DRIVERS Jules Bianchi, Max Chilton
RACE ENGINEER (BIANCHI) Paul Davison
RACE ENGINEER (CHILTON) Gary Gannon
CHIEF MECHANIC Richard Wrenn
NO 1 MECHANICS Kieron Marchant, Ian Staniforth
RESERVE DRIVER Rodolfo Gonzalez
TOTAL NUMBER OF EMPLOYEES 210
NUMBER IN RACE TEAM 47
TEAM BASE Banbury, England
TELEPHONE +44 (0)1295 517270
WEBSITE www.marussiaf1team.com

TEAM STATS
IN F1 SINCE 2010 as Virgin Racing until 2011
FIRST GRAND PRIX Bahrain 2010
CONSTRUCTORS' TITLES 0 **DRIVERS' TITLES** 0

SPONSORS
A-Gas, Armin Strom, Avelo, Bifold, Free radio, LDC, Liga Stavok, Marussia, Pirelli, QNET, RBC, Rototrade, Royals, Sage ERP X3

  22 JULES BIANCHI   **23 MAX CHILTON**

"WE FORCED CATERHAM TO FOCUS ON 2013"

BY JOHN BOOTH
TEAM PRINCIPAL

"The MR-02 was the first of our cars to have a full development programme. It had been in the wind tunnel since the previous June, so was a big step forward, probably by a couple of per cent. As a result, the first four or five grands prix went as well as we could have hoped. We'd closed the gap on the front-runners and Jules Bianchi got us an important 13th place in the Malaysian GP.

"I think Caterham came into the year hoping not to do a lot on their car and to put all their efforts into the 2014 car, and we sort of forced their hand a little. The last major update we had on the car was for the Spanish GP, with a small update for the British GP, which was pretty much the last things we brought to the car.

"We have a design team of maybe 70-80 people, as opposed to the several hundred that a lot of teams have, so we just had to commit to the 2014 car. We had no choice. It's a massive challenge for anyone to get a car built for the new regulations but, for us, it's particularly difficult.

"The updates were all bodywork. Silverstone was just drumlets, a new front wing endplate and flaps, although the updates for the Spanish GP were more comprehensive: engine cover, sidepods and turning vanes. We did have an attempt at another update later in the year, but it didn't quite work out in the wind tunnel and we decided to shelve it.

"From the moment that Pat Symonds arrived as technical consultant, he instilled some real discipline into the whole programme. Nothing ever came to the track that wasn't either fit to go on the car or a worthwhile performance gain. In previous years, we'd been bolting stuff onto the car that we weren't sure about and which often didn't work, which was demoralising for the guys in the garage.

"We've got a very young group with some experienced heads of department: John McQuilliam, the chief designer, Rich Taylor, head of aero, and Rob Taylor, head of mechanical, have been around for a long time. Pat really put a structure in place more than the people. We'll miss Pat, but he doesn't design a car, so it doesn't affect the 2014 car. I spoke at length with Pat before he left for Williams and went through every area and every person in every department. He was very happy with everything we've got.

"Firming the driver line-up was pretty last minute. Luiz Razia was with us as a reserve driver and we were looking forward to running him in 2013, but then he had difficulties with his sponsorship. We ran out of patience and time just as Force India decided on their driver line-up, so the timing was perfect with Jules Bianchi.

"The whole deal was done in one afternoon. We started talking lunchtime of the second day at the Barcelona test, he had a seat fit that evening and was in the car the following day. Nicolas Todt, his manager, knows the game and was a straightforward chap to deal with.

"The biggest concern for me was that it would have been very easy for Jules to be thinking about what he could have had. He'd driven a lot of miles in a Ferrari and came very close to getting the Force India race seat, but he couldn't have been more positive.

"Although neither Jules nor Max Chilton had raced in a grand prix before, Jules had done quite a lot of testing in much better cars than ours. Even from his very first day he gave us pointers in the direction we needed to be working. We could have had a load of shunts, but that just didn't happen. They were bloody great, the pair of them.

"Max really stepped up his game. He was overshadowed by Jules at the

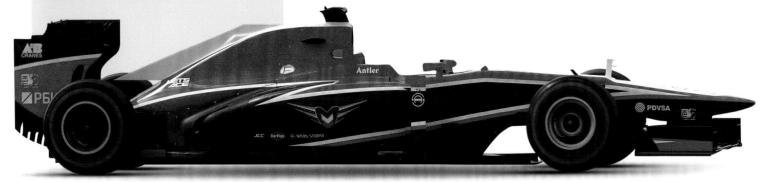

TECHNICAL SPECIFICATIONS

ENGINE
MAKE/MODEL
Cosworth CA2013K
CONFIGURATION
2400cc V8 (90 degree)
SPARK PLUGS Champion
ECU FIA standard issue
FUEL BP Castrol
OIL BP Castrol
BATTERY Braille

TRANSMISSION
GEARBOX Xtrac/Marussia
FORWARD GEARS Seven
CLUTCH AP

CHASSIS
CHASSIS MODEL Marussia MR-02
FRONT SUSPENSION LAYOUT
Pushrod-operated double wishbone

REAR SUSPENSION LAYOUT
Pullrod-operated double wishbone
DAMPERS Penske
TYRES Pirelli
WHEELS BBS
BRAKE DISCS Hitco
BRAKE PADS Hitco
BRAKE CALIPERS AP Racing
FUEL TANK ATL
INSTRUMENTS McLaren
Electronic Systems

DIMENSIONS
LENGTH 4900mm
WIDTH 1800mm
HEIGHT 950mm
WHEELBASE 3300mm
TRACK, FRONT 1800mm
TRACK, REAR 1800mm
WEIGHT 642kg (including driver and camera)

start of the year but showed great character and dug deep. He looks quite an angelic guy, but he's got plenty of steel down there, he really has. He never once whinged or complained, just worked really hard. It would be great to keep the same two next year as they've been a delight to work with.

"Our shortfall has simply been lack of downforce. Marc Hynes goes out on track and watches quite a lot and says our car displays similar traits to the others, just with less downforce. Mechanically we were pretty pleased as the MR-02 handled pretty well, drove quite nicely and the drivers gave good feedback. But, if you haven't got downforce, you're going nowhere.

"The tenth place battle was important and we were hanging on by our fingernails. At the end of the season, Caterham had a 0.5s advantage over us. That takes some getting around. In 2012, we had bad luck at the very end when Caterham moved past us at the final race in Brazil. We spent all those years with Timo Glock praying for a wet race, but this time we were praying for sunshine!

"Fate can be very fickle. Going back to Brazil 2012, without Jean-Eric Vergne's moment of madness under the safety car we could have scored a point that day. We got the strategy dead right and had Pic so far in front of the Caterhams. It was only when we switched onto intermediates and he hadn't had much experience on

them, that it cost us dear. We didn't want to lose it at the last minute again!

"Over the year, the absolute high was Australia, as the car was brilliant out of the box. Spa qualifying was pretty good, for the guys to take the chance when we were given it. The low was Monaco, Jules's home race, when we let him down in qualifying and it went against us in the race too without doing very much wrong.

"Next year will be interesting. We got the engine deal done early enough to incorporate it into the design plans, but it was pretty borderline, right on the cusp. Ferrari were giving us some information even before the deal was signed, enabling us to progress. Not hyper-sensitive stuff, but enough to get us going. They've been first class people to deal with, very open and proactive.

"It's a challenge for everyone, and not just the money side. Try telling Boeing or Airbus, 'Sorry lads, you're losing a third of your fuel next year, but you've still got to get to Australia! You've got two years to sort it out'..."

THE RACES

With 19 grands prix located in 19 different nations spread across four continents, the 2013 FIA Formula One World Championship™ was the most global sporting competition on Earth

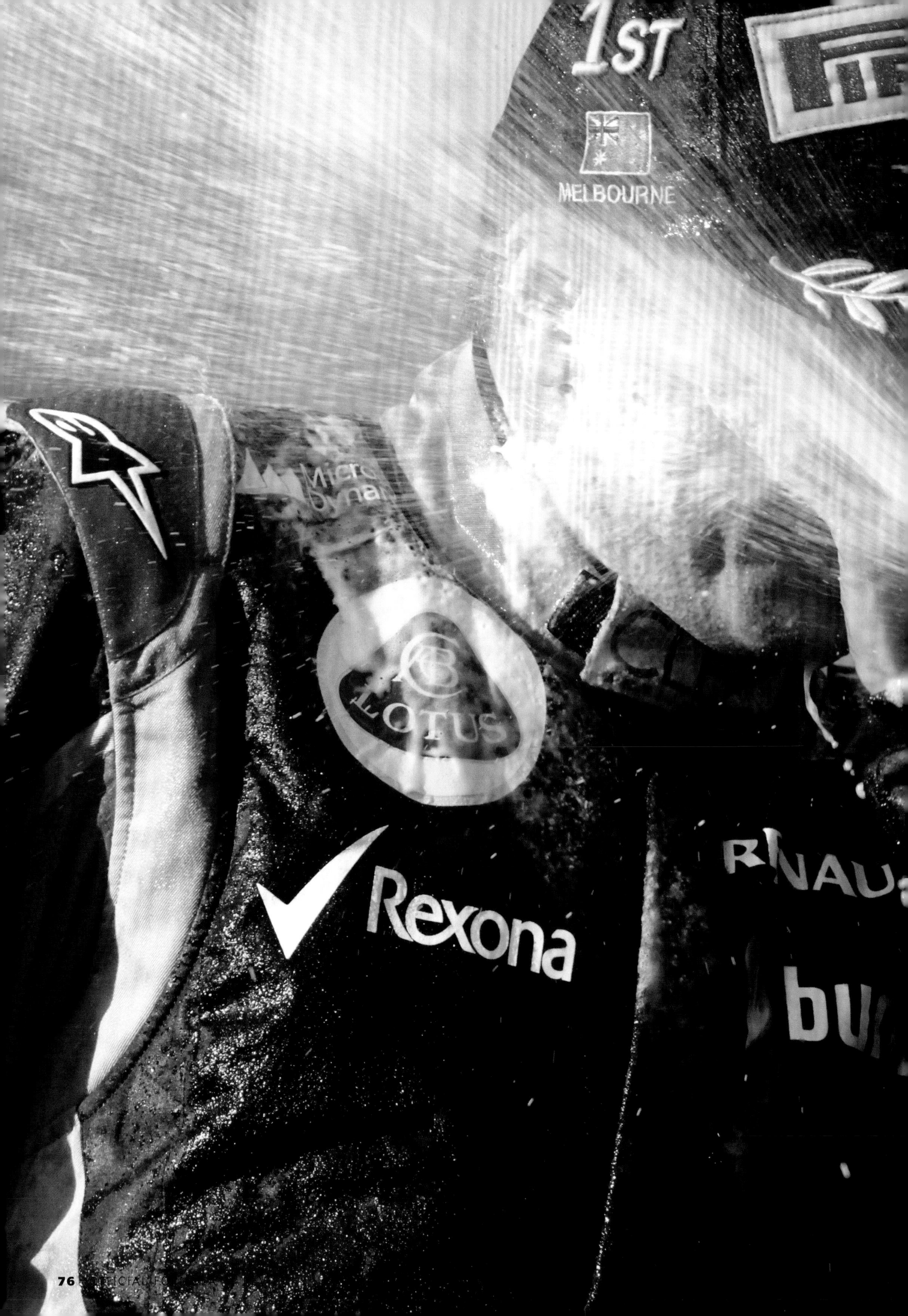
1ST
MELBOURNE
Rexona

2013 FORMULA 1 ROLEX AUSTRALIAN GRAND PRIX

15-17 MARCH
ALBERT PARK
MELBOURNE

IMPOSSIBLE TO PREDICT

Pre-season testing had suggested that the Lotus was able to preserve its tyres better than its rivals, and Kimi Räikkönen took full advantage to win an intriguing 2013 season opener from seventh on the grid

Looking at the grid, it would have been impossible to predict how things would turn out, the only guaranteed outcome being that McLaren would be miles behind the frontrunning teams. In fact, a pecking order that over one lap read "Red Bull Racing, Mercedes, Ferrari, Lotus" was very nearly reversed on Sunday afternoon, becoming instead "Lotus, Ferrari, Red Bull Racing, Mercedes".

Qualifying, started late due to heavy rain, and there was plenty of drama as drivers explored the limits. Felipe Massa, Giedo van der Garde, Esteban Gutierrez and Charles Pic all made heavy front-end contact with the wall, although the first two were at least able to return to the pits and resume the session with new wings. Lewis Hamilton also touched the wall with his rear wing after a spin, and was lucky to get back on track after being forced to find reverse gear.

There was more heavy rain in the break between sessions, which led to a further delay before Q2, and then another. At 18:47, with sunset officially just 50 minutes away, the decision was taken to postpone the session until 11:00 on Sunday.

After more rain in the morning, the session got underway on schedule on a damp but drying track,

OPPOSITE TOP Sebastian Vettel gets the power down best to lead away from pole, chased by a fast-starting Felipe Massa and Lewis Hamilton, as Mark Webber is slow off the mark after his KERS failed

BELOW Charles Pic gets his Caterham crossed up on his first outing for the team in which he worked his way past his team-mate

OPPOSITE BOTTOM After switching from Sauber, Sergio Perez prepares for the start of his first race for McLaren, albeit way back in 15th place on the grid

with high winds and a low 13°C track temperature adding to the challenge. Drivers started the Q3 session on intermediate tyres, but in the final five minutes began to pit for dry tyres, giving themselves two or three flying laps in which to set a time.

Hamilton went top before Sebastian Vettel moved the goalposts while crossing the line with a second to go, giving himself one more lap. Mark Webber then went second but, with no one else beating his time, Vettel was able to pull into the pits and abort his final lap.

Behind Webber, Hamilton held onto third, while the Ferraris had solid runs to qualify fourth and fifth, with Felipe Massa besting Fernando Alonso by 0.003s. After being fast when the track was wet, Nico Rosberg had to settle for sixth, with the top ten completed by Räikkönen, Romain Grosjean, Paul di Resta and a frustrated Jenson Button.

Tyres were always going to be the key to the race, and specifically how long the supersofts would last in the opening stint. There was also the question of a potential surprise being sprung by anyone starting outside the top ten on the medium tyre and then running a long first stint.

INSIDE LINE
ERIC BOULLIER
LOTUS
TEAM PRINCIPAL

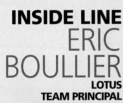

"It's great to start the year with a win. It was in the second stint of the race that I really thought it was going to happen for us. I could see that the others were on a three-stop strategy and that we had good pace and were planning just two stops.

"Obviously, we were just a bit

nervous about the tyre degradation but, when we achieved our target number of laps early on, we knew that the win was feasible. We knew we could do two stints, but there's always a risk and we couldn't be complacent.

"The car was very good, but Kimi is also capable of changing his driving style to save the tyres. I think he only spun up the rear tyres three times in the whole race. The combination of car and driver worked very well.

"At the beginning we were a little concerned that Hamilton was going to do a two-stop race as well, but then I saw the Mercedes' pace and realised that, even if they did manage that, it was all right for us. I hope the fact that we did it comfortably bodes well for the rest of the year.

"Romain had bad luck. He had a poor start and got into the traffic.

Being stuck there destroying his tyres was no good, so we switched him to a three-stop strategy to try to help him clear it. We never could achieve that though, so he had a frustrating race. If we had managed to spring him, he'd have been capable of running at a similar pace to Kimi.

"Abu Dhabi was a good win last year, but this one was clearly on merit. We now need to extract the potential of the car as the season progresses. People talk about budgets and that's important, but, even if you have money and don't find the right development path, it doesn't work.

"We have a pretty good team. In 2012, we were more or less able to follow developments and so we should be able to do it this year as well. When we won in Abu Dhabi last year it might have been late

but really it was just delivering something that we had been expecting since the beginning of the season. It was a just reward.

"This is a different story: new win, new car. I think my guys have done a good job. We can't take too much out of it, though. The Red Bull qualifying pace was very impressive. There's no doubt they are going to be fast on one lap, but as long as they are not as quick as that on long runs, I'll be happy!"

AUSTRALIA

MELBOURN

UBS

Vettel led away at the start from Massa, Alonso, Hamilton and Räikkönen. Meanwhile, Webber found himself swamped after experiencing KERS and telemetry problems on the way to the grid.

Initially, it appeared that Vettel was well set, but tyre degradation came into play and he was one of the first to pit, coming in on lap 7. Massa and Alonso both led a lap before their stops, then Hamilton and Rosberg also took turns in the lead prior to coming in.

The surprise package was Force India's Adrian Sutil, who started 12th on the mediums and worked his way into the lead as those ahead pitted. He then stayed comfortably in front of Vettel and the Ferraris before his first stop coincided with the second stops of those behind him, and that kept him in the fight.

It was at that stage that Räikkönen entered the equation. Having stopped relatively early on lap 9, he was able to run a second stint that was both long and extremely fast, and it soon became apparent that he would be able to make it on two stops while his main rivals were set for three. Räikkönen finally pitted for a second time on lap 34.

He briefly dropped to fifth, but as Massa, Vettel and Alonso all made their third stops, he moved up

TALKING POINT
NO PACE –
NO ANSWER

The opening round of 2013 marked a nightmarish start for McLaren. The team knew that the final Barcelona pre-season test didn't look promising and Jenson Button did well to put the new MP4-28 on the fifth row of the grid in Melbourne and go on to collect two points for ninth. Qualifying told the tale, though, as he was

almost 2.5s off Red Bull's ultimate pace. On-track, the car looked stiff, disconnected and as much a handful as the Lotus E21 was compliant.

McLaren Team Principal Martin Whitmarsh was honest. "It's been one of the most difficult first days to a season that I can remember," he said on Friday. "The car suffered from lack of grip, understeer, poor ride and we didn't go forward."

McLaren was pretty much alone in a radical redesign for 2013, with pullrod front suspension and significant changes elsewhere. Button was surprised by the car's complexity in testing, with set-up changes taking longer than before.

Had the team bitten off too much in a year preceding such fundamental changes to the engine/powertrain regulations?

If there's a team with the resources and capability to pursue aggressive simultaneous race development, you have to fancy it being McLaren. But at the same time, Vodafone – only the team's fourth title sponsor in 50 years (after Yardley, Marlboro and West) – had already announced that it wouldn't be renewing its McLaren contract after seven years, which left Whitmarsh fielding awkward questions.

Could he categorically kill off the story that McLaren was going to bring back its 2012 car? "Yes, I can categorically kill it off. For the time being..."

Then: "Why is it that on many forums, fans of the team want Ron Dennis to run McLaren?" Whitmarsh batted back: "Because he's such a warm and cuddly sort of individual."

In the background were stories linking Honda to an F1 return, with McLaren. It made perfect sense. The technical synergies between the pursuit of efficiency for the 2014 regulations and their direct application to the road car sphere were designed to lure back the manufacturers.

For a manufacturer like Honda, it isn't every day that a team of McLaren's calibre, with its resources and ever-growing brand image, is looking for a new partner. It's inevitable that McLaren will go a different route from Mercedes in the long-term, so what better time to renew a partnership that won them four drivers' titles in five years between 1988 and 1992?

For the moment, though, McLaren had some fires to put out.

to second. The leader at this stage was Sutil, who had done a magnificent job to stay in the fight by running two stints on mediums, and leaving his compulsory supersoft run to the end. However, he was unable to hold off Räikkönen, who moved into the lead on lap 43. When Sutil made his stop for supersofts on lap 48, he dropped back, leaving Räikkönen well clear of Alonso, Vettel and Massa as the final laps ran out.

Räikkönen's victory was a truly remarkable performance, and a reminder of what a clever and canny driver the 2007 champion has become. Lotus has given him a great car, but its creators admitted that even they couldn't pinpoint just why they were able to hit the sweet spot with the tyres in Australia. It was also a reminder that this is a team still packed with guys who won a championship as recently as 2006, and know how to do it, as Kimi's two-stop strategy was executed brilliantly.

"The team worked very well and we had a good plan. We followed it and it worked out perfectly for us," said Räikkönen. "I could save the tyres and I could go fast if I needed to and I could really drive very easily. It was one of the easiest races I've done to win. Hopefully, we can have many more of these kinds of races."

"We had no doubts even though we were in the same position last year in China and had some issues," said Lotus boss Eric Boullier. "Now we were quite confident that we could do it, but Kimi's second stint was the key, although the first one was important, too, to be able to last long enough on the supersoft. It was long enough and fast enough."

It seemed appropriate that 2012 title rivals Alonso and Vettel finished second and third, carrying on their fight. The Spaniard was happy to get a handy helping of points after such a bad start to the 2012 season. He put in a typically committed race, jumping both Vettel and his team-mate at the second round of stops, a

development that left Massa somewhat frustrated. Later the Brazilian accepted that had he pitted as early as Alonso, and thus stayed ahead of the Spaniard, he would have faced tyre troubles later in the race.

"For sure the global picture of what I've seen during these three days, which were very intense, was more or less what I was expecting if you look back at the testing," explained Ferrari Team Principal Stefano Domenicali.

"We had a group of cars that are quite competitive, we had a qualifying where – even if it's difficult to understand from the pure performance point-of-view because of the conditions – we saw Red Bull being

OPPOSITE Vettel led until his first pit stop, but couldn't get the performance he wanted from his tyres, so fell to an eventual third

ABOVE The sun appeared to be shining on Hamilton when he outqualified the McLarens, but he had to settle for fifth place

BELOW Fernando Alonso drove an extremely dogged race to bring his Ferrari F138 home in second place

very strong and Mercedes very strong as expected. Then we saw a different picture during the race. As was clear during the test, we saw a very consistent Lotus, with good race pace. In that respect, there wasn't a really big surprise."

For Vettel, third was good damage limitation on a day when things didn't quite go right, and the cool conditions didn't favour the Red Bull. The three-time champion was also well aware that while this time it didn't play out for him, the rest of the weekend demonstrated that the RB9 is very competitive.

"I think the first thing is to have a fast car, and then the second thing is to make sure that car uses its tyres correctly," said Red Bull Team Principal Christian Horner. "There are lot of lessons that we've learned from today which will hopefully be relevant for cool races in the future. Nobody in the team is leaving here despondent or disheartened by today's race. We've had a very, very solid weekend, and found ourselves a bit out of the window with the tyres in the race, but we've got a quick car."

Hamilton could have done what Räikkönen did, as he was even better set for a two-stop run after a surprisingly long first stint. However, the Mercedes

wasn't as happy on the medium tyre as on the supersoft. After switching to Plan B and joining the majority on three stops, Lewis finished fifth. He was beaming afterwards, though, encouraged massively by the potential he had discovered at Mercedes.

The recovering Webber took sixth, again disappointed at his home race. Sutil struggled badly on his supersofts at the end and slipped to a still encouraging seventh, ahead of team-mate di Resta.

Button made it home ninth, two places ahead of new team-mate Sergio Perez. There was a huge gulf in performance to McLaren's usual rivals, and it was apparent that bridging this isn't going to be the work of a moment. As ever, Team Principal Martin Whitmarsh remained optimistic, although he appeared to be clutching at straws.

"We struggled to have a proper understanding in testing – I think a lot of people did," he said. "Winter testing was very strange this year. We knew we weren't coming here with masses of confidence. I think it frankly was a little bit worse than expected.

"We knew to an extent that this circuit would play to our weaknesses, and I think it certainly managed to do that. We didn't have enough of an understanding to fix it, but I think we're gaining that. I think you've got to know what you're trying to do, you've got to understand what the problems are, and then you've got to work hard to fix it. Sadly, there's no magic and we've just got to work hard now and get it right."

Grosjean struggled more than Räikkönen with his tyres and could not better tenth place in the second Lotus, just ahead of Perez who, like Sutil, had started on mediums. Among those out of luck was Rosberg, who had been destined for a good helping of points until hitting electrical problems; and Nico Hulkenberg, who failed even to make the start after Sauber discovered a fuel system problem shortly before his car was due to go to the grid.

BELOW Pastor Maldonado gets it all wrong and spins his Williams FW35 out of the race at Turn 1

BOTTOM It was a good start to the 2013 season with three teams represented on the podium, and not in the expected order, after Lotus racer Räikkönen beat Ferrari's Alonso and Red Bull Racing's Vettel

SNAPSHOT FROM
AUSTRALIA

CLOCKWISE FROM RIGHT

Melbourne's distinctive skyline provides an iconic backdrop when viewed from Turn 13; Lewis Hamilton parks his Mercedes after technical problems, but went on to score 10 points in the race; Felipe Massa arrives in the pits but later rued his strategy; Jean-Eric Vergne surprises some birds at Albert Park; Jenson Button managed only ninth; Sebastian Vettel started the season out in front, but could only hold onto third at the chequered flag; Giedo van der Garde made his Formula 1 debut for Caterham; Alonso continues to be a focus of media attention; the Lotus pit crew celebrate Kimi Räikkönen's race victory; McLaren's top brass check the latest weather conditions during the disrupted qualifying sessions

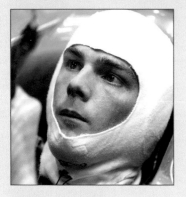

AUSTRALIA
MELBOURNE
ROUND 1

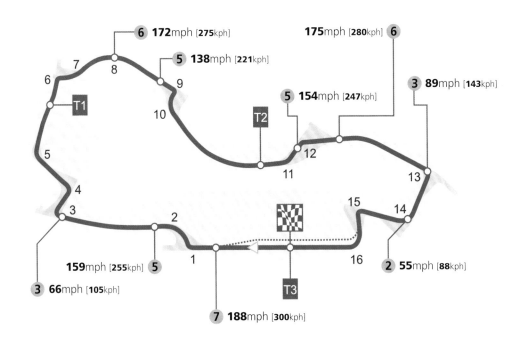

6 172mph [275kph]
5 138mph [221kph]
6 175mph [280kph]
3 89mph [143kph]
5 154mph [247kph]
5 159mph [255kph]
3 66mph [105kph]
7 188mph [300kph]
2 55mph [88kph]

RACE RESULTS

RACE DATE 17 March 2013
CIRCUIT LENGTH 3.295 miles
NO. OF LAPS 58
RACE DISTANCE 191.110 miles
WEATHER Overcast, 18°C
TRACK TEMP 25°C
LAP RECORD Michael Schumacher,
1m24.125s, 141.016mph, 2004

PRACTICE 1

	Driver	Time	Laps
1	S Vettel	1m27.211s	16
2	F Massa	1m27.289s	17
3	F Alonso	1m27.547s	16
4	L Hamilton	1m27.552s	18
5	M Webber	1m27.668s	18
6	K Räikkönen	1m27.887s	17
7	N Rosberg	1m28.013s	17
8	A Sutil	1m28.426s	19
9	J Button	1m28.440s	19
10	R Grosjean	1m28.520s	15
11	S Perez	1m28.597s	19
12	N Hulkenberg	1m28.786s	19
13	P di Resta	1m28.910s	18
14	P Maldonado	1m29.443s	20
15	V Bottas	1m29.928s	19
16	E Gutierrez	1m30.203s	17
17	J-E Vergne	1m30.729s	17
18	D Ricciardo	1m30.969s	19
19	J Bianchi	1m31.263s	24
20	M Chilton	1m32.176s	23
21	C Pic	1m32.274s	21
22	G van der Garde	1m32.388s	18

PRACTICE 2

	Driver	Time	Laps
1	S Vettel	1m25.908s	33
2	M Webber	1m26.172s	31
3	N Rosberg	1m26.322s	26
4	K Räikkönen	1m26.361s	38
5	R Grosjean	1m26.680s	32
6	F Alonso	1m26.748s	35
7	L Hamilton	1m26.772s	28
8	F Massa	1m26.855s	32
9	A Sutil	1m27.435s	35
10	N Hulkenberg	1m28.187s	34
11	J Button	1m28.294s	30
12	P di Resta	1m28.311s	37
13	S Perez	1m28.566s	33
14	D Ricciardo	1m28.627s	31
15	E Gutierrez	1m28.772s	33
16	P Maldonado	1m28.852s	36
17	J-E Vergne	1m28.968s	36
18	V Bottas	1m29.386s	39
19	J Bianchi	1m29.696s	32
20	C Pic	1m30.165s	37
21	M Chilton	1m30.600s	36
22	G van der Garde	1m32.450s	11

PRACTICE 3

	Driver	Time	Laps
1	R Grosjean	1m26.929s	14
2	F Alonso	1m27.000s	7
3	F Massa	1m27.241s	10
4	P di Resta	1m27.533s	9
5	K Räikkönen	1m27.625s	12
6	D Ricciardo	1m27.849s	19
7	J-E Vergne	1m27.860s	16
8	A Sutil	1m28.069s	15
9	N Hulkenberg	1m28.253s	18
10	E Gutierrez	1m28.253s	20
11	N Rosberg	1m28.486s	13
12	S Vettel	1m29.808s	9
13	M Webber	1m30.073s	16
14	J Bianchi	1m30.388s	17
15	G van der Garde	1m30.598s	20
16	C Pic	1m30.959s	19
17	J Button	1m33.236s	7
18	S Perez	1m33.527s	8
19	P Maldonado	1m39.232s	13
20	V Bottas	1m39.779s	13
21	M Chilton	1m42.872s	13
22	L Hamilton	1m47.246s	9

QUALIFYING 1

	Driver	Time
1	N Rosberg	1m43.380s
2	F Alonso	1m43.850s
3	R Grosjean	1m44.284s
4	S Perez	1m44.300s
5	M Webber	1m44.472s
6	F Massa	1m44.635s
7	S Vettel	1m44.657s
8	J Button	1m44.688s
9	J-E Vergne	1m44.871s
10	L Hamilton	1m45.456s
11	K Räikkönen	1m45.545s
12	P di Resta	1m45.601s
13	N Hulkenberg	1m45.930s
14	D Ricciardo	1m46.450s
15	V Bottas	1m47.328s
16	A Sutil	1m47.330s
17	P Maldonado	1m47.614s
18	E Gutierrez	1m47.776s
19	J Bianchi	1m48.147s
20	M Chilton	1m48.909s
21	G van der Garde	1m49.519s
22	C Pic	1m50.626s

QUALIFYING 2

	Driver	Time
1	N Rosberg	1m36.194s
2	M Webber	1m36.524s
3	L Hamilton	1m36.625s
4	J Button	1m36.644s
5	F Massa	1m36.666s
6	F Alonso	1m36.691s
7	S Vettel	1m36.745s
8	P di Resta	1m36.901s
9	K Räikkönen	1m37.517s
10	R Grosjean	1m37.641s
11	N Hulkenberg	1m38.067s
12	A Sutil	1m38.134s
13	J-E Vergne	1m38.778s
14	D Ricciardo	1m39.042s
15	S Perez	1m39.900s
16	V Bottas	1m40.290s

Best sectors – Practice
Sec 1	S Vettel	28.459s
Sec 2	S Vettel	22.968s
Sec 3	S Vettel	34.223s

Speed trap – Practice
1	L Hamilton	194.489mph
2	S Perez	193.930mph
3	J Button	193.930mph

Best sectors – Qualifying
Sec 1	S Vettel	28.427s
Sec 2	S Vettel	23.312s
Sec 3	S Vettel	35.299s

Speed trap – Qualifying
1	L Hamilton	193.308mph
2	F Massa	192.438mph
3	P di Resta	191.568mph

Sebastian Vettel

"You're disappointed when you start first but don't win. We were a bit too aggressive with the tyres and lost the fronts and the rears, while others did a little better."

Fernando Alonso

"The three-stop strategy was right with the degradation we had, and bringing forward the second stop by a few laps meant I was able to pass Vettel and Sutil."

Jenson Button

"Our car isn't quick enough yet, so the team did a great job to achieve even as much as we did. The car needs a lot of work before it's properly competitive."

Kimi Räikkönen

"I made up a few places and then had a good battle with Lewis but, after that, it was probably one of my easiest wins. You can't start the year much better than that."

Nico Rosberg

"An electric problem finished my race, which was a shame as I was on a two-stop strategy and all set to score a decent result. There were lots of positives though."

Nico Hulkenberg

"I'm bitterly disappointed, but things like this – fuel system failure – can happen. What bothers me is that I lost all this mileage, which is so vital early in the year."

Mark Webber

"We had issues on the grid, getting the telemetry to the pits. We lost KERS early on and had a slow stop (due to a front-jack failure), which put me behind Jenson."

Felipe Massa

"I had an attacking start, in which I was fighting for the top places. Maybe if we'd brought forward the second stop, the podium would have been on."

Sergio Perez

"I got a good start, which is a bonus. After that, even though the team did a great job with strategy, we didn't have enough pace to make further progress."

Romain Grosjean

"My car felt so good until the race, but the race was long and quite difficult. We know Albert Park can be a tricky circuit and the weather really didn't help."

Lewis Hamilton

"I had a strong first stint and made the supersofts last longer than the others. We'd planned two stops, but then converted to a three-stop strategy."

Esteban Gutierrez

"My main goal was to finish, so I want to thank the team, because in qualifying we had a good chance and today we were able to recover some of what we lost."

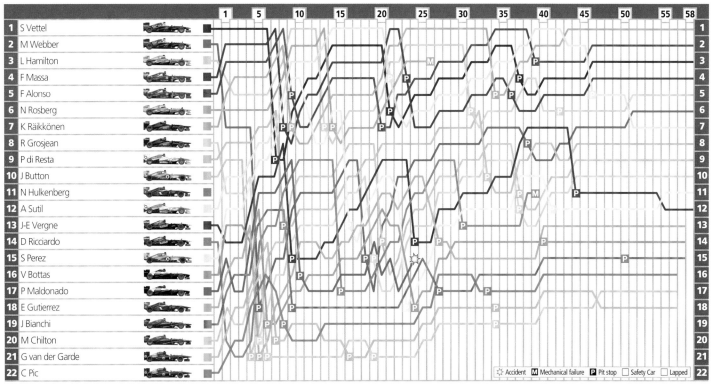

Accident | M Mechanical failure | P Pit stop | Safety Car | Lapped

QUALIFYING 3

	Driver	Time
1	S Vettel	1m27.407s
2	M Webber	1m27.827s
3	L Hamilton	1m28.087s
4	F Massa	1m28.490s
5	F Alonso	1m28.493s
6	N Rosberg	1m28.523s
7	K Räikkönen	1m28.738s
8	R Grosjean	1m29.013s
9	P di Resta	1m29.305s
10	J Button	1m30.357s

GRID

	Driver	Time
1	S Vettel	1m27.407s
2	M Webber	1m27.827s
3	L Hamilton	1m28.087s
4	F Massa	1m28.490s
5	F Alonso	1m28.493s
6	N Rosberg	1m28.523s
7	K Räikkönen	1m28.738s
8	R Grosjean	1m29.013s
9	P di Resta	1m29.305s
10	J Button	1m30.357s
11	N Hulkenberg	1m38.067s
12	A Sutil	1m38.134s
13	J-E Vergne	1m38.778s
14	D Ricciardo	1m39.042s
15	S Perez	1m39.900s
16	V Bottas	1m40.290s
17	P Maldonado	1m47.614s
18	E Gutierrez	1m47.776s
19	J Bianchi	1m48.147s
20	M Chilton	1m48.909s
21	G van der Garde	1m49.519s
22	C Pic	1m50.626s

RACE

	Driver	Car	Laps	Time	Avg. mph	Fastest	Stops
1	K Räikkönen	Lotus-Renault E21	58	1h30m03.225s	127.335	1m29.274s	2
2	F Alonso	Ferrari F138	58	1h30m15.676s	127.042	1m29.560s	3
3	S Vettel	Red Bull-Renault RB9	58	1h30m25.571s	126.810	1m30.409s	3
4	F Massa	Ferrari F138	58	1h30m36.802s	126.549	1m30.239s	3
5	L Hamilton	Mercedes F1 W04	58	1h30m48.786s	126.270	1m29.759s	3
6	M Webber	Red Bull-Renault RB9	58	1h30m50.025s	126.242	1m29.732s	3
7	A Sutil	Force India-Mercedes VJM06	58	1h31m08.293s	125.820	1m30.710s	2
8	P di Resta	Force India-Mercedes VJM06	58	1h31m11.674s	125.742	1m30.894s	2
9	J Button	McLaren-Mercedes MP4-28	58	1h31m24.855s	125.440	1m30.198s	3
10	R Grosjean	Lotus-Renault E21	58	1h31m25.984s	125.414	1m30.395s	3
11	S Perez	McLaren-Mercedes MP4-28	58	1h31m26.592s	125.401	1m29.926s	3
12	J-E Vergne	Toro Rosso-Ferrari STR8	58	1h31m27.082s	125.389	1m29.498s	3
13	E Gutierrez	Sauber-Ferrari C32	57	1h30m32.317s	124.470	1m31.415s	2
14	V Bottas	Williams-Renault FW35	57	1h30m39.768s	124.299	1m30.652s	3
15	J Bianchi	Marussia-Cosworth MR-02	57	1h31m41.295s	122.909	1m30.454s	3
16	C Pic	Caterham-Renault CT03	56	1h30m18.894s	122.589	1m32.261s	2
17	M Chilton	Marussia-Cosworth MR-02	56	1h30m53.253s	121.816	1m32.210s	3
18	G van der Garde	Caterham-Renault CT03	56	1h31m19.879s	121.224	1m32.636s	3
R	D Ricciardo	Toro Rosso-Ferrari STR8	39	Exhaust	-	1m30.881s	2
R	N Rosberg	Mercedes F1 W04	26	Electrics	-	1m32.259s	1
R	P Maldonado	Williams-Renault FW35	24	Spun off	-	1m32.915s	1
NS	N Hulkenberg	Sauber-Ferrari C32	0	Fuel leak	-	-	-

CHAMPIONSHIP

	Driver	Pts
1	K Räikkönen	25
2	F Alonso	18
3	S Vettel	15
4	F Massa	12
5	L Hamilton	10
6	M Webber	8
7	A Sutil	6
8	P di Resta	4
9	J Button	2
10	R Grosjean	1

Grid penalties
None

Fastest lap
K Räikkönen 1m29.274s
(132.883mph) on lap 56

Fastest speed trap	
J-E Vergne	193.060mph
Slowest speed trap	
N Rosberg	183.304mph

Fastest pit stop		
1	F Massa	21.509s
2	F Massa	21.5s11
3	M Webber	21.515s

	Constructor	Pts
1	Ferrari	30
2	Lotus-Renault	26
3	Red Bull-Renault	23
4	Mercedes	10
5	Force India-Mercedes	10
6	McLaren-Mercedes	2

Paul di Resta
"Seventh and eighth is a great result. We've shown that our car is kind to its tyres, and that helped us today. We made fewer stops than some of our rivals."

Pastor Maldonado
"It was a disappointing end to a difficult weekend. The car wasn't responding as we hoped today, and unfortunately I lost the back end and finished in the gravel."

Jean-Eric Vergne
"I was pushed to the outside at the start and ran through a gravel trap. The last two sections of the race on Primes were very good, and I was even in the points."

Charles Pic
"The supersofts fell away quickly, but the mediums held up well, so I could push the second stint longer than planned. Towards the end, I had a KERS failure."

Jules Bianchi
"I can't imagine a better start to my F1 career. I felt very calm, and everything went smoothly in the race as I worked my way through the tyre-management issues."

Adrian Sutil
"Unlike most, I started on medium tyres. My final stint on supersofts was tricky, as they grained. I was thinking that I might need to pit, but they came back."

Valtteri Bottas
"I had a good start, but then a mistake cost me places. We got the full performance from the car, and although the pace isn't there yet, there are still positives."

Daniel Ricciardo
"I had to retire with an exhaust problem. I reported back to the team that I could hear noises, and I tried to fix it by changing a few functions, but it wasn't to be."

Giedo van der Garde
"It was important to finish my first race. I started on supersofts, passed a few people and kept up with Bianchi until the first pit stop. Unluckily, I had a slow puncture."

Max Chilton
"I'm happy with my F1 debut, but the clash with van der Garde early in the race damaged my front wing, which meant that I had to stop for a wing change."

2013 FORMULA 1 PETRONAS MALAYSIA GRAND PRIX

22-24 MARCH
SEPANG INTERNATIONAL
CIRCUIT, KUALA LUMPUR

RED MIST AT RED BULL

Sebastian Vettel won the race in controversial circumstances, but Red Bull Racing were left to manage the fallout after the German defied team orders to overtake Mark Webber in the latter stages of a race they had dominated

Leading after the final round of pit stops, Mark Webber was on course for his tenth grand prix victory. Mindful of tyre wear and the value of a safe one-two finish, the Red Bull Racing team told Sebastian Vettel to hold station in second place. But instead, the reigning world champion caught and passed Webber in a move that left the Australian fuming and the team management keen to confirm that Vettel had disobeyed instructions. The bottom line, though, was that Vettel had secured a win and 25 priceless points.

In qualifying, he also earned his second pole position in the second race of 2013, but it certainly wasn't straightforward, as a damp track made the final qualifying session something of a lottery.

The rain came part way through Q2, and it caught out those drivers who hadn't managed to do a banker lap. The highest-profile victim was Romain Grosjean, who found himself stuck in 11th. The rain had stopped by the time Q3 got underway, so the session started on a wet but drying track, with everyone pounding around, trying to get a lap in.

The crucial decision came in the dying minutes when half of the ten runners – Vettel, the two

Ferraris, Force India's Adrian Sutil and Lotus team leader Kimi Räikkönen – pitted for a new set of intermediates, which gave them a better chance on their final flying laps. It worked spectacularly well for the top three as Vettel emerged the quickest, ahead of Felipe Massa and Fernando Alonso, making this the fourth race in a row that the Brazilian had outqualified his team-mate. Of those who stayed out on old intermediates, Lewis Hamilton was the best placed in fourth, ahead of Webber and his Mercedes team-mate, Nico Rosberg.

The tyre change didn't work well for Räikkönen who ended up seventh fastest. Worse was to come, though – he was then given a three-place penalty for impeding Rosberg after his pit stop in Q3. That dropped the Australian GP winner to tenth, behind Jenson Button, Sutil, and Sergio Perez.

The race itself started on a damp but drying track following a shower as the cars went to the grid. Everyone knew that they would have to make an early switch to slick tyres and that timing it right would be crucial. Vettel led away from pole, but at the second corner he was tapped by Alonso, who suffered front wing damage. Ferrari looked at its

data and hoped that the wing would stay in place at least until the change to dry tyres. However the TV showed that it was a forlorn hope, and at the start of the second lap the wing fell under Alonso's front wheels, sending him spearing off into the gravel and out of the race. It was an expensive mistake...

Vettel continued to lead from Webber until he pitted for slicks, a little prematurely as it turned out, on lap 5. Webber stayed out for a further lap, which proved to be crucial. He was faster than his team-mate, and emerged from the pits just ahead.

The two Red Bulls continued to run at the front for the remainder of the race, Webber staying ahead after both the second and third rounds of pit stops, while Hamilton led the chase.

"I got myself into a position where we were controlling the race," said Webber. "I was being told the target lap times, again in relation to how the tyres are. Obviously Seb and Lewis came back to me at one point in the race, I responded and lifted the pace and got away around the stop. Then we had a pretty good situation teed up towards the end of the race."

After his fourth stop on lap 44, the Australian again squeezed out ahead of Vettel. It was then that the controversy happened. Despite being told

OPPOSITE TOP Fernando Alonso's Ferrari spears straight on at Turn 1 after its damaged front wing collapsed as he started lap 2

OPPOSITE BOTTOM The red, yellow and white gravel Alonso kicked up even matched his Ferrari

ABOVE Lewis Hamilton got ahead in his battle with Mercedes team-mate Nico Rosberg, to be the best of the rest behind the Red Bulls

INSIDE LINE
SEBASTIAN VETTEL
RED BULL RACING DRIVER

"I got quite a good launch off the grid and kept the lead into Turn 1. I then tried to defend into Turn 2, but it was slippery there and I got a bit sideways and took a bit of a hit from Alonso. I think Mark passed him straight away.

"Throughout the race it was very close. It was certainly an interesting one to start with on the intermediate tyres in mixed conditions. I think we weren't too bad on the crossover going to dries, but maybe we did it a little too soon as some places on the track looked pretty dry, but turned out to be still damp. Coming back out in traffic also didn't help, so I lost the lead then.

"It was quite a long race, trying to look after the tyres. Towards the end, I had quite strong pace and obviously at the very end on a new set of medium tyres I had a bit more speed than Mark. It was a close fight but I think… yeah, as you can see, I'm not entirely happy with how it all went.

"I think I made a big mistake today. I think we should have stayed in the positions that we were. I didn't ignore the instruction on purpose, but I messed up in that situation and obviously took the lead and I can see that Mark's upset. I want to be honest, stick to the truth and apologise, but I know that it doesn't really help his feelings right now.

"The difference in pace at the end probably wasn't fair because he was trying to save the car and tyres. As I said, I didn't ignore that, but I should have been more aware.

"Obviously, I took quite a lot of risk to pass him and then that was the end of the race. I'm the black sheep right now. I put myself in that position so, as I said, all I can say is apologies to Mark.

"Other than that, it was obviously a very good race for the team. We handled the tyres pretty well. It's very different racing to how it used to be in the past, even to last year. It's another step, a bit more extreme, just trying to look after the tyres and driving into the unknown.

"You see on television how pieces of rubber are flying off and how we suffer on those tyres. The last thing you want is to risk a puncture and not finish the race, so I think we would all enjoy it if we had a tyre that was stronger and which we could race harder on."

TALKING POINT
RED BULL'S STRIFE

Before Sebastian Vettel's move on Mark Webber, tyres had been the issue. We'd seen Kimi Räikkönen win in Australia because he alone had been able to get through competitively on two tyre stops. Sepang was different, and again there was a huge difference between the one-lap pace of a Red Bull and its race pace. Team Principal Christian Horner wanted a return to 2012 tyres that, by the end of that year at least, had been understood by the teams. He didn't want Adrian Newey's brilliance as a designer being restrained by what had been labelled 'chocolate' tyres.

Yet, unless you were Red Bull or Mercedes – which were in trouble with this year's steel- rather than Kevlar-belted rubber, because it ran around 10°C hotter – you were happy to see Newey being restrained. You simply claimed that your car, with its more benign tyre usage, had been designed around the 2013 tyre regulations.

Like the tyres themselves, this almost sounded like so much hot air, but nobody needed to worry, as the tyres couldn't be changed without the unanimous agreement of all competing teams. And that, quite simply, was never going to be forthcoming.

The arguments were already raging: the racing was artificial; this was supposed to be the pinnacle of motor racing; it made a mockery of the whole thing. But no it didn't: F1 has always been about designing a car around the rules. Some had simply done a better job of grasping what was most important.

Human wars will always generate more column inches than technical ones, so after the race we had two: one at Red Bull and another at Mercedes. Webber had a face like thunder after Vettel ignored the 'Multi 21' team order not to pass him after the final round of pit stops, and Rosberg was distinctly unimpressed by a Ross Brawn instruction preventing him from trying to pass Hamilton.

By the time Vettel got to the post-race press conference, he was apologising, but probably more in the interests of his own personal safety! Perhaps he didn't actually mean it. Was he thinking about Mark's chop at Interlagos six months earlier when he'd been trying to clinch his third title, and about Webber backing him into range of the Mercedes during this very race, and about how he, Seb, was deliberately saving a set of option Pirellis that he was damn well going to use? Multi 21? To hell with it.

Webber's comment was telling: Sebastian would get away with it and the team would protect him. Did that moment guarantee his signature on a Porsche sportscar contract?

made a decision, which we always say before the race is probably how it's going to be – we look after the tyres, get the car to the end. And in the end, Seb made his own decisions today..."

However, Red Bull Racing wasn't the only team to face a team orders controversy in Malaysia. Immediately behind the two RB9s, the Mercedes pair of Hamilton and Rosberg ran third and fourth and, after exchanging places several times, they were told to hold station, with Hamilton in front.

Both men had to save fuel, although the British driver was in the more serious situation. An unhappy Rosberg had to be told several times to stay in position by team boss Ross Brawn. To his credit, the German abided by the rules.

"We just had a big team talk just now, and everyone's been fantastic," said a sheepish Hamilton after the race. "The guys did a great job today, and Nico in particular did an exceptional job and showed great maturity. It was a unique and difficult position for me to be in, and I'm going to work hard to make sure I'm not in that position again.

"We looked at the positives. We're the second fastest team, which is a massive bonus. To be that close at some stages of the grand prix – you've got to remember that I was competing with the Red Bulls at some stages in the race – and to be in that position was a great feeling. Unfortunately, we didn't have enough fuel in the car, more so on my side, so I was fuel saving from lap 25 or something.

"Because of this, it was very much an impossible task to challenge the guys in front. Towards the end, I was fuel saving like you couldn't believe: I was lifting and coasting everywhere, so there was no way that I could compete with any of the people around me. But that's motor racing. I'm sure if we were all on the same fuel it would have been a different situation. I'm confident about that."

LEFT Mercedes pair Hamilton and Rosberg swapped positions several times as they fought over third place, and were then told to hold station, with Hamilton in front, much to Rosberg's disappointment

BELOW The McLaren pit crew run down the pit lane to Jenson Button's MP4-28 after it had been released from its pit stop before the front right tyre had been fully attached

to stay behind for the run to the flag via the radio codephrase "Multi 21" – which also guaranteed Webber that he wasn't under threat from his team-mate – Vettel made it clear that he had his own ideas, getting by after instigating a spectacular fight between the pair that lasted for several corners.

On the podium, it was clear that both were unhappy with the way the race had unfolded, and celebrations were muted, to say the least.

Vettel apologised to Webber, but curiously he also claimed that he hadn't ignored the team orders "deliberately" (see Inside Line, left).

However, Red Bull Racing Team Principal Christian Horner made it clear that the triple world champion knew precisely what was being asked of him.

Not surprisingly, Webber had his own thoughts on what had unfolded between him and his team-mate, explaining "After the last stop, I thought that it would be interesting to see how the team would deal with the situation, and I was ready for a sprint to the end. Then the team obviously rang up and said 'the pressure is off now. We need to look after the tyres to the end'. Basically, don't fight each other.

"I wanted to race as well, but in the end the team

Massa salvaged fifth place for Ferrari after starting from the front row. The Brazilian driver suffered from serious tyre graining, and couldn't match the pace of those running ahead of him.

Both Lotus drivers struggled in the wet conditions in the early laps, after which they both had to fight to recover ground, Räikkönen being further hampered by front wing damage. They fought both with each other and with Nico Hulkenberg's Sauber before eventually finishing in sixth and seventh places, with Frenchman Grosjean crossing the finish line some 12s ahead.

After missing out on a race start in Australia, Hulkenberg enjoyed a busy race that saw him fight with Button and both Lotus drivers. At one point, he made contact with Räikkönen when he didn't see the Finn coming up alongside. He went on to secure eighth place, scoring his first points for Sauber after his move from Force India.

Almost 20s further back at the finish, Perez scored his first McLaren points with ninth place, making a late pit stop for tyres that not only didn't cost him a place, but allowed him to set the race's fastest lap on his return. McLaren team leader Button had a strong

race and had been set to finish as high as fifth place until a mistake at his final pit stop saw him leave with a wheel not fully tightened. Realising this, he stopped and was pulled back to the pit for attention, but he lost so much time that the team later decided to retire the car, citing a vibration as its reason.

Scuderia Toro Rosso racer Jean-Eric Vergne lost time after a pit collision with Charles Pic's Caterham, but the French driver still managed to score the final point by finishing in tenth place.

The last of the unlapped finishers was Williams rookie Valtteri Bottas who had a moment on the laps to the grid and then another on the first lap, but after that the Finn recovered well to finish 11th, having run inside the top ten at one stage of the race.

Further down the race order, Force India suffered a disastrous race. Sutil had run in eighth place early on, but when he came into the pits to change to slick tyres he lost time with a wheelnut problem. Coming in behind him on the same lap, team-mate Paul di Resta was also delayed. Then, after the very same thing happened at subsequent stops, and the nuts couldn't be secured, the team were forced to retire both cars.

BELOW As Vettel stays in his car, gathering his thoughts on how he won the race, Webber storms away looking for answers on why Vettel ignored orders to stay behind him

SNAPSHOT FROM
MALAYSIA

CLOCKWISE FROM RIGHT

Kimi Räikkönen flew in practice when conditions were dry, but couldn't repeat his Melbourne victory here; Alonso climbs from his Ferrari after qualifying third; Red Bull's Mark Webber reflects on what might have been his tenth F1 win; even 'Ice Man' Räikkönen needs to get into the shade to stay cool; Jenson Button keeps hydrated in the garage; Felipe Massa gathers his thoughts before going out to qualify; a bad weekend for Force India as wheelnut trouble ended their hopes; with rain spattering his helmet, Lewis Hamilton studies the timing screens ahead of Q3; when it rains in Malaysia, it *really* rains, so Caterham made sure that Giedo van der Garde had cover; the Dutchman's helmet sported a new livery at Sepang

MALAYSIA
KUALA LUMPUR
ROUND 2

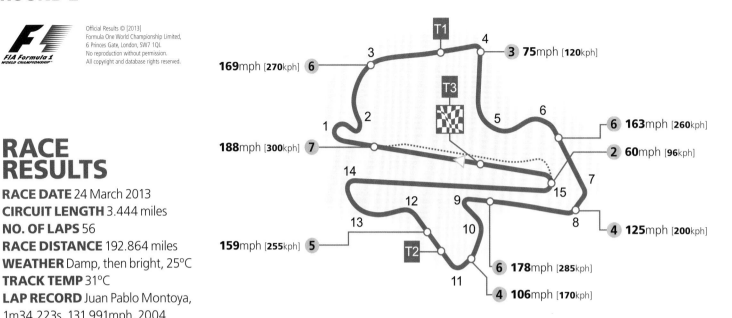

169mph [270kph] 6
3 75mph [120kph]
6 163mph [260kph]
2 60mph [96kph]
188mph [300kph] 7
4 125mph [200kph]
159mph [255kph] 5
6 178mph [285kph]
4 106mph [170kph]

RACE RESULTS

RACE DATE 24 March 2013
CIRCUIT LENGTH 3.444 miles
NO. OF LAPS 56
RACE DISTANCE 192.864 miles
WEATHER Damp, then bright, 25°C
TRACK TEMP 31°C
LAP RECORD Juan Pablo Montoya, 1m34.223s, 131.991mph, 2004

PRACTICE 1

	Driver	Time	Laps
1	M Webber	1m36.935s	15
2	K Räikkönen	1m37.003s	15
3	S Vettel	1m37.104s	21
4	F Alonso	1m37.319s	13
5	N Rosberg	1m37.588s	19
6	A Sutil	1m37.769s	17
7	F Massa	1m37.771s	15
8	P di Resta	1m37.773s	15
9	L Hamilton	1m37.840s	18
10	R Grosjean	1m37.915s	17
11	J Button	1m38.173s	16
12	P Maldonado	1m38.673s	16
13	S Perez	1m38.830s	17
14	N Hulkenberg	1m39.054s	17
15	E Gutierrez	1m39.204s	16
16	V Bottas	1m39.208s	19
17	J-E Vergne	1m39.284s	17
18	D Ricciardo	1m39.567s	16
19	G van der Garde	1m40.728s	17
20	J Bianchi	1m40.996s	14
21	C Pic	1m41.163s	18
22	M Chilton	1m41.513s	14

PRACTICE 2

	Driver	Time	Laps
1	K Räikkönen	1m36.569s	28
2	S Vettel	1m36.588s	27
3	F Massa	1m36.661s	33
4	F Alonso	1m36.985s	23
5	M Webber	1m37.026s	29
6	R Grosjean	1m37.206s	26
7	N Rosberg	1m37.448s	32
8	P di Resta	1m37.571s	30
9	L Hamilton	1m37.574s	32
10	A Sutil	1m37.788s	10
11	S Perez	1m37.838s	21
12	J Button	1m37.865s	29
13	N Hulkenberg	1m38.068s	31
14	E Gutierrez	1m38.645s	23
15	J-E Vergne	1m38.738s	30
16	P Maldonado	1m38.801s	26
17	D Ricciardo	1m38.904s	30
18	J Bianchi	1m39.508s	29
19	V Bottas	1m39.660s	27
20	C Pic	1m40.757s	29
21	G van der Garde	1m40.768s	32
22	M Chilton	1m41.438s	22

PRACTICE 3

	Driver	Time	Laps
1	S Vettel	1m36.435s	20
2	L Hamilton	1m36.568s	17
3	A Sutil	1m36.588s	19
4	M Webber	1m36.613s	20
5	K Räikkönen	1m36.806s	19
6	P di Resta	1m36.807s	18
7	J Button	1m36.822s	16
8	F Massa	1m36.946s	14
9	N Rosberg	1m36.949s	25
10	F Alonso	1m37.302s	14
11	P Maldonado	1m37.359s	11
12	S Perez	1m37.538s	12
13	N Hulkenberg	1m37.685s	23
14	R Grosjean	1m37.690s	14
15	V Bottas	1m37.936s	16
16	E Gutierrez	1m38.294s	17
17	J-E Vergne	1m38.376s	16
18	D Ricciardo	1m38.425s	15
19	C Pic	1m38.995s	18
20	J Bianchi	1m39.717s	21
21	G van der Garde	1m40.209s	18
22	M Chilton	1m40.495s	18

QUALIFYING 1

	Driver	Time
1	A Sutil	1m36.809s
2	K Räikkönen	1m36.959s
3	N Rosberg	1m37.239s
4	F Alonso	1m37.314s
5	R Grosjean	1m37.363s
6	J Button	1m37.487s
7	P di Resta	1m37.493s
8	L Hamilton	1m37.513s
9	M Webber	1m37.619s
10	S Perez	1m37.702s
11	E Gutierrez	1m37.707s
12	F Massa	1m37.712s
13	D Ricciardo	1m37.722s
14	P Maldonado	1m37.867s
15	S Vettel	1m37.899s
16	N Hulkenberg	1m37.931s
17	J-E Vergne	1m38.157s
18	V Bottas	1m38.207s
19	J Bianchi	1m38.434s
20	C Pic	1m39.314s
21	M Chilton	1m39.672s
22	G van der Garde	1m39.932s

QUALIFYING 2

	Driver	Time
1	N Rosberg	1m36.190s
2	M Webber	1m36.449s
3	L Hamilton	1m36.517s
4	K Räikkönen	1m36.640s
5	A Sutil	1m36.834s
6	F Massa	1m36.874s
7	F Alonso	1m36.877s
8	J Button	1m37.117s
9	S Vettel	1m37.245s
10	S Perez	1m37.342s
11	R Grosjean	1m37.636s
12	N Hulkenberg	1m38.125s
13	D Ricciardo	1m38.822s
14	E Gutierrez	1m39.221s
15	P di Resta	1m44.509s
16	P Maldonado	No time

Best sectors – Practice

Sec 1	R Grosjean	24.878s
Sec 2	S Vettel	32.038s
Sec 3	S Vettel	39.016s

Speed trap – Practice

1	A Sutil	190.450mph
2	K Räikkönen	190.388mph
3	F Alonso	190.263mph

Best sectors – Qualifying

Sec 1	K Räikkönen	24.932s
Sec 2	N Rosberg	32.048s
Sec 3	N Rosberg	39.159s

Speed trap – Qualifying

1	A Sutil	190.823mph
2	P di Resta	190.698mph
3	R Grosjean	190.698mph

Sebastian Vettel
"We could have ended up eighth or ninth after destroying the tyres in those two laps; I put myself above a team decision, which was wrong and I apologise."

Fernando Alonso
"After a good start, Vettel and I touched at Turn 2. My car was damaged, but we decided to keep going. It's easy to criticise this decision, but it seemed right."

Jenson Button
"Strategy-wise, we did everything right. We pitted on the correct laps and looked after the tyres. We'd have finished fifth but for the problem in the pit stop."

Kimi Räikkönen
"Since Saturday, the car hasn't been behaving as we expected, especially in the wet. It was a tough race, and I lost part of my front wing which didn't help."

Nico Rosberg
"It was good to be competitive. Of course, it was disappointing having to hold position, but I understood the team's decision to safeguard our positions."

Nico Hulkenberg
"At the start, we were quite quick on the intermediates, but then I was stuck in traffic and couldn't find my way past other drivers. I think eighth was well deserved."

Mark Webber
"I think Sebastian has respect for me and I have respect for him, but the situation today wasn't handled well. It's hard to put your finger on it all after the race."

Felipe Massa
"Starting on new intermediates, on a track that was very damp at some points and dry at others, prevented me from finding a good pace and I lost ground."

Sergio Perez
"My engineers sorted out a very good strategy that enabled me to pass the cars in front of me. Sadly, towards the end, my tyres began to degrade a bit too much."

Romain Grosjean
"I spent a lot of time behind Felipe mid-race, and I'm sure if I could have passed him earlier then I'd have stayed ahead, but by the end my tyres were finished."

Lewis Hamilton
"The team made the call to hold positions and we respected that. We were fighting with Red Bull and went aggressive on strategy, but they were too good today."

Esteban Gutierrez
"Late in the race, we lost time, as we stayed on the same tyres too long. We tried to change strategy, and I did my best. That was all we could do at that stage."

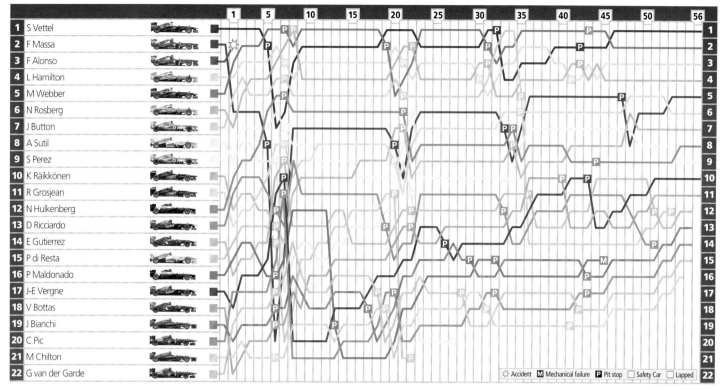

	Driver	
1	S Vettel	
2	F Massa	
3	F Alonso	
4	L Hamilton	
5	M Webber	
6	N Rosberg	
7	J Button	
8	A Sutil	
9	S Perez	
10	K Räikkönen	
11	R Grosjean	
12	N Hulkenberg	
13	D Ricciardo	
14	E Gutierrez	
15	P di Resta	
16	P Maldonado	
17	J-E Vergne	
18	V Bottas	
19	J Bianchi	
20	C Pic	
21	M Chilton	
22	G van der Garde	

☆ Accident　Ⓜ Mechanical failure　Ⓟ Pit stop　☐ Safety Car　☐ Lapped

QUALIFYING 3

	Driver	Time
1	S Vettel	1m49.674s
2	F Massa	1m50.587s
3	F Alonso	1m50.727s
4	L Hamilton	1m51.699s
5	M Webber	1m52.244s
6	N Rosberg	1m52.519s
7	K Räikkönen	1m52.970s
8	J Button	1m53.175s
9	A Sutil	1m53.439s
10	S Perez	1m54.136s

GRID

	Driver	Time
1	S Vettel	1m49.674s
2	F Massa	1m50.587s
3	F Alonso	1m50.727s
4	L Hamilton	1m51.699s
5	M Webber	1m52.244s
6	N Rosberg	1m52.519s
7	K Räikkönen	1m52.970s
8	J Button	1m53.175s
9	A Sutil	1m53.439s
10	S Perez	1m54.136s
11	R Grosjean	1m37.636s
12	N Hulkenberg	1m38.125s
13	D Ricciardo	1m38.822s
14	E Gutierrez	1m39.221s
15	P di Resta	1m44.509s
16	P Maldonado	No time
17	J-E Vergne	1m38.157s
18	V Bottas	1m38.207s
19	J Bianchi	1m38.434s
20	C Pic	1m39.314s
21	M Chilton	1m39.672s
22	G van der Garde	1m39.932s

RACE

	Driver	Car	Laps	Time	Avg. mph	Fastest	Stops
1	S Vettel	Red Bull-Renault RB9	56	1h38m56.681s	116.967	1m40.446s	4
2	M Webber	Red Bull-Renault RB9	56	1h39m00.979s	116.877	1m40.685s	4
3	L Hamilton	Mercedes F1 W04	56	1h39m08.862s	116.721	1m41.001s	4
4	N Rosberg	Mercedes F1 W04	56	1h39m09.321s	116.713	1m40.755s	4
5	F Massa	Ferrari F138	56	1h39m22.329s	116.458	1m39.805s	4
6	R Grosjean	Lotus-Renault E21	56	1h39m32.245s	116.265	1m41.226s	3
7	K Räikkönen	Lotus-Renault E21	56	1h39m45.160s	116.014	1m41.769s	4
8	N Hulkenberg	Sauber-Ferrari C32	56	1h39m49.725s	115.925	1m40.727s	4
9	S Perez	McLaren-Mercedes MP4-28	56	1h40m09.038s	115.552	1m39.199s	4
10	J-E Vergne	Toro Rosso-Ferrari STR8	56	1h40m23.805s	115.269	1m40.492s	3
11	V Bottas	Williams-Renault FW35	56	1h40m25.291s	115.241	1m41.373s	3
12	E Gutierrez	Sauber-Ferrari C32	55	1h39m01.194s	114.785	1m40.929s	4
13	J Bianchi	Marussia-Cosworth MR-02	55	1h39m55.128s	113.752	1m42.423s	4
14	C Pic	Caterham-Renault CT03	55	1h40m29.370s	113.106	1m42.942s	4
15	G van der Garde	Caterham-Renault CT03	55	1h40m38.354s	112.938	1m43.157s	4
16	M Chilton	Marussia-Cosworth MR-02	54	1h39m14.486s	112.446	1m43.150s	4
17	J Button	McLaren-Mercedes MP4-28	53	Vibration	-	1m40.556s	3
18	D Ricciardo	Toro Rosso-Ferrari STR8	51	Exhaust	-	1m42.581s	3
R	P Maldonado	Williams-Renault FW35	45	KERS	-	1m43.465s	3
R	A Sutil	Force India-Mercedes VJM06	27	Wheelnuts	-	1m42.791s	2
R	P di Resta	Force India-Mercedes VJM06	22	Wheelnuts	-	1m43.094s	2
R	F Alonso	Ferrari F138	1	Accident	-	-	-

CHAMPIONSHIP

	Driver	Pts
1	S Vettel	40
2	K Räikkönen	31
3	M Webber	26
4	L Hamilton	25
5	F Massa	22
6	F Alonso	18
7	N Rosberg	12
8	R Grosjean	9
9	A Sutil	6
10	P di Resta	4
11	N Hulkenberg	4
12	S Perez	2
13	J Button	2
14	J-E Vergne	1

Grid penalties
K Räikkönen Three-place penalty for impeding Nico Rosberg

Fastest lap
S Perez 1m39.199s
(125.000mph) on lap 56

Fastest speed trap
E Gutierrez　191.444mph
Slowest speed trap
F Alonso　171.933mph

Fastest pit stop
1	M Webber	20.736s
2	S Vettel	20.757s
3	M Webber	20.767s

	Constructor	Pts
1	Red Bull-Renault	66
2	Lotus-Renault	40
3	Ferrari	40
4	Mercedes	37
5	Force India-Mercedes	10
6	Sauber-Ferrari	4
7	McLaren-Mercedes	4
8	Toro Rosso-Ferrari	1

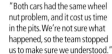

Paul di Resta

"It's frustrating to come away with nothing, given how competitive we have looked all weekend. The good news is that we have the performance in the car."

Pastor Maldonado

"The intermediates made the start difficult, as it was slippery. After a new set of tyres, my second stint was good, but my race ended when I had a KERS problem."

Charles Pic

"It's good to finish in the points, but a shame that a mistake in the pits cost us so much. So, overall I feel rather frustrated, but I will take the point gladly."

Jules Bianchi

"I spent a lot of time stuck behind Giedo's Caterham. After 18 laps, I was able to get back into position, though, and from then on I was very happy with my progress."

Adrian Sutil

"Both cars had the same wheel nut problem, and it cost us time in the pits. We're not sure what happened, so the team stopped us to make sure we understood."

Valtteri Bottas

"I had a good start, but drove off the dry line racing van der Garde, and dropped to the back of the field. Once the track began to dry, I was able to start overtaking."

"I compromised my race before the start, aquaplaning off at Turn 3. I kept going, but had damaged the floor. That probably played a part in my problem at the end."

Giedo van der Garde

"Just when the conditions were going from wet to dry, I heard that I had a puncture, but it was exactly at the time that we were coming in to switch to the dry tyres."

Max Chilton

"I lost time on the opening lap. Being stuck behind the Caterhams defined my race which is tough, as you know the blue-flag period is going to come much sooner."

国际汽联 FIA
Santander
KASPERSKY
Santander
潍柴动力
WEICHAI POWER

2013 FORMULA 1 UBS CHINESE GRAND PRIX

12-14 APRIL
SHANGHAI INTERNATIONAL CIRCUIT, SHANGHAI

FERRARI ON TOP AGAIN

Fernando Alonso made it three different winners in three races with a superb victory in China. In a race inevitably dominated by strategy, Alonso and Ferrari got everything just right, timing their stops to perfection

Fernando Alonso's victory was a tonic after his early retirement in the Malaysian GP, and it gave both driver and team the belief that they could challenge for the 2013 FIA Formula One World Championship™.

As the meeting unfolded, Nico Rosberg, Felipe Massa and Alonso topped the timesheets in the three practice sessions, as Red Bull Racing's Sebastian Vettel and Mark Webber managed only fourth and fifth respectively in the last session. When it came to qualifying, though, Lewis Hamilton proved to be the star, topping the times in Q1 and Q2 before securing pole position on only his third start with Mercedes. Nobody went out in the opening minutes of the final session, apart from Vettel, who didn't do a flying lap. It was anticipated that some drivers might wait in the garage for the duration and save precious tyres, but in the end everyone did emerge, with Vettel and Button opting for the medium rather than the soft tyre as they looked towards the race.

Hamilton was once again fastest, just ahead of Kimi Räikkönen and Alonso, making it three different teams in the top three. Potential pole challenger Rosberg made a mistake on his lap and had to settle for fourth, and so qualified ahead of Massa, Romain Grosjean and Toro Rosso's surprise package, Daniel Ricciardo. Button didn't

complete his lap at proper racing pace, but still qualified eighth after Vettel locked up and aborted his attempt.

Meanwhile, Vettel's team-mate, Webber, was out of luck, the Australian running out of fuel in Q2 and so being sent to the back of the grid. Because of this, Red Bull Racing decided to change his set-up and start him from the pit lane.

Hamilton led away at the start, while a bad getaway dropped Räikkönen to fourth behind Alonso and Massa. As expected, tyre degradation became an issue almost immediately, and Hamilton soon lost out to both Ferraris. He pitted as early as lap 5, and others who had started on the soft tyre soon followed him in.

Drivers who had started on the longer-lasting medium stayed out and thus moved to the front of the field. After a good start, tenth qualifier Nico Hulkenberg led for several laps in impressive style from Vettel, Button and Perez. Hulkenberg and Vettel swapped positions when they pitted, while Button moved into the lead as he planned to make a very late first stop, and come in only twice. However, he was caught by quicker cars on newer tyres, and Alonso moved into the lead on lap 20 before making his second stop. This in turn passed the lead to Vettel, who had pitted only once.

RIGHT Lewis Hamilton leads the field through Turn 3, followed by Alonso, Massa, Räikkönen, Rosberg, Grosjean, Ricciardo and Button

BELOW Fernando Alonso leaves the Ferrari garage to go to the grid for what would be the near perfect tactical race performance

BOTTOM The 22 drivers, from Mercedes' Hamilton on pole to Caterham's Giedo van der Garde, wait for the five red lights to go out

INSIDE LINE
FERNANDO ALONSO
FERRARI DRIVER

"It was a fantastic race for us from start to finish. It's a long time since I've won here, eight years in fact, so that was good too! The tyre degradation was better than expected, so we could more or less manage the pace. It feels particularly great after my retirement from the race in Malaysia. After that, there was definitely pressure to finish here.

"It's true that today we maybe had some pace left in our pocket, and it's not easy to know when to use it, because it depends on the state of the tyres. I think there was a little bit more potential and hopefully we can show that in Bahrain next week.

"This was nearly a perfect Sunday for us. The start was clean and good and I managed to overtake both Kimi and Lewis as well in that opening stint. The car also felt a little better on the tyre degradation side.

"For the rest of the race obviously you need to take care of the tyres, you need to manage the gap to the guys behind and, with all the different strategies, it wasn't so easy to understand the race at times. We were overtaking the McLarens, Hulkenberg, Sebastian, so it was all a bit of a mix. It must have been even more difficult for the spectators.

"There were some moments of action as well and the risk is that when you do an overtaking manoeuvre you have to manage that as well. But the team did a perfect job with the set-up of the car for qualifying, the race and perfect, well-executed pit stops.

"We've had a win and a second place in the two races that we've finished here and in Melbourne, so I'm quite optimistic about the season although it's a little bit too early to say where everyone is. We'll probably need to wait until after the summer break to see the real contenders. Hopefully we'll be in that group.

"At the moment, Lotus, Red Bull and Mercedes are in the same position as us. I don't see that anyone has a clear advantage. Red Bull was dominant in Australia in all the free practice sessions but in qualifying and the race they suffered from tyre degradation. In Malaysia, they were a bit more in the groove, but here they were similar to the others, so let's wait and see what the car updates bring.

"Luck will also play a part. Nico Rosberg didn't finish in Australia because of car problems. It happened to us in Malaysia. The same with Webber here, who had the problem with a tyre and didn't finish. It can happen to anyone, but you just hope that it evens out."

When Vettel came in on lap 31, a clearer picture emerged. All the top runners had one more pit stop to do, but while some planned a long stint on medium tyres, others were saving their final change to the soft until the closing laps. At this point, Alonso led from Hamilton, Räikkönen, Button and Vettel.

The order changed once again as the final round of pit stops played out, with Räikkönen getting ahead of Hamilton. By now, it was apparent that Alonso had the advantage as he was well clear of any of his rivals after his car proved consistently fast throughout each stint. He lost the lead briefly to Vettel at his final pit stop on lap 41, but on new tyres he soon got it back. Vettel then dropped to fourth when he made his own final stop for softs on lap 51, with just five laps to go. Thereafter, Alonso held his lead ahead of Räikkönen to the finish.

"Definitely it was nearly a perfect Sunday for us, with not any problem in the race," said Alonso (see Inside Line, p99). The Spaniard also admitted that even he struggled to comprehend what was a complicated race, given the teams' various strategies.

Ferrari Team Principal Stefano Domenicali said that a good strategy, consistent pace and getting past traffic had been the keys to Alonso's win. "I think what we

saw already on Friday was that it seemed that we would have a good pace for the race, and so what I believe is the most important thing today is that we were really spot-on with the strategy," said the Ferrari boss.

"The difference today was the consistency in all the different situations with the race pace, which was very strong. We had a good start, and this is another thing that was very important. And I have to say that the key factor was to try to be in front of the traffic as soon as possible, because that could present a real problem later on during the race."

Conversely, Räikkönen had made a bad start and lost out to the Ferraris, although he later passed Massa in the first pit-stop sequence. On lap 16, though, he damaged his car's nose and a couple of winglets against the right rear tyre of Perez's out of sequence McLaren at Turn 6, which certainly didn't help his car's performance. Nevertheless, the Finn was eventually able to move ahead of Hamilton and secure second place to log 18 valuable points towards his title challenge.

"I think we just had wrong settings," said Räikkönen of his poor start. "The practice start was very good, but then it was really bad at the real start, and I lost some positions. After that, the car was all right, but I had a

little accident, some problems with Perez, and damaged the nose and the front wing. I was surprised there was no more damage, because I hit him quite hard. I was also a bit surprised that I didn't have any more problems after that. There was a bit too much understeer, and we were destroying the front tyre because of that, but we were still able to fight for second place and get quite a good result in the end. Obviously, we wanted to try to win, but today with all the issues it wasn't possible."

A second successive third place was a useful reward for Hamilton given the tyre issues from which Mercedes was clearly suffering, although he only just scraped home in front of Vettel. Hamilton's team-mate, Rosberg, wasn't as fortunate as the German retired at just past one-third race distance after a rear anti-roll-bar failure.

"It was a good race for me, I'm quite happy with third," said Hamilton. "Of course I would have liked to have won, but congratulations to Fernando as he did a great job and so did Kimi. They were both a little too fast for us during the race. I seemed to be able to apply some pressure on Kimi, but not enough to get sufficiently close to overtake. My tyres were shot at the end, and there was nothing I could do really to hold off Sebastian. I was a little unlucky with some traffic,

BELOW Mark Webber's Red Bull RB9 shed a rear wheel at Turn 14 shortly after he had emerged from his pit stop following a clash with Jean-Eric Vergne's Toro Rosso

TALKING POINT
IS IT TOO ARTIFICIAL?

Is Formula 1 about ultimate excellence or is it a 'show'? Can it legitimately be both? You could argue that Red Bull Racing has dominated since 2010 and would have done so to a much greater degree had Adrian Newey's designs not been restricted by degrading tyres. Privately, some say that if the tyres were built for

ultimate performance, nobody would see which way the Red Bulls went.

You could also argue, however, that the team has still been winning, that the racing has been entertaining, and so it's a win-win situation. Of concern, though, were Fernando Alonso's post-race comments about tyre management, the need even to 'manage' overtaking moves, and his observation that if he was struggling to keep track of varying strategies, what chance did spectators watching at the circuit have?

"It's all a bit WWF wrestling at the moment," Mark Webber grimaced. By which he meant 'artificial'.

"I'm not sure it's that great for people to watch, because a lot of overtakes are pretty straightforward," Sebastian Vettel added. "What I mean is, to look after the tyres and

manage gaps, you wave people by or they wave you by. You don't resist because you'll slow yourself down."

Do we really want to be listening to engineers telling drivers: "Don't fight because you're in a different race"? That was the instruction that went out to both Jenson Button and Vettel at differing stages of the Chinese GP.

If it happened to the same extent as Shanghai every fortnight, F1 might have a problem, but China was atypical as it's not often you have such a performance difference between the two tyre compounds and such extreme wear. That led directly to the strategy battles, the chess game, that some liked but others did not.

Whenever there's unrestricted freedom to excel, somebody does.

And dominance results. That's been the case throughout F1 history. We've had McLaren domination in the mid- to late-80s and again in the late '90s, Williams in the early '90s, Ferrari in the '00s. Would we really like to be heading off to races knowing the outcome in advance, as was true of much of the Schumacher/Ferrari era?

It's a difficult balance. On leaving China, opinion was polarised. Some were adamant: 80-odd pit stops, meaningless passing and confusing strategy were no good. Others were more cautious, saying it was better to avoid knee-jerk responses. The 'show' was still good, TV coverage better than ever and such a multi-faceted sport more than capable of entertaining its audience. So let's hang fire. And, as Bahrain proved, they were right.

ABOVE Alonso acknowledges his pit crew as he flashes past the chequered flag to make it three different winners in the 2013 season's first three rounds

though. Still, to get on the podium, I'm delighted, and really happy with the points as well."

Vettel was able to lap fast on his soft tyres over the final laps of the race, and closed right up on third-placed Hamilton. Fourth place was better than nothing, but in the end the strategy of qualifying and starting on the medium tyre hadn't really played out as planned. Red Bull Racing Team Principal Christian Horner insisted that Vettel would have finished at least third had he not got caught behind Hulkenberg's Sauber in the opening stint and lost valuable time.

"Seb managed to pass Jenson, who he knew he had to clear quickly," said Horner, "but then Hulkenberg cruised past both of them, and that cost him quite a bit of time in that first stint. If Sebastian had found one more second in that first stint and not been locked up behind Hulkenberg then his race would have been quite different. He would certainly have been on the podium, and maybe even able to finish second. I think it was the right thing to do. It was certainly worth giving it a go."

Button opted for a two-stop strategy, moving up to third when those who had started the race on soft tyres pitted, then taking the lead when Hulkenberg and Vettel came in. Ultimately, he didn't have the consistent

pace he needed and so had to settle for fifth, ahead of Massa, who suffered badly from tyre graining.

Ricciardo damaged his car's nose in a clash with Rosberg, which necessitated an earlier-than-planned first pit stop, but thereafter the Australian drove a strong race to seventh place for Toro Rosso.

A collision between the two Force India drivers at the hairpin at the end of the back straight on the first lap cost Paul di Resta some time, but fortunately both drivers were able to continue. However, after just five laps, Adrian Sutil was hit by Esteban Gutierrez as they braked hard for the same corner, and was forced to retire. Di Resta ran in the top ten for much of the race, and after a late pit stop for soft tyres, finished eighth. Grosjean and Hulkenberg completed the top ten.

Webber followed a bold strategy of starting from the pit lane, running one lap with the soft tyre, and pitting immediately to off-load it, so leaving him free to run on mediums for the rest of the race. The choice paid off and he made good progress early on. However, he was then delayed by a collision with Jean-Eric Vergne's Toro Rosso at Turn 6, then lost a rear wheel after a pit stop, which earned him a three-place grid penalty for the Bahrain GP. All of which meant it didn't appear to be Mark's year…

SNAPSHOT FROM CHINA

CLOCKWISE FROM RIGHT

Tower blocks provide a backdrop beyond the swampy land on which the circuit was built; race winner Fernando Alonso acknowledges the applause after climbing out of his car in parc ferme; Mercedes adviser Niki Lauda raises a smile from Lewis Hamilton; pit stop practice makes perfect; Caterham gave Chinese driver Ma Qing Hua a run in practice on Friday; one Red Bull RB9 put away for the night; Daniel Ricciardo's helmet; Valtteri Bottas tops up and checks the times as he waits in his Williams during practice; Red Bull tech chief Adrian Newey shares a joke with Sebastian Vettel; Romain Grosjean's Lotus E21 appears to be floating as it enters the pits

CHINA
SHANGHAI
ROUND 3

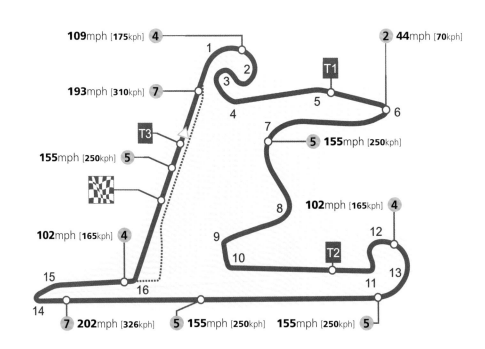

109mph [175kph] 4

2 44mph [70kph]

T1

193mph [310kph] 7

5

6

T3

5 155mph [250kph]

155mph [250kph] 5

102mph [165kph] 4

8

102mph [165kph] 4

12

9

10

T2

13

11

15

16

14

7 202mph [326kph]

5 155mph [250kph]

155mph [250kph] 5

RACE RESULTS

RACE DATE 14 April 2013
CIRCUIT LENGTH 3.390 miles
NO. OF LAPS 56
RACE DISTANCE 189.680 miles
WEATHER Sunny, 17°C
TRACK TEMP 25°C
LAP RECORD Michael Schumacher, 1m32.238s, 132.202mph, 2004

PRACTICE 1	Driver	Time	Laps
1	N Rosberg	1m36.717s	21
2	L Hamilton	1m37.171s	20
3	M Webber	1m37.658s	21
4	S Vettel	1m37.942s	20
5	F Alonso	1m37.965s	17
6	J Button	1m38.069s	24
7	F Massa	1m38.095s	14
8	A Sutil	1m38.125s	21
9	R Grosjean	1m38.398s	17
10	P di Resta	1m38.561s	15
11	K Räikkönen	1m38.790s	16
12	J-E Vergne	1m39.057s	19
13	P Maldonado	1m39.158s	22
14	N Hulkenberg	1m39.180s	21
15	D Ricciardo	1m39.336s	19
16	S Perez	1m39.360s	20
17	V Bottas	1m39.392s	21
18	E Gutierrez	1m40.032s	22
19	J Bianchi	1m41.966s	16
20	M Chilton	1m42.056s	18
21	G van der Garde	1m42.083s	21
22	M Qing Hua	1m43.545s	20

PRACTICE 2	Driver	Time	Laps
1	F Massa	1m35.340s	32
2	K Räikkönen	1m35.492s	32
3	F Alonso	1m35.755s	30
4	N Rosberg	1m35.819s	35
5	M Webber	1m36.092s	31
6	J Button	1m36.432s	29
7	L Hamilton	1m36.496s	39
8	A Sutil	1m36.514s	32
9	P di Resta	1m36.595s	33
10	S Vettel	1m36.791s	27
11	S Perez	1m36.940s	16
12	R Grosjean	1m36.963s	31
13	E Gutierrez	1m37.103s	22
14	D Ricciardo	1m37.206s	39
15	J-E Vergne	1m38.127s	34
16	V Bottas	1m38.185s	18
17	N Hulkenberg	1m38.211s	32
18	P Maldonado	1m38.276s	34
19	J Bianchi	1m38.725s	29
20	G van der Garde	1m39.271s	21
21	C Pic	1m39.814s	27
22	M Chilton	1m43.227s	5

PRACTICE 3	Driver	Time	Laps
1	F Alonso	1m35.391s	13
2	F Massa	1m36.013s	11
3	L Hamilton	1m36.065s	18
4	S Vettel	1m36.286s	17
5	M Webber	1m36.420s	15
6	A Sutil	1m36.549s	16
7	K Räikkönen	1m36.605s	16
8	J Button	1m36.693s	16
9	S Perez	1m36.777s	16
10	N Hulkenberg	1m36.853s	15
11	J-E Vergne	1m37.072s	15
12	D Ricciardo	1m37.205s	18
13	P Maldonado	1m37.300s	11
14	N Rosberg	1m37.349s	12
15	V Bottas	1m37.457s	16
16	P di Resta	1m37.487s	13
17	E Gutierrez	1m37.740s	20
18	R Grosjean	1m37.813s	16
19	J Bianchi	1m38.496s	17
20	C Pic	1m38.821s	18
21	M Chilton	1m39.627s	16
22	G van der Garde	1m39.652s	18

QUALIFYING 1	Driver	Time
1	L Hamilton	1m35.793s
2	N Rosberg	1m35.959s
3	F Massa	1m35.972s
4	M Webber	1m36.148s
5	F Alonso	1m36.253s
6	S Vettel	1m36.537s
7	J Button	1m36.667s
8	R Grosjean	1m36.929s
9	S Perez	1m36.952s
10	N Hulkenberg	1m36.985s
11	D Ricciardo	1m36.993s
12	K Räikkönen	1m37.046s
13	P Maldonado	1m37.281s
14	A Sutil	1m37.349s
15	P di Resta	1m37.478s
16	J-E Vergne	1m37.508s
17	V Bottas	1m37.769s
18	E Gutierrez	1m37.990s
19	J Bianchi	1m38.780s
20	M Chilton	1m39.537s
21	C Pic	1m39.614s
22	G van der Garde	1m39.660s

QUALIFYING 2	Driver	Time
1	L Hamilton	1m35.078s
2	F Alonso	1m35.148s
3	S Vettel	1m35.343s
4	F Massa	1m35.403s
5	N Rosberg	1m35.537s
6	K Räikkönen	1m35.659s
7	J Button	1m35.784s
8	R Grosjean	1m36.035s
9	D Ricciardo	1m36.258s
10	N Hulkenberg	1m36.261s
11	P di Resta	1m36.287s
12	S Perez	1m36.314s
13	A Sutil	1m36.405s
14	M Webber	1m36.679s
15	P Maldonado	1m37.139s
16	J-E Vergne	1m37.199s

Best sectors – Practice			Speed trap – Practice			Best sectors – Qualifying			Speed trap – Qualifying		
Sec 1	F Massa	24.935s	1	E Gutierrez	199.460mph	Sec 1	K Räikkönen	24.604s	1	N Rosberg	198.714mph
Sec 2	F Massa	28.337s	2	N Hulkenberg	198.901mph	Sec 2	F Massa	28.287s	2	L Hamilton	198.466mph
Sec 3	F Alonso	41.410s	3	L Hamilton	198.838mph	Sec 3	F Alonso	41.362s	3	D Ricciardo	198.217mph

 Sebastian Vettel

"When I saw Lewis at the end of the straight, I thought 'that's too far', but we had more speed on the fresher tyres. It was a shame to lose out by such a tiny bit."

Fernando Alonso

"It couldn't have gone any better than this! We had a good feeling all weekend, and qualifying third fastest gave us the possibility of fighting for the top positions."

Jenson Button

"I'm very happy to have finished fifth. We weren't fast enough to adopt the same strategy as the others, so we had to run longer and make two stops, not three."

 Kimi Räikkönen

"I'm not 100 per cent happy because we didn't win, but it is what it is, and second place is a good result after a bad start and the incident with Sergio."

Nico Rosberg

"I had an unexpected level of understeer. After my second stop, it got worse and I had one front wheel in the air in corners, as the rear anti-roll bar had broken."

 **Nico Hulkenberg**

"It was nice to be leading again. I had an okay start and some nice battles in the first few laps but, somehow, towards the end, we were lacking enough pace."

 Mark Webber

"We elected to get rid of the soft tyre quickly, and came back through the field well. But when Vergne turned in I was already committed and we collided."

Felipe Massa

"It's difficult to understand what happened, as the start went well. At the first stop, I fitted the medium tyres, but after a few laps I began to suffer graining."

Sergio Perez

"I had a reasonably good first stint and thought I could achieve a good result with the strategy, but then we encountered tyre degradation, slowing my pace."

 **Romain Grosjean**

"It was a long, tough race, and I'm definitely not happy with ninth, as I started sixth and thought I had a good chance to end up in the top five."

Lewis Hamilton

"While I'd have loved to win, I'm happy with being on the podium for the second race in a row. Fernando and Kimi were too fast for us and my tyres were shot."

 **Esteban Gutierrez**

"I had a good first lap. Going onto the straight I had Sergio behind me, and I approached the corner too fast. I tried my best to stop, but didn't succeed."

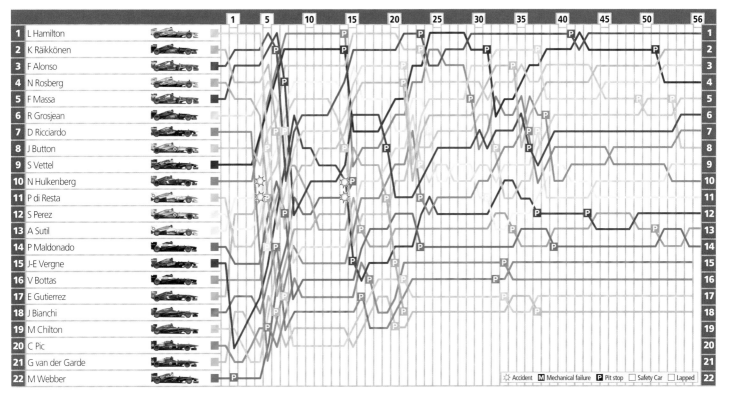

	Driver
1	L Hamilton
2	K Räikkönen
3	F Alonso
4	N Rosberg
5	F Massa
6	R Grosjean
7	D Ricciardo
8	J Button
9	S Vettel
10	N Hulkenberg
11	P di Resta
12	S Perez
13	A Sutil
14	P Maldonado
15	J-E Vergne
16	V Bottas
17	E Gutierrez
18	J Bianchi
19	M Chilton
20	C Pic
21	G van der Garde
22	M Webber

☆ Accident　Ⓜ Mechanical failure　Ⓟ Pit stop　☐ Safety Car　☐ Lapped

QUALIFYING 3

	Driver	Time
1	L Hamilton	1m34.484s
2	K Räikkönen	1m34.761s
3	F Alonso	1m34.788s
4	N Rosberg	1m34.861s
5	F Massa	1m34.993s
6	R Grosjean	1m35.364s
7	D Ricciardo	1m35.998s
8	J Button	2m05.673s
9	S Vettel	No time
10	N Hulkenberg	No time

GRID

	Driver	Time
1	L Hamilton	1m34.484s
2	K Räikkönen	1m34.761s
3	F Alonso	1m34.788s
4	N Rosberg	1m34.861s
5	F Massa	1m34.993s
6	R Grosjean	1m35.364s
7	D Ricciardo	1m35.998s
8	J Button	2m05.673s
9	S Vettel	No time
10	N Hulkenberg	No time
11	P di Resta	1m36.287s
12	S Perez	1m36.314s
13	A Sutil	1m36.405s
15	P Maldonado	1m37.139s
16	J-E Vergne	1m37.199s
16	V Bottas	1m37.769s
17	E Gutierrez	1m37.990s
18	J Bianchi	1m38.780s
19	M Chilton	1m39.537s
20	C Pic	1m39.614s
21	G van der Garde	1m39.660s
22	M Webber	1m36.679s

RACE

	Driver	Car	Laps	Time	Avg. mph	Fastest	Stops
1	F Alonso	Ferrari F138	56	1h36m26.945s	117.928	1m39.506s	3
2	K Räikkönen	Lotus-Renault E21	56	1h36m37.113s	117.715	1m39.955s	3
3	L Hamilton	Mercedes F1 W04	56	1h36m39.267s	117.672	1m39.981s	3
4	S Vettel	Red Bull-Renault RB9	56	1h36m39.470s	117.668	1m36.808s	3
5	J Button	McLaren-Mercedes MP4-28	56	1h37m02.230s	117.208	1m38.058s	2
6	F Massa	Ferrari F138	56	1h37m07.772s	117.096	1m40.284s	3
7	D Ricciardo	Toro Rosso-Ferrari STR8	56	1h37m09.636s	117.059	1m40.240s	3
8	P di Resta	Force India-Mercedes VJM06	56	1h37m18.029s	116.890	1m40.101s	3
9	R Grosjean	Lotus-Renault E21	56	1h37m20.368s	116.844	1m40.563s	3
10	N Hulkenberg	Sauber-Ferrari C32	56	1h37m23.543s	116.780	1m40.630s	3
11	S Perez	McLaren-Mercedes MP4-28	56	1h37m30.805s	116.635	1m41.281s	2
12	J-E Vergne	Toro Rosso-Ferrari STR8	56	1h37m39.549s	116.461	1m40.138s	3
13	V Bottas	Williams-Renault FW35	56	1h38m00.806s	116.040	1m38.200s	3
14	P Maldonado	Williams-Renault FW35	56	1h38m02.398s	116.009	1m40.968s	3
15	J Bianchi	Marussia-Cosworth MR-02	55	1h36m38.818s	115.578	1m41.537s	3
16	C Pic	Caterham-Renault CT03	55	1h36m40.872s	115.537	1m41.997s	3
17	M Chilton	Marussia-Cosworth MR-02	55	1h37m16.746s	114.827	1m41.978s	3
18	G van der Garde	Caterham-Renault CT03	55	1h37m47.991s	114.216	1m42.357s	3
R	N Rosberg	Mercedes F1 W04	21	Anti-roll bar	-	1m43.378s	3
R	M Webber	Red Bull-Renault RB9	15	Lost wheel	-	1m43.416s	2
R	A Sutil	Force India-Mercedes VJM06	5	Accident damage	-	1m44.257s	-
R	E Gutierrez	Sauber-Ferrari C32	4	Accident	-	1m44.775s	-

CHAMPIONSHIP

	Driver	Pts
1	S Vettel	52
2	K Räikkönen	49
3	F Alonso	43
4	L Hamilton	40
5	F Massa	30
6	M Webber	26
7	N Rosberg	12
8	J Button	12
9	R Grosjean	11
10	P di Resta	8
11	D Ricciardo	6
12	A Sutil	6
13	N Hulkenberg	5
14	S Perez	2
15	J-E Vergne	1

Grid penalties
M Webber Excluded for not having enough fuel on board after qualifying

Fastest lap
S Vettel 1m36.808s
(125.962mph) on lap 53

Fastest speed trap
D Ricciardo　199.398mph
Slowest speed trap
P Maldonado　189.704mph

Fastest pit stop
1	S Vettel	19.323s
2	F Alonso	19.719s
3	N Rosberg	19.894s

	Constructor	Pts
1	Red Bull-Renault	78
2	Ferrari	73
3	Lotus-Renault	60
4	Mercedes	52
5	McLaren-Mercedes	14
6	Force India-Mercedes	14
7	Toro Rosso-Ferrari	7
8	Sauber-Ferrari	5

Paul di Resta
"I was battling with Nico on the first lap, but had contact with Adrian at the hairpin, which cost me three or four positions. After that, I was stuck in the pack."

Pastor Maldonado
"It was a difficult race. We lost a lot of time on the Option tyres in the first stint, and didn't have the pace, which gave us no chance to fight for any higher positions."

Jean-Eric Vergne
"I think Mark couldn't have got through from where he tried. I'm not even sure if he was trying to pass. The impact put me into a spin and damaged my floor."

Charles Pic
"I had a decent start on the soft tyres, pitted as they degraded, and came out ahead of Bianchi. On my third stop, I came out 16th and didn't have enough pace."

Jules Bianchi
"I'm very happy to finish 15th, but it was a tough race, and so I was happy to see the chequered flag after quite a difficult final stint, trying to hold onto the tyres."

Adrian Sutil
"It was going well in the opening laps. Then, under braking for the final hairpin, I got hit from behind as I turned in. I guess Gutierrez missed his braking point."

Valtteri Bottas
"I knew it was going to be close with Pastor, so I was pushing hard in my final stint. I was right behind him on the Option tyres and so able to make a move."

Daniel Ricciardo
"The last time I qualified this well was Bahrain 2012 and I failed to score. The pit stop to change the nose affected our plans, and by the end I was catching Massa."

Giedo van der Garde
"I had another strong start, passing three cars, but from the moment the first set of soft tyres started going off, I couldn't find any pace and was struggling."

Max Chilton
"I didn't get the best start, but things improved through the race and that was reflected in my lap time relative to van der Garde. So it's all starting to come together."

2013 FORMULA 1 GULF AIR BAHRAIN GRAND PRIX

19-21 APRIL
BAHRAIN INTERNATIONAL CIRCUIT, SAKHIR

TRAILING IN SEB'S DUST

Sebastian Vettel won an intriguing Bahrain GP, as tyre strategy became the hot topic. While Fernando Alonso suffered technical glitches and other teams struggled, Red Bull got the best out of the Pirellis in the desert heat

Reigning champion Sebastian Vettel became the first two-time winner of 2013, and headed into the short break before the first European race in Spain leading closest title rival Kimi Räikkönen by 10 points.

However, on Saturday, another German grabbed the headlines when Nico Rosberg took a surprise pole position, following a tense qualifying session. Mercedes had appeared to be the only one of the four main contenders not to be in with a shot of the top spot in qualifying, but the German popped up when it mattered in Q3 to claim the best place on the grid.

That meant the men thought most likely to battle for pole, Vettel and Fernando Alonso, had to settle for second and third positions as Robserg's best lap was an impressive quarter-second better than Vettel's. Rosberg's team-mate Lewis Hamilton qualified fourth, but he went into the session knowing he had a five-place gearbox change penalty as a rear tyre failure in that morning's practice session had broken the rear suspension which caused gearbox damage as he returned to the pits.

Mark Webber was fifth fastest on the timing screens, but the Aussie carried his own three-place collision penalty from the Chinese GP. Hamilton's penalty meant

tangled with Valtteri Bottas's Williams and was then hit hard by Giedo van der Garde's Caterham, leaving Vergne with a puncture and a damaged floor. He carried on after pitting but, owing to the damage, he became the race's only retirement after 16 laps.

Unfortunately for Mercedes, its cars soon suffered tyre problems, and as early as lap 4 both Vettel and Alonso had got past Rosberg. A fascinating race between the 2012 title rivals appeared to be in prospect, but on the seventh lap Alonso's DRS wing became stuck in the open position. The Spaniard dashed into the pits and had it reset manually, only for it to happen again, and force another pit stop a lap later. After that, Alonso was faced with a long slog to get back into the points.

"When the DRS remained open the first time, I informed the team that we had finished the rear tyres, because at that stage I thought the rear tyres had gone completely," Alonso explained. "But they told me, 'No, no, the tyres are okay, it's just the DRS, so we pit this lap.'

"It was very light at the rear, and I had very strange snap braking for Turn 10, but at that point I wasn't looking in the mirror or anything. I really thought that it was the tyres going away. It wasn't good. I was keeping the position, because no one could overtake me on the straight, as I was keeping the DRS open all the time, but it was obviously not the way to continue.

"They fixed it, and there was some kind of feeling that it was stuck there. We thought that this had fixed it, but obviously it wasn't okay, as on the out lap it happened again and I had to pit again."

Ferrari's troubles left Vettel away clear in the lead, able to control the race, and the German continued to put in fast and consistent laps while keeping his tyres alive and while being under no real threat from behind. He made it to the chequered flag on three stops and it looked all too easy.

"I certainly didn't expect that," admitted Vettel.

ABOVE Nico Rosberg started from pole but soon dropped back. By lap 6, he was fourth and holding off Felipe Massa and Mark Webber

OPPOSITE Sebastian Vettel found himself in a class of his own, controlling the race after passing Alonso and Rosberg in the early laps

BELOW Pastor Maldonado locks up his Williams car en route to a frustrating 11th place finish at Sakhir

that, in the end, Webber lost only two places.

The main beneficiary of all this was Felipe Massa, who qualified sixth but moved up to fourth, after qualifying on the hard tyre. Force India had a good day, with Paul di Resta and Adrian Sutil taking seventh and eighth, and moving up to fifth and sixth after the penalties were applied. Webber would line up seventh, ahead of Räikkönen, Hamilton and Jenson Button.

At the start, Rosberg got away from pole position safely in front, while behind him Alonso initially got past Vettel to claim second. However, just a few corners into the lap, Vettel surged back past.

Down the order, Toro Rosso's Jean-Eric Vergne

INSIDE LINE
SEBASTIAN VETTEL
RED BULL RACING DRIVER

"I knew that it was crucial to lead so that I could go from there and look after the tyres. It was very tight in the first corner, with Fernando on the outside. I had to give way, but then I got him back, which was crucial. I saved some KERS and was able to out-accelerate him into Turn 6.

"Then Nico Rosberg was a tough one. I really had to think as he was quite quick down the straights. Obviously the headwind helped all the cars behind, but it still wasn't straightforward. Out of Turn 4, I again managed to save a bit of KERS and got by him on the inside of Turn 5.

"The car was very quick and it just started to get better and better towards the end. It was a beautiful race where you could push every single lap. I was pretty dominant and that certainly wasn't what I expected. I could feel that I was able to pull away and the medium compound tyre felt pretty strong, but we also had three sets of new hard tyres and the car seemed to work very well on those.

"I realised in the second stint that I could open a gap and did it because you don't know what's going to

happen. It buys you some flexibility. Fortunately, we never got into a pressure situation again. I think the pace was related to the way that we worked with the tyres. We know the car's quick, which we saw again in qualifying, and leading always helps because if you sit behind someone you lose grip, you start to slide and the tyres go off, then you have a different race.

"As for what we've been saying about the tyres, I think the fact that we've won the constructors' championship for the last three years makes people listen a bit more. I did talk about the tyres, I did complain, but I always said that as long as there are other people doing a better job then we have no right to complain really. We just need to catch up.

"I don't think you have

to be a genius to see that from race to race some people suffer with their tyres and can't go at the true pace of their cars. It's obviously very strategic, but it's the same for all of us. Out of four races, we've had two good ones and two average ones, but the average ones weren't disastrous.

"Comparing it to a couple of years ago, though, the fact that you can't push as hard as you like every lap and have to hold a certain pace and take it from there is very different and to some extent less enjoyable than in the past.

ABOVE Exciting times: Ferrari's Felipe Massa tries a move on Nico Rosberg who, in turn, tries to overtake Jenson Button

OPPOSITE The circuit provides a backdrop like no other, mixing arid and rocky desert with oases

"I was pretty dominant today, as I said, but certainly didn't expect to be. Early on, it was quite tight, wheel-to-wheel racing. I knew it would be crucial to get into the lead if I could, because then you have a little bit of an advantage, looking after your tyres and managing the race from there.

"In the second stint, I was able to open a gap so I thought, 'Right, I'll take my chance as much as I can to pull away'. It probably buys us some flexibility. We were then able to look after the tyres, and really manage every stint the best way we could."

Fortunately, there was plenty of action behind Vettel. Di Resta ran in a strong second place for Force India for a while as his two-stop schedule kept him out on track when others running ahead of him pitted. However, the Scot was eventually overhauled by Räikkönen, who was on the same strategy.

The Finn did well to recover from eighth on the grid to claim an eventual second, proving once again that the Lotus E21 is light on its tyres. However, he didn't blame the grid position for losing out to Vettel.

"I think my grid position didn't help, but I think overall we wouldn't have had the speed for beating Red Bull here this weekend anyway," said Kimi. "Even if yesterday we could have qualified a few places higher on the grid, I don't think speed-wise we could really have challenged Vettel for the win.

"Second place is obviously better than third, but we haven't won, and that's what we try to do. Today we got good points, and we didn't lose too many to Sebastian, but obviously it doesn't help to finish second if he's winning all the time."

With a free choice of tyres from a lowly 11th on the grid, Romain Grosjean started the other Lotus on the hard tyres and made three pit stops to Räikkönen's two. He was also able to get ahead of di Resta in the last part of the race to claim third, helped by his fresher rubber. This first podium finish of the season came despite the Frenchman being forced into an early first pit stop after picking up debris that raised both brake and water temperatures.

"We've had a difficult start to the season," said Grosjean. "I think we've put in a lot of work and a lot of effort to understand what exactly was going on – and it wasn't easy to find out, but basically I think we came back to where we should be. Qualifying was a bit disappointing, but never mind, we had a lot of new sets of tyres for today, which was good.

TALKING POINT
FAR ENDS OF
THE SPECTRUM

It was so typically Formula 1 that – having left China amid lots of hand-wringing about strategy that was too complex, and overtaking that wasn't overtaking – we should turn up a few days later in Bahrain and witness a fantastic, skilled and pure racing battle throughout the field.

Nowhere did it get more physical than in the scrap between McLaren team-mates Jenson Button and Sergio Perez (above). The Mexican, already starting to come under pressure from detractors just three races into his McLaren career, had passed Button by taking an earlier second pit stop. But Jenson re-passed him a few laps later with the help of his DRS into Turn 1.

Following the Malaysian GP, McLaren team principal Martin Whitmarsh had suggested that perhaps Perez needed to "get his elbows out a little more". At the Bahrain GP, though, Whitmarsh must have had quite an exciting time of it as he contemplated the possible elimination of both MP4-28s...

First, they banged wheels through Turn 2 on lap 30 as they fought over fifth place, then made much more solid contact as Perez clipped the back of Button's car as he tried to undercut Jenson out of Turn 4.

Even more robust wheel-banging then followed between Turns 3 and 4, before Button drove Perez wide and hung him out to dry on the exit of Turn 4. But Perez finally made a move stick and proved that he'd learned by deploying a similar tactic against a very indignant Alonso. Finally, his dander well and truly up, he dived inside Webber at Turn 5 to snatch sixth place on the final lap.

Post-race, Button was a bit chippy about Perez's driving, but Whitmarsh played it all down.

"Checo needed that," he said. "People were starting to get on his case, expecting to see a bit more spark. I was being asked to control Sergio during that race, but I wasn't about to. And, while we saw that Jenson had a bit more trouble than Checo with tyres today, neither was it right for us to tell Jenson to wave him by. I've not done that sort of thing yet and I don't think I'm likely to start any time soon.

"What you don't do, though, is hit your team-mate from behind, potentially giving him a puncture and taking off your own front wing. That was going a bit too far and I told Checo so. But he definitely had the spark today!"

That was just one snapshot in a superb race that featured committed fighting almost wherever you looked.

ABOVE Force India's Paul di Resta led the race at one point by opting for a two-stop run before settling for fourth place

BELOW Caterham's Giedo van der Garde accelerates past the circuit's distinctive tower in his damage-delayed run to last place

"After the first few laps there wasn't much optimism because we had a lot of big debris coming into the radiator and the rear brakes, and so we had to pit very early because the temperature was going up. I knew then that the two first stints would be normally quite long on hard tyres before a short stint on mediums, but we had to pit and change the tyres. Fortunately, the car was then good and I think it was one of the races where I had the most overtaking manoeuvres and fights on track."

Di Resta managed to hang onto fourth after a weekend that underlined the competitiveness of the Force India VJM06. Behind him, there were fraught battles for the other points positions. On the fringes of the top ten initially, Hamilton moved up the order in the second half of the race and claimed fifth right at the end from Webber.

After a storming race, Sergio Perez also got past Webber – whose tyres were finished – on the final lap. For a large chunk of the race, the Mexican driver had been involved in a fight with his McLaren team-mate, Jenson Button, and after the pair made contact more than once, the more experienced British racer made his displeasure pretty clear. Nevertheless, Perez did much to boost his confidence after a difficult start to his McLaren career.

Webber had run second in the second stint, but the Australian Red Bull driver struggled with rear tyre wear, which led to an early pit stop. In the closing laps, he was unable to defend himself against Hamilton and Perez, who demoted him to an eventual seventh.

At least he finished ahead of Alonso, who had lost his DRS and also made contact with the charging Perez as they battled for position. Pole man Rosberg tumbled down to a frustrated ninth after being forced to make four tyre stops, while Button slipped back to tenth after an unplanned fourth pit stop.

Pastor Maldonado started on the hard tyre and made good progress up to 11th at the flag, although the Williams driver was still almost 20s off the points. Nico Hulkenberg had an untroubled race, but his Sauber punished its rear tyres and simply lacked speed, so he finished out of the points in 12th.

An unlucky Sutil suffered a first lap puncture after being hit by Massa. Thereafter, he was actually the fastest car on the track for much of the race, but following the early delay he could recover only to 13th. Meanwhile, Massa himself had been set to score some useful points for Ferrari, but two rear punctures cost him dearly and left the Brazilian only 15th at the end. It just wasn't Ferrari's day.

SNAPSHOT FROM
BAHRAIN

CLOCKWISE FROM RIGHT

Nico Rosberg (Mercedes) leads Sebastian Vettel, Fernando Alonso, Paul di Resta, Felipe Massa, Mark Webber, Kimi Räikkönen, Jenson Button, Sergio Perez and Romain Grosjean; Ferrari Team Principal Stefano Domenicali listens to a Sebastian Vettel punchline; a pit stop for Romain Grosjean; Adrian Newey, Vettel and Christian Horner celebrate the German's second win in four races; multiple world champions Sir Jackie Stewart and Niki Lauda share a joke; Perez contemplates Martin Whitmarsh's advice while waiting in the pits; elevation is everything for these photographers; Force India driver Paul di Resta gets in a reconnaissance lap; Kimi Räikkönen checks his tyres after finishing second in Bahrain

BAHRAIN
SAKHIR
ROUND 4

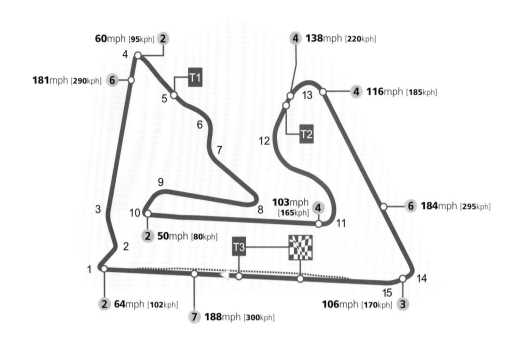

60mph [95kph] 2
4
4 138mph [220kph]
181mph [290kph] 6
T1
4 116mph [185kph]
5
13
6
12
T2
7
9
103mph [165kph] 4
6 184mph [295kph]
3
10
8
11
2
2 50mph [80kph]
T3
1
2 64mph [102kph]
14
15
106mph [170kph] 3
7 188mph [300kph]

RACE RESULTS

RACE DATE 21 April 2013
CIRCUIT LENGTH 3.363 miles
NO. OF LAPS 57
RACE DISTANCE 191.691 miles
WEATHER Sunny, 26°C
TRACK TEMP 37°C
LAP RECORD Michael Schumacher,
1m30.252s, 134.262mph, 2004

PRACTICE 1

	Driver	Time	Laps
1	F Massa	1m34.487s	11
2	F Alonso	1m34.564s	19
3	N Rosberg	1m34.621s	22
4	S Vettel	1m34.790s	20
5	P di Resta	1m34.949s	17
6	J Button	1m35.069s	22
7	M Webber	1m35.101s	19
8	A Sutil	1m35.119s	19
9	K Räikkönen	1m35.345s	17
10	R Grosjean	1m35.611s	14
11	S Perez	1m35.640s	23
12	V Bottas	1m35.783s	16
13	L Hamilton	1m35.792s	16
14	J-E Vergne	1m36.014s	19
15	D Ricciardo	1m36.485s	20
16	P Maldonado	1m36.498s	17
17	N Hulkenberg	1m36.755s	20
18	E Gutierrez	1m37.214s	21
19	C Pic	1m37.850s	20
20	H Kovalainen	1m38.401s	20
21	M Chilton	1m39.445s	12
22	R Gonzalez	1m40.215s	7

PRACTICE 2

	Driver	Time	Laps
1	K Räikkönen	1m34.154s	31
2	M Webber	1m34.184s	26
3	S Vettel	1m34.282s	29
4	F Alonso	1m34.310s	29
5	P di Resta	1m34.543s	35
6	F Massa	1m34.552s	34
7	R Grosjean	1m34.631s	33
8	N Rosberg	1m34.666s	37
9	A Sutil	1m34.932s	33
10	L Hamilton	1m34.976s	29
11	J Button	1m35.356s	32
12	J-E Vergne	1m35.506s	36
13	S Perez	1m35.589s	37
14	D Ricciardo	1m35.761s	33
15	N Hulkenberg	1m36.133s	36
16	P Maldonado	1m36.279s	33
17	V Bottas	1m36.579s	28
18	E Gutierrez	1m36.616s	34
19	C Pic	1m37.061s	33
20	M Chilton	1m37.313s	33
21	J Bianchi	1m37.363s	29
22	G van der Garde	1m37.970s	34

PRACTICE 3

	Driver	Time	Laps
1	F Alonso	1m33.247s	12
2	S Vettel	1m33.348s	15
3	M Webber	1m33.380s	19
4	K Räikkönen	1m33.446s	21
5	L Hamilton	1m33.455s	19
6	R Grosjean	1m33.464s	19
7	A Sutil	1m33.596s	17
8	P di Resta	1m33.700s	15
9	N Rosberg	1m33.764s	19
10	N Hulkenberg	1m33.922s	17
11	F Massa	1m33.949s	20
12	J Button	1m34.117s	17
13	S Perez	1m34.282s	18
14	D Ricciardo	1m34.577s	16
15	V Bottas	1m34.611s	17
16	J-E Vergne	1m34.678s	16
17	P Maldonado	1m34.833s	17
18	C Pic	1m35.816s	16
19	J Bianchi	1m36.731s	17
20	G van der Garde	1m36.939s	16
21	M Chilton	1m37.630s	7
22	E Gutierrez	1m39.592s	29

QUALIFYING 1

	Driver	Time
1	F Alonso	1m32.878s
2	S Vettel	1m33.327s
3	N Rosberg	1m33.364s
4	L Hamilton	1m33.498s
5	R Grosjean	1m33.498s
6	P di Resta	1m33.762s
7	F Massa	1m33.780s
8	K Räikkönen	1m33.827s
9	M Webber	1m33.966s
10	A Sutil	1m34.048s
11	J Button	1m34.071s
12	D Ricciardo	1m34.120s
13	S Perez	1m34.310s
14	J-E Vergne	1m34.314s
15	N Hulkenberg	1m34.409s
16	V Bottas	1m34.425s
17	P Maldonado	1m34.425s
18	E Gutierrez	1m34.730s
19	C Pic	1m35.283s
20	J Bianchi	1m36.178s
21	G van der Garde	1m36.304s
22	M Chilton	1m36.476s

QUALIFYING 2

	Driver	Time
1	S Vettel	1m32.746s
2	N Rosberg	1m32.867s
3	M Webber	1m33.098s
4	K Räikkönen	1m33.146s
5	F Alonso	1m33.316s
6	P di Resta	1m33.335s
7	L Hamilton	1m33.346s
8	F Massa	1m33.358s
9	A Sutil	1m33.378s
10	J Button	1m33.702s
11	R Grosjean	1m33.762s
12	S Perez	1m33.914s
13	D Ricciardo	1m33.974s
14	N Hulkenberg	1m33.976s
15	V Bottas	1m34.105s
16	J-E Vergne	1m34.284s

Best sectors – Practice

Sec 1	A Sutil	29.759s
Sec 2	F Alonso	40.020s
Sec 3	M Webber	23.227s

Speed trap – Practice

1	L Hamilton	196.291mph
2	K Räikkönen	196.291mph
3	R Grosjean	196.229mph

Best sectors – Qualifying

Sec 1	N Rosberg	29.416s
Sec 2	N Rosberg	39.847s
Sec 3	N Rosberg	22.987s

Speed trap – Qualifying

1	P di Resta	195.234mph
2	A Sutil	195.172mph
3	F Alonso	194.799mph

Sebastian Vettel
"It's important to get to the front. I love to be in clean air, so I was pushing hard to get into the lead and, with the speed we had mid-race, it was comfortable today."

Fernando Alonso
"In the early laps, I thought the rear tyres had gone off, but the team told me that the DRS was stuck. It wasn't fixed at first, so I had to come in for another one."

Jenson Button
"The race was fun, but I didn't get the result I wanted, as I used up my tyres fending off Checo. There was a lot of action and so I wasn't able to conserve my tyres."

Kimi Räikkönen
"You're never really happy if you don't win, but second is as close as you can get. I drove to the maximum and the car had the pace we missed in qualifying."

Nico Rosberg
"As nice as it was to start from pole, it was just as hard to finish ninth. We switched to four stops at the end of my third stint, as we were using the rears too much."

Nico Hulkenberg
"We lacked speed and ate up the rear tyres too much. I pitted a bit late, as we expected to have more problems on low fuel. That cost me at least one position."

Mark Webber
"We went aggressive on the first out-lap, which meant we jumped people, but the tyres didn't like it. That meant the second stint was a disaster at the end."

Felipe Massa
"I lost ground after the collision with Sutil, and then lost more time coming back to the pits to change tyres. That wiped out any chance of having a good race."

Sergio Perez
"That was an incredible race, really enjoyable. I was a little aggressive; banging wheels with Jenson was perhaps too risky, but the team never told us to stop."

Romain Grosjean
"It's great to be back on the podium. I felt more comfortable in the car and the result is a deserved reward. To come from 11th to the podium is really satisfying."

Lewis Hamilton
"Finishing fifth was damage limitation. I struggled in the first two stints but, as temperatures fell, the car picked up and then I had the grip that I needed to push."

Esteban Gutierrez
"I expected a difficult race and I got one. On the first lap, I had contact into Turn 10, which was really hard to avoid. Apart from that, things were quite okay."

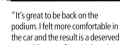

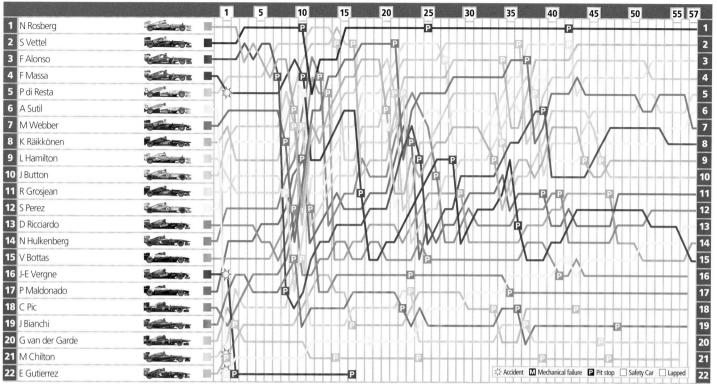

	Driver		
1	N Rosberg		
2	S Vettel		
3	F Alonso		
4	F Massa		
5	P di Resta		
6	A Sutil		
7	M Webber		
8	K Räikkönen		
9	L Hamilton		
10	J Button		
11	R Grosjean		
12	S Perez		
13	D Ricciardo		
14	N Hulkenberg		
15	V Bottas		
16	J-E Vergne		
17	P Maldonado		
18	C Pic		
19	J Bianchi		
20	G van der Garde		
21	M Chilton		
22	E Gutierrez		

☼ Accident ■ Mechanical failure P Pit stop ☐ Safety Car ☐ Lapped

QUALIFYING 3

	Driver	Time
1	N Rosberg	1m32.330s
2	S Vettel	1m32.584s
3	F Alonso	1m32.667s
4	L Hamilton	1m32.762s
5	M Webber	1m33.078s
6	F Massa	1m33.207s
7	P di Resta	1m33.235s
8	A Sutil	1m33.246s
9	K Räikkönen	1m33.327s
10	J Button	No time

GRID

	Driver	Time
1	N Rosberg	1m32.330s
2	S Vettel	1m32.584s
3	F Alonso	1m32.667s
4	F Massa	1m33.207s
5	P di Resta	1m33.235s
6	A Sutil	1m33.246s
7	M Webber	1m33.078s
8	K Räikkönen	1m33.327s
9	L Hamilton	1m32.762s
10	J Button	No time
11	R Grosjean	1m33.762s
12	S Perez	1m33.914s
13	D Ricciardo	1m33.974s
14	N Hulkenberg	1m33.976s
15	V Bottas	1m34.105s
16	J-E Vergne	1m34.284s
17	P Maldonado	1m34.425s
18	C Pic	1m35.283s
21	J Bianchi	1m36.178s
20	G van der Garde	1m36.304s
21	M Chilton	1m36.476s
22	E Gutierrez	1m34.730s

RACE

	Driver	Car	Laps	Time	Avg. mph	Fastest	Stops
1	S Vettel	Red Bull-Renault RB9	57	1h36m00.498s	119.696	1m36.961s	3
2	K Räikkönen	Lotus-Renault E21	57	1h36m09.609s	119.506	1m38.164s	2
3	R Grosjean	Lotus-Renault E21	57	1h36m20.005s	119.291	1m37.627s	3
4	P di Resta	Force India-Mercedes VJM06	57	1h36m22.225s	119.246	1m38.336s	2
5	L Hamilton	Mercedes F1 W04	57	1h36m35.728s	118.968	1m38.204s	3
6	S Perez	McLaren-Mercedes MP4-28	57	1h36m36.496s	118.952	1m37.913s	3
7	M Webber	Red Bull-Renault RB9	57	1h36m37.742s	118.926	1m38.557s	3
8	F Alonso	Ferrari F138	57	1h36m38.072s	118.920	1m37.204s	4
9	N Rosberg	Mercedes F1 W04	57	1h36m41.624s	118.847	1m37.588s	4
10	J Button	McLaren-Mercedes MP4-28	57	1h36m47.129s	118.734	1m37.743s	4
11	P Maldonado	Williams-Renault FW35	57	1h37m06.948s	118.331	1m38.962s	3
12	N Hulkenberg	Sauber-Ferrari C32	57	1h37m13.431s	118.199	1m38.770s	3
13	A Sutil	Force India-Mercedes VJM06	57	1h37m17.217s	118.122	1m37.070s	3
14	V Bottas	Williams-Renault FW35	57	1h37m22.009s	118.026	1m38.192s	3
15	F Massa	Ferrari F138	57	1h37m26.862s	117.927	1m38.839s	4
16	D Ricciardo	Toro Rosso-Ferrari STR8	56	1h36m06.584s	117.470	1m39.579s	3
17	C Pic	Caterham-Renault CT03	56	1h36m16.347s	117.271	1m39.546s	3
18	E Gutierrez	Sauber-Ferrari C32	56	1h36m16.937s	117.259	1m38.202s	4
19	J Bianchi	Marussia-Cosworth MR-02	56	1h36m54.150s	116.509	1m38.756s	4
20	M Chilton	Marussia-Cosworth MR-02	56	1h37m06.434s	116.263	1m39.279s	4
21	G van der Garde	Caterham-Renault CT03	55	1h36m55.737s	114.395	1m39.334s	5
R	J-E Vergne	Toro Rosso-Ferrari STR8	16	Accident damage	-	1m43.107s	1

CHAMPIONSHIP

	Driver	Pts
1	S Vettel	77
2	K Räikkönen	67
3	L Hamilton	50
4	F Alonso	47
5	M Webber	32
6	F Massa	30
7	R Grosjean	26
8	P di Resta	20
9	N Rosberg	14
10	J Button	13
11	S Perez	10
12	A Sutil	6
13	D Ricciardo	6
14	N Hulkenberg	5
15	J-E Vergne	1

Grid penalties

M Webber Three-place penalty for causing a collision in the previous race
L Hamilton Five-place penalty for changing the gearbox
E Gutierrez Five-place penalty for causing a collision in the previous race

Fastest lap
S Vettel 1m36.961s
(124.857mph) on lap 55

Fastest speed trap
F Massa 195.234mph
Slowest speed trap
G van der Garde 188.213mph

Fastest pit stop
1	M Webber	21.031s
2	F Alonso	21.123s
3	S Perez	21.161s

	Constructor	Pts
1	Red Bull-Renault	109
2	Lotus-Renault	93
3	Ferrari	77
4	Mercedes	64
5	Force India-Mercedes	26
6	McLaren-Mercedes	23
7	Toro Rosso-Ferrari	7
8	Sauber-Ferrari	5

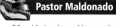

Paul di Resta
"It's great to finish the flyaways with fourth. With our strategy, we were going to be vulnerable, especially to Grosjean, who had two new sets of medium tyres."

Pastor Maldonado
"Considering the problems we've been having, we got 100 per cent out of the car. We put everything together, working well as a team and managing the tyres."

Fernando Alonso
"I was pushed by Bottas as I overtook him on the outside of Turn 4 and he clipped my car. The impact caused a lot of damage to the floor as well as a puncture."

Charles Pic
"I passed both Marussias after starting on the medium tyres. I then kept pace with Ricciardo, and kept Gutierrez back, and so did a long stint on the hards."

Jules Bianchi
"We struggled with the tyres. On my fourth stint the plan was to go to the end of the race, but we had to pit again. From there, it was just about making it to the finish."

Adrian Sutil
"I was racing Massa into Turn 4. I was on the outside; I gave him space, but he hit my front-right tyre. I had a puncture, so had to pit and lost a lot of time."

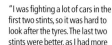

Valtteri Bottas
"I was fighting a lot of cars in the first two stints, so it was hard to look after the tyres. The last two stints were better, as I had more clean air and made up ground."

Daniel Ricciardo
"I made an okay start and got ahead of Grosjean. Then I locked up and lost a place or two. We struggled with speed as we were limited in terms of downforce."

Giedo van der Garde
"I didn't have a great start, but I was up to 16th going into Turn 4 and saw that Vergne had spun. I tried to miss him, but couldn't, destroying my front wing."

Max Chilton
"I got a good start and leapfrogged both Caterhams. Unfortunately, we struggled on the tyres, and it wasn't long into each stint before I hit that window again."

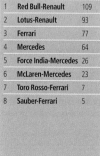

FORMULA 1 GRAN PREMIO DE ESPAÑA 2013

10-12 MAY
CIRCUIT DE CATALUNYA
MONTMELO

VIVA ESPAÑA!

Fernando Alonso delivered exactly what an expectant home crowd wanted when he won the Spanish GP in superb style, despite starting only fifth. It had been a long wait since his last home success in 2006.

A lthough he did score a surprise triumph in the European GP in Valencia in 2012, this win for Fernando Alonso was perfectly timed. He'd already lost priceless points when he suffered an early retirement in the Malaysian GP and then a DRS problem last time out in Bahrain. In a race dominated by tyres at the Circuit de Catalunya, Alonso showed superb speed and left everyone behind to win by a comfortable margin.

Although perhaps not a classic contest, it certainly improved on many of the processions we've seen at this circuit in years gone by, when the winner was pretty sure to come from the first couple of rows of the grid. This time the four-stop schedule settled on by most teams left drivers, never mind the fans in the stands, in a state of excited doubt for most of the race.

Mercedes made it three pole positions in as many races when Nico Rosberg and Lewis Hamilton secured a front-row lockout. The Silver Arrows had not shown front-running pace earlier in the weekend, and indeed people expected the pole battle to be fought out between Ferrari, Red Bull Racing and surprise contenders Lotus, after the black and gold cars impressed in the third practice session.

ABOVE Sebastian Vettel edges his RB9 out of his pit garage and into the Spanish sunshine in practice

OPPOSITE ABOVE Mercedes to the fore as Rosberg leads the charge to Turn 1 from Hamilton and Vettel, chased by Räikkönen and Alonso

OPPOSITE BELOW Vettel is through to second place by Turn 2 and Alonso is preparing to pounce on both Räikkönen and Hamilton

When it mattered, though, the Mercedes F1 W04 was fast again, the drivers finding chunks of time in the twisty third sector of the lap. Hamilton was quickest in both Q1 and Q2, but come Q3 he was beaten to pole by Rosberg by 0.254s.

Sebastian Vettel qualified third for Red Bull Racing and, given that the Mercedes duo were expected to struggle with their Pirellis during the race, the three-time champion looked well set. However, he had Kimi Räikkönen slotted in immediately behind him, and Lotus had once again demonstrated very good pace over long runs.

Alonso had looked fast for much of the weekend,

INSIDE LINE
FERNANDO ALONSO
FERRARI DRIVER

"I felt the support from everybody today – fantastic! I'm lucky to have won three times now in my home country. Maybe I'm not as emotional as at Valencia last year because that was very different. It's not that we expected to win today, rather that we were completely surprised last year when we did.

"We knew that if everything went well today we could win, but in Valencia last year we thought that our optimum strategy would maybe deliver fifth or sixth place. That's what the simulations said. To win from 11th, in front of everyone, wasn't something we even dreamed about. That's why it was so emotional, but it's always very special to win at home. It doesn't matter how many times you do it, it's always like starting from zero and you have emotional last laps. They are long laps because you want to finish as soon as possible!

"I'm happy for the team to have both cars in the first three after a difficult qualifying. We were only fifth and ninth but knew we had the pace on the long runs and wanted to have some clear air to exploit the potential. We had that and everything worked perfectly.

"Today was actually not so difficult. We had pace in the car, we had clean air and only a little bit of traffic in the first stint behind Vettel and Rosberg. Then we undercut Sebastian in the pits and passed Nico two laps later at the first corner. From that point on, we just pushed 90 per cent. We had enough pace to open the necessary gap, and if you push 100 per cent maybe you kill the tyres. It was more or less normal driving, let's say, for 2013 races. You try to control the pace and tyres, balancing the two.

"In spite of that, it wasn't until after the last stop that I knew I had things under control. We knew that Kimi was on a different strategy, but you never know how the tyres are going to behave. When I pitted two or three laps later than

Kimi and was still in front with fresher tyres, that's when I knew we were OK.

"I don't want to talk about the championship as we've only had five races and some ups and downs. But, yes, in terms of car performance, this could probably be my best chance at Ferrari. We should have won in 2010 but last year maybe we didn't deserve it because we were 1.0s off the pace even if we managed to stay in the title fight until the final round. This year we have a package that's maybe still not the fastest, but we're working on it."

but had to settle for fifth, ahead of Ferrari team-mate Felipe Massa. The top 10 was completed by Romain Grosjean, Mark Webber, Sergio Perez (who did a good job to wrestle his McLaren into Q3) and Paul di Resta.

At the start, Rosberg managed to stay safely in front, while Hamilton locked up at Turn 1 and was passed by Vettel. An inspired Alonso then pulled off an amazing overtaking move, getting ahead of Räikkönen between Turns 1 and 2 and then powering past Hamilton to snatch third place with a little help from his KERS. Those early moves were crucial, as they propelled the crowd's hero up the order and got him ahead of Räikkönen, who would turn out to be his main rival.

"I think we knew that to win the race we needed to pass people right away," said Alonso. "The start was very good, but then it was very narrow and we didn't have the space to move even a little bit. So, I waited for a better opportunity. It came straight after Turn 1. I saw Kimi and Lewis running a little bit wide in Turn 1, so I changed trajectory and had a clean exit from Turn 2. I passed Kimi and I thought, 'Why not Hamilton too?' I had a little bit of KERS that I saved from the start for Turn 3, so I used that to pass him."

TALKING POINT
HEAT OVER TYRE 'TEST'

In the week following the Spanish GP, Mercedes undertook a three-day Pirelli test at Barcelona's Circuit de Catalunya with Lewis Hamilton and Nico Rosberg driving a current F1 W04 chassis with their identity concealed by wearing plain black helmets.

The test remained a secret until the Saturday of the following week's Monaco GP meeting, when FIA race director Charlie Whiting was discussing the tyre situation with GPDA directors Sebastian Vettel, Jenson Button and Pedro de la Rosa.

When the news got out, it was like a bomb going off in the F1 paddock. The F1 regulations outlaw in-season testing with contemporary chassis other than the pre-arranged Young Driver Test and limited straightline aerodynamic running and filming days.

The complication, however, was that Pirelli's own tyre supplier contract has a provision for 1,000 kilometres of testing, provided that the tyre company rather than the team runs the test, and that all teams are given the chance to participate.

Considering that nobody else knew about the run, that was evidently not the case. Red Bull Racing and Ferrari immediately protested and, after careful consideration, it was decided that Pirelli and Mercedes would be called before the first FIA International Tribunal, an initiative of Jean Todt's in the interests of greater judicial transparency.

There was some sympathy for Pirelli. Ferrari's Felipe Massa, Force India's Paul di Resta and Lewis Hamilton had already suffered delaminations that were image-damaging for the Italian company, who would also soon be faced with visits to high-speed tracks such as Montreal and Silverstone. And, although as yet without a firm 2014 supplier contract, Pirelli also had to prepare for the new drivetrains due in 2014 that will undoubtedly put greater stress through the cars' rear tyres.

The use of Mercedes was both logical and incendiary. Logical because Hamilton also suffered a suspension failure when he had his delamination during free practice in Bahrain. Incendiary because Mercedes had sufficient one-lap pace to have taken the previous three pole positions but was in trouble with rear thermal degradation in the races. It was inevitable, said their rivals, that the team would gain a significant advantage through the test.

Mercedes Team Principal Ross Brawn claimed that it had been Pirelli's responsibility to inform the other teams and that Mercedes had checked with the FIA before undertaking the test. There seemed to be some confusion over this last point, but all would be revealed at the Tribunal, which was scheduled for Paris on 20 June.

From there, it was always going to be all about tyres, and who did the best job of preserving them – especially the left front which is under constant stress at this circuit. Ferrari took an aggressive approach, going for four pit stops rather than the widely anticipated three, thus giving Alonso five sets of tyres with which to run the race's 66 laps, and this meant that he could pretty much push as hard as he wanted for the duration.

Rosberg managed to stay in the lead until his early first pit stop. As everyone piled into the pits, Sauber's rookie Esteban Gutierrez enjoyed a brief spell in the lead by staying out longer than anyone else, but the key outcome of the initial pit-stop sequence was that Alonso moved ahead of Vettel to secure second place. He then passed Rosberg – already struggling on his second set of tyres – to claim the lead.

Like Alonso, most drivers opted for a four-stop strategy that allowed them to push the tyres hard for most of the race. Bucking this trend, Räikkönen went for just three stops and, after getting ahead of Vettel for second place, the Finn confirmed that he was Alonso's main threat.

Emerging from his third pit stop, Alonso dropped behind Räikkönen's Lotus but, with extra life in his fresh tyres, he was soon able to power back past.

"Obviously, we were leading, but when we were on old tyres and he had newer tyres, it's too easy to overtake," said Räikkönen. "There's no point really in fighting, because you can't hold him behind. I knew if I could somehow stay a bit closer, even with old tyres, maybe I would have some chance, even if I'm already behind and will be with old tyres towards the end, as you never know."

At that stage, both men had just one pit stop to come – Alonso's fourth and Kimi's third – and it was apparent that the Ferrari driver had the trump card. He opened up a gap of 13s at one stage, but allowed it to drop back down to 9s at the flag. This victory clearly meant a huge amount to Alonso, and not just in the context of the title battle.

"Maybe we weren't too fast yesterday," he explained, "but we knew we had the pace for the long runs and we did it. I am so happy for the team, for the fans and hopefully this result won't be a one-off."

Lotus had no regrets about Räikkönen stopping three times rather than four, the team feeling that Alonso would have won the race in any case. Crucially, the Finn lost time stuck behind other cars early in the race. Yet Räikkönen still earned his third straight second place and fourth podium of the year to keep himself firmly in the title battle, although he expressed doubts about the strategy.

"I think we had the speed, but we should have done it differently," said Kimi. "Maybe we should have made more pit stops, then you can push all the time – but I think this was our best way of doing the race. That's what we planned and that's what we did, and I think we deserved to be second and not really winning. It's okay for the team, the guys did a good job and we'll go to the next race to try to do better and get the best out of it."

Massa underlined Ferrari's strong form by finishing in third place, albeit some 26s behind his team-mate.

Vettel collected priceless points with a somewhat subdued fourth place as the Red Bull RB9 again proved tough on its tyres. Afterwards, the German couldn't disguise his frustration with the role of Pirelli in 2013. "I think there were obviously three people that did better today, and we need to catch up," he said. "We're not going at the pace of the car, we're going at the pace of the tyres."

Vettel downplayed the suggestion that by going

OPPOSITE **Mark Webber dives past Max Chilton's Marussia as he recovers from a terrible first lap**

BELOW **Kimi Räikkönen powers his Lotus E21 out of the pit lane en route to his third consecutive second-place finish**

ABOVE Thumbs up from Ferrari as Fernando Alonso flashes across the win line. Jules Bianchi, two laps down, is in the background

for four pit stops, winner Alonso was able to push throughout with no apparent concern for the tyres, as he himself switched to four stops. "We were trying to do it on three pit stops at the beginning, but we had to admit that our tyre wear was too big for us today and we couldn't stay with the cars ahead so we adapted our strategy."

His team-mate Webber, who tumbled down to 11th place after a bad first lap, managed to recover to fifth. Despite tyre issues, Rosberg hung on to finish in sixth place, which was a poor reward for Mercedes after the team's competitive showing in qualifying. He just managed to hold off the Force India of Paul di Resta. Jenson Button and Sergio Perez finished close together in eighth and ninth as the last of the unlapped runners after another low-key afternoon for McLaren, while Daniel Ricciardo took the final point for Scuderia Toro Rosso.

Hamilton experienced much worse tyre degradation than Rosberg, and ultimately finished out of the points, a despondent 12th. He admitted that the engineers were still in the dark about where to go next. "There was no grip today, just sliding around on all fours," he said ruefully. "I was just tip-

toeing around, basically. It doesn't matter whether I go slow or go fast, it doesn't do anything different. It's very, very strange – one of the strangest feelings I've had for a long time.

"We've just got to understand where we went wrong, and how we can improve it for the upcoming races, but it's something to do with how you prepare the tyres, or use the tyres, or something like that. It seemed to work quite well in Bahrain, but it didn't work here. It's something that we haven't quite caught up with just yet."

Also out of luck were Adrian Sutil, who lost almost a minute with a wheel problem at a pit stop, and Grosjean, who retired his Lotus early on after suspension failure.

Afterwards, Pirelli conceded that four pit stops was one too many, and promised that revised tyres, with less dramatic degradation, would be used for the British GP at Silverstone at the end of June. That came as a relief to those who, like Red Bull Racing and Mercedes, felt that tyres were overshadowing the true strengths of their cars. The Pirelli promise would prove a little premature, however. Nevertheless, tyres would remain in the news...

SNAPSHOT FROM
SPAIN

CLOCKWISE FROM RIGHT

With so many pit stops, the race was a little confusing, but the fans in the grandstands certainly knew that local hero Fernando Alonso was the winner; a quiet pre-qualifying moment for Sergio Perez who, with team-mate Jenson Button, scored a rare double finish in the top ten for McLaren; Button and his double; a group interview at McLaren; parc ferme colour; tyre wear continued to confuse the teams; with both drivers on the podium, there was every reason for Ferrari to celebrate in Spain; understanding the data is a never-ending task; Kimi Räikkönen checks his mirrors – in the race it was Ferrari's Felipe Massa behind him; darkness falls, but hard preparation work continues in the Red Bull Racing garage

SPAIN
CATALUNYA
ROUND 5

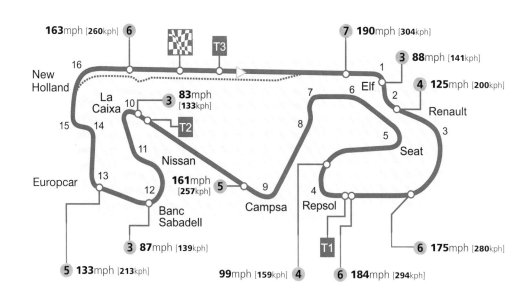

163mph [260kph] 6 — New Holland — 16
7 190mph [304kph]
3 88mph [141kph]
T3
La Caixa — 3 83mph [133kph]
15 — 14 — 10 — T2
1 — Elf — 6
4 125mph [200kph]
Renault
11 — Nissan
7
8
2
3
Europcar — 13 — 12 — 161mph [257kph] 5 — 9
Seat
5
Campsa
Banc Sabadell — 3 87mph [139kph]
4 — Repsol
T1
5 133mph [213kph]
99mph [159kph] 4
6 184mph [294kph]
6 175mph [280kph]

RACE RESULTS

RACE DATE 12 May 2013
CIRCUIT LENGTH 2.893 miles
NO. OF LAPS 66
RACE DISTANCE 190.904 miles
WEATHER Sunny, 20°C
TRACK TEMP 38°C
LAP RECORD Kimi Räikkönen,
1m21.670s, 127.500mph, 2008

PRACTICE 1

	Driver	Time	Laps
1	F Alonso	1m25.252s	20
2	F Massa	1m25.455s	20
3	J-E Vergne	1m25.667s	25
4	R Grosjean	1m26.042s	21
5	A Sutil	1m26.212s	24
6	L Hamilton	1m26.374s	19
7	V Bottas	1m26.456s	20
8	K Räikkönen	1m26.614s	21
9	N Rosberg	1m26.621s	21
10	P di Resta	1m26.755s	16
11	D Ricciardo	1m26.940s	26
12	N Hulkenberg	1m27.061s	24
13	S Perez	1m27.135s	6
14	E Gutierrez	1m27.250s	26
15	P Maldonado	1m27.576s	24
16	H Kovalainen	1m28.373s	14
17	G van der Garde	1m28.600s	19
18	J Bianchi	1m28.887s	14
19	S Vettel	1m29.457s	11
20	M Webber	1m29.473s	21
21	R Gonzalez	1m30.314s	13
22	J Button	No time	6

PRACTICE 2

	Driver	Time	Laps
1	S Vettel	1m22.808s	34
2	F Alonso	1m22.825s	35
3	M Webber	1m22.891s	36
4	K Räikkönen	1m23.030s	32
5	F Massa	1m23.110s	37
6	L Hamilton	1m23.140s	35
7	N Rosberg	1m23.398s	45
8	A Sutil	1m23.840s	37
9	J-E Vergne	1m24.058s	31
10	P di Resta	1m24.104s	25
11	D Ricciardo	1m24.175s	32
12	J Button	1m24.306s	35
13	S Perez	1m24.854s	31
14	V Bottas	1m24.888s	38
15	N Hulkenberg	1m25.167s	38
16	P Maldonado	1m25.321s	32
17	E Gutierrez	1m25.441s	37
18	R Grosjean	1m25.851s	36
19	G van der Garde	1m25.963s	30
20	J Bianchi	1m26.078s	31
21	C Pic	1m26.930s	35
22	M Chilton	1m26.970s	26

PRACTICE 3

	Driver	Time	Laps
1	F Massa	1m21.901s	13
2	K Räikkönen	1m21.907s	14
3	M Webber	1m22.044s	17
4	R Grosjean	1m22.069s	13
5	S Vettel	1m22.229s	17
6	F Alonso	1m22.254s	15
7	P di Resta	1m22.574s	11
8	A Sutil	1m22.729s	17
9	L Hamilton	1m22.740s	24
10	J-E Vergne	1m22.759s	15
11	N Rosberg	1m22.839s	26
12	J Button	1m23.151s	13
13	E Gutierrez	1m23.371s	21
14	S Perez	1m23.373s	13
15	P Maldonado	1m23.385s	17
16	N Hulkenberg	1m23.388s	18
17	V Bottas	1m23.660s	16
18	D Ricciardo	1m23.767s	17
19	C Pic	1m24.775s	18
20	J Bianchi	1m24.793s	16
21	M Chilton	1m25.135s	17
22	G van der Garde	1m25.250s	18

QUALIFYING 1

	Driver	Time
1	L Hamilton	1m21.728s
2	N Rosberg	1m21.913s
3	S Vettel	1m22.158s
4	K Räikkönen	1m22.210s
5	F Alonso	1m22.264s
6	M Webber	1m22.342s
7	F Massa	1m22.492s
8	R Grosjean	1m22.613s
9	P di Resta	1m22.663s
10	J-E Vergne	1m22.775s
11	D Ricciardo	1m22.905s
12	A Sutil	1m22.952s
13	N Hulkenberg	1m23.058s
14	S Perez	1m23.116s
15	J Button	1m23.166s
16	E Gutierrez	1m23.218s
17	V Bottas	1m23.260s
18	P Maldonado	1m23.318s
19	G van der Garde	1m24.661s
20	J Bianchi	1m24.713s
21	M Chilton	1m24.996s
22	C Pic	1m25.070s

QUALIFYING 2

	Driver	Time
1	L Hamilton	1m21.001s
2	S Vettel	1m21.602s
3	F Alonso	1m21.646s
4	K Räikkönen	1m21.676s
5	M Webber	1m21.718s
6	N Rosberg	1m21.776s
7	S Perez	1m21.790s
8	F Massa	1m21.978s
9	R Grosjean	1m21.998s
10	P di Resta	1m22.019s
11	D Ricciardo	1m22.127s
12	J-E Vergne	1m22.166s
13	A Sutil	1m22.346s
14	J Button	1m22.355s
15	N Hulkenberg	1m22.389s
16	E Gutierrez	1m22.793s

Best sectors – Practice			Speed trap – Practice			Best sectors – Qualifying			Speed trap – Qualifying		
Sec 1	R Grosjean	22.709s	1	F Alonso	198.093mph	Sec 1	K Räikkönen	22.512s	1	F Alonso	197.906mph
Sec 2	K Räikkönen	30.683s	2	S Perez	197.099mph	Sec 2	F Massa	30.224s	2	D Ricciardo	197.161mph
Sec 3	M Webber	28.261s	3	J-E Vergne	197.099mph	Sec 3	N Rosberg	27.738s	3	S Perez	196.974mph

---

Sebastian Vettel
"I think we can be happy with fourth today. The first three cars were a little bit too fast for us, and with regard to looking after the tyres, they did a better job."

Fernando Alonso
"Even if this is the third time that I've won my home grand prix, the emotion is still very strong, especially at a time when the country is in crisis."

Jenson Button
"I had no grip due to a very slow lap to the grid, so Turn 1 was a mess and I fell to 17th. To finish eighth shows what a good job the team did with the strategy."

Kimi Räikkönen
"Unfortunately, it's second place again. The car felt good, and we did pretty much all we could today, but simply didn't have the pace to challenge Fernando."

Nico Rosberg
"I managed my first stint to keep quicker cars behind me. I then had to drive my own race, and as I began to go backwards it made no sense to destroy my tyres."

Nico Hulkenberg
"The start went well, and until the incident in the pits, it looked quite good. We planned three stops, but had to convert it to four. Then I had the incident."

Mark Webber
"I was struggling for range and pace. The Ferraris and Lotuses were in a different league. We got the most out of what we had, especially as by Turn 1 I was 14th."

Felipe Massa
"When you start from far back, everything's more complicated, but I managed to pull off a few passing moves because the car was very competitive."

Sergio Perez
"It's so difficult to manage these tyres. We didn't do a perfect job, and, like many drivers, I needed four pit stops. So I didn't maximise the full potential of our car."

Romain Grosjean
"I made a poor start, but then I was on the pace, so there was potential for a strong result. The car was feeling good until I had an issue with the rear suspension."

Lewis Hamilton
"Going backwards is no fun. We switched to a four-stop strategy, but I suffered from a lack of grip and balance, and we were never able to get the tyres working."

Esteban Gutierrez
"At the start, I was quite surprised about how much I could get out of the tyres. The last two stints were a bit more difficult, but this is a step forward."

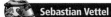  

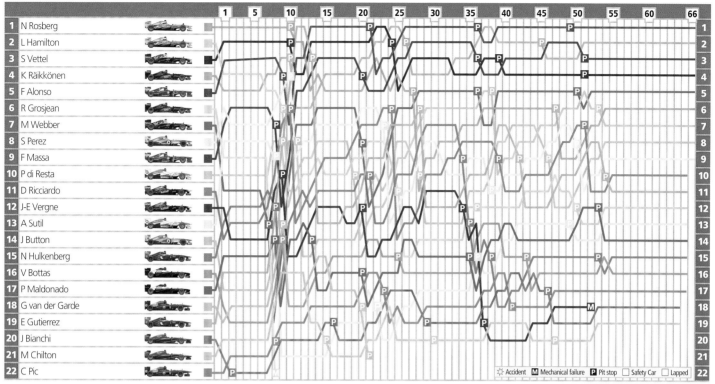

	Driver		
1	N Rosberg		
2	L Hamilton		
3	S Vettel		
4	K Räikkönen		
5	F Alonso		
6	R Grosjean		
7	M Webber		
8	S Perez		
9	F Massa		
10	P di Resta		
11	D Ricciardo		
12	J-E Vergne		
13	A Sutil		
14	J Button		
15	N Hulkenberg		
16	V Bottas		
17	P Maldonado		
18	G van der Garde		
19	E Gutierrez		
20	J Bianchi		
21	M Chilton		
22	C Pic		

☆ Accident   Ⓜ Mechanical failure   Ⓟ Pit stop   ☐ Safety Car   ☐ Lapped

QUALIFYING 3

	Driver	Time
1	N Rosberg	1m20.718s
2	L Hamilton	1m20.972s
3	S Vettel	1m21.054s
4	K Räikkönen	1m21.177s
5	F Alonso	1m21.218s
6	F Massa	1m21.219s
7	R Grosjean	1m21.308s
8	M Webber	1m21.570s
9	S Perez	1m22.069s
10	P di Resta	1m22.233s

GRID

	Driver	Time
1	N Rosberg	1m20.718s
2	L Hamilton	1m20.972s
3	S Vettel	1m21.054s
4	K Räikkönen	1m21.177s
5	F Alonso	1m21.218s
6	R Grosjean	1m21.308s
7	M Webber	1m21.570s
8	S Perez	1m22.069s
9	F Massa	1m21.219s
10	P di Resta	1m22.233s
11	D Ricciardo	1m22.127s
12	J-E Vergne	1m22.166s
13	A Sutil	1m22.346s
14	J Button	1m22.355s
15	N Hulkenberg	1m22.389s
16	V Bottas	1m23.260s
17	P Maldonado	1m23.318s
18	G van der Garde	1m24.661s
19	E Gutierrez	1m22.793s
20	J Bianchi	1m24.713s
21	M Chilton	1m24.996s
22	C Pic	1m25.070s

RACE

	Driver	Car	Laps	Time	Avg. mph	Fastest	Stops
1	F Alonso	Ferrari F138	66	1h39m16.596s	115.329	1m26.681s	4
2	K Räikkönen	Lotus-Renault E21	66	1h39m25.934s	115.149	1m26.757s	3
3	F Massa	Ferrari F138	66	1h39m42.645s	114.827	1m26.394s	4
4	S Vettel	Red Bull-Renault RB9	66	1h39m54.869s	114.593	1m27.036s	4
5	M Webber	Red Bull-Renault RB9	66	1h40m04.559s	114.408	1m27.017s	4
6	N Rosberg	Mercedes F1 W04	66	1h40m24.616s	114.027	1m27.591s	3
7	P di Resta	Force India-Mercedes VJM06	66	1h40m25.584s	114.009	1m26.776s	4
8	J Button	McLaren-Mercedes MP4-28	66	1h40m36.102s	113.810	1m27.957s	3
9	S Perez	McLaren-Mercedes MP4-28	66	1h40m38.334s	113.768	1m27.251s	4
10	D Ricciardo	Toro Rosso-Ferrari STR8	65	1h39m22.402s	113.470	1m28.083s	4
11	E Gutierrez	Sauber-Ferrari C32	65	1h39m22.706s	113.465	1m26.217s	4
12	L Hamilton	Mercedes F1 W04	65	1h39m27.565s	113.372	1m27.895s	4
13	A Sutil	Force India-Mercedes VJM06	65	1h39m28.040s	113.363	1m26.564s	4
14	P Maldonado	Williams-Renault FW35	65	1h39m45.740s	113.028	1m27.849s	4
15	N Hulkenberg	Sauber-Ferrari C32	65	1h39m47.162s	113.001	1m26.586s	5
16	V Bottas	Williams-Renault FW35	65	1h40m35.040s	112.104	1m29.747s	3
17	C Pic	Caterham-Renault CT03	65	1h40m37.441s	112.060	1m29.362s	3
18	J Bianchi	Marussia-Cosworth MR-02	64	1h39m20.860s	111.753	1m28.844s	4
19	M Chilton	Marussia-Cosworth MR-02	64	1h39m48.230s	111.242	1m28.011s	3
R	J-E Vergne	Toro Rosso-Ferrari STR8	52	Accident damage	-	1m28.231s	4
R	G van der Garde	Caterham-Renault CT03	21	Lost wheel	-	1m30.597s	2
R	R Grosjean	Lotus-Renault E21	8	Suspension	-	1m31.136s	0

CHAMPIONSHIP

	Driver	Pts
1	S Vettel	89
2	K Räikkönen	85
3	F Alonso	72
4	L Hamilton	50
5	F Massa	45
6	M Webber	42
7	R Grosjean	26
8	P di Resta	26
9	N Rosberg	22
10	J Button	17
11	S Perez	12
12	D Ricciardo	7
13	A Sutil	6
14	N Hulkenberg	5
15	J-E Vergne	1

Grid penalties
F Massa Three-place penalty for impeding Mark Webber in qualifying
E Gutierrez Three-place penalty for impeding Kimi Räikkönen in qualifying

Fastest lap
E Gutierrez 1m26.217s
(120.776mph) on lap 56

Fastest speed trap
F Alonso 198.093mph
Slowest speed trap
M Webber 190.139mph

Fastest pit stop
1	F Alonso	18.471s
2	S Vettel	18.606s
3	S Vettel	18.694s

	Constructor	Pts
1	Red Bull-Renault	131
2	Ferrari	117
3	Lotus-Renault	111
4	Mercedes	72
5	Force India-Mercedes	32
6	McLaren-Mercedes	29
7	Toro Rosso-Ferrari	8
8	Sauber-Ferrari	5

Paul di Resta
"We said before the race that seventh would be a good result, and late on I was even fighting for sixth. So we can take a lot of positives from the weekend."

Pastor Maldonado
"The pace wasn't in the car. We made one more stop than we hoped, as I was given a drive-through for speeding in the pits, but we did the best we could."

"After a good start, I had understeer and we had to keep adding more wing. The strategy we adopted was right as, even with a damaged floor, I could do good lap times."

Charles Pic
"Finishing 17th doesn't tell the story, as I ended right with one of the Williamses, showing we've made good progress, although the blue flags didn't help."

Jules Bianchi
"I drove a hard race, but there's not much to show for it. I had strong middle stints, but the damage was done early on when I had to pit for a new nose."

Adrian Sutil
"It was all going to plan until the first stop when the team told me to switch the engine off while they sorted the problem, but it cost me the chance of points."

Valtteri Bottas
"I couldn't feel the grip and was sliding a lot from the start. We made a three-stop strategy work, but Pastor switched to a four-stop race that seemed to be better."

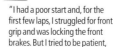

"I had a poor start and, for the first few laps, I struggled for front grip and was locking the front brakes. But I tried to be patient, and eventually it improved."

Giedo van der Garde
"I fought with Button and both Williamses in the first two stints, but when I came in for my second pit stop there was a problem with the left rear tyre as I rejoined."

Max Chilton
"It was disappointing to have such a problematic start, then we had the pit stop issue, which was a further set-back. What is encouraging is my lap times in free air."

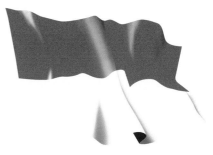

FORMULA 1 GRAND PRIX DE MONACO 2013

**23-26 MAY
CIRCUIT DE MONACO
MONTE CARLO**

ROSBERG'S HOME RULE

In a race punctuated by safety cars and a red flag, Nico Rosberg reigned supreme. A local resident his whole life, the Mercedes driver did everything right to win 30 years after his father, Keke, triumphed here

Quick in Monaco in 2012, Nico Rosberg had again looked good throughout practice for Mercedes AMG Petronas, and he duly backed up that form by taking pole position ahead of his team-mate, Lewis Hamilton. Although the outcome followed the expected pattern, it was a far from straightforward Saturday afternoon as rain intervened in the early stages of the session.

The story began in the third official practice session held that morning, when Ferrari's Felipe Massa, Force India's Adrian Sutil and Lotus's Romain Grosjean all had major accidents, and their teams were left having to make rush repair jobs to get the cars ready for the start of qualifying.

In the end, Ferrari didn't quite make it and, while Massa was ready and waiting, the job couldn't be completed on time. In any case, the team had opted for a gearbox change – which would have cost him five places on the grid – but, instead, the Brazilian was demoted to the back of the grid.

Meanwhile, it began to rain just 30 minutes before qualifying started. The track then remained damp for the whole of the first qualifying session, forcing drivers to run on intermediate tyres. But while

INSIDE LINE
NICO ROSBERG
MERCEDES AMG PETRONAS DRIVER

"It's amazing! This is my home; I've grown up here, lived all my life here, gone to school here...

"It's a very, very special day for me. The whole weekend really went perfectly. Everything. Qualifying was difficult because of the conditions, but that was the same for everyone and

we got the pole. Then I had a bad start. These are the two keys at Monaco.

"Even though the start wasn't great, it still worked out and once those two things were done, from then on it was okay. There were still some challenges with the safety car because the tyres, the primes, got very cold, but the main ones were qualifying and the start.

"I was close to Sebastian and then with Lewis also in Turn 1, but after that I could control the pace. The car was really good, the tyres held on OK and so a massive thanks to the team for having improved so much from Barcelona. I'm just ecstatic.

"The final part of the race was tricky. I was in a great rhythm on those prime tyres, trying to nurse them towards the end and then, all of a sudden, there was a race stoppage...

It's never nice to lose your rhythm, especially around Monaco, because if you do lose concentration it's so easy to make a quick error, then you're in the barrier and that's the end of your race.

"Just two weeks ago in the Spanish GP we ago were more than a minute away [from victory] in the race, and even today tyre degradation was still an issue. We were in a better position, much better, but it's also a different track, different tyres and very different circumstances. I had the possibility of taking it easy and dictating the pace initially to save tyres, so we probably shouldn't get over-excited now about the next couple of races.

"If maybe I had a childhood dream... when I was quite young I was watching this race, always. My first memories are of Ayrton Senna with his yellow helmet,

the red-and-white of McLaren winning. It became a dream to one day win the Grand Prix of Monaco.

"The feeling at the end of the race was just incredible. It was unreal. That's what's so special about this sport: these emotions you get that make up for all the difficult moments that have gone before. Winning provides these moments of joy.

It's amazing. There was a lot going through my mind, definitely, as I drove around to parc ferme at the end. Various things. Even, to be honest, winning Monaco in a Silver Arrow. That's very special to me.

and instead drove at a pace steady enough to preserve his tyres. He also ensured that the whole field remained backed up sufficiently to ensure those immediately behind couldn't try strategy tricks and pit earlier, because, if they did so, they'd emerge mired in traffic. Indeed, the pace was such that many drivers felt that for much of the afternoon they were playing cat-and-mouse, following the car in front.

"I had a fantastic start, but no room," said Vettel. "I think I could have gone past both Mercedes, but didn't have the room and had to lift. Then Mark came and it was tight into the first corner. After that, I was a bit surprised by the slow pace in the opening laps. Usually you expect two Silver Arrows in front of you, and there were two buses today, going for a cruise – at least in the first couple of laps. But obviously the strategy was clear, and they did a very good job..."

So, at the front of the field at least, the racing was more close than spectacular, and it was clear that the need to keep tyres alive throughout put an emphasis on tactical driving. Rosberg was going for a long opening stint in order to make it into a one-stop race, but his hand was forced when Massa crashed heavily at Ste Devote on lap 29 in an apparent repeat of his incident in the Saturday morning practice session.

Inevitably, the safety car came out. In the subsequent pit-stop sequence, Hamilton lost two priceless spots to the Red Bulls simply by returning to the pits too slowly, as he miscalculated the necessity to leave a gap for Rosberg to pit in front of him and so allowed too much time.

At the restart, Rosberg continued to reign supreme up front. The Red Bulls remained in second and third, despite a big effort by Hamilton to get past Webber.

Any chance of worn tyres coming into the equation in the second half of the race was ended by a red flag on lap 45, after Pastor Maldonado collided with Max Chilton's Marussia at Tabac. Bizarrely, a

LEFT Nico Rosberg didn't make the best start, but was still able to lead into Ste Devote, chased by Lewis Hamilton and the Red Bulls

BELOW Esteban Gutierrez raced to 13th place on his Monaco debut

there were a few trips up escape roads, there were no major incidents. It was still wet for the start of the second session too, but in the closing minutes everyone could switch to the supersoft tyre, when Sebastian Vettel proved fastest of all. Among the sextet eliminated at this point was Romain Grosjean.

The final, 10-minute, Q3 session was a thriller. Vettel and Mark Webber were on top in the closing stages, before strong laps from Rosberg and Hamilton secured them the front row as Vettel's last-gasp response wasn't quite good enough to topple the Mercedes duo. He and Webber thus had to settle for third and fourth on the grid, while Kimi Räikkönen qualified fifth for Lotus. Ferrari's Fernando Alonso was disappointed to start sixth, ahead of Sergio Perez, Sutil, Jenson Button and Jean-Eric Vergne.

On Sunday morning, all hell broke loose when it emerged that Mercedes had conducted a 'secret' Pirelli test at Barcelona after the Spanish GP and, for a few hours, prospects for the race took a back seat in all discussions in the paddock (see p120).

When the real action finally got underway, Rosberg slipped safely into the lead ahead of Hamilton, Vettel and Webber, but he didn't disappear,

TALKING POINT
LIKE FATHER LIKE SON

Sometimes there's a romantic force to something that makes it seem almost inevitable. Such was the feeling around Nico Rosberg's victory in Monaco.

Keke Rosberg's swashbuckling win in 1983, when he made the right tyre choice for his normally-aspirated Williams while the drivers of vastly more powerful turbocharged cars ahead of him on the grid did not, was a defining moment. Yes, Keke had already claimed the championship, but he'd won it with only a single victory in 1982 in a season of 11 different winners in a campaign that had seen fatal and career-ending accidents to championship favourites Gilles Villeneuve and Didier Pironi in the Ferraris.

Keke had a reputation for being quick and spectacular, but he was never a Williams driver in quite the same way Alan Jones had been a Williams driver. His brio in keeping it on the island without losing too much time in the early laps of that grand prix allowing him to take full advantage when everyone ahead had to pit,

was hailed around the world. Although Keke had been around for six years by then, he hadn't been in a competitive car, and even a 1982-83 Williams was not the same thing as the Williams FW07 of 1979 through to 1981.

For Nico, the momentum was building. Far from being blown away by team-mate Lewis Hamilton, he had thus far looked the more impressive and, already, people were starting to re-evaluate Michael Schumacher's three years with Mercedes. Privately, it had got up Nico's nose that for three years he coped with Schumacher in a manner nobody foresaw and got very little credit for it. He knew how quick Michael still was.

Hamilton is awesome around Monte Carlo, loves the place, and yet it was Nico who was in control throughout, from the first moment the cars left the pit lane on the previous Thursday. It had been close but it was Nico who had taken the crucial pole, Nico who had controlled every lap of the race, not making a single mistake.

That's something that can quickly and easily be written in a sentence but which was a towering achievement that takes immense natural ability allied to years of commitment and application to achieve. It was Nico's Olympic gold.

"These emotions that you get that make up for all the difficult moments that have gone before..." Nico wasn't born until two years after his father won in Monte Carlo but, like Keke's, his win number two has been his defining moment.

large section of plastic Tecpro barrier was dislodged by the Williams, and it slid across the track, blocking it completely. After the red flag was shown, marshals were able to make a big enough gap for everyone to crawl past the rearranged barrier and get back to the grid. A lengthy delay followed while the track was cleared.

The race was finally restarted with a lap behind the safety car before the green flag was flown, everyone having had a welcome opportunity to change to fresh tyres during the stoppage. Thus, all drivers were able to push a little harder after the restart without too much fear of running out of rubber.

On lap 62, there was a third safety car period after Grosjean ran into the back of Daniel Ricciardo down the slope to the chicane. The Toro Rosso was out on the spot, but the Frenchman continued, then retired after a pit stop and was later given a 10-place grid penalty for the Canadian GP.

Despite the safety car closing everyone up, the top four remained in the same order for the rest of the race, Rosberg staying just far enough ahead to be safe and Vettel accepting that second place would be a satisfactory result.

It was a well deserved victory for Mercedes. They had looked so strong in qualifying in recent races. However, inevitably, it was tainted somewhat by the testing scandal that had erupted on Sunday morning, and led to an FIA enquiry after the race. Fortunately for the team, it had no impact on the result.

Rosberg admitted that the safety car periods and red flag hadn't helped his progress. "It wasn't very nice, because I was in a great rhythm and then all of a sudden there was a race stoppage," he said. "So it was really important today to remain concentrated and that didn't make it easy, all those safety cars and the red flag and everything – but fortunately, in the end, it all worked out."

Vettel meanwhile was satisfied with second, not least because he increased his points lead over main his title rivals, Alonso and Räikkönen.

"I think overall I'm very happy and pleased with the result," said Vettel. "We know that it's very difficult to overtake here. First of all, though, congratulations to Nico, as he did a very good job and ran a very controlled race. I think he had the pace and the tyres to respond whenever I tried to get a little bit closer. Obviously, Lewis lost a couple of positions with the safety car – I'm sure he's not too pleased about that – but we took that, no question."

Double Monaco winner Webber was pleased to be

OPPOSITE Kimi Räikkönen sweeps through Massenet in his Lotus on his way to a 10th-place finish after a late-race charge following a puncture

ABOVE Sebastian Vettel had no answer to Nico Rosberg's race tactics. Red Bull team-mate Mark Webber follows him through the tunnel

BELOW Force India's Paul di Resta rounds Portier as he climbs the order from 17th on the grid to finish ninth

on the podium again in third place, while Hamilton was left to rue the extremely costly mistake that saw him gift two positions to the Red Bulls during that first safety car period.

While a stalemate settled on the top four, much was happening behind, notably in the group that included Räikkönen, Alonso, the two McLarens and Force India's Sutil. There was some spectacular racing, and we even saw overtaking, although some clumsy moves resulted in contact.

It was a bad day for title contender Räikkönen. He held fifth place for much of the race, but suffered a puncture after being hit hard by Perez under braking for the chicane. The Mexican's McLaren suffered overheating brakes after the incident, and a huge queue formed behind him before he was forced to pull off and retire in the closing laps.

In the end, Sutil emerged from the chaos to take a fine fifth place ahead of Button. Alonso – forced over the chicane by another tough Perez move – simply didn't have the pace, ultimately earning a chastening seventh place for Ferrari.

Like Räikkönen, Alonso clearly wasn't happy with Perez: "He was lucky this year with two or three incidents," he said. "In Bahrain, he nearly had contact with Jenson, and I went off the track to avoid the contact, while here I cut the chicane to avoid contact with him again. Kimi wasn't lucky because he didn't avoid the contact, and at the end he retired. Only McLaren can be happy with him – all the others, we just need to do our work."

Over the course of the race, Alonso, was overtaken several times, notably at the hairpin. He made the good point that it was much harder for a title contender to take risks in wheel-to-wheel combat. "Why did we find ourselves in that position? Because we didn't have the pace, and we didn't have the pace in qualifying especially. You start at the front, you fight with the top guys, if you start seventh or eighth, there is the risk of these battles with people who have nothing to lose."

Behind him, an impressive Vergne claimed eighth for Scuderia Toro Rosso, while di Resta negotiated his way forward from 17th on the grid after a disastrous qualifying session to finish ninth.

Following a costly pit stop for a puncture sustained in the Perez incident, Räikkönen initially dropped out of the top 10. However, a superb charge and some fraught last-minute overtaking that included Sauber's Nico Hulkenberg on the final lap, earned the Finn the final point for 10th place, which at least maintained his extraordinary scoring streak. The result did little for his title prospects, though.

ABOVE LEFT Force India's Paul di Resta and Mercedes' Lewis Hamilton chase through the dappled light

LEFT A delighted Nico Rosberg shows off his winner's trophy from on top of the Mercedes team base

SNAPSHOT FROM
MONACO

CLOCKWISE FROM RIGHT

The photographers are pleased not to have any barriers between them and Max Chilton's Marussia at the chicane; Sergio Perez shares his thoughts with an engineer; a rare moment of reflection for Sebastian Vettel; Jules Bianchi after crashing at St Devote; the Caterham garage at the start of practice; Kimi Räikkönen is kept cool by trainer Mark Arnall; Pastor Maldonado had a smile but it didn't last all meeting; "Could you keep the noise down – we're in the jacuzzi!"; Räikkönen and Lotus team-mate Romain Grosjean take the harder, better, faster route to the grid with the band Daft Punk; Caterham's co-owner Tony Fernandes and Team Principal Cyril Abiteboul are forging ever-closer links with Renault Sport

MONACO
MONTE CARLO
ROUND 6

Official Results © [2013]
Formula One World Championship Limited,
6 Princes Gate, London, SW7 1QJ.
No reproduction without permission.
All copyright and database rights reserved.

RACE RESULTS

RACE DATE 26 May 2013
CIRCUIT LENGTH 2.075 miles
NO. OF LAPS 78
RACE DISTANCE 161.850 miles
WEATHER Dry and sunny, 19°C
TRACK TEMP 43°C
LAP RECORD Michael Schumacher, 1m14.439s, 100.373mph, 2004

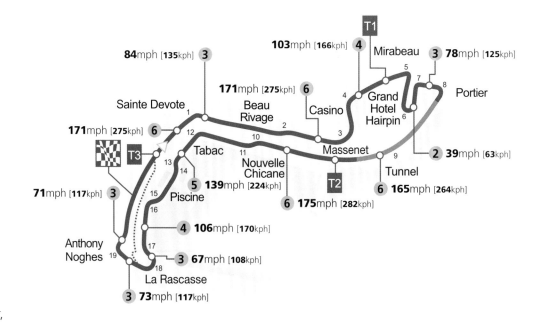

PRACTICE 1				PRACTICE 2				PRACTICE 3				QUALIFYING 1			QUALIFYING 2	
	Driver	Time	Laps		Driver	Time	Laps		Driver	Time	Laps		Driver	Time		Driver	Time
1	N Rosberg	1m16.195s	31	1	N Rosberg	1m14.759s	46	1	N Rosberg	1m14.378s	22	1	P Maldonado	1m23.452s	1	S Vettel	1m15.988s
2	F Alonso	1m16.282s	27	2	L Hamilton	1m15.077s	51	2	R Grosjean	1m15.039s	13	2	J-E Vergne	1m23.699s	2	K Räikkönen	1m16.040s
3	R Grosjean	1m16.380s	21	3	F Alonso	1m15.196s	38	3	S Vettel	1m15.261s	17	3	F Alonso	1m23.712s	3	N Rosberg	1m16.135s
4	F Massa	1m16.394s	23	4	F Massa	1m15.278s	39	4	F Alonso	1m15.286s	17	4	R Grosjean	1m23.738s	4	L Hamilton	1m16.265s
5	L Hamilton	1m16.469s	28	5	M Webber	1m15.404s	42	5	L Hamilton	1m15.311s	20	5	J Button	1m23.744s	5	F Alonso	1m16.510s
6	P Maldonado	1m16.993s	27	6	K Räikkönen	1m15.511s	39	6	K Räikkönen	1m15.380s	19	6	L Hamilton	1m23.779s	6	A Sutil	1m17.261s
7	M Webber	1m17.010s	27	7	R Grosjean	1m15.718s	10	7	M Webber	1m15.550s	20	7	S Vettel	1m24.243s	7	M Webber	1m17.322s
8	J Button	1m17.129s	29	8	J Button	1m15.959s	40	8	P di Resta	1m15.594s	17	8	N Rosberg	1m24.620s	8	J Button	1m17.420s
9	S Perez	1m17.378s	25	9	S Vettel	1m16.014s	33	9	P Maldonado	1m15.861s	15	9	V Bottas	1m24.681s	9	J-E Vergne	1m17.623s
10	S Vettel	1m17.380s	23	10	P di Resta	1m16.046s	43	10	N Hulkenberg	1m15.926s	25	10	S Perez	1m24.682s	10	S Perez	1m17.748s
11	K Räikkönen	1m17.509s	26	11	A Sutil	1m16.349s	44	11	S Perez	1m15.958s	23	11	D Ricciardo	1m24.852s	11	N Hulkenberg	1m18.331s
12	P di Resta	1m17.548s	27	12	S Perez	1m16.434s	41	12	J Button	1m15.976s	19	12	A Sutil	1m25.108s	12	D Ricciardo	1m18.344s
13	A Sutil	1m17.625s	20	13	N Hulkenberg	1m16.823s	43	13	J-E Vergne	1m15.976s	21	13	M Webber	1m25.352s	13	R Grosjean	1m18.603s
14	N Hulkenberg	1m18.193s	26	14	P Maldonado	1m16.857s	41	14	D Ricciardo	1m16.060s	16	14	N Hulkenberg	1m25.547s	14	V Bottas	1m19.077s
15	J-E Vergne	1m18.454s	25	15	E Gutierrez	1m16.935s	45	15	A Sutil	1m16.068s	12	15	K Räikkönen	1m25.835s	15	G van der Garde	1m19.408s
16	E Gutierrez	1m18.754s	28	16	D Ricciardo	1m17.145s	38	16	F Massa	1m16.105s	8	16	G van der Garde	1m26.095s	16	P Maldonado	1m21.688s
17	V Bottas	1m18.830s	28	17	J-E Vergne	1m17.184s	43	17	E Gutierrez	1m16.427s	26	17	P di Resta	1m26.322s			
18	D Ricciardo	1m19.067s	25	18	V Bottas	1m17.264s	47	18	V Bottas	1m16.933s	17	18	C Pic	1m26.633s			
19	G van der Garde	1m19.203s	21	19	J Bianchi	1m17.892s	41	19	C Pic	1m17.902s	20	19	E Gutierrez	1m26.917s			
20	C Pic	1m19.438s	28	20	C Pic	1m18.212s	44	20	G van der Garde	1m18.102s	20	20	M Chilton	1m27.303s			
21	J Bianchi	1m19.773s	20	21	M Chilton	1m18.784s	41	21	J Bianchi	1m18.706s	22	21	J Bianchi	No time			
22	M Chilton	1m20.225s	21	22	G van der Garde	1m19.031s	31	22	M Chilton	1m19.228s	22	22	F Massa	No time			

Best sectors – Practice			Speed trap – Practice			Best sectors – Qualifying			Speed trap – Qualifying		
Sec 1	S Vettel	19.416s	1	J Button	176.034mph	Sec 1	N Rosberg	19.343s	1	M Webber	176.531mph
Sec 2	N Rosberg	34.683s	2	L Hamilton	175.972mph	Sec 2	L Hamilton	34.295s	2	A Sutil	175.723mph
Sec 3	N Rosberg	20.172s	3	P di Resta	175.848mph	Sec 3	L Hamilton	20.092s	3	S Perez	175.661mph

 Sebastian Vettel

"I had a fantastic start and could have gone past both Mercedes, but there was no space and I had to lift. A good strategy from our team got us past Lewis."

Fernando Alonso

"If I hadn't cut the chicane, I wouldn't have been able to avoid Perez. The same happened with Sutil at Loews. As for what Sergio did, I don't have much to say."

Jenson Button

"Things weren't looking very good, but Monaco is one race where you need to hang in there until the end, because anything can happen – and today it did."

 **Kimi Räikkönen**

"Because of one stupid move from Sergio we've lost a lot of points, and you can't afford that. He hit me from behind and that's about all there is to it."

Nico Rosberg

"Monaco is a special place to win. It was a childhood dream to win this race. To do it in a Silver Arrow on the streets where I've lived all of my life is fantastic."

Nico Hulkenberg

"We lacked speed through the race. Unlike most others, I started on soft tyres at the restart. But, after another safety car, the tyres never came back to life again."

  Mark Webber

"We knew we were up against it starting on row two, but I got an incredible start, yet Seb and I had nowhere to go. After that, it was about saving the tyres."

Felipe Massa

"My race ended after an accident at Ste Devote, just as happened yesterday. I was taken to hospital for precautionary checks, but I've just got a slight pain in my neck."

Sergio Perez

"I'd been passing cars through the race, but Kimi didn't leave me enough room when I tried to pass him as we exited the tunnel, and I got squeezed into the wall."

 **Romain Grosjean**

"Daniel seemed to be struggling with his rear tyres. I'd followed him almost all race, but was caught out by him braking early in the middle of the circuit."

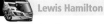 **Lewis Hamilton**

"When the safety car came out, I needed to maintain a gap to not get delayed with the double pit stop, but the gap was too big and we lost out to the Red Bulls."

 **Esteban Gutierrez**

"The first safety car compromised our strategy and we had to make the best out of that situation. We couldn't expect to score points, but I did my best."

POSITIONS LAP BY LAP

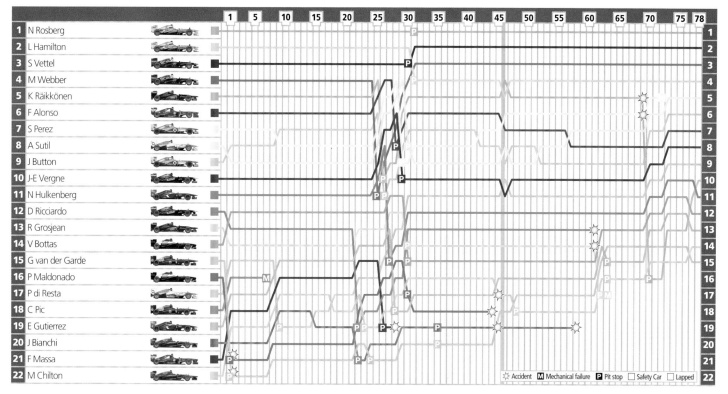

	Lap markers: 1 5 10 15 20 25 30 35 40 45 50 55 60 65 70 75 78
1	N Rosberg
2	L Hamilton
3	S Vettel
4	M Webber
5	K Räikkönen
6	F Alonso
7	S Perez
8	A Sutil
9	J Button
10	J-E Vergne
11	N Hulkenberg
12	D Ricciardo
13	R Grosjean
14	V Bottas
15	G van der Garde
16	P Maldonado
17	P di Resta
18	C Pic
19	E Gutierrez
20	J Bianchi
21	F Massa
22	M Chilton

☆ Accident M Mechanical failure P Pit stop ☐ Safety Car ☐ Lapped

QUALIFYING 3

	Driver	Time
1	N Rosberg	1m13.876s
2	L Hamilton	1m13.967s
3	S Vettel	1m13.980s
4	M Webber	1m14.181s
5	K Räikkönen	1m14.822s
6	F Alonso	1m14.824s
7	S Perez	1m15.138s
8	A Sutil	1m15.383s
9	J Button	1m15.647s
10	J-E Vergne	1m15.703s

GRID

	Driver	Time
1	N Rosberg	1m13.876s
2	L Hamilton	1m13.967s
3	S Vettel	1m13.980s
4	M Webber	1m14.181s
5	K Räikkönen	1m14.822s
6	F Alonso	1m14.824s
7	S Perez	1m15.138s
8	A Sutil	1m15.383s
9	J Button	1m15.647s
10	J-E Vergne	1m15.703s
11	N Hulkenberg	1m18.331s
12	D Ricciardo	1m18.344s
13	R Grosjean	1m18.603s
14	V Bottas	1m19.077s
15	G van der Garde	1m19.408s
16	P Maldonado	1m21.688s
17	P di Resta	1m26.322s
18	C Pic	1m26.633s
19	E Gutierrez	1m26.917s
20	J Bianchi	No time
21	F Massa	No time
22	M Chilton	1m27.303s

RACE

	Driver	Car	Laps	Time	Avg. mph	Fastest	Stops
1	N Rosberg	Mercedes F1 W04	78	2h17m52.056s	70.450	1m18.327s	1
2	S Vettel	Red Bull-Renault RB9	78	2h17m55.944s	70.417	1m16.577s	1
3	M Webber	Red Bull-Renault RB9	78	2h17m58.370s	70.396	1m18.262s	1
4	L Hamilton	Mercedes F1 W04	78	2h18m05.950s	70.332	1m18.133s	1
5	A Sutil	Force India-Mercedes VJM06	78	2h18m13.533s	70.267	1m18.292s	1
6	J Button	McLaren-Mercedes MP4-28	78	2h18m15.159s	70.253	1m18.720s	1
7	F Alonso	Ferrari F138	78	2h18m18.790s	70.223	1m19.340s	1
8	J-E Vergne	Toro Rosso-Ferrari STR8	78	2h18m19.279s	70.219	1m19.151s	1
9	P di Resta	Force India-Mercedes VJM06	78	2h18m19.664s	70.215	1m19.215s	1
10	K Räikkönen	Lotus-Renault E21	78	2h18m28.638s	70.140	1m17.392s	2
11	N Hulkenberg	Sauber-Ferrari C32	78	2h18m34.628s	70.089	1m19.853s	1
12	V Bottas	Williams-Renault FW35	78	2h18m34.747s	70.088	1m20.921s	1
13	E Gutierrez	Sauber-Ferrari C32	78	2h18m35.268s	70.084	1m18.685s	2
14	M Chilton	Marussia-Cosworth MR-02	78	2h18m41.941s	70.027	1m19.016s	1
15	G van der Garde	Caterham-Renault CT03	78	2h18m54.646s	69.920	1m20.494s	2
16	S Perez	McLaren-Mercedes MP4-28	72	Brakes	-	1m19.530s	1
R	R Grosjean	Lotus-Renault E21	63	Accident damage	-	1m20.969s	2
R	D Ricciardo	Toro Rosso-Ferrari STR8	61	Accident	-	1m19.426s	1
R	J Bianchi	Marussia-Cosworth MR-02	58	Brakes	-	1m20.617s	2
R	P Maldonado	Williams-Renault FW35	44	Accident	-	1m20.881s	1
R	F Massa	Ferrari F138	28	Suspension	-	1m20.064s	1
R	C Pic	Caterham-Renault CT03	7	Gearbox	-	1m22.772s	-

CHAMPIONSHIP

	Driver	Pts
1	S Vettel	107
2	K Räikkönen	86
3	F Alonso	78
4	L Hamilton	62
5	M Webber	57
6	N Rosberg	47
7	F Massa	45
8	P di Resta	28
9	R Grosjean	26
10	J Button	25
11	A Sutil	16
12	S Perez	12
13	D Ricciardo	7
14	N Hulkenberg	5
15	J-E Vergne	5

Grid penalties
M Chilton 5-place grid penalty for gearbox change

Fastest lap
S Vettel 1m16.577s
(97.566mph) on lap 77

Fastest speed trap
J Button 179.576mph
Slowest speed trap
N Rosberg 171.995mph

Fastest pit stop
1	M Webber	24.316s
2	S Vettel	24.375s
3	K Räikkönen	24.420s

Constructor

	Constructor	Pts
1	Red Bull-Renault	164
2	Ferrari	123
3	Lotus-Renault	112
4	Mercedes	109
5	Force India-Mercedes	44
6	McLaren-Mercedes	37
7	Toro Rosso-Ferrari	12
8	Sauber-Ferrari	5

Paul di Resta
"I was stuck behind Vergne after the restart and had one chance to overtake, but he defended well. Luckily, with cars making contact I made up places and scored."

Pastor Maldonado
"I had an unfortunate incident with the Marussia car, and the impact was quite big. Fortunately, I am all right and the stewards took immediate action."

Jean-Eric Vergne
"Near the end, Sutil did a good job of passing Jenson and Fernando at the hairpin, but I was coming up behind and couldn't get past as they blocked me."

Charles Pic
"It looks like my retirement was due to a gearbox problem. The fire was from the exhausts which had overheated. It looked more dramatic than it felt in the car."

Jules Bianchi
"I had to start from the pit lane. When Pastor hit the barrier, it came back out and my nose was damaged. Then I had a front brake-disc failure that took me out."

Adrian Sutil
"Fifth feels fantastic. It was hard to move forward in the first half of the race when I was stuck in the train of cars, but the red flag opened up some opportunities."

Valtteri Bottas
"It was hard to pass, and even though I sometimes felt I had the pace, I couldn't make the moves. There was a lot of action, so I was happy to bring the car home."

Daniel Ricciardo
"I could see that Grosjean had got a good run out of the tunnel and was close, so I defended my line and the next thing I knew he was over the back of me."

Giedo van der Garde
"Pastor hit me, so I had to pit. I rejoined 22nd, but when the safety car came out for Massa's crash I was able to unlap myself and get back into the action."

Max Chilton
"I fought hard in the latter stages to ensure we had something to take away, and I'm happy that I was able to get past van der Garde on the penultimate lap."

FORMULA 1 GRAND PRIX DU CANADA 2013

7-9 JUNE
CIRCUIT DE GILLES-VILLENEUVE
MONTREAL

SEBASTIAN DOMINATES

Sebastian Vettel extended his points chase for the championship with a dominant victory in the Canadian Grand Prix, as both the driver and his Red Bull Racing team registered their first-ever wins at the Circuit Gilles Villeneuve

Just a few races earlier, the 2013 world title fight had looked wide open, but Sebastian Vettel's consistent high scoring rate now put him firmly in the box seat. And, while there was still a long way to go, he was already looking like a good bet for a fourth championship. Despite Red Bull Racing's protestations about the unsuitability of Pirelli's tyres, he continued to be the man to beat.

For once, the fans were treated to a race in Montreal without any rain or safety car interruptions, or indeed any major dramas among the front-runners. And that made it untypical of the event, and Vettel's easy run at the front made for a superb exhibition of driving of the highest class. Despite the hot conditions and lack of dry running in practice, tyre degradation wasn't an issue either, and most drivers were able to push harder than at many other grands prix this year.

Unusually, the whole of qualifying was run on intermediate tyres, although the lap times varied between the three sessions as conditions changed. It was potentially something of a lottery, but Vettel did everything right as he secured top spot and ended a run of pole positions for Mercedes. It was close, though, and had he not jumped the final chicane on

ABOVE Sebastian Vettel raced
into the lead from Lewis Hamilton
and Nico Rosberg as Valtteri Bottas
started his slide down the order

OPPOSITE Pastor Maldonado
assaults Adrian Sutil's Force India
under braking for the chicane

BELOW Fernando Alonso was
frustrated to qualify sixth on a damp
track but raced through to second

his last lap, Lewis Hamilton might have continued that inspired streak.

The real star of the day, though, was Valtteri Bottas. The Finn was fast throughout the soggy qualifying session and ultimately secured a sensational third grid spot, giving his Williams team a huge boost, and demonstrating that he really is a man to watch. Nico Rosberg qualified fourth after being hampered by radio problems, but he was still ahead of Mark Webber and Ferrari's disappointed Fernando Alonso. Title contender Kimi Räikkönen could manage only ninth grid position, and a penalty dropped him a further place.

After the rain of the previous two days, Sunday turned out to be dry and considerably warmer than the rest of the weekend. From pole position, Vettel opened up a big lead on Hamilton in the early laps and thereafter was never challenged.

However, he clearly had to work to keep up his concentration and was lucky to escape a brush with a wall, and on another occasion he ran wide at Turn 1 and took a short cut across the grass. Otherwise, it was a perfect performance on a day when tyres weren't much of an issue, and his two-stop strategy unfolded without drama.

Inevitably, it hadn't looked quite as easy from where he was sitting. "I was pushing very hard at the beginning to get away and open a gap," said Vettel. "It's Canada, you obviously go close to the walls here or there, sometimes a little bit closer than I wanted.

"I was really just trying to open as much of a gap as I could. I felt I had more pace in the early stages. It's difficult to foresee what's going to happen later on, when you swap tyres, also in terms of range how far we were going to get on each set of tyres.

"We weren't sure if it was a one-stop or a two-stop. You don't know any of these things, so it's good to have a little bit of time in hand, which was the reason why I pushed very hard in the beginning. Obviously, it was clear quickly after the first stint that I had a good gap and controlled it. It was difficult with the traffic, but I think we had a great car and we always had enough pace in hand to react and control the gap."

Vettel celebrated by heading to Sunday night's Rolling Stones concert in downtown Montreal.

There was a little more excitement behind him, at least. Hamilton held second for most of the race, having run a very strong opening stint. However, tyres remained an Achilles' heel for Mercedes and in the closing laps he was caught and passed by Alonso, who had moved up well from his lowly grid position.

INSIDE LINE
CHRISTIAN HORNER

**RED BULL RACING
TEAM PRINCIPAL**

"We won that one – despite not having done three days of testing... I'm only joking!

"It was a really strong race and what was good about it was that everybody seemed to be pushing flat-out from start to finish, unlike in Monaco. Sebastian was mighty

today, got his head down, built up a comfortable lead and that was that.

"Going into the race, we thought it might be a one-stop but, because of the temperature rise, it became more obvious it was going to be a two-stop, yet Seb never looked threatened. He managed to build up a 15s margin by mid-distance. That's the time it takes to do a pit stop and drive through the pit lane, and from there it was about managing the gap.

"He had a couple of wake-up calls: one when he touched the barrier in the middle sector and a little 'off' at Turn 1.

"It's been a strong performance for us here, like it was in Bahrain and in Malaysia. We see with these tyres that once you're in the window with them, you can extract a lot of lap time. We were certainly in the right window here.

"With Mark, it was a shame his race

was compromised by the backmarker [Giedo van der Garde] because I'm convinced that we'd have had him on the podium as well.

"The backmarkers weren't at all helpful to Mark and he sustained a bit of front wing damage that affected him for a while. But the balance wasn't too bad and I think he got fastest lap on the penultimate lap. I'm sure that without that front wing problem he could have held Fernando off or closed down Lewis.

"We looked at changing the wing but the performance loss was outweighed by the time loss to change the nose box in the pit lane, so we decided to leave it, particularly when he did a green time [personal best] the lap after it came off!

"Today wasn't Mark's fault at all: van der Garde left the door open, it was under blue flags and it was his

responsibility to make way for the race leaders coming through. Then he just turned back in and it was a silly move.

"Set-up wise, we made progress here and hopefully that will continue into the Silverstone weekend. We weren't great in Barcelona, which has higher speed corners, but Malaysia also had very quick corners and we were strong there. I think we've understood some of the issues we had in Barcelona and hopefully we can carry this form through into the next few races."

TALKING POINT
SINGING IN THE RAIN

One of the sensations of qualifying in Montreal was Finn Valtteri Bottas, in his rookie F1 season with Williams.

After a promising 2012 season in which Pastor Maldonado won the Spanish GP, the Williams FW35 had been a great disappointment. Maldonado and Bottas often had a fight on their hands to escape Q1. Coming to Canada, Bottas had qualified 16th, 18th, 16th, 15th, 16th and 14th. But, even that run put him 4-2 up in a head-to-head comparison with his more experienced team-mate.

Then in Montreal, came that great leveller: rain. The result? Third on the grid as the highly-rated Finn outqualified everyone except Sebastian Vettel and Lewis Hamilton…

Williams Chief Race Engineer, Xevi Pujolar, congratulated Bottas on 'a perfect job' and added: "If we could give them a better car, both drivers have got the potential. Pastor proved it by winning a race last year and, if we had a good car again, I've no doubt that Valtteri can win a race as well. He has shown the speed and consistency in races, even if you can't really see it from the outside because of the performance we lack in the car."

Williams had brought a revised front wing to Canada, but there was no mistaking that Bottas's performance was all about the man in the cockpit. He has been compared to countryman and double world champion Mika Hakkinen in terms of ability, but this was the first true opportunity he'd had to show it.

There was no doubt about Bottas's preferred conditions for the race. "It looks like the weather might be tricky again," he said hopefully, on Saturday night. "At first the forecast for race day was dry, but it now seems there's a chance of some rain."

If Bottas performed a rain dance on Saturday evening, it was unsuccessful and from the moment the starting lights extinguished, he and his FW35 began an inexorable slide down the order to an eventual 14th place. It was entirely predictable and no reflection on the driver. Williams was still searching for its first points of 2013, but Bottas had sounded a warning.

In the paddock, the rumour mill was suggesting that Pat Symonds, approaching the end of his ban for his involvement in the 2008 'Crashgate' saga at the Singapore GP – where Nelson Piquet Jr crashed deliberately to bring out the safety car at an opportune moment for team-mate Fernando Alonso to win – was about to be confirmed as the new Williams Technical Director.

front-wing damage. However, the team chose not to replace his nose at the pit stop and the Australian was still able to maintain a good pace, even setting the race's fastest lap right at the end.

"The car was very damaged from that," Webber said of the clash. "It was very difficult from there. I was very keen to get on the podium, as I think we had everything teed up very well to do that, but you can't have a bleeding car with Fernando around you. He's going to capitalise on that."

After his superb Monaco win, Rosberg was unable to match team-mate Hamilton over the course of the weekend. He jumped up to third at the start, but struggled more with his tyres than Hamilton did. In the end, he was passed by Webber and Alonso and, after stopping three times, had to settle for fifth.

Following a strong race in Monaco, Jean-Eric Vergne impressed again for Scuderia Toro Rosso. Having qualified seventh, he broke away from the midfield pack and soon moved into a solid sixth place, which he held for the duration. It was the team's best result since the Vettel days of 2008.

The driver of the race, arguably, was Paul di Resta. After frustrations in qualifying, the team opted for a one-stop strategy, and the Scot ran a marathon 56-lap opening stint on the medium tyres. By the time he finally came in, he was firmly established in seventh, having gained 10 places with an impressively controlled performance.

Felipe Massa took a low-key eighth place in the other Ferrari, after failing to match Alonso's pace. He spent a lot of time trying to pass Adrian Sutil's Force India and struggled on the supersoft tyre.

It was another disappointing weekend for Räikkönen, who was beset by brake issues and simply didn't have the speed with which to challenge those ahead. He ran a one-stop strategy, using the supersoft tyre initially and, after losing a few precious

LEFT The Lotus team's form was not its best in Canada and Kimi Räikkönen could manage only ninth place, a lap down

BELOW Force India's Paul di Resta drove an exceptional 56-lap opening stint en route to seventh place

The pair made contact when racing each other, but without any ill effects for either driver. Having managed only seventh place in Monaco, Alonso was relieved to score a solid helping of points to keep Vettel in sight during the title battle.

"I think the pace difference was very, very small," Alonso said of the fight with Hamilton. "With other battles we did, maybe I was a little bit faster than the people I was catching. With Lewis, we were really very close on pace and we had some moments going out of Turn 8 where we fought to see who had the DRS detection point and then the same thing in Turn 10 and also at the last chicane, so there was some action out there.

"It was nice to have these battles, particularly with such talented and intelligent drivers that you know, so you can fight wheel-to-wheel at 315km/h and feel safe. You feel you are racing and you are competing. It can go your way or it can go the other way, but this is real racing."

Behind Hamilton, Webber took fourth after an eventful afternoon. At one point, he made contact with backmarker Giedo van der Garde, sending the Dutchman into a spin and leaving the Red Bull with

The final point went to Sutil. The German would have finished ahead of his team-mate, but he had a spin after making contact with Bottas. Later, he was handed a drivethrough penalty for failing to obey blue flags, although he was far from happy with that decision.

Incredibly, McLaren failed to score a point after a troubled weekend. Both drivers started on the option tyre, but with Sergio Perez running a two-stop strategy and Jenson Button one. They ran close together early on, with the English driver getting ahead when Sergio pitted, but the speed simply wasn't there and they finished 11th and 12th, the Mexican keeping his nose ahead by 2.6s at the flag.

Romain Grosjean went into the weekend with a 10-place grid penalty after his collision with Daniel Ricciardo in Monaco. He started on the mediums and did a long first stint that lifted him to eighth before he came in. However, tyre issues dictated an unplanned second pit stop and he fell back to 13th.

Inevitably, Bottas couldn't sustain the pace in the dry conditions on race day, tumbling down to sixth on the opening lap and then to seventh. He would drop all the way down to 14th, finishing ahead of Ricciardo and Pastor Maldonado.

Nico Hulkenberg lost out to both the penalised drivers and he had a quiet race in the middle of the pack until contact with the lapped van der Garde forced his retirement after 45 laps. Esteban Gutierrez managed to crash exiting the pits after his second stop, making Sauber the only team to retire both cars.

Sadly, the weekend was tragically marred by an accident that took place shortly after the race. Marshal Mark Robinson was escorting a tractor crane that was retrieving Gutierrez's Sauber when he stumbled and was struck by the vehicle. The 38-year-old volunteer, who had served at the race for the previous 10 years, later succumbed to his injuries.

ABOVE Jean-Eric Vergne drove a superb race for Scuderia Toro Rosso, using all the track available to qualify seventh and race to sixth

BELOW Applause for Sebastian Vettel after he made winning look easy with a dominant performance

seconds in the pits, couldn't do better than ninth. He did at least equal Michael Schumacher's record of 24 consecutive finishes in the points.

"My race didn't start very well and then my brakes were fading with the pedal going soft," said Kimi. "It was similar to the problem we had on Friday, but at least the brakes were good enough to slow me down for the corners. Unfortunately, it meant I lost a lot of time and wasn't able to attack, plus we lost a few seconds in the pit stop which didn't help either. Most of my race was just following the cars in front, and defending from those behind, so it wasn't the most enjoyable day nor the most enjoyable result."

SNAPSHOT FROM
CANADA

CLOCKWISE FROM RIGHT

Montreal provides a fine backdrop when viewed from the hairpin; Sebastian Vettel meets the Mounties; McLaren mechanics watch the race as they wait for the next pit stop; Nico Rosberg accelerates out of Coin Senna en route to fifth place in the race; Vettel grabs a snap of his muddied Infiniti for the weekend; the dominant Red Bull Racing team celebrates its third win of the season and its first in Canada; rain through the first two days (and fireworks from his team-mate) didn't wipe the smile off Pastor Maldonado's face; Romain Grosjean takes his engineers for a lap of the track, here rounding the hairpin; Jenson Button waits as his McLaren MP4-28 is prepared for action ahead of practice

CANADA
MONTRÉAL
ROUND 7

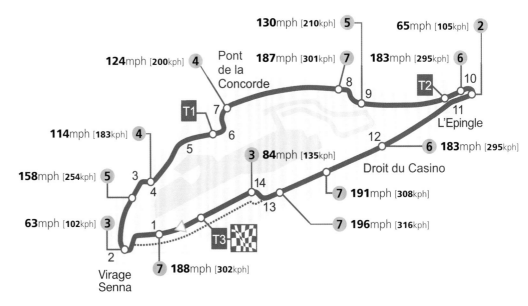

- 130mph [210kph] 5
- 65mph [105kph] 2
- 124mph [200kph] 4
- Pont de la Concorde
- 187mph [301kph] 7
- 183mph [295kph] 6
- T1 7
- 8 9 T2 10 11
- L'Epingle
- 114mph [183kph] 4
- 6
- 5
- 158mph [254kph] 5 3
- 4
- 3 84mph [135kph]
- 14
- 12 6 183mph [295kph]
- Droit du Casino
- 63mph [102kph] 3
- 1
- 13
- 7 191mph [308kph]
- 2
- T3
- 7 196mph [316kph]
- 7 188mph [302kph]
- Virage Senna

RACE RESULTS

RACE DATE 9 June 2013
CIRCUIT LENGTH 2.710 miles
NO. OF LAPS 70
RACE DISTANCE 189.686 miles
WEATHER Part cloudy, 24°C
TRACK TEMP 30°C
LAP RECORD Rubens Barrichello, 1m13.622s, 132.511mph, 2004

PRACTICE 1

	Driver	Time	Laps
1	P di Resta	1m21.020s	10
2	J Button	1m21.108s	20
3	R Grosjean	1m21.258s	21
4	F Alonso	1m21.308s	16
5	K Räikkönen	1m21.608s	22
6	D Ricciardo	1m22.068s	18
7	N Rosberg	1m22.402s	22
8	S Perez	1m22.587s	17
9	S Vettel	1m23.047s	26
10	M Webber	1m23.131s	16
11	F Massa	1m23.341s	13
12	V Bottas	1m23.352s	17
13	J-E Vergne	1m23.386s	19
14	A Sutil	1m23.417s	19
15	E Gutierrez	1m23.957s	33
16	L Hamilton	1m25.054s	21
17	N Hulkenberg	1m25.354s	22
18	G van der Garde	1m25.753s	21
19	M Chilton	1m25.821s	19
20	A Rossi	1m27.143s	20
21	P Maldonado	1m27.522s	11
22	J Bianchi	1m29.306s	8

PRACTICE 2

	Driver	Time	Laps
1	F Alonso	1m14.818s	48
2	L Hamilton	1m14.830s	45
3	R Grosjean	1m15.083s	40
4	M Webber	1m15.212s	46
5	N Rosberg	1m15.249s	46
6	F Massa	1m15.245s	43
7	S Vettel	1m15.280s	41
8	A Sutil	1m15.396s	43
9	J Button	1m15.422s	29
10	D Ricciardo	1m15.566s	38
11	K Räikkönen	1m15.599s	35
12	S Perez	1m15.661s	39
13	P di Resta	1m15.855s	22
14	P Maldonado	1m16.319s	46
15	J-E Vergne	1m16.351s	38
16	V Bottas	1m16.374s	40
17	E Gutierrez	1m16.475s	45
18	N Hulkenberg	1m16.929s	35
19	J Bianchi	1m17.070s	41
20	C Pic	1m17.236s	35
21	M Chilton	1m17.888s	45
22	G van der Garde	1m18.392s	39

PRACTICE 3

	Driver	Time	Laps
1	M Webber	1m17.895s	7
2	A Sutil	1m18.248s	8
3	L Hamilton	1m18.732s	7
4	F Alonso	1m18.977s	10
5	S Vettel	1m19.131s	6
6	N Rosberg	1m19.457s	7
7	P di Resta	1m19.496s	6
8	F Massa	1m19.750s	9
9	J Button	1m19.790s	9
10	K Räikkönen	1m20.316s	8
11	R Grosjean	1m20.596s	9
12	P Maldonado	1m21.035s	12
13	D Ricciardo	1m21.364s	7
14	M Chilton	1m21.652s	9
15	N Hulkenberg	1m22.021s	14
16	E Gutierrez	1m22.720s	15
17	J-E Vergne	1m23.058s	7
18	G van der Garde	1m23.132s	14
19	S Perez	1m23.309s	8
20	C Pic	1m23.620s	12
21	V Bottas	1m24.314s	12
22	J Bianchi	1m26.195s	9

QUALIFYING 1

	Driver	Time
1	S Vettel	1m22.318s
2	F Alonso	1m23.224s
3	M Webber	1m23.247s
4	V Bottas	1m23.446s
5	F Massa	1m23.735s
6	L Hamilton	1m23.801s
7	N Rosberg	1m23.840s
8	N Hulkenberg	1m23.899s
9	J Button	1m24.021s
10	J-E Vergne	1m24.159s
11	S Perez	1m24.176s
12	E Gutierrez	1m24.408s
13	K Räikkönen	1m24.451s
14	A Sutil	1m24.551s
15	D Ricciardo	1m24.770s
16	P Maldonado	1m24.776s
17	P di Resta	1m24.908s
18	C Pic	1m25.626s
19	R Grosjean	1m25.716s
20	J Bianchi	1m26.508s
21	M Chilton	1m27.062s
22	G van der Garde	1m27.110s

QUALIFYING 2

	Driver	Time
1	L Hamilton	1m27.649s
2	M Webber	1m28.145s
3	S Vettel	1m28.166s
4	V Bottas	1m28.419s
5	N Rosberg	1m28.420s
6	J-E Vergne	1m28.527s
7	K Räikkönen	1m28.667s
8	F Alonso	1m28.788s
9	A Sutil	1m28.799s
10	D Ricciardo	1m29.359s
11	N Hulkenberg	1m29.435s
12	S Perez	1m29.761s
13	P Maldonado	1m29.917s
14	J Button	1m30.068s
15	E Gutierrez	1m30.315s
16	F Massa	1m30.354s

Best sectors – Practice

Sec 1	F Alonso	20.656s
Sec 2	S Vettel	23.926s
Sec 3	L Hamilton	29.964s

Speed trap – Practice

1	D Ricciardo	200.765mph
2	E Gutierrez	199.646mph
3	K Räikkönen	199.335mph

Best sectors – Qualifying

Sec 1	S Vettel	23.153s
Sec 2	M Webber	27.608s
Sec 3	S Vettel	31.415s

Speed trap – Qualifying

1	S Perez	200.205mph
2	M Chilton	200.081mph
3	P di Resta	200.081mph

 Sebastian Vettel

"I was pushing hard, especially at the start, trying to get away from the field. It turned out that we could control things in the later stages, but you don't know that."

Fernando Alonso

"At the end of a very complicated weekend, this second place tastes like a win, because we were competitive and managed to fight with the leading drivers."

 Jenson Button

"With hindsight, I'd have been better off starting on the prime tyre. During my first stint, the two-stoppers pitted ahead of me, then came back to overtake me."

 **Kimi Räikkönen**

"My race didn't start well, then my brakes were fading, which meant I lost a lot of time and wasn't able to attack, plus we lost a few seconds in the stop."

Nico Rosberg

"I went for the option tyre at my first stop to protect track position against Webber and Alonso, but it would probably have been better to have gone the other way."

 **Nico Hulkenberg**

"I lapped Giedo and braked. I didn't feel anything until I exited the corner and realised that the car wasn't going straight, so I decided to stop."

 **Mark Webber**

"I lost some time with Nico in the first stint, and the car was getting hot behind him. Once I got in free air, the car handled better. Then I had the incident with Giedo."

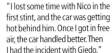 **Felipe Massa**

"My race was a battle from start to finish. After going off the track yesterday, it wasn't going to be easy starting 16th, but I managed to pull off several nice moves."

 **Sergio Perez**

"This wasn't the race we were hoping to have. We tried our best to score a few points, but it was impossible, as the car didn't work that well on the option tyre."

Romain Grosjean

"It was always going to be a tough race from the back, but it's disappointing to miss out on points. Things were looking good until we switched to the options."

Lewis Hamilton

"The car felt fantastic and I had good grip for low-speed corners, but wasn't quite on the pace of Seb and Fernando. I got absolutely everything out of the car."

 **Esteban Gutierrez**

"The first set of tyres was difficult to drive on. When I came out from my second stop into Turn 1, I went over one of the bumps, the front locked and I couldn't stop."

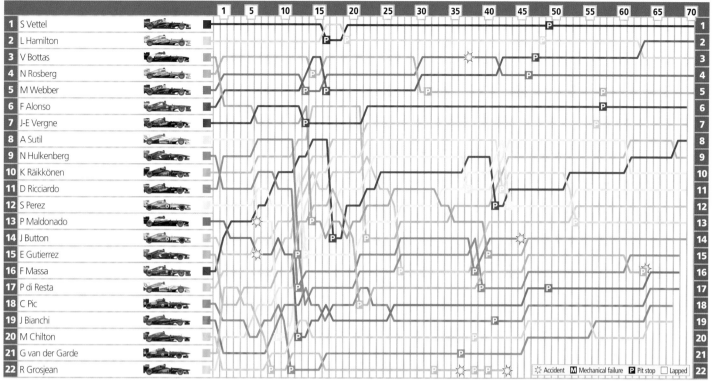

		1	5	10	15	20	25	30	35	40	45	50	55	60	65	70	
1	S Vettel																1
2	L Hamilton																2
3	V Bottas																3
4	N Rosberg																4
5	M Webber																5
6	F Alonso																6
7	J-E Vergne																7
8	A Sutil																8
9	N Hulkenberg																9
10	K Räikkönen																10
11	D Ricciardo																11
12	S Perez																12
13	P Maldonado																13
14	J Button																14
15	E Gutierrez																15
16	F Massa																16
17	P di Resta																17
18	C Pic																18
19	J Bianchi																19
20	M Chilton																20
21	G van der Garde																21
22	R Grosjean																22

☆ Accident   Ⓜ Mechanical failure   Ⓟ Pit stop   ☐ Lapped

QUALIFYING 3

	Driver	Time
1	S Vettel	1m25.425s
2	L Hamilton	1m25.512s
3	V Bottas	1m25.897s
4	N Rosberg	1m26.008s
5	M Webber	1m26.208s
6	F Alonso	1m26.504s
7	J-E Vergne	1m26.543s
8	A Sutil	1m27.348s
9	K Räikkönen	1m27.432s
10	D Ricciardo	1m27.946s

GRID

	Driver	Time
1	S Vettel	1m25.425s
2	L Hamilton	1m25.512s
3	V Bottas	1m25.897s
4	N Rosberg	1m26.008s
5	M Webber	1m26.208s
6	F Alonso	1m26.504s
7	J-E Vergne	1m26.543s
8	A Sutil	1m27.348s
9	N Hulkenberg	1m29.435s
10	K Räikkönen	1m27.432s
11	D Ricciardo	1m27.946s
12	S Perez	1m29.761s
13	P Maldonado	1m29.917s
14	J Button	1m30.068s
15	E Gutierrez	1m30.315s
16	F Massa	1m30.354s
17	P di Resta	1m24.908s
18	C Pic	1m25.626s
19	J Bianchi	1m26.508s
20	M Chilton	1m27.062s
21	G van der Garde	1m27.110s
22	R Grosjean	1m25.716s

RACE

	Driver	Car	Laps	Time	Avg. mph	Fastest	Stops
1	S Vettel	Red Bull-Renault RB9	70	1h32m09.143s	123.503	1m16.561s	2
2	F Alonso	Ferrari F138	70	1h32m23.551s	123.182	1m16.203s	2
3	L Hamilton	Mercedes F1 W04	70	1h32m25.085s	123.148	1m16.354s	2
4	M Webber	Red Bull-Renault RB9	70	1h32m34.874s	122.931	1m16.182s	2
5	N Rosberg	Mercedes F1 W04	70	1h33m18.868s	121.965	1m16.534s	3
6	J-E Vergne	Toro Rosso-Ferrari STR8	69	1h32m27.572s	121.334	1m17.909s	2
7	P di Resta	Force India-Mercedes VJM06	69	1h32m36.957s	121.129	1m17.841s	1
8	F Massa	Ferrari F138	69	1h32m38.951s	121.086	1m16.939s	2
9	K Räikkönen	Lotus-Renault E21	69	1h32m41.642s	121.027	1m17.766s	1
10	A Sutil	Force India-Mercedes VJM06	69	1h32m44.121s	120.973	1m17.694s	2
11	S Perez	McLaren-Mercedes MP4-28	69	1h32m45.406s	120.945	1m17.369s	2
12	J Button	McLaren-Mercedes MP4-28	69	1h32m48.028s	120.889	1m17.458s	1
13	R Grosjean	Lotus-Renault E21	69	1h33m00.532s	120.618	1m17.607s	2
14	V Bottas	Williams-Renault FW35	69	1h33m22.484s	120.145	1m18.004s	2
15	D Ricciardo	Toro Rosso-Ferrari STR8	68	1h32m15.612s	119.710	1m18.257s	2
16	P Maldonado	Williams-Renault FW35	68	1h32m51.037s	119.073	1m18.105s	2
17	J Bianchi	Marussia-Cosworth MR-02	68	1h33m12.754s	118.610	1m18.873s	1
18	C Pic	Caterham-Renault CT03	67	1h32m09.998s	118.192	1m19.380s	2
19	M Chilton	Marussia-Cosworth MR-02	67	1h32m31.141s	117.742	1m19.566s	1
20	E Gutierrez	Sauber-Ferrari C32	63	Accident damage	-	1m19.478s	2
R	N Hulkenberg	Sauber-Ferrari C32	45	Accident damage	-	1m19.056s	2
R	G van der Garde	Caterham-Renault CT03	43	Accident damage	-	1m21.811s	3

CHAMPIONSHIP

	Driver	Pts
1	S Vettel	132
2	F Alonso	96
3	K Räikkönen	88
4	L Hamilton	77
5	M Webber	69
6	N Rosberg	57
7	F Massa	49
8	P di Resta	34
9	R Grosjean	26
10	J Button	25
11	A Sutil	17
12	J-E Vergne	13
13	S Perez	12
14	D Ricciardo	7
15	N Hulkenberg	5

	Constructor	Pts
1	Red Bull-Renault	201
2	Ferrari	145
3	Mercedes	134
4	Lotus-Renault	114
5	Force India-Mercedes	51
6	McLaren-Mercedes	37
7	Toro Rosso-Ferrari	20
8	Sauber-Ferrari	5

Grid penalties

K Räikkönen Two-place grid penalty for pit exit error
D Ricciardo Two-place grid penalty for pit exit error
R Grosjean Ten-place grid penalty for causing a collision in the Monaco GP

Fastest lap

M Webber 1m16.182s
(128.052mph) on lap 69

Fastest speed trap

N Hulkenberg 199.833mph

Slowest speed trap

G van der Garde 194.737mph

Fastest pit stop

1	J Button	20.212s
2	F Massa	20.372s
3	S Perez	20.427s

 Paul di Resta

"To finish seventh, having started 17th, is a great result. As soon as I felt the tyres starting to drop off, I came in. Then it was a case of looking after the supersofts."

 **Pastor Maldonado**

"We knew we didn't have the top speed to challenge at the front. The car felt better in the wet than in the hot weather we had today, so we need to understand why."

Jean-Eric Vergne

"As it was a normal race in the dry with no one going out in front of me, it's even more satisfying. I passed Bottas and Räikkönen and then managed my race."

Charles Pic

"My start was okay, but I had to brake to avoid hitting one of the cars ahead and lost two places. With 10 laps left, I passed Chilton and was told to push to the flag."

Jules Bianchi

"It was a bit daunting to know we were planning a one-stop strategy and would have to go so long on the medium tyre, but my engineers and I kept in close contact."

Adrian Sutil

"I spun when I tried to pass Bottas. I fell back and the pack was bunched up, which is when Maldonado ran into the back of me and damaged my rear wing."

Valtteri Bottas

"I fought hard to try to secure some points, but ultimately we just didn't have the pace. Also, I didn't get a great start, which allowed a few cars to jump me."

Daniel Ricciardo

"I made up two places off the line, but Hulkenberg got me back. He ran wide at the chicane, I got ahead of him and gained another position when Sutil went off."

Giedo van der Garde

"After I pitted for a second set of medium tyres I had to take the stop-go I had from contact with Mark, but the temperatures soared and I had to come back in."

Max Chilton

"I started on mediums and ran just under 40 laps. The early part of the second stint worked well, then I struggled with tyre wear and wasn't able to keep Pic back."

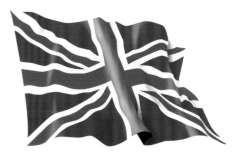

2013 FORMULA 1
SANTANDER
BRITISH GRAND PRIX

28-30 JUNE
SILVERSTONE

NICO FLIES TO VICTORY

Nico Rosberg scored his second win of 2013 in an entertaining British GP, but only after leader Sebastian Vettel had suffered a late gearbox failure and team-mate Lewis Hamilton became one of five to suffer tyre blow-outs

Nico Rosberg's win came as a huge boost to Mercedes in light of the FIA's investigation into its 'secret' Pirelli test at Barcelona, which resulted in a ban from the upcoming rookie test at Silverstone. However, the big story on a dramatic afternoon was a succession of spectacular tyre failures that left Pirelli, the FIA and the teams with a lot of investigating to do.

Lewis Hamilton delighted the crowd by pipping Rosberg to pole after an enthralling qualifying session had the pair battling for supremacy. The Mercedes team-mates were first and second in Q1 but were in the middle of the top-10 in Q2 as they saved their tyres. They went for it again when it mattered in Q3.

Hamilton was ahead after the first runs and then Rosberg briefly took pole with his final effort. But then the local hero crossed the line just seconds later to reclaim the top spot. Both drivers used option tyres throughout qualifying, ensuring that they would have plenty of fresh hard rubber available for the race.

Mercedes was kept on its toes by Red Bull Racing, but Sebastian Vettel and Mark Webber had to settle for third and fourth, the Australian having made the headlines earlier in the weekend by announcing his plans to quit F1 for a Porsche sportscar drive in 2014.

ABOVE Lewis Hamilton leads
Sebastian Vettel, Nico Rosberg,
Adrian Sutil, Fernando Alonso et al
into Luffield on the opening lap

OPPOSITE The track sign gives
a clue to the joys of the Becketts
sweepers awaiting Kimi Räikkönen

Paul di Resta put in a great effort to qualify fifth
for Force India. However, he was later excluded from
qualifying after his car was found to be underweight
for reasons the team couldn't fathom. That promoted
Daniel Ricciardo, who did a great job for Toro Rosso
just at the time Red Bull Racing was beginning to
evaluate candidates for Webber's seat. The only good
news for Force India was that di Resta's penalty moved
team-mate Adrian Sutil from seventh to sixth.

Lotus had a below par day as Romain Grosjean
and Kimi Räikkönen – running different aero packages
– qualified seventh and eighth. It was even more
frustrating for Ferrari as Fernando Alonso could not
better ninth on the grid, the F138 suffering a disastrous
lack of one-lap pace.

Hamilton led away at the start, while Rosberg was
overtaken immediately by Vettel and dropped to third,
ahead of Sutil, Massa and Räikkönen. The biggest
loser was Webber, who got away badly and suffered
front-wing damage after contact with Grosjean.

"I haven't a clue what happened off the line," said
the Australian. "We've had two or three good starts
in the past few races and then the lights went out and
we're back to our normal tactics. We need to have

a look at why they pop up. Then I had, I think it was
Grosjean, take the front wing in the first corner, so the
first stint was compromised by that."

Alonso also made a bad getaway. "The start was
probably the worst start for years," he said. "I was
fighting with [Nico] Hulkenberg in Village and The
Loop, and I remembered he hadn't started from near
the front of the grid, so I realised I was quite far down."

Hamilton looked in control in the early stages,
but on lap 8 the race was turned on its head when
he suffered a spectacular left-rear tyre failure. He faced
a long crawl back to the pits, which dropped him to
the tail of the field, and handed the lead to Vettel.

Shortly afterwards, Massa had a similar rear Pirelli
failure, and it became apparent that something was up.
There followed nervous moments in race control and
on the pit wall. In an attempt to address the problem,
drivers were told to avoid the kerbs, and pressures were
increased on the tyres waiting to be fitted.

After the first round of pit stops, Vettel continued
to lead strongly from Rosberg, Sutil and Alonso – until
Jean-Eric Vergne had his left-rear let go. This time tyre
debris led to a lengthy safety car period, which at least
allowed both Hamilton and Massa to rejoin the pack.

INSIDE LINE
PAUL HEMBERY
PIRELLI MOTORSPORT DIRECTOR

As the British GP approached, Pirelli could be forgiven for feeling nervous. After delamination issues earlier in the year, some development tyres had been tried during free practice in Canada but mixed conditions limited the opportunity for data gathering, and Montreal, with its absence of high-speed corners and lateral loads, was hardly representative of conditions at Silverstone. Teams such as Red Bull had been pushing for a return to the 2012-specification Pirellis, but the requirement for unanimous agreement among the teams for a specification change was never going to be forthcoming, as Paul Hembery's answers to questions asked in Montreal made clear:

How did the development tyres go? "Some teams did between five and eight laps in the second practice session. We didn't see any difference in terms of peak performance. Some of the running temperatures were between eight and 10 degrees lower, which is quite a lot, but in terms of handling we had some positive feedback."

What happens at Silverstone and beyond? "There are a number of approaches. But you need to get agreement with all teams, which is unlikely. We've some other ideas that would keep us even closer to the current tyre. We've developed some indoor drum testing that allows us to simulate the delaminations that we've seen. We've been working on some process changes – in basic terms, to the glue and so increase the adhesion between the components in the tyre. You can imagine, the situation we've got is that you have a number of teams who want no change, and they're very insistent on that. And one or maybe two teams that would like to have a change. And we're in the middle. You're trying to find something that's almost impossible: a consensus."

Is the push for change coming from Pirelli or the teams? "It's coming from us. The teams would like to see us find a solution. They want a win/win situation that doesn't dramatically change the performance characteristics of the tyre. Because you've got a number of teams that believe they've taken a design direction based on the information we gave them, that's affected their car design and that's something they want to maintain."

That was Pirelli's problem in a nutshell. The 2012-spec tyres to which Red Bull Racing and Mercedes were keen to return, used Kevlar rather than steel belts. Being lighter, they ran at lower temperatures. Mercedes had been struggling with rear tyre temperatures in races, while many feared that the cooler-running tyres would also favour Red Bull. Teams with more benign tyre usage, such as Ferrari, Lotus and Force India wanted no change.

TALKING POINT
A LUCKY ESCAPE

In the run-up to the British GP, the FIA International Tribunal looking into the controversial Pirelli/Mercedes tyre test at Barcelona the previous month had rather diverted attention away from the fact that real tyre issues dating back to April were still in evidence and no closer to being solved.

When the paddock assembled at Silverstone, it was against a backdrop of tribunal reprimands for both Mercedes and Pirelli, the only action against the team being exclusion from the impending Silverstone Young Driver Test at the end of July, seemingly as a way of balancing the books.

Then what happened on race day changed all that. It was Pirelli's worst nightmare, save for the fact that F1 escaped without any injuries.

Early race leader Lewis Hamilton suffered a delamination and, shortly afterwards, so did Felipe Massa. Sergio Perez's McLaren, which had a problem in free practice on Friday, had another one in the race, as did Jean-Eric Vergne's Toro Rosso and Esteban Gutierrez's Sauber. Less evident, were failure to Fernando

Alonso's Ferrari and race winner Nico Rosberg's Mercedes. In the latter two cases, they were fortunate enough to be close to the pits when they occurred and there was little effect on their respective races.

Up in race control, Race Director Charlie Whiting had a dilemma on his hands and admitted that he came close to red-flagging the race.

Pirelli's Paul Hembery said all he could say: "There have obviously been some issues with rear-left failures which we have not seen before. We are taking the situation very seriously and are investigating all tyres to determine the cause as soon as possible, ahead of the next grand prix in Germany. We can't really say much more until we have fully investigated and analysed all these incidents."

By the Nürburgring a week later, Pirelli had highlighted a number of problems: Teams mounting tyres the wrong way around; the use of lower than recommended tyre pressures; extreme camber angles; and the aggressive kerbing at Silverstone.

Yet, there could be procrastination no longer. In the face of the Silverstone debacle, teams opposing a return to the 2012-spec Kevlar-belted tyres capitulated and there would be a return to that type of tyre in two stages over the following two races in Germany and Hungary, and the FIA initiated a rule change that would in future allow Pirelli to change the tyre specification without unanimity being required from the teams.

After the restart, Rosberg kept Vettel in his sights but the Red Bull Racing driver appeared to have plenty in hand until he slowed at the end of lap 41 with gearbox failure and parked by the pit wall, handing the lead to Rosberg.

Vettel's parked Red Bull RB9 triggered another safety car period. Alonso was coming in anyway just as the safety car emerged, and he lost some ground but did at least rejoin the queue with fresh tyres.

Next time around, some drivers pitted for fresh tyres. Rosberg was among those who pitted and, having retained the lead, was able to stay safely in front of Webber after what proved to be a seven-lap dash to the flag. He also survived a post-race scare when he was investigated for speeding under yellows, and escaped with a reprimand.

"It's a very special day and I think what makes it more special is that our factory is so close, and our team has done such a fantastic job to come through during the season," said Rosberg. "We have such momentum at the moment, progressing all the time. We're really massively quick in qualifying, and are also getting faster and faster in the race. I think today we had equally the fastest race car as well. So, it's a very special day for me."

His boss, Ross Brawn, said that the win came as a huge boost after the testing saga. "Getting back to racing was just great, and getting back to racing with the result we had is obviously very special," he noted. "It was partly frustrating as Lewis had a great weekend, but just one event took it away from him. We're greatly encouraged for the rest of the season."

He also acknowledged that we'll never know what would have happened had Hamilton and Vettel both enjoyed clean races: "We were keeping in touch, Nico managed to keep in touch the whole time. Lewis had got the gap we'd asked him to get, and he was holding that, so it would have been close."

Räikkönen and Sutil were still on old tyres for that final seven-lap sprint to the finish, and both were unable to defend from those who'd pitted. The two really on charges were Webber and Alonso, who moved up from fifth and eighth to second and third in the course of those busy closing laps. It was a great effort by Webber, who'd dropped as low as 14th after his disastrous first lap.

"The boys did a great job to put a fresh front wing on at the stop," he said. "Then we started to get the race underway from there. Obviously, there were a lot of people with issues with the tyres which helped a bit, but we were lucky not to have anything like that. It was a clean race, a good strategy.

"I'd have liked a few more laps aiming at Nico, but he deserved the win. He was quick all day, obviously. He had a little bit of fortune, but you've got to be there to capitalise."

For Alonso, third place represented 15 very useful points on a day when rival Vettel failed to score any, although he still felt frustrated. "Mixed feelings to be honest," said the Spaniard. "Happy for the points, as we've reduced the gap a little bit in this race, but the pace we saw this weekend isn't good enough. There

OPPOSITE Felipe Massa was the second of five drivers to suffer a blow-out during the grand prix

BELOW Sebastian Vettel leaves his parked car after its gearbox failed when he was leading

BOTTOM Mark Webber fought his way up from 14th, after an awful opening lap, to just short of victory

ABOVE Nico Rosberg celebrates his second win of 2013 after a race that came to him after Lewis Hamilton then Sebastian Vettel hit trouble

were some other Sundays that we lost some points and maybe I was more optimistic. Today we recovered some points, but we know there's a lot of work to do. I trust the team, though, as we're united. We have a difficult weekend, we put it behind us and now we think of the next one."

Despite having older tyres himself, Hamilton also made progress over the closing laps to claim fourth place, a pretty good reward given how far back he dropped after his early puncture. Without that, he could certainly have won his home race.

Frustrated by the team's decision not to pit him for new tyres, Räikkönen tumbled to fifth, but a top-10 finish at least meant that he set a new record of 25 consecutive races in the points.

A charge in the last stint got Massa up to sixth, the Brazilian helped, like his team-mate, by a tyre stop before the final sprint after the second safety car period. Sutil made a good start and ran fourth initially, moving up to third when Hamilton had his blow-out. He was still running third at the second restart, but the decision not to pit for new tyres cost him, and he slipped back to sixth.

Ricciardo dropped a couple of places to seventh

at the start, and ultimately crossed the line eighth. From the back, di Resta charged strongly throughout the race and eventually recovered to ninth, having enjoyed a fraught battle with Hamilton at one stage. Nico Hulkenberg had a strong race from 15th on the grid, but like many others was compromised by a puncture. However, he crossed the line in 10th place to secure a useful point.

McLaren's Sergio Perez had looked likely to finish in the top six, but just after the final restart he too suffered a rear tyre failure, which led to his retirement just a few laps from the flag. Team-mate Jenson Button finished 13th after struggling to get temperature into his worn tyres in the closing laps after the safety car. As also happened in the Canadian GP, McLaren failed to score a single point.

Inevitably, the tyre failures were the only topic of conversation after the race and there were a lot of unhappy people in the paddock. It also became apparent that, at one stage, race control had given serious consideration to stopping the race. With just a few days to go until practice kicked off for the German GP at the Nürburgring, Pirelli were under serious pressure to come up with some answers.

SNAPSHOT FROM
GREAT BRITAIN

CLOCKWISE FROM RIGHT

Lotus hoped for divine intervention at Silverstone, but got just ten points from the weekend; few grands prix draw the crowds like the British race; tyres proved to be a real focus at Silverstone; Jenson Button appears surprisingly cheery, but his car's handling and speed left him frustrated; the Sauber C32 Ferrari of Nico Hulkenberg arrives on the grid for the race and despite suffering a puncture he managed to get into the points; Charles Pic contemplates his strategy; Alain Prost and Adrian Newey; the four British drivers pose together ahead of their home race; McLaren get set for a pit stop; Vettel walks down the pit lane after retiring with gearbox issues

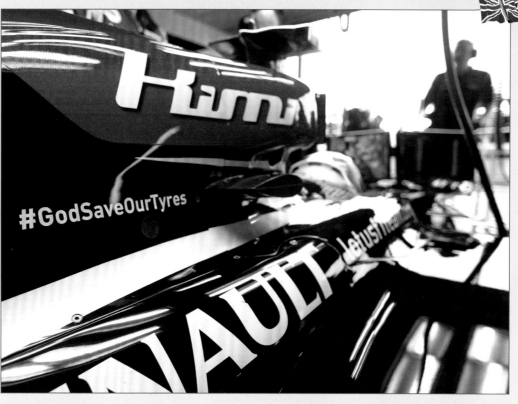

#GodSaveOurTyres

GREAT BRITAIN
SILVERSTONE
ROUND 8

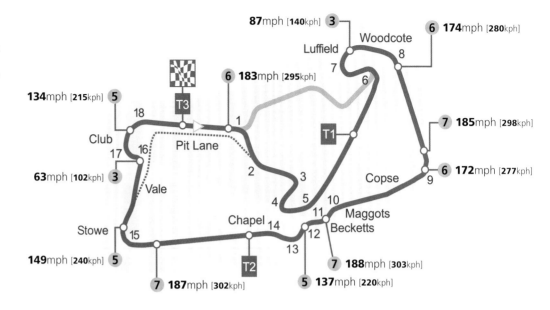

87mph [**140**kph] **3**

6 174mph [**280**kph]

Woodcote
8

Luffield
7

6 183mph [**295**kph]

T3

134mph [**215**kph] **5**

18

7 185mph [**298**kph]

Club
T1

17 16

Pit Lane

1

6 172mph [**277**kph]

63mph [**102**kph] **3**

Vale

2

3

Copse
9

4 5 10

11 Maggots

Chapel 14 12 Becketts

188mph [**303**kph] **7**

Stowe 15

13

149mph [**240**kph] **5**

T2

5 137mph [**220**kph]

7 187mph [**302**kph]

Official Results © [2013]
Formula One World Championship Limited,
6 Princes Gate, London, SW7 1QJ.
No reproduction without permission.
All copyright and database rights reserved.

RACE RESULTS

RACE DATE 30 June 2013
CIRCUIT LENGTH 3.659 miles
NO. OF LAPS 52
RACE DISTANCE 190.262 miles
WEATHER Sunny, 34°C
TRACK TEMP 22°C
LAP RECORD Fernando Alonso,
1m30.874s, 145.011mph, 2011

PRACTICE 1

	Driver	Time	Laps
1	D Ricciardo	1m54.249s	10
2	N Hulkenberg	1m55.033s	7
3	P Maldonado	1m55.354s	7
4	L Hamilton	1m55.458s	5
5	E Gutierrez	1m55.825s	9
6	V Bottas	1m56.361s	7
7	J-E Vergne	1m57.891s	4
8	G van der Garde	1m58.859s	6
9	M Chilton	1m59.719s	7
10	J Bianchi	1m59.876s	8
11	F Massa	2m06.534s	6
12	F Alonso	No time	4
13	P di Resta	No time	4
14	A Sutil	No time	4
15	S Vettel	No time	4
16	C Pic	No time	3
17	N Rosberg	No time	3
18	J Button	No time	1
19	R Grosjean	No time	1
20	S Perez	No time	1
21	M Webber	No time	1
22	K Räikkönen	No time	0

PRACTICE 2

	Driver	Time	Laps
1	N Rosberg	1m32.248s	33
2	M Webber	1m32.547s	26
3	S Vettel	1m32.680s	31
4	P di Resta	1m32.832s	34
5	L Hamilton	1m32.911s	28
6	D Ricciardo	1m33.171s	34
7	J-E Vergne	1m33.290s	38
8	A Sutil	1m33.313s	34
9	R Grosjean	1m33.322s	38
10	F Alonso	1m33.494s	32
11	J Button	1m33.740s	29
12	N Hulkenberg	1m33.896s	36
13	K Räikkönen	1m34.120s	30
14	S Perez	1m34.130s	29
15	E Gutierrez	1m34.998s	32
16	V Bottas	1m35.070s	29
17	P Maldonado	1m35.127s	35
18	J Bianchi	1m35.802s	27
19	G van der Garde	1m35.984s	32
20	C Pic	1m36.079s	35
21	M Chilton	1m37.329s	33
22	F Massa	1m43.366s	7

PRACTICE 3

	Driver	Time	Laps
1	N Rosberg	1m31.487s	18
2	L Hamilton	1m31.633s	20
3	S Vettel	1m32.037s	20
4	M Webber	1m32.078s	17
5	R Grosjean	1m32.391s	18
6	D Ricciardo	1m32.440s	19
7	F Alonso	1m32.454s	18
8	K Räikkönen	1m32.459s	22
9	A Sutil	1m32.536s	17
10	P di Resta	1m32.571s	17
11	J-E Vergne	1m32.580s	15
12	J Button	1m32.926s	18
13	P Maldonado	1m33.133s	17
14	N Hulkenberg	1m33.225s	16
15	F Massa	1m33.273s	16
16	V Bottas	1m33.309s	25
17	E Gutierrez	1m33.370s	19
18	S Perez	1m33.607s	9
19	C Pic	1m34.971s	18
20	J Bianchi	1m34.990s	17
21	M Chilton	1m36.694s	16
22	G van der Garde	1m37.443s	18

QUALIFYING 1

	Driver	Time
1	L Hamilton	1m30.995s
2	N Rosberg	1m31.355s
3	K Räikkönen	1m31.400s
4	R Grosjean	1m31.466s
5	S Vettel	1m31.559s
6	M Webber	1m31.605s
7	S Perez	1m31.953s
8	J Button	1m31.979s
9	A Sutil	1m32.002s
10	P di Resta	1m32.062s
11	D Ricciardo	1m32.097s
12	J-E Vergne	1m32.105s
13	N Hulkenberg	1m32.168s
14	F Massa	1m32.241s
15	F Alonso	1m32.266s
16	P Maldonado	1m32.512s
17	V Bottas	1m32.664s
18	E Gutierrez	1m32.666s
19	C Pic	1m33.866s
20	J Bianchi	1m34.108s
21	G van der Garde	1m35.481s
22	M Chilton	1m35.858s

QUALIFYING 2

	Driver	Time
1	S Vettel	1m30.990s
2	M Webber	1m31.002s
3	N Rosberg	1m31.028s
4	A Sutil	1m31.097s
5	D Ricciardo	1m31.182s
6	L Hamilton	1m31.224s
7	P di Resta	1m31.291s
8	F Alonso	1m31.387s
9	R Grosjean	1m31.530s
10	K Räikkönen	1m31.592s
11	J Button	1m31.649s
12	F Massa	1m31.779s
13	J-E Vergne	1m31.785s
14	S Perez	1m32.082s
15	N Hulkenberg	1m32.211s
16	P Maldonado	1m32.359s

Best sectors – Practice

Sec 1	L Hamilton	29.025s
Sec 2	N Rosberg	37.355s
Sec 3	N Rosberg	24.960s

Speed trap – Practice

1	F Massa	193.557mph
2	J Button	193.432mph
3	M Chilton	192.687mph

Best sectors – Qualifying

Sec 1	L Hamilton	28.537s
Sec 2	L Hamilton	36.499s
Sec 3	L Hamilton	24.571s

Speed trap – Qualifying

1	F Massa	193.743mph
2	J Bianchi	192.749mph
3	M Chilton	192.563mph

Sebastian Vettel
"It was disappointing to retire only a few laps from the end. I think fifth gear broke and damaged the rest of the gearbox, so it wasn't possible to carry on."

Fernando Alonso
"I was lucky on a few occasions, with Perez's blow-out and then, at the first pit stop, with a worn-out tyre at the last corner and then with Vettel's retirement."

Jenson Button
"My primes soon grained. After the final safety car there wasn't a lot of tread left on the option, so getting them up to heat was tricky, leaving me vulnerable."

Kimi Räikkönen
"I tried to hold on at the end, but with tyres 20 laps older than the others' it was impossible to keep them behind. It's a shame, as the race went pretty well until then."

Nico Rosberg
"This is a great moment for me and the team to win at the home of motor racing. This win is for every person who has been involved in building our car."

Nico Hulkenberg
"At one point, I lost the overview of what was going on, with the two safety cars and tyre debris. I had a slow puncture in my second stint, so had to pit early."

Mark Webber
"My start was bad, then my wing was damaged by Grosjean. I made the most of the safety car periods. Then it was Nico and I left. I needed a few more laps."

Felipe Massa
"After a fantastic start and a perfect first lap, I drove an attacking first stint. On lap 10, when I was in the middle of the corner at Turn 5, my left-rear tyre failed."

Sergio Perez
"I'd been running inside the top 10 for most of the afternoon, when my left-rear tyre suddenly exploded. I just felt an explosion along the Hangar Straight."

Romain Grosjean
"Towards the end, I lost part of the front wing, making it hard to drive, so it was best to retire due to safety concerns. We don't know if it was caused by debris."

Lewis Hamilton
"The grand prix started well: I felt comfortable in the lead and was managing my pace. The tyre problem was a shame, but from then on, it was just a case of giving it my all."

Esteban Gutierrez
"It was a crazy race. I had to pit because of a problem with my front-left tyre. This also damaged my front wing, which forced me to pit again two laps later."

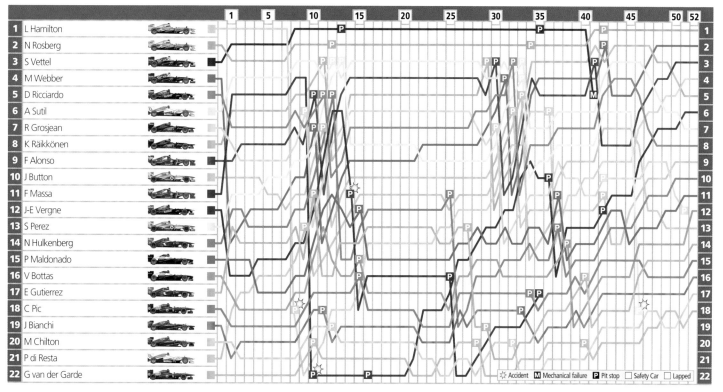

	Driver	
1	L Hamilton	
2	N Rosberg	
3	S Vettel	
4	M Webber	
5	D Ricciardo	
6	A Sutil	
7	R Grosjean	
8	K Räikkönen	
9	F Alonso	
10	J Button	
11	F Massa	
12	J-E Vergne	
13	S Perez	
14	N Hulkenberg	
15	P Maldonado	
16	V Bottas	
17	E Gutierrez	
18	C Pic	
19	J Bianchi	
20	M Chilton	
21	P di Resta	
22	G van der Garde	

☆ Accident ■ Mechanical failure P Pit stop □ Safety Car □ Lapped

QUALIFYING 3

	Driver	Time
1	L Hamilton	1m29.607s
2	N Rosberg	1m30.059s
3	S Vettel	1m30.211s
4	M Webber	1m30.220s
5	P di Resta	1m30.736s
6	D Ricciardo	1m30.757s
7	A Sutil	1m30.908s
8	R Grosjean	1m30.955s
9	K Räikkönen	1m30.962s
10	F Alonso	1m30.979s

GRID

	Driver	Time
1	L Hamilton	1m29.607s
2	N Rosberg	1m30.059s
3	S Vettel	1m30.211s
4	M Webber	1m30.220s
5	D Ricciardo	1m30.757s
6	A Sutil	1m30.908s
7	R Grosjean	1m30.955s
8	K Räikkönen	1m30.962s
9	F Alonso	1m30.979s
10	J Button	1m31.649s
11	F Massa	1m31.779s
12	J-E Vergne	1m31.785s
13	S Perez	1m32.082s
14	N Hulkenberg	1m32.211s
15	P Maldonado	1m32.359s
16	V Bottas	1m32.664s
17	E Gutierrez	1m32.666s
18	C Pic	1m33.866s
19	J Bianchi	1m34.108s
20	M Chilton	1m35.858s
21	P di Resta	1m30.736s
22	G van der Garde	1m35.481s

RACE

	Driver	Car	Laps	Time	Avg. mph	Fastest	Stops
1	N Rosberg	Mercedes F1 W04	52	1h32m59.456s	122.762	1m33.531s	3
2	M Webber	Red Bull-Renault RB9	52	1h33m00.221s	122.745	1m33.401s	3
3	F Alonso	Ferrari F138	52	1h33m06.580s	122.605	1m34.090s	3
4	L Hamilton	Mercedes F1 W04	52	1h33m07.212s	122.591	1m34.159s	3
5	K Räikkönen	Lotus-Renault E21	52	1h33m10.713s	122.514	1m35.384s	2
6	F Massa	Ferrari F138	52	1h33m14.029s	122.442	1m35.273s	4
7	A Sutil	Force India-Mercedes VJM06	52	1h33m15.791s	122.403	1m35.961s	2
8	D Ricciardo	Toro Rosso-Ferrari STR8	52	1h33m15.999s	122.399	1m35.927s	2
9	P di Resta	Force India-Mercedes VJM06	52	1h33m17.399s	122.368	1m35.330s	3
10	N Hulkenberg	Sauber-Ferrari C32	52	1h33m19.165s	122.329	1m36.013s	3
11	P Maldonado	Williams-Renault FW35	52	1h33m20.591s	122.298	1m35.907s	2
12	V Bottas	Williams-Renault FW35	52	1h33m24.550s	122.212	1m36.312s	2
13	J Button	McLaren-Mercedes MP4-28	52	1h33m25.425s	122.193	1m36.356s	2
14	E Gutierrez	Sauber-Ferrari C32	52	1h33m25.741s	122.186	1m36.439s	4
15	C Pic	Caterham-Renault CT03	52	1h33m31.069s	122.070	1m37.091s	2
16	J Bianchi	Marussia-Cosworth MR-02	52	1h33m33.553s	121.972	1m37.978s	2
17	M Chilton	Marussia-Cosworth MR-02	52	1h34m07.116s	121.291	1m39.156s	2
18	G van der Garde	Caterham-Renault CT03	52	1h34m07.215s	121.288	1m38.722s	3
19	R Grosjean	Lotus-Renault E21	51	Front wing	-	1m35.614s	3
20	S Perez	McLaren-Mercedes MP4-28	46	Tyre failure	-	1m36.131s	2
R	S Vettel	Red Bull-Renault RB9	41	Gearbox	-	1m35.018s	2
R	J-E Vergne	Toro Rosso-Ferrari STR8	35	Tyre failure	-	1m38.370s	2

CHAMPIONSHIP

	Driver	Pts
1	S Vettel	132
2	F Alonso	111
3	K Räikkönen	98
4	L Hamilton	89
5	M Webber	87
6	N Rosberg	82
7	F Massa	57
8	P di Resta	36
9	R Grosjean	26
10	J Button	25
11	A Sutil	23
12	J-E Vergne	13
13	S Perez	12
14	D Ricciardo	11
15	N Hulkenberg	6

Grid penalties

P di Resta Excluded from qualifying for car being underweight
G van der Garde Five-place grid penalties for ignoring blue flags in the Canadian GP & for a gearbox change

Fastest lap	Fastest speed trap		Fastest pit stop	
M Webber 1m33.401s	**F Massa**	193.495mph	1 S Vettel	24.092s
(141.094mph) on lap 52	**Slowest speed trap**		2 S Vettel	24.159s
	N Rosberg	182.559mph	3 J Button	24.357s

	Constructor	Pts
1	Red Bull-Renault	219
2	Mercedes	171
3	Ferrari	168
4	Lotus-Renault	124
5	Force India-Mercedes	59
6	McLaren-Mercedes	37
7	Toro Rosso-Ferrari	24
8	Sauber-Ferrari	6

 Paul di Resta

"It was a scruffy race, as I lost my front wing trying to get ahead of Nico. We chose to change it when the safety car came out, which cost me two places."

 **Pastor Maldonado**

"We were close to scoring our first point, but before the second restart I was on the inside when Hulkenberg went off, then he hit me when he rejoined."

Jean-Eric Vergne

"I got a bad start, but it wouldn't have made a difference due to the problem I had when my tyre failed. I didn't feel any warning signs, as it let go under braking."

 Charles Pic

"I was managing the tyre wear, but just before the last safety car I was ahead of Bottas and looking at an exciting last few laps. I ended up 15th, which isn't bad."

Jules Bianchi

"It was a tricky race, which began with a bad start. After that I just had to follow Charles, but it was a fight to stay with him, as the Caterham was a bit stronger."

Adrian Sutil

"At the second safety car, the cars around me pitted. I stayed out and was third at the restart, but the cars with fresh rubber had an advantage and passed me easily."

Valtteri Bottas

"It wasn't an easy race, as the car was quite hard to handle. I didn't have the best set-up for qualifying or the race, and we also lost some time in the pit stops."

Daniel Ricciardo

"At the end, I was on used tyres, and those who changed for a third time were able to pass me. Eighth place is a good result, but I see it as a missed opportunity."

Giedo van der Garde

"I started running with a strategy we'd begun in qualy, which was all about managing the deg as long as I could to take advantage of anything that happened."

 **Max Chilton**

"I was really psyched up and got a great start. I got past Jules and Pic, then they passed me again and I took back position and we had a close tussle for the first few laps."

FORMULA 1 GROSSER PREIS SANTANDER VON DEUTSCHLAND 2013

**5-7 JULY
NÜRBURGRING**

HOME WIN AT LAST

Sebastian Vettel bounced back from the disappointment of his retirement at Silverstone to take the win in front of his home crowd. But the local hero had to work very hard just to edge out Lotus's Kimi Räikkönen

Despite this being Sebastian Vettel's 30th grand prix victory, it was his first in his own country and also, oddly enough, his first in the month of July. The real significance was that it indicated that he would now be hard to beat in the title race, given the inconsistency of the opposition. Had he not retired a week earlier in Britain, Vettel's lead would have been substantially more than the 34-point advantage he now assumed over Alonso.

After the Silverstone dramas, an exciting race passed without tyre issues, although it was marred by an incident in the pit lane when an errant wheel from Mark Webber's Red Bull struck FOM TV cameraman Paul Allen (see Talking Point, p161).

Lewis Hamilton gave Mercedes another pole position on the manufacturer's home ground, but it was a day of mixed emotions for the team as a strategy error in qualifying kept his team-mate, Nico Rosberg, out of Q3.

The temperatures rose during the day and that contributed to an unpredictable session, as form from practice appeared to mean little. Having struggled in the second practice session and then in the third – when he was only seventh and calling his

ABOVE Red Bull's Sebastian Vettel and Mark Webber both got the jump on Lewis Hamilton at the start and were ahead by the first corner

OPPOSITE Tyre problems forced Lewis Hamilton to have a lonely run, taking fifth on the race's final lap

BELOW Lotus racer Kimi Räikkönen managed to pass Nico Rosberg for sixth place early in the race

car undriveable – Hamilton found performance just at the right time. He was fastest on the first runs in Q3 and, having briefly ceded pole to Vettel, stole it back right at the end with his final run. Vettel was happy enough to secure a front row spot, just ahead of Red Bull Racing team-mate Mark Webber. Lotus looked strong throughout and, having been second fastest in Q1 and Q2, Räikkönen claimed the fourth grid spot in the session that mattered, ahead of his Lotus team-mate, Romain Grosjean.

Daniel Ricciardo further staked his claim for a 2014 Red Bull race seat with an excellent run to sixth on the grid for Toro Rosso, repeating his Silverstone performance. Felipe Massa and Alonso were first and third in both Q1 and Q2, but Ferrari knew that the positions were flattering and, rather than lose out to the expected pacesetters, took the bold gamble of qualifying on the medium tyre, which would allow for a much longer first stint than the more fragile soft tyre that those ahead were using. They qualified seventh and eighth, with the Brazilian in front.

Rosberg was the highest profile victim of Q2. Having set a time, he waited in the garage, but the team failed to judge how much faster the track would become and he tumbled down to 11th as others improved, and it was too late to respond.

Hamilton's hopes of beating the Red Bulls were dashed when he was overtaken by both Vettel and Webber at the start. Massa remained in front of Alonso at the start, but on only the fourth lap he spun to a halt at Turn 1 and, stuck in fifth gear, couldn't get going.

Webber dropped out of victory contention at the first pit stop when he was waved out with an unsecured right rear wheel. The wheel bounced past the Lotus and Mercedes pits and hit cameraman Allen (who was facing the other way) in the back. Webber lost a lap while the car was retrieved from the end of the pit lane and fitted with a fresh set of wheels.

As the first pit stops played out, Grosjean surprised everyone by running a long opening stint on the more fragile soft tyre. It was enough to lift him into a solid second place, behind Vettel and ahead of team-mate Räikkönen.

Vettel then lost the small advantage he had built up when a safety car came out on lap 23 after Jules Bianchi's Marussia stopped just before the chicane with an engine failure that set the rear of the car ablaze. In a bizarre incident, the car then rolled back across the track after the Frenchman had abandoned it, fortunately without causing any problems for oncoming traffic.

The safety car allowed the top runners to make their

INSIDE LINE
SEBASTIAN VETTEL
RED BULL RACING DRIVER

"I'm very, very happy to finally win my home race! Kimi was pushing hard at the end and obviously they tried to do something with different compound tyres.

"We had a very solid, controlled race, but I was pushing every lap except during those behind the safety car. I had a couple of laps where it was quite close with Romain as well, and in the middle of the race we lost KERS for a couple of laps, so it was very difficult. Fortunately, the system recovered, which was important so that I could defend, but I was happy that the race ended after 60 laps – not 61 or 62!

"I knew that it would be very close with Kimi once he got past Romain. Lotus were incredibly quick and looking after their tyres, probably a little bit better than others.

"It's a great relief to get the German GP under my belt. There are a lot of expectations, especially when you've got a good car and for a couple of years you've had a good run. When you come to home soil people expect you to win. I think the whole team, including me, never ever let that go to our heads, but it feels very, very sweet to have succeeded after a few tries.

"The team did a fantastic job with strategy and pit stops, but on the track it was so difficult. It's so tough when you know that you can't abuse the tyres too much because then you won't reach the end of the stint. Equally, passing people, you know that you have to get through traffic as quickly as you can.

"Last but not least, compliments to Pirelli. They did a very good job within a couple of days to react and bring a different rear tyre to this event, but I don't think that this win has anything to do with that. Whenever I spoke about using the 2012 tyres, it was purely targeted at safety, because we can't go out and have a race like we did at Silverstone. We step into the car, want to race at the limit and can't be driving into the unknown. I pushed hard from the drivers' point-of-view. I think we're happier overall, all the drivers, with the tyres we raced on this weekend. Whether it suits your car or not, is secondary.

"The most important thing is that we learn the lesson from previous races, especially the British GP. Nothing happened here, which is good, but it's also good to have another proper look, especially around Silverstone. Pirelli can do that at next week's Young Driver Test that the race drivers can now attend, then decide for the remainder of the season."

second stops, and at the restart Vettel continued to lead from Grosjean and Räikkönen. Grosjean then pitted for a final time on lap 40, forcing Vettel to react a lap later.

"It was a tough call in some respects and not in others," said Christian Horner of Vettel's final pit stop. "Obviously, the pace car came out when a Marussia started a life of its own, and that was at a very awkward point in the race, because it was still potentially too far to go on a set of the harder tyres. With this in mind, we elected to fit a set of scrubbed tyres to Sebastian's car, leaving one new set available for the last stint.

"So, we intended to stop, and were thinking that the Lotuses might actually try to brave it out to the end. Once Grosjean stopped, though, it made perfect sense for us to cover him. The risk with that was conceding the lead to Kimi if he didn't need to stop, and he was looking in pretty good shape at that stage..."

Räikkönen duly took the lead when Vettel stopped, and he stayed out as the team kept its options open. In theory, he could have run to the chequered flag without pitting again, but in the end Lotus brought him in on lap 49, giving him an 11-lap sprint to the flag on the more fragile soft tyre. This dropped him back to third place behind Vettel and Grosjean.

"We made the stop, covered Grosjean," said Horner. "We then focused on keeping the gap to Kimi to less than a pit stop obviously, so that when he did stop for the soft tyres Sebastian had just enough to cover him. We saw that the Lotus was very quick on the soft tyre at the beginning of the race, but Sebastian kept just enough performance up his sleeve to fend him off over the last few laps."

Could Räikkönen get the job done? Traffic didn't help his cause, and it was a few laps before team-mate Grosjean reluctantly let him by. Over the final five laps, Räikkönen brought down the margin to Vettel, eventually crossing the finish line just 1s behind, having run out of time to make a pass, much to his frustration.

RIGHT Sergio Perez (left in picture) and Jenson Button were relieved to both score points for McLaren

BELOW Felipe Massa's race came to an early end when he lost control into Turn 1, spun off and stalled

TALKING POINT
DANGER IN THE PIT LANE

An accident to FOM TV cameraman Paul Allen during the German GP highlighted the dangers of working in a Formula One pit lane.

Allen was knocked over by the right rear wheel from Mark Webber's Red Bull RB9 which had come loose after not being attached properly at the Australian's pit stop.

Allen was removed from the pit lane and then treated at the Nürburgring's medical centre before being taken to hospital in Koblenz, suffering from both a broken shoulder and cracked ribs.

"The camera guys are getting very close to the action, getting some great pictures, but it's still a dangerous environment," said Red Bull Racing Team Principal Christian Horner. "It's something that needs looking at. Things do go wrong.

"Mechanics have to wear safety gear and helmets and maybe it's time that we looked at other operational working people having to have safety equipment as well."

While the tyre issues affecting F1 had been allowed to drift up until the jolt provided by the multiple blow-outs during the British GP,

action on the issue of pit lane safety was swift.

From the Hungarian GP onwards, F1 camera crews and broadcast personnel were to be banned from the pit lane during all F1 sessions, rather than just during qualifying sessions and the grand prix itself. Access to the pit lane would be limited, and granted to select media on a rotational basis, who would need to be stationed on the pit wall rather than walking the pit lane.

Former Jordan and Jaguar technical chief Gary Anderson, who works for the BBC from the pit lane, joked about needing to head for the Job Centre but, on a more serious note, he wasn't sure that the right issue was being addressed.

"It looks like a knee-jerk reaction that isn't fixing the problem of

wheels coming off racing cars, but actually making another one," he said. "With a 2s pit stop, the lollipop man or jack man has no hope of seeing a problem. Why do we need 2s pit stops? The viewers can't see anything. If it were left to me, I'd limit pit stops to 10 or 11 people working on the car – two on each corner, front and rear jack men and a lollipop man. That would probably give you 4s stops and more chance of a problem being spotted.

"As for the pit wall, we'd better put up warnings to let loose wheels know that they can't go there! They have huge energy and the way those prat perches are designed, with nowhere to go, if a wheel does get up there, it's going to take out a lot of high-dollar people staring at their screens and laptops!"

TOP It had been a long time coming, but Sebastian Vettel finally added a German GP to his collection

ABOVE Pirelli's changes to its tyres worked as hoped and there were no tyre-related problems at the event

"After the safety car we were pretty okay and the cars, three of us, had similar speed, but it's very difficult to overtake anybody," said the Finn. "I could run longer and we had a think about it, if we could try to run until the end. But we had a massive problem with the radio: I could hear them, but they could only hear me between two corners. So I'm wondering if we should have done it, taken a gamble and tried to go to the end because the tyres were okay so was my speed, so it was hard to know what would happen in the next 10 laps. We decided to come in and put on the soft tyres. We still had good speed. Obviously, I got some help from Romain to get past but we would have had a big fight anyhow. I could have probably passed him in a normal situation but obviously it could have cost me a lot of time."

Grosjean hung onto to a solid third place, finishing just ahead of Alonso. The Ferrari driver had a much stronger latter part of the race following a disappointing opening stint on the medium tyre, which saw him make his first pit stop earlier than anticipated. Later on, the safety car helped him out.

After falling out of contention in the middle part of the race, Hamilton fought back to claim fifth place,

passing Jenson Button right at the end. Nevertheless, it was a poor reward for Mercedes.

"The first half of the race was pretty horrible," said Ross Brawn. "In the second half, when the fuel weight went down, it got a touch cooler and we got back in the window again. And it was respectable, our times not so bad. It just shows how critical we are. On high fuel at the beginning of the race, trying to push, we just overstressed the tyres and we have to try and find more solutions to resolve that.

"I think it's something you fall over the edge of. The track temperature did take it over that threshold, and the fact that it came back a bit towards us for the second half of the race demonstrated that. The fuel weight went down. I don't think it necessarily did get much cooler in the second half, but certainly when the fuel weight went down we were in a better position."

Starting on the medium tyre, Button had run a long 21-lap first stint that saw him run third for many laps, his two-stop strategy ultimately earning him sixth place. Meanwhile, Webber finally had some good luck and got back the lap he'd lost with his pit drama under the safety car. Thereafter, a charging drive took him from last place to seventh. In contrast to his team-mate, Sergio Perez preferred to start on the softer tyre, which meant an early first pit stop. He finished two places behind Button in eighth, having lost out to the flying Webber right at the end. Rosberg started on primes, but struggled throughout for grip on his way to ninth.

Nico Hulkenberg put in a charging performance for Sauber, starting on the medium tyre and running as high as fourth before his late first pit stop dropped him back. After the safety car, he still ran as high as sixth, but the yellow flag interruption had helped others gain ground and he eventually finished 10th. Paul di Resta braved it out on two stops, but his 36-lap-old tyres were past their best by the end, and the Scot slipped out of the points on the penultimate lap to finish 11th.

SNAPSHOT FROM
GERMANY

CLOCKWISE FROM RIGHT

The giant grandstands form a distinctive backdrop to Turn 1 (thankfully, the rather ominous dark clouds cleared before Sunday); Williams' Valtteri Bottas gets accustomed to meeting fans young and not-so-young; Charles Pic in pensive mood as he contemplates his race strategy; Red Bull fans check on home favourite Sebastian Vettel's progress; Nico Rosberg shows off his ball skills; Lewis Hamilton and his mirror image as he helmets up; a rare moment of quiet in the McLaren pit garage; the Nürburgring can sometimes be swept by rain, but not on race day as Romain Grosjean uses an umbrella to ensure a bit of shade; Jenson Button gathers his thoughts; FOM President Bernie Ecclestone points the way forward

GERMANY
NÜRBURGRING
ROUND 9

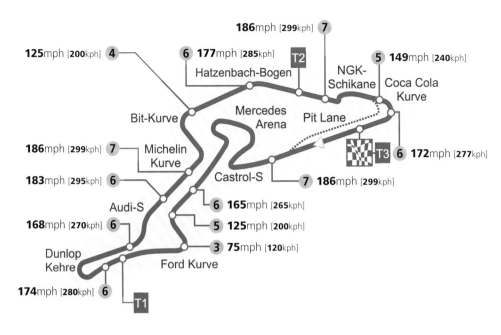

- **186**mph [**299**kph] ⑦
- **125**mph [**200**kph] ④
- ⑥ **177**mph [**285**kph] T2
- ⑤ **149**mph [**240**kph]
- Hatzenbach-Bogen
- NGK-Schikane
- Coca Cola Kurve
- Bit-Kurve
- Mercedes Arena
- Pit Lane
- **186**mph [**299**kph] ⑦ Michelin Kurve
- ⑥ **172**mph [**277**kph] T3
- **183**mph [**295**kph] ⑥
- Castrol-S
- ⑦ **186**mph [**299**kph]
- Audi-S
- ⑥ **165**mph [**265**kph]
- **168**mph [**270**kph] ⑥
- ⑤ **125**mph [**200**kph]
- ③ **75**mph [**120**kph]
- Dunlop Kehre
- Ford Kurve
- **174**mph [**280**kph] ⑥ T1

RACE RESULTS

RACE DATE 7 July 2013
CIRCUIT LENGTH 3.199 miles
NO. OF LAPS 60
RACE DISTANCE 191.940 miles
WEATHER Dry and bright, 24°C
TRACK TEMP 42°C
LAP RECORD Michael Schumacher, 1m29.468s, 128.721mph, 2004

PRACTICE 1

	Driver	Time	Laps
1	L Hamilton	1m31.754s	25
2	N Rosberg	1m31.973s	25
3	M Webber	1m32.789s	22
4	A Sutil	1m32.822s	16
5	K Räikkönen	1m32.956s	22
6	F Massa	1m33.065s	18
7	J Button	1m33.139s	24
8	S Vettel	1m33.213s	20
9	R Grosjean	1m33.260s	27
10	S Perez	1m33.456s	18
11	P di Resta	1m33.493s	18
12	N Hulkenberg	1m33.810s	20
13	D Ricciardo	1m33.901s	23
14	J-E Vergne	1m33.976s	26
15	P Maldonado	1m34.025s	20
16	V Bottas	1m34.200s	22
17	E Gutierrez	1m34.437s	24
18	C Pic	1m35.674s	23
19	M Chilton	1m35.987s	19
20	G van der Garde	1m36.078s	23
21	R Gonzalez	1m37.459s	21
22	F Alonso	No time	2

PRACTICE 2

	Driver	Time	Laps
1	S Vettel	1m30.416s	39
2	N Rosberg	1m30.651s	38
3	M Webber	1m30.683s	41
4	R Grosjean	1m30.843s	32
5	K Räikkönen	1m30.848s	27
6	F Alonso	1m31.056s	39
7	F Massa	1m31.059s	41
8	L Hamilton	1m31.304s	35
9	J Button	1m31.568s	37
10	P di Resta	1m31.797s	40
11	A Sutil	1m31.824s	34
12	D Ricciardo	1m31.855s	42
13	J-E Vergne	1m32.055s	39
14	S Perez	1m32.086s	36
15	N Hulkenberg	1m32.495s	39
16	E Gutierrez	1m32.762s	44
17	V Bottas	1m32.879s	35
18	P Maldonado	1m32.880s	36
19	C Pic	1m33.695s	38
20	G van der Garde	1m33.804s	40
21	J Bianchi	1m34.017s	10
22	M Chilton	1m34.667s	39

PRACTICE 3

	Driver	Time	Laps
1	S Vettel	1m29.517s	19
2	N Rosberg	1m30.193s	19
3	M Webber	1m30.211s	18
4	F Alonso	1m30.621s	16
5	F Massa	1m30.639s	17
6	K Räikkönen	1m30.671s	19
7	L Hamilton	1m30.744s	20
8	R Grosjean	1m30.781s	18
9	N Hulkenberg	1m30.966s	20
10	A Sutil	1m31.009s	18
11	J Button	1m31.326s	22
12	E Gutierrez	1m31.405s	20
13	P di Resta	1m31.733s	21
14	J-E Vergne	1m31.855s	18
15	S Perez	1m31.855s	23
16	D Ricciardo	1m31.898s	19
17	P Maldonado	1m31.969s	20
18	V Bottas	1m32.036s	23
19	C Pic	1m33.230s	19
20	J Bianchi	1m33.470s	22
21	G van der Garde	1m33.964s	21
22	M Chilton	1m34.683s	20

QUALIFYING 1

	Driver	Time
1	F Massa	1m30.547s
2	K Räikkönen	1m30.676s
3	F Alonso	1m30.709s
4	D Ricciardo	1m31.081s
5	L Hamilton	1m31.131s
6	N Hulkenberg	1m31.132s
7	J Button	1m31.181s
8	R Grosjean	1m31.242s
9	S Vettel	1m31.269s
10	A Sutil	1m31.320s
11	N Rosberg	1m31.322s
12	P di Resta	1m31.322s
13	M Webber	1m31.428s
14	S Perez	1m31.498s
15	J-E Vergne	1m31.629s
16	E Gutierrez	1m31.681s
17	V Bottas	1m31.693s
18	P Maldonado	1m31.707s
19	C Pic	1m32.937s
20	J Bianchi	1m33.063s
21	G van der Garde	1m33.734s
22	M Chilton	1m34.098s

QUALIFYING 2

	Driver	Time
1	F Massa	1m29.825s
2	K Räikkönen	1m29.852s
3	F Alonso	1m29.962s
4	S Vettel	1m29.992s
5	R Grosjean	1m30.005s
6	L Hamilton	1m30.152s
7	M Webber	1m30.217s
8	D Ricciardo	1m30.223s
9	N Hulkenberg	1m30.231s
10	J Button	1m30.269s
11	N Rosberg	1m30.326s
12	P di Resta	1m30.697s
13	S Perez	1m30.933s
14	E Gutierrez	1m31.010s
15	A Sutil	1m31.010s
16	J-E Vergne	1m31.104s

Best sectors – Practice
Sec 1	S Vettel	29.400s
Sec 2	S Vettel	37.245s
Sec 3	S Vettel	22.817s

Speed trap – Practice
1	P di Resta	189.083mph
2	J Button	188.648mph
3	A Sutil	188.586mph

Best sectors – Qualifying
Sec 1	K Räikkönen	29.253s
Sec 2	R Grosjean	37.162s
Sec 3	S Vettel	22.813s

Speed trap – Qualifying
1	P di Resta	188.524mph
2	S Perez	188.027mph
3	F Massa	187.716mph

Sebastian Vettel
"It was a tough race and I'm happy it wasn't two or three laps longer, as Kimi was a bit quicker towards the end. I'm pleased it worked out and it's very special."

Fernando Alonso
"I paid the price for being on used tyres, as by lap 12 they were finished, which cost us some of the advantage that we hoped to gain from our strategic choice."

Jenson Button
"There are a lot of positives to take from this weekend. Our lap times compared to the four cars at the front weren't too bad, and today's points are badly needed right now."

Kimi Räikkönen
"After my first stop, I was stuck behind a Mercedes. Then, after the safety car, three of us pulled away, but we were too close on speed to change the order."

Nico Rosberg
"We struggled with the rear tyres, and that's why we weren't able to match the pace of the guys in the front. Even so, I had fun when I changed to the option tyres."

Nico Hulkenberg
"It was a very tough race. I was fighting every lap, but this is what we were able to get out of it. To be honest, I expected we'd have better pace today, but we didn't."

Mark Webber
"I knew we'd lost the tyre in the pit stop, but not that someone got hit by it. Today was a nightmare and you want to wake up and have another go at it."

Felipe Massa
"I'm disappointed with what happened. At the start of lap 4, at the moment when I braked, the rear wheels locked and I couldn't stop the car from spinning."

Sergio Perez
"After the safety car, it was like the start of a second race. I focused on preserving the tyres, and the car performed well, but I just lost out at the final corner."

Romain Grosjean
"After some difficult races, everything went right, and it was pretty special when I was leading the race, and returning to the podium is naturally a good thing."

Lewis Hamilton
"I didn't make a great start, and the Red Bulls were quicker off the line. I struggled with the second set of tyres, which compromised the remainder of my race."

Esteban Gutierrez
"From the beginning to the end we were fighting for positions, so it was very tough. It was difficult to overtake, because we were lacking speed on the straights."

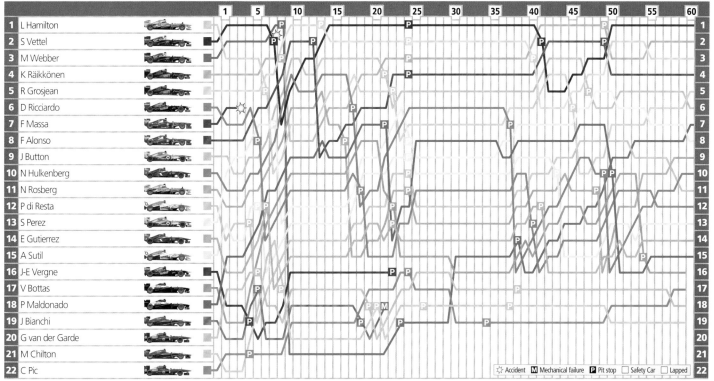

Accident | M Mechanical failure | P Pit stop | Safety Car | Lapped

QUALIFYING 3

	Driver	Time
1	L Hamilton	1m29.398s
2	S Vettel	1m29.501s
3	M Webber	1m29.608s
4	K Räikkönen	1m29.892s
5	R Grosjean	1m29.959s
6	D Ricciardo	1m30.528s
7	F Massa	1m31.126s
8	F Alonso	1m31.209s
9	J Button	No time
10	N Hulkenberg	No time

GRID

	Driver	Time
1	L Hamilton	1m29.398s
2	S Vettel	1m29.501s
3	M Webber	1m29.608s
4	K Räikkönen	1m29.892s
5	R Grosjean	1m29.959s
6	D Ricciardo	1m30.528s
7	F Massa	1m31.126s
8	F Alonso	1m31.209s
9	J Button	No time
10	N Hulkenberg	No time
11	N Rosberg	1m30.326s
12	P di Resta	1m30.697s
13	S Perez	1m30.933s
14	E Gutierrez	1m31.010s
15	A Sutil	1m31.010s
16	J-E Vergne	1m31.104s
17	V Bottas	1m31.693s
18	P Maldonado	1m31.707s
19	J Bianchi	1m33.063s
20	G van der Garde	1m33.734s
21	M Chilton	1m34.098s
22	C Pic	1m32.937s

RACE

	Driver	Car	Laps	Time	Avg. mph	Fastest	Stops
1	S Vettel	Red Bull-Renault RB9	60	1h41m14.711s	113.646	1m34.164s	3
2	K Räikkönen	Lotus-Renault E21	60	1h41m15.719s	113.627	1m33.767s	3
3	R Grosjean	Lotus-Renault E21	60	1h41m20.541s	113.537	1m34.576s	3
4	F Alonso	Ferrari F138	60	1h41m22.432s	113.502	1m33.468s	3
5	L Hamilton	Mercedes F1 W04	60	1h41m41.638s	112.934	1m34.156s	3
6	J Button	McLaren-Mercedes MP4-28	60	1h41m42.707s	112.777	1m34.201s	2
7	M Webber	Red Bull-Renault RB9	60	1h41m52.273s	112.720	1m34.782s	3
8	S Perez	McLaren-Mercedes MP4-28	60	1h41m53.017s	112.649	1m36.134s	2
9	N Rosberg	Mercedes F1 W04	60	1h42m01.532s	112.777	1m34.181s	3
10	N Hulkenberg	Sauber-Ferrari C32	60	1h42m04.603s	112.720	1m34.244s	3
11	P di Resta	Force India-Mercedes VJM06	60	1h42m08.482s	112.649	1m36.566s	2
12	D Ricciardo	Toro Rosso-Ferrari STR8	60	1h42m11.686s	112.590	1m35.982s	3
13	A Sutil	Force India-Mercedes VJM06	60	1h42m12.449s	112.576	1m35.816s	3
14	E Gutierrez	Sauber-Ferrari C32	60	1h42m14.871s	112.531	1m35.792s	3
15	P Maldonado	Williams-Renault FW35	60	1h42m16.640s	112.499	1m34.293s	2
16	V Bottas	Williams-Renault FW35	59	1h41m23.946s	111.581	1m33.972s	2
17	C Pic	Caterham-Renault CT03	59	1h41m50.508s	111.095	1m37.584s	3
18	G van der Garde	Caterham-Renault CT03	59	1h41m55.601s	111.003	1m38.509s	3
19	M Chilton	Marussia-Cosworth MR-02	59	1h42m00.415s	110.916	1m38.383s	4
R	J-E Vergne	Toro Rosso-Ferrari STR8	22	Hydraulics	-	1m39.281s	1
R	J Bianchi	Marussia-Cosworth MR-02	21	Engine	-	1m39.844s	2
R	F Massa	Ferrari F138	3	Spun off	-	1m38.890s	0

CHAMPIONSHIP

	Driver	Pts
1	S Vettel	157
2	F Alonso	123
3	K Räikkönen	116
4	L Hamilton	99
5	M Webber	93
6	N Rosberg	84
7	F Massa	57
8	R Grosjean	41
9	P di Resta	36
10	J Button	33
11	A Sutil	23
12	S Perez	16
13	J-E Vergne	13
14	D Ricciardo	11
15	N Hulkenberg	7

Grid penalties
C Pic Five-place grid penalty for changing the gearbox

Fastest lap
F Alonso 1m33.468s
(123.205mph) on lap 51

Fastest speed trap
N Rosberg 191.568mph
Slowest speed trap
F Massa 174.667mph

Fastest pit stop
1	S Vettel	19.118s
2	L Hamilton	19.316s
3	L Hamilton	19.321s

	Constructor	Pts
1	Red Bull-Renault	250
2	Mercedes	183
3	Ferrari	180
4	Lotus-Renault	157
5	Force India-Mercedes	59
6	McLaren-Mercedes	49
7	Toro Rosso-Ferrari	24
8	Sauber-Ferrari	7

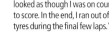

Paul di Resta
"It hasn't been the easiest of weekends, but late in the race it looked as though I was on course to score. In the end, I ran out of tyres during the final few laps."

Pastor Maldonado
"It was a good race for us, as we put everything together and were on for points. It's disappointing to finish where we did today after the problem with the pit stops."

Jean-Eric Vergne
"I found the car hard to drive from the start, then there was the moment at my pit stop when I had to brake to avoid di Resta who was released in front of me."

Charles Pic
"I had to brake hard in Turn 1, and soon had a vibration from the front right. I was going to pit early, so didn't have to change strategy much, coming in on lap 4."

Jules Bianchi
"I got a really poor start, and it was a battle to recover and stay ahead of Pic. I'd just made my second pit stop and got ahead of van der Garde when the engine let go."

Adrian Sutil
"I struggled with the tyres and had to convert from a two-stop race to a three-stopper. I lost time at my final stop, and after that points were just too far away."

Valtteri Bottas
"I didn't get a good start as I had a few problems getting away from the line. I also lost time in both pit stops, so we need to work out what happened there."

Daniel Ricciardo
"I was able to hold position on the option tyre but, once we pitted for the prime tyre, I really struggled for pace and couldn't push as hard as I wanted to."

Giedo van der Garde
"I got up to 17th on lap 1. We got the soft tyres out of the way by coming in early for mediums, then pitted on lap 20 for another set of the harder compound."

Max Chilton
"There was nothing between us and Caterham, and then the safety car came out and we made the right call, but suffered with rear tyre wear with 10 laps to go."

FORMULA 1 MAGYAR NAGYDÍJ 2013

26-28 JULY
HUNGARORING
BUDAPEST

A SURPRISE FOR LEWIS

Lewis Hamilton surprised even himself by scoring the victory after a dominant performance in an exciting Hungarian GP. The Briton's first win with Mercedes AMG Petronas came in his 10th start for the team

Although Lewis Hamilton secured pole position, he admitted after qualifying that he wasn't looking forward to the race, fearing that, as so often this year, Mercedes would struggle to keep its tyres alive. In fact, he maintained a superb pace throughout the 70 laps and won in style as he left his pursuers behind.

The Mercedes driver was helped by some decisive overtaking manoeuvres that made sure he kept in clean air and not stuck behind cars that were out of sequence. In contrast to Hamilton's run, Sebastian Vettel did get caught up and also damaged his front wing while trying to fight his way through. For once, the German and Red Bull Racing simply didn't get it right, and the team headed into the summer break knowing that they had some homework to do.

The key to the Hungarian GP meeting was adapting to the revised Pirelli tyres, now featuring the 2012 construction. They had recently been tested by all the teams, bar the banned Mercedes, at Silverstone. Indeed, Mercedes didn't show much one-lap pace over the course of the meeting until the first qualifying session, when Nico Rosberg and Hamilton topped the timesheet. The pair then repeated the feat in Q2. At the start of Q3, though, Vettel made the

INSIDE LINE
LEWIS HAMILTON

MERCEDES DRIVER

"I think you could tell I was 'hungry' for it today – excuse the pun. I was going all-out. I needed to get past people and usually I get stuck in traffic. Today, I wasn't having it: I was going for every move!

"This is one of the most important grand prix wins of my career. To move to a new team and to win for Mercedes-Benz is a real privilege. The guys have done an exceptional job and I hope there are many more to come.

"I really didn't expect it as it's probably been one of the toughest weeks for me. I know I've been on pole for the last three races, but I wasn't expecting this and it was great to finally be able to maintain it throughout the race.

"I came here praying that when we put on these tyres they would come towards us more than go away from us, and it seems like they've done that. It was 52-55°C track temperatures today, one of the hottest races I can remember doing, and for a team that really struggles with tyre degradation, it was a walk in the park. I'm really baffled...

"I used all the techniques I could possibly use to look after the tyres, which I'm sure everyone was doing, but it worked. I really, really, hope that when we go to the next race, we'll be able to do the same again.

"At the start, the pace was okay. I think maybe Sebastian was just as quick or a little bit quicker, but fortunately he was behind. I think I called the first pit stop just right and after that it was about managing the gap.

"On three pit stops, I had to make sure I got past people. When I came out behind Jenson, I thought it was just my luck, but I got past him and was surprised to see Sebastian and the others get stuck behind. But I think generally we had the pace on everyone today.

"Coming into the race, we were making improvements but not big enough to make the difference we saw today, so I'm assuming that a large part of that was tyres. I really wasn't expecting it, which is why I said after qualifying that it would take a miracle to win. Our long runs didn't look that great in the second practice session, but I got the balance just spot on with the front wing and the car felt great.

"If we can be quick in a race with these track temperatures, I'm very hopeful that we can be competitive everywhere else, so this could be really good. It could be a turning point for us."

most of being the only driver to have new soft tyres for the first of his two runs and set a stunning provisional pole lap of 1m19.506s.

Everyone had new rubber for their second attempts, and one after another driver took a shot at Vettel's time. Kimi Räikkönen could only go second before he was bumped down by Rosberg, who in turn lost out to Romain Grosjean. Fernando Alonso got amongst them with fourth quickest time before Hamilton popped up with a brilliant lap of 1m19.388s to push everyone down a position. Vettel was right behind and, while he improved on his previous best, it wasn't fast enough to secure him the pole.

Grosjean had looked good all weekend, and did well to claim third on the grid, ahead of Rosberg. Alonso was happy with fifth fastest time after some recent mediocre qualifying performances from Ferrari, while Räikkönen slipped down to an eventual sixth, ahead of Felipe Massa, Daniel Ricciardo and Sergio Perez. The last named was compromised by a heavy crash in the third practice session that morning that left his crew racing to finish the repairs in time. Mark Webber had KERS problems throughout qualifying and, having made Q3, didn't do a flying lap, and therefore finally qualified a frustrated 10th.

Crucially, Hamilton got into the first corner in the lead and, against all expectations, soon opened up a small advantage over the pursuing Vettel. Then, after his first pit stop, the British driver made a decisive pass on Jenson Button – who had started with prime tyres on his McLaren and so had yet to pit – which ensured that he had a clear track.

In contrast, Vettel got caught behind Button. He not only lost time but damaged the right hand side of his front wing against the McLaren in his attempts to get by, which took the edge off his performance. He was also told by the team to drop back from Button's slipstream in order to keep temperatures down.

Later, Hamilton had to make another important pass on Webber, who was also out of synch after starting on the prime tyre, and once again the Mercedes driver managed to give himself a clear track. He eventually came home some 11s clear of Räikkönen, his nearest pursuer.

"It's been a great weekend, really a great weekend," enthused Hamilton. "I really didn't expect it. Obviously, we hadn't had the test at Silverstone, so were on the back foot when we came in. I really wasn't even expecting to be on pole. I was really surprised with that, and then at the start of the race my pace was okay. Fortunately, Sebastian was

OPPOSITE Romain Grosjean chases Sebastian Vettel in the early laps as they battle over second place

ABOVE Williams finally won its first points of the season when Pastor Maldonado raced to 10th

BELOW Jenson Button proved a stumbling block for Vettel, keeping him from chasing after Hamilton

behind me and my tyres went off just maybe a lap or two before his.

"I thought that it was just my luck when I came out behind Jenson, because that's what usually happens when you're having to pass people if you're on a three-stop strategy, when others might be stopping just twice. But I was able to get past him and I guess he did me a favour there as others also got stuck behind him.

"I know I was really controlling the pace, particularly through the second, third and last stint, and especially on the last stint. This win is just down to an exceptional job from the team. We came here with upgrades and constantly doing work to try and understand these tyres. I think today we bolted them on and they just worked for us."

Räikkönen had started only sixth but, with typically canny tyre management, the Finn was able to run a two-stop strategy, while all his key rivals stopped three times. That moved him ahead of Vettel in the latter part of the race and, despite having to make his final set of tyres last for 28 laps – while the chasing Vettel's were 13 laps younger – he was just able to stay ahead. It was some kind of revenge

for losing out in the opposite circumstances in the German GP, although the reward this time was second place rather than a win.

"I knew that my tyres were okay and I was good through the last sector, so I was pretty sure that there was no chance for Sebastian to try to overtake me into the first corner," Räikkönen said. "But then, obviously, Turn 2 was a bit more tricky for me all race. Sebastian got a good run once before, and then a second time, and I defended. Maybe I'm over a bit on the right and it's a bit tight, but then I kept him behind me and that was the only time he had a good run on me. In there, it's very difficult to overtake because it's so narrow on top of the hill.

"After that, I had no issues. That was the only part of the circuit where I really had some problems with the tyres. Overall, it was good work for the team, the car was working well but unfortunately our Saturday form keeps making the race a bit difficult for me. Hopefully we can fix that and so be a bit nearer the front at the beginning of the race."

Despite his disappointment, Vettel kept his title campaign firmly on course with third place, leaving him with a 38-point lead over Räikkönen heading into the summer break.

"It's not the best circuit at which to be stuck in traffic, because it's quite difficult to overtake," said Vettel. "I think we hadn't got enough speed on the straights to put people under enough pressure, so obviously I got stuck behind Jenson for a long time. I damaged my front wing on his car as well, which dropped us back and after that obviously it was about fighting back as much as we could. In the middle of the race, I didn't know where I was so I just tried to hang in there and then attempt to come back as much as I could."

Having started only 10th after his KERS problems in qualifying, Webber used the strategy of starting

OPPOSITE Vettel made three pit stops en route to third, but Kimi Räikkönen's two stops worked better

BELOW Paul di Resta pulled up four laps short to become the second Force India to be sidelined

BOTTOM Sergio Perez struggled for grip but brought his MP4-28 home ninth, the first lapped runner

TALKING POINT
IS LEWIS IN THE HUNT?

Lewis Hamilton's Hungarian GP victory, on merit and in scorching track temperatures, certainly got the attention of Mercedes' rivals as F1 headed into its summer break.

A look at the points table was making happy reading for Sebastian Vettel in his quest for four successive world titles. The reigning champion had 172 points, to Kimi Räikkönen's 134, Fernando Alonso's 133 and Hamilton's 124.

Yet, while the evidence was suggesting that Lotus and Ferrari didn't have the ultimate pace to unseat Vettel, the Hungarian GP hinted that Mercedes just might have, notwithstanding the competitive picture changing from circuit to circuit. That Hamilton had no tyre concerns in such high temperatures had certainly started tongues wagging.

According to Pirelli's Paul Hembery, it wasn't the change of tyre spec, as it was something Mercedes had done. He wasn't being specific, obviously, but even so it seemed to fly in the face of what Hamilton himself was saying.

Lewis's win was his fourth at the Hungaroring, where he is always super-competitive, and the track was expected to suit the Mercedes, but it was interesting to see that his pole margin of 0.038s was less than predicted. Had set-up changes very effectively traded qualifying pace for more benign tyre usage in the race?

While Hamilton conceded that he hoped Hungary was a turning point, he was coy about his chances of challenging for the championship.

"I think it's still far too early," he said. "When you have a win like this, you get excited and start thinking that anything is possible. I think it's still too early to say whether or not we can challenge for the titles. I know the guys are working hard so that we can close the gap and I hope today is the first step towards doing so, but we've got a lot of tough races coming up. I just hope that's not the last time my tyres work for me..."

Vettel's 48-point advantage over Hamilton seemed huge but was less than two grand prix wins. Fernando Alonso lost a similar margin in 2012.

Vettel and Hamilton's respective team-mates could also play a part. While Rosberg wouldn't enjoy a supporting role, Nico was 40 points behind Lewis and realistic enough to know that he may be called upon to do so. At Red Bull Racing, however, Vettel was unlikely to receive much help from Mark Webber. Their relationship has always been strained and the Australian had confirmed at the British GP that he'll be a Porsche sportscar driver in 2014...

ABOVE Jubilation in the Mercedes pit as Hamilton takes his first win for the team, with Perez coming home a lapped ninth behind him

on prime tyres to good effect, working his way up through the field to a solid fourth place.

Alonso got ahead of Rosberg on the first lap, but it was soon apparent that Ferrari were struggling badly for race pace, and he was never a contender for a podium finish. In fact, Alonso ultimately lost out to Webber and thus, unusually, finished in the same place he started, namely fifth.

Grosjean had been many people's favourite to win the race but, after a good early run, he picked up a controversial drive-through penalty for putting all four wheels off track while passing Massa, a move that many considered to have been a great bit of driving. Earlier, the French Lotus driver had made contact with Button and, after a post-race investigation, he received a further 20s penalty. However, that didn't affect the eight points he collected for sixth place, as he had crossed the finish line 21.5s in front of the McLaren.

Seventh place was a respectable outcome for Button after his strategy of starting on prime tyres gave him an early boost. From 13th on the grid, he made a great start to promote himself to eighth place on the opening lap. He then rose as high

as third ahead of Vettel before his first pit stop, surviving contact both with the Red Bull RB9 and with Grosjean's Lotus before his two-stop strategy played out successfully.

Massa made contact with Rosberg at Turn 5 on the opening lap and carried front wing damage throughout. Struggling like his team-mate for pace, the Brazilian finished in eighth place.

Perez struggled on used prime tyres in the opening stint on his way to ninth place as the first of the lapped runners after Rosberg pulled up short with engine failure with six laps to go. Behind him, Pastor Maldonado had a good first lap, and by jumping up to 11th the Williams racer gave himself a shot at the points. He ran a three-stop strategy and was still 11th in the closing laps until Rosberg's retirement handed the team its first point for 2013.

Nico Hulkenberg lost several places at the start of the grand prix, which didn't make his life any easier, but a two-stop strategy had the Sauber driver on course for a potential 10th place and a useful point – until he was handed a drive-through penalty for speeding in the pit lane, the result of a gear change issue. He finished in 11th place.

SNAPSHOT FROM
HUNGARY

CLOCKWISE FROM RIGHT

Lewis Hamilton has plenty to smile
about at the Hungaroring; Charles
Pic cools down with piped cold air;
safety marshals entertain themselves
trackside on race day; the Red Bull pit
crew recorded the fastest pit stop of
the weekend but it wasn't enough for
victory; McLaren were forced to reflect
on further misfortune; Lotus racer
Romain Grosjean gets his autograph-
signing arm ready; Sergio Perez waits
to go out; fresh from her run at the
Silverstone Young Driver tests, Williams
development driver Susie Wolff listens in
to the engineers' chat; Bernie Ecclestone
and Red Bull's Christian Horner swap
thoughts; Vettel races out to try to
take pole, but would end up just short,
pipped by Mercedes' Hamilton

HUNGARY
BUDAPEST
ROUND 10

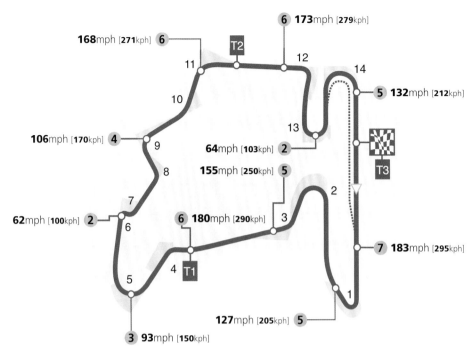

168mph [**271**kph] ⑥
173mph [**279**kph] ⑥
106mph [**170**kph] ④
132mph [**212**kph] ⑤
64mph [**103**kph] ②
155mph [**250**kph] ⑤
62mph [**100**kph] ②
180mph [**290**kph] ⑥
183mph [**295**kph] ⑦
127mph [**205**kph] ⑤
93mph [**150**kph] ③

RACE RESULTS

RACE DATE 28 July 2013
CIRCUIT LENGTH 2.719 miles
NO. OF LAPS 70
RACE DISTANCE 190.30 miles
WEATHER Sunny, 35°C
TRACK TEMP 52°C
LAP RECORD Michael Schumacher,
1m19.071s, 123.828mph, 2004

PRACTICE 1				PRACTICE 2				PRACTICE 3		
	Driver	Time	Laps		Driver	Time	Laps		Driver	Time	Laps
1	S Vettel	1m22.723s	19	1	S Vettel	1m21.264s	34	1	R Grosjean	1m20.730s	20
2	M Webber	1m22.982s	24	2	M Webber	1m21.308s	42	2	F Alonso	1m20.898s	13
3	K Räikkönen	1m23.010s	20	3	R Grosjean	1m21.417s	40	3	S Perez	1m21.052s	10
4	F Alonso	1m23.099s	22	4	F Alonso	1m21.426s	34	4	S Vettel	1m21.125s	27
5	R Grosjean	1m23.111s	20	5	F Massa	1m21.544s	37	5	F Massa	1m21.151s	14
6	J Button	1m23.370s	26	6	L Hamilton	1m21.802s	42	6	L Hamilton	1m21.158s	19
7	A Sutil	1m23.390s	20	7	N Rosberg	1m21.991s	40	7	M Webber	1m21.254s	17
8	N Rosberg	1m23.531s	28	8	K Räikkönen	1m22.011s	32	8	N Rosberg	1m21.356s	23
9	S Perez	1m23.591s	26	9	J Button	1m22.180s	41	9	J Button	1m21.499s	15
10	P Maldonado	1m23.911s	21	10	A Sutil	1m22.304s	41	10	A Sutil	1m21.519s	20
11	E Gutierrez	1m24.119s	21	11	P di Resta	1m22.526s	39	11	K Räikkönen	1m21.589s	17
12	V Bottas	1m24.150s	27	12	S Perez	1m22.529s	37	12	P Maldonado	1m21.646s	19
13	L Hamilton	1m24.157s	28	13	P Maldonado	1m22.781s	36	13	P di Resta	1m21.963s	21
14	J-E Vergne	1m24.204s	15	14	E Gutierrez	1m22.837s	42	14	N Hulkenberg	1m21.964s	21
15	F Massa	1m24.299s	19	15	N Hulkenberg	1m22.841s	39	15	D Ricciardo	1m22.180s	18
16	N Hulkenberg	1m24.314s	23	16	J-E Vergne	1m23.369s	34	16	J-E Vergne	1m22.423s	19
17	D Ricciardo	1m24.383s	24	17	D Ricciardo	1m23.411s	41	17	V Bottas	1m23.028s	16
18	P di Resta	1m24.608s	21	18	V Bottas	1m23.646s	34	18	G van der Garde	1m23.975s	21
19	C Pic	1m25.827s	24	19	C Pic	1m24.325s	38	19	C Pic	1m23.987s	19
20	G van der Garde	1m26.808s	25	20	G van der Garde	1m25.065s	36	20	J Bianchi	1m24.298s	20
21	J Bianchi	1m27.617s	20	21	J Bianchi	1m25.143s	39	21	M Chilton	1m25.122s	20
22	R Gonzalez	1m28.927s	25	22	M Chilton	1m26.647s	33	22	E Gutierrez	No time	2

QUALIFYING 1			QUALIFYING 2		
	Driver	Time		Driver	Time
1	N Rosberg	1m20.350s	1	N Rosberg	1m19.778s
2	L Hamilton	1m20.363s	2	L Hamilton	1m19.862s
3	R Grosjean	1m20.447s	3	S Vettel	1m19.992s
4	S Vettel	1m20.646s	4	R Grosjean	1m20.101s
5	F Alonso	1m20.652s	5	F Alonso	1m20.183s
6	P Maldonado	1m20.816s	6	K Räikkönen	1m20.243s
7	K Räikkönen	1m20.867s	7	F Massa	1m20.460s
8	F Massa	1m21.004s	8	M Webber	1m20.503s
9	N Hulkenberg	1m21.028s	9	D Ricciardo	1m20.527s
10	J Button	1m21.131s	10	S Perez	1m20.545s
11	V Bottas	1m21.135s	11	A Sutil	1m20.569s
12	D Ricciardo	1m21.181s	12	N Hulkenberg	1m20.580s
13	M Webber	1m21.264s	13	J Button	1m20.777s
14	J-E Vergne	1m21.345s	14	J-E Vergne	1m21.029s
15	A Sutil	1m21.471s	15	P Maldonado	1m21.133s
16	S Perez	1m21.612s	16	V Bottas	1m21.219s
17	E Gutierrez	1m21.724s			
18	P di Resta	1m22.043s			
19	C Pic	1m23.007s			
20	G van der Garde	1m23.333s			
21	J Bianchi	1m23.787s			
22	M Chilton	1m23.997s			

Best sectors – Practice			Speed trap – Practice		
Sec 1	S Perez	29.052s	1	V Bottas	186.908mph
Sec 2	R Grosjean	28.911s	2	P Maldonado	185.790mph
Sec 3	R Grosjean	22.544s	3	G van der Garde	185.790mph

Best sectors – Qualifying			Speed trap – Qualifying		
Sec 1	L Hamilton	28.549s	1	G van der Garde	187.032mph
Sec 2	R Grosjean	28.299s	2	V Bottas	185.790mph
Sec 3	S Vettel	22.146s	3	N Rosberg	185.790mph

Sebastian Vettel
"I lost more time than expected on the way into the first pit stop, and came out just behind Jenson. I tried to force it and damaged my wing, which was my mistake."

Fernando Alonso
"Finishing fifth, maybe we did better than we should, as Mercedes, Lotus and Red Bull were quicker than us, a fact we'd known since Friday's practice."

Jenson Button
"Seb tried many times to get past me, and clipped my rear wheel into Turn 2. I was lucky not to get a puncture. Had I not taken to the grass, we would have touched."

Kimi Räikkönen
"I did two long stints on the tyres, but the car felt strong, so it let us make one less stop. Seb got the run on me twice, but luckily it was where you can't really pass."

Nico Rosberg
"I got a good start, but Felipe and I clashed, which was unfortunate as I was in front and had left some space for him at Turn 5, but his front wing hit my rear tyre."

Nico Hulkenberg
"At the second pit stop, I had trouble shifting from first to second. I must have released the button too early. Without the drive-through, I could have scored."

Mark Webber
"I had a tricky car for the first few laps, as I knew the option tyres were quite grippy, and after that just got my head down. I don't think I could've got much more."

Felipe Massa
"The race was difficult from start to finish, because right from the first lap, at Turn 5, after making contact with Rosberg, I lost the left part of my front wing."

Sergio Perez
"We needed the starting tyre in the best condition to make a two-stopper work, but I struggled with the rear of the car, had to pit early and then ran into traffic."

Romain Grosjean
"This is a race that got away. Maybe the strategy didn't quite work out how we wanted, but the car felt really good and it was the traffic that cost us."

Lewis Hamilton
"I said that I needed a miracle to win. Well, just maybe they do happen. The team called the strategy just right, and then it was all about managing the gap."

Esteban Gutierrez
"I was on a good strategy, and everything was going as planned. Unfortunately, I had to retire due to a gearbox problem after an engine problem yesterday."

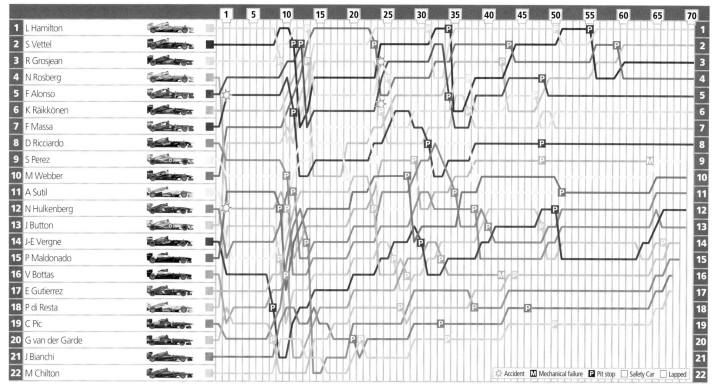

	Driver			
1	L Hamilton			
2	S Vettel			
3	R Grosjean			
4	N Rosberg			
5	F Alonso			
6	K Räikkönen			
7	F Massa			
8	D Ricciardo			
9	S Perez			
10	M Webber			
11	A Sutil			
12	N Hulkenberg			
13	J Button			
14	J-E Vergne			
15	P Maldonado			
16	V Bottas			
17	E Gutierrez			
18	P di Resta			
19	C Pic			
20	G van der Garde			
21	J Bianchi			
22	M Chilton			

☼ Accident   M Mechanical failure   P Pit stop   ☐ Safety Car   ☐ Lapped

QUALIFYING 3

	Driver	Time
1	L Hamilton	1m19.388s
2	S Vettel	1m19.426s
3	R Grosjean	1m19.595s
4	N Rosberg	1m19.720s
5	F Alonso	1m19.791s
6	K Räikkönen	1m19.851s
7	F Massa	1m19.929s
8	D Ricciardo	1m20.641s
9	S Perez	1m22.398s
10	M Webber	No time

GRID

	Driver	Time
1	L Hamilton	1m19.388s
2	S Vettel	1m19.426s
3	R Grosjean	1m19.595s
4	N Rosberg	1m19.720s
5	F Alonso	1m19.791s
6	K Räikkönen	1m19.851s
7	F Massa	1m19.929s
8	D Ricciardo	1m20.641s
9	S Perez	1m22.398s
10	M Webber	No time
11	A Sutil	1m20.569s
12	N Hulkenberg	1m20.580s
13	J Button	1m20.777s
14	J-E Vergne	1m21.029s
15	P Maldonado	1m21.133s
16	V Bottas	1m21.219s
17	E Gutierrez	1m21.724s
18	P di Resta	1m22.043s
19	C Pic	1m23.007s
20	G van der Garde	1m23.333s
21	J Bianchi	1m23.787s
22	M Chilton	1m23.997s

RACE

	Driver	Car	Laps	Time	Avg. mph	Fastest	Stops
1	L Hamilton	Mercedes F1 W04	70	1h42m29.445s	111.540	1m24.647s	3
2	K Räikkönen	Lotus-Renault E21	70	1h42m40.383s	111.342	1m25.260s	2
3	S Vettel	Red Bull-Renault RB9	70	1h42m41.904s	111.314	1m24.553s	3
4	M Webber	Red Bull-Renault RB9	70	1h42m47.489s	111.213	1m24.069s	3
5	F Alonso	Ferrari F138	70	1h43m00.856s	111.197	1m25.394s	3
6	R Grosjean	Lotus-Renault E21	70	1h43m21.740s	110.560	1m25.328s	3
7	J Button	McLaren-Mercedes MP4-28	70	1h43m23.264s	110.572	1m26.195s	2
8	F Massa	Ferrari F138	70	1h43m25.892s	110.526	1m25.176s	3
9	S Perez	McLaren-Mercedes MP4-28	69	1h42m31.566s	109.909	1m26.143s	2
10	P Maldonado	Williams-Renault FW35	69	1h42m49.449s	109.590	1m25.597s	3
11	N Hulkenberg	Sauber-Ferrari C32	69	1h43m18.840s	109.070	1m26.740s	2
12	J-E Vergne	Toro Rosso-Ferrari STR8	69	1h43m19.299s	109.062	1m26.491s	3
13	D Ricciardo	Toro Rosso-Ferrari STR8	69	1h43m19.910s	109.051	1m26.863s	2
14	G van der Garde	Caterham-Renault CT03	68	1h43m05.916s	107.714	1m27.473s	3
15	C Pic	Caterham-Renault CT03	68	1h43m12.290s	107.603	1m27.725s	2
16	J Bianchi	Marussia-Cosworth MR-02	67	1h42m46.176s	106.469	1m28.250s	3
17	M Chilton	Marussia-Cosworth MR-02	67	1h43m29.075s	105.734	1m28.160s	3
18	P di Resta	Force India-Mercedes VJM06	66	Hydraulics	-	1m26.608s	3
19	N Rosberg	Mercedes F1 W04	64	Engine	-	1m25.089s	3
R	V Bottas	Williams-Renault FW35	42	Hydraulics	-	1m27.127s	2
R	E Gutierrez	Sauber-Ferrari C32	28	Gearbox	-	1m29.135s	1
R	A Sutil	Ford India-Mercedes VJM06	19	Hydraulics	-	1m28.548s	0

CHAMPIONSHIP

	Driver	Pts
1	S Vettel	172
2	K Räikkönen	134
3	F Alonso	133
4	L Hamilton	124
5	M Webber	105
6	N Rosberg	84
7	F Massa	61
8	R Grosjean	49
9	J Button	39
10	P di Resta	36
11	A Sutil	23
12	S Perez	18
13	J-E Vergne	13
14	D Ricciardo	11
15	N Hulkenberg	7
16	P Malonado	1

Race penalties
R Grosjean 20s penalty for causing a collision

Fastest lap
M Webber 1m24.069s
(116.571mph) on lap 61

Fastest speed trap
N Rosberg   189.580mph
Slowest speed trap
A Sutil   181.005mph

Fastest pit stop
1	S Vettel	21.343s
2	L Hamilton	21.454s
3	F Alonso	21.599s

	Constructor	Pts
1	Red Bull-Renault	277
2	Mercedes	208
3	Ferrari	194
4	Lotus-Renault	183
5	Force India-Mercedes	59
6	McLaren-Mercedes	57
7	Toro Rosso-Ferrari	24
8	Sauber-Ferrari	7
9	Williams-Renault	1

Paul di Resta
"I made a good start, and was aggressive on lap 1. I was up to about 12th, but from there on it was tricky as I struggled with the balance and tyre performance."

Pastor Maldonado
"I had a really good start, and made a few overtaking moves that were on the limit, which is especially pleasing, as at this track it's very hard to overtake."

Jean-Eric Vergne
"I made a bad start, which meant I had to fight to get back to where I was. Beating my team-mate? It means nothing, especially when we are outside the points."

Charles Pic
"After my first stop I came out behind Bianchi and Chilton, but passed them and caught Giedo. After that second pit stop, I had to make the tyres last 32 laps."

Jules Bianchi
"I struggled with balance and having to work so hard to preserve the rear tyres. On the plus side, we remained reliable in a race which is very demanding for the cars."

Adrian Sutil
"Just before my pit stop I couldn't shift up any more. I came into the pits, and it became clear I had a hydraulic problem, so the team told me to park up."

Valtteri Bottas
"It's a shame to have my first retirement of 2013. We need to investigate what happened, but it felt like hydraulics, as I lost the power steering, then the engine."

Esteban Gutierrez
"We couldn't match our rivals today, as we lacked speed when we had a heavy fuel load, which is the opposite of what we used to see with last year's car."

Giedo van der Garde
"That was the best race of the year for me. I was right on the pace that we'd targeted until, with about six laps to go, the tyres were pretty much gone."

Max Chilton
"That was easily the hardest race of my career. The track is really challenging, and compounding things further for us was a balance shift on the medium tyres."

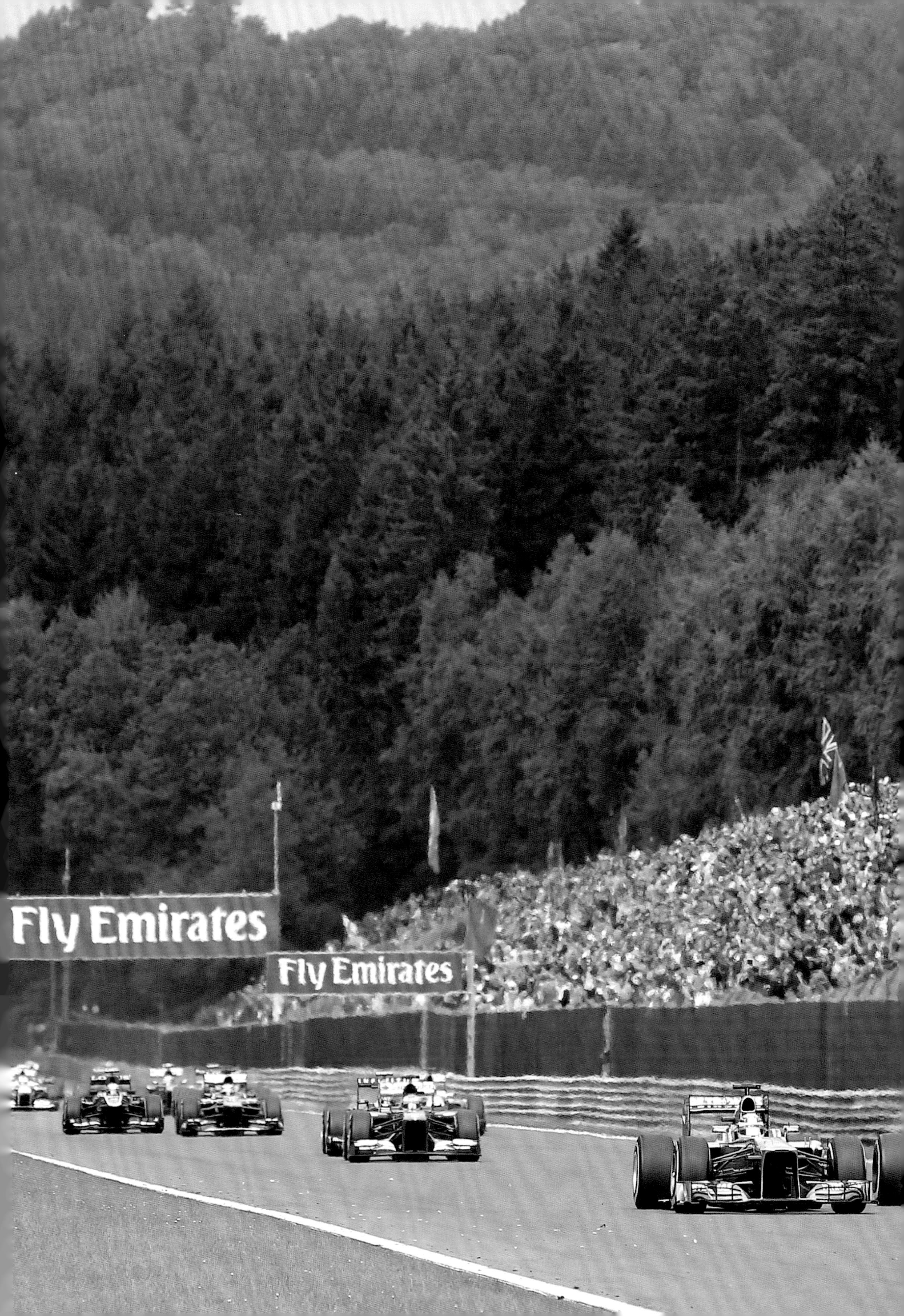
Fly Emirates
Fly Emirates

2013 FORMULA 1 SHELL BELGIAN GRAND PRIX

23-25 AUGUST
SPA-FRANCORCHAMPS

RED BULL REFRESHED

Sebastian Vettel returned from the summer break to extend his championship lead to 46 points. The expected rain never arrived, allowing the German to dominate a surprisingly straightforward Belgian Grand Prix

While Sebastian Vettel claimed maximum points at Spa-Francorchamps, Fernando Alonso and Lewis Hamilton did at least add to their scores with podium finishes, but it was a bad day for Kimi Räikkönen, who had looked like Vettel's most likely title challenger.

Hamilton made it four pole positions in a row after rain helped to turn qualifying into a lottery. The opening session started in light drizzle, but towards the end the track began to dry. Most drivers opted for new intermediate tyres for their crucial first run, but a few backmarkers gambled on slicks, and it proved to be a risk well worth taking.

Alonso was fastest for Ferrari but, with his final lap, Caterham's Giedo van der Garde vaulted up to an impressive third, while Marussia drivers Jules Bianchi and Max Chilton also made it through to Q2. Thus several more fancied cars didn't make it, including both Williamses and both Toro Rossos. Things calmed down a bit in Q2 when it was dry, and Räikkönen was fastest ahead of Alonso. Meanwhile, a relieved Hamilton was lucky just to scrape through in tenth.

The rain returned just as the drivers headed out for the start of Q3. Most went out on slicks, but discovered by the end of their out laps that the track was already too wet. There then followed a mad scramble into the pits for intermediates.

One man was already on them, Paul di Resta having opted to go straight out on inters. The Force India driver thus managed to get a lap in before the rain really began to come down. He hung on to pole for several minutes until a great lap from Nico Rosberg in increasingly tricky conditions put the German top.

Everything turned around once again as the rain eased off, and the track became marginally drier. One after the other, Mark Webber, Vettel and finally Hamilton went top as they crossed the line a few seconds apart, bumping Rosberg down to fourth.

Given the chances of getting it wrong, second was a pretty good outcome for Vettel. Behind him, Webber took third and Rosberg fourth, while di Resta – who was in the pits when the quickest times were set – managed to hang onto fifth. Jenson Button qualified sixth, ahead of Romain Grosjean. However, title contenders Räikkönen and Alonso didn't have any luck when it mattered, and would line up eighth and ninth, with Felipe Massa completing the top 10.

Pole man Hamilton led the field away from the gird before, for once, everyone made it through the La Source hairpin intact. However, Vettel had more momentum heading into Eau Rouge and was able to drag past the Mercedes on the following uphill straight, and slot easily into the lead. Hamilton just didn't have the pace to stay with him.

"I had a half-decent start," said Hamilton, "and I felt like I got a good exit out of Turn 1, but Sebastian just caught me massively, particularly through Eau Rouge. There was no defending, really. I could only move once, so I moved once and just had to watch him glide by. After that, it was very, very difficult to hold onto him."

"I think Sebastian had worked it out in his own mind," said Red Bull Racing principal Christian Horner. "He didn't have a great start, but he went to the left

RIGHT Lewis Hamilton leads the field into La Source, as Jenson Button makes an excellent start from sixth, Sebastian Vettel holds the middle ground, and Nico Rosberg locks up

BELOW The arrival of rain for qualifying made life interesting for the drivers. Here, Sebastian Vettel tiptoes his way around La Source

INSIDE LINE
SEBASTIAN VETTEL
RED BULL RACING DRIVER

"That was a fantastic race for us from start to finish, with very good tactics. Obviously it helped my first lap to have the tow from Lewis through Eau Rouge, and then I was flying.

"It's certainly very difficult around here to plan your start because first you need to have a good launch off the line and then there's a long straight coming. It's a bit like Korea in that respect. I tried my best to line up behind Lewis and basically benefit from a massive tow through Eau Rouge. It's especially important on the opening lap of the race. When the tyres are not yet completely there and the fuel tank is full, and obviously the cars are quite heavy up the hill and produce a lot of drag.

"In the tow, I was able to make up a lot of speed and when I got side-by-side with Lewis I had a big advantage over him and was able to get straight by. After that, I just settled into a rhythm and then tried to open a gap to be flexible at the first pit stop.

"The car was much better than we expected going into the race and we had a bit of pace in hand to control it. I really enjoyed that a lot and I think the guys on the pit wall were not as stressed as at other times. The rain staying away also meant that there were no critical calls to make. It was a very good afternoon and bodes well for the Italian GP where we also don't expect, maybe, to be that strong.

"You need to optimise the set-up at Spa-Francorchamps and whether it was us over-performing or the others under-performing, I'm not entirely sure. So, in that regard, it's always nice to have speed on the straights if you have to overtake. If you're limited by straightline speed, it's really very difficult to pass. We've had some bad experiences around here with that, so maybe this year we were a little bit on the higher side in terms of straightline speed.

"We've had painful years where we just got hammered down the straights both here and at Monza, and we've had years where the loss down the straight was limited and so we could come back at our rivals in the corners. For sure, the 2011 experience was great like that.

"Now, I think, we can be quite confident for Monza. We had a good race in Canada and a very good race here – both on medium downforce types of track – so let's hope our low downforce package goes in the same direction."

TALKING POINT
CHANGES AT WILLIAMS

It's a funny old game! Twenty years ago, Williams was winning everything, but there was clearly a Benetton threat on the horizon. Michael Schumacher had shown himself to be a freakish talent and, technically, Enstone was getting it together with a formidable combination of drive and technical

brainstorming from the likes of Tom Walkinshaw, Ross Brawn, Rory Byrne and Pat Symonds. Intense rivalry between the two outfits dominated the next two seasons.

And so it was that you did an involuntary double-take when Symonds arrived in the F1 paddock wearing his Williams team gear for the first time… His ban in the wake of Renault 'Crashgate' at Singapore 2008 was now over. He'd been consulting in the meantime, most recently with Marussia, but was now back full-time as Williams Technical Director, replacing Mike Coughlan.

After Pastor Maldonado won so well at Barcelona in 2012, Williams's 2013 season has been the paddock's greatest disappointment. Some fundamental issues with the FW35 mean that the car lacks the front-

end feel that the Venezuelan needs and which hampers rising talent Valtteri Bottas. Symonds arrived to contemplate a situation in which the team had scored just one point, for Pastor's 10th place in Hungary.

Symonds, 60, is an old-school engineer from the days when teams raced with a handful of people. Back then you did it all, which makes men of such experience highly valuable when integrating an effective structure into teams that now employ many hundreds of people. Bigger is not necessarily better, unless teams are well defined and well organised.

Williams has to hope that 2013 is a one-off. With hugely different powertrains and technical regulations due in 2014, Symonds said: "Fundamentally, the focus has

to be on 2014. It's the most difficult programme we've had to tackle for a long time. We've obviously started work on the FW36, but my influence will be more on process than detail, so I hope that pays off and leads to the sort of structure that builds ongoing success."

If the glory days of Williams seem to be a receding memory, Maldonado's win a year ago proved that a return to the sharp end isn't just a pipe dream and, with a Mercedes powertrain agreed for 2014 and a talented young driver like Bottas, whose capabilities have been masked by the FW35, Canada notwithstanding, there are some roses in the garden. Symonds is out to return the team to a position where it can add to its nine constructors' and nine drivers' world titles.

hand side and focused on getting a clean exit out of La Source and then a good run through Eau Rouge.

"I think, with the gearing that we ran, if he hadn't made the pass at that point it would have been very difficult for him to overtake Lewis, so he used his KERS where he needed to, timed it just right and grabbed his one opportunity. As soon as he'd made his pass around the outside, he then just got his head down and got on with it."

Within a few laps, Vettel had built a 4.0s margin, and it was soon clear that the race was his to lose. In the end, everything unfolded perfectly for him and he won at what appeared to be a canter.

"He had tremendous pace in the early laps," said Horner, "and of course what we don't know with the modern way of racing in F1 is how severe the degradation is going to be. You can burn up your tyres quickly and then see heavy degradation in later laps.

"It was a matter then of making sure that he built up a gap, but also made sure that he had the range with the tyres as well. So it's that fine balance between how hard you push and how much you protect your tyres to get the range. I think we just about managed to get the balance right with that."

Vettel put in a dominant performance, stopping on laps 14 and 30 before finishing 16s ahead of Alonso after 44 laps. He acknowledged that passing Hamilton on the first lap was crucial.

"It worked very well, what I was trying to, let's say, plan at the exit of Turn 2," said the German. "After that, I just tried to settle into the rhythm. I tried to open a gap to be flexible at the first pit stop and I had incredible pace until the end. We didn't expect that. We knew going in that, in the dry, that we should probably be able to beat Mercedes on the track, but we knew other cars – Lotus, Ferrari – had looked very competitive in the dry, so in that regard we had massive pace and could control the race until the end."

Despite extending his lead, Vettel insisted he wasn't yet thinking about the championship. "I'm honestly more happy to win the race today," he said. "Spa is a fantastic track and, especially when the car works well, you really don't want the race to stop. The car was getting lighter and lighter and I was very comfortable at the end on the prime tyres. The car was just a pleasure to drive."

From ninth on the grid, Alonso had enjoyed a great first lap and quickly moved up to fifth place. He then passed Button and Rosberg to move into third. Then, immediately after the first round of pit stops, he overtook Hamilton at La Source to claim second.

OPPOSITE Sergio Perez (left) was adjudged to have been too hard on Romain Grosjean and was hit with a drive-through penalty

ABOVE Pastor Maldonado and Adrian Sutil drive on after the Venezuelan had hit Paul di Resta

BELOW After the clash, Maldonado pitted for a new nose for his Williams, but then lost more ground when hit with a stop-go penalty

Although he was able to edge clear of the Mercedes, he could do nothing about Vettel's Red Bull. So while the Spaniard lost more ground in the title race, he was pleased to secure 18 points after recent disappointments. "The weekend was more or less good for us as we recovered some feelings that we lost in July with the car," he said. "We felt a little bit more competitive here this weekend. Not maybe for pole, but to be in the first four or five positions on the grid, maybe that was possible, but I think we were extremely unlucky with the situation in Q3: we were in the wrong place at the wrong time. I remember Q3 at the Malaysian GP when we were in the right place at the right time, and we were second and third on the grid. Yesterday was the opposite. So we had to plan a perfect race from the start to the pace of the car, to the strategy and everything worked fine, and we could recover some places which is extremely important for the championship after three races that weren't so good."

Hamilton lacked speed on the straights and through Eau Rouge, but he still managed to hang on to third place, keeping his fading championship hopes alive. "They were both too fast for us today," he said. "It's the best we could have done. Yesterday, the weather helped us to get up to where we were. In the final analysis, we just need to work a little bit harder."

In the last part of the race, Hamilton was chased by team-mate Rosberg who had passed Webber at the start to take third, but lost out to Alonso on lap 6. Webber had had clutch issues and tumbled down to sixth at the start and, lacking straightline speed with which to overtake – he was set-up to run in clear air – he gained just a single place to finish fifth.

Button had a good first lap and got past Webber and di Resta. He was aiming for a one-stop run, but lap 17 proved to be too early. After running third in the middle of the race, he eventually had to make a second stop and eventually finished sixth.

Massa lost places avoiding Grosjean on the opening lap and also had problems with his steering wheel electronics. He recovered to finish seventh while, after losing a couple of positions at the start, Grosjean ran a rare one-stop strategy on the way to eighth.

Both Force India drivers made poor starts, with di Resta dropping to seventh and Adrian Sutil to 13th. The pair spent much of the race in close company and were involved in an incident at the chicane on lap 27 when Pastor Maldonado struck Sutil and then di Resta, putting the latter out of the race. Sutil continued to finish ninth, while Maldonado pitted for a new nose and later received a 10s stop-go penalty before finishing 17th.

After a disastrous time in qualifying, Daniel Ricciardo ran a long opening stint on the harder tyre, and in the closing laps was able to move ahead of Sergio Perez to claim tenth. The Mexican had a busy race that earned him a drive-through penalty after an incident with Grosjean. He finished just outside the points in 11th.

Finally, it was a bad day for Räikkönen, who suffered front brake overheating problems, apparently after a visor tear-off strip became lodged in the brake duct. The Finn retired his Lotus after 25 laps while running eighth, ending his record streak of finishes in the points.

BELOW Max Chilton's Marussia kicks up sparks as it powers through Eau Rouge en route to 19th place

BOTTOM Jean-Eric Vergne finished 12th, two places and 13s behind Toro Rosso team-mate Daniel Ricciardo

SNAPSHOT FROM
BELGIUM

CLOCKWISE FROM RIGHT

The upper stretch of Eau Rouge feeds directly into Raidillon; Ferrari's Fernando Alonso enjoys the drivers parade; Lotus F1 Team's main men, Gerard Lopez and Eric Boullier; the cars of Jenson Button, Mark Webber and Nico Rosberg in parc ferme after qualifying; second-placed Alonso congratulates Sebastian Vettel on another Red Bull victory; Valtteri Bottas listens to the years of experience brought by new Williams technical chief Pat Symonds; Vettel has every reason to smile as he once again leaves his main rivals trailing behind; Pirelli tyres for every occasion; McLaren's Sergio Perez prepares to go out during qualifying, but he fails to reach Q3

BELGIUM
SPA-FRANCORCHAMPS
ROUND 11

Official Results © [2013]
Formula One World Championship Limited,
6 Princes Gate, London, SW7 1QJ.
No reproduction without permission.
All copyright and database rights reserved.

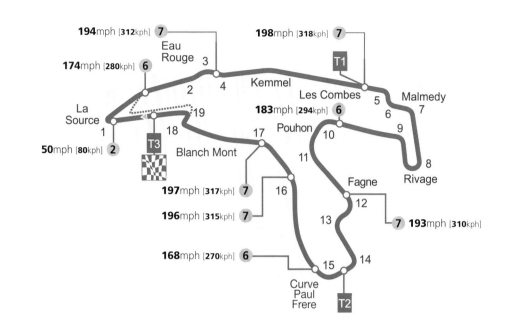

RACE RESULTS

RACE DATE 25 August 2013
CIRCUIT LENGTH 4.352 miles
NO. OF LAPS 44
RACE DISTANCE 191.488 miles
WEATHER Overcast but dry, 20°C
TRACK TEMP 26°C
LAP RECORD Sebastian Vettel,
1m47.263s, 146.065mph, 2009

	PRACTICE 1				PRACTICE 2				PRACTICE 3				QUALIFYING 1			QUALIFYING 2	
	Driver	Time	Laps		Driver	Time	Laps		Driver	Time	Laps		Driver	Time		Driver	Time
1	F Alonso	1m55.198s	11	1	S Vettel	1m49.331s	22	1	S Vettel	1m48.327s	16	1	F Alonso	2m00.190s	1	K Räikkönen	1m48.296s
2	P di Resta	1m55.224s	10	2	M Webber	1m49.390s	34	2	F Alonso	1m48.432s	14	2	L Hamilton	2m00.368s	2	F Alonso	1m48.309s
3	A Sutil	1m55.373s	11	3	R Grosjean	1m50.149s	34	3	M Webber	1m48.533s	16	3	G van der Garde	2m00.564s	3	N Rosberg	1m48.552s
4	S Perez	1m55.518s	14	4	F Massa	1m50.164s	27	4	J-E Vergne	1m48.776s	15	4	N Rosberg	2m01.099s	4	M Webber	1m48.641s
5	N Rosberg	1m55.614s	10	5	J-E Vergne	1m50.253s	28	5	F Massa	1m48.788s	15	5	K Räikkönen	2m01.151s	5	J Button	1m48.641s
6	S Vettel	1m55.636s	14	6	K Räikkönen	1m50.318s	33	6	J Button	1m48.882s	13	6	J Button	2m01.301s	6	S Vettel	1m48.646s
7	E Gutierrez	1m55.934s	18	7	F Alonso	1m50.510s	21	7	E Gutierrez	1m48.930s	18	7	F Massa	2m01.462s	7	R Grosjean	1m48.649s
8	N Hulkenberg	1m56.110s	11	8	S Perez	1m50.536s	27	8	R Grosjean	1m48.967s	14	8	M Webber	2m01.597s	8	P di Resta	1m48.925s
9	D Ricciardo	1m56.770s	14	9	N Rosberg	1m50.601s	33	9	N Rosberg	1m48.993s	16	9	N Hulkenberg	2m01.712s	9	F Massa	1m49.020s
10	V Bottas	1m56.858s	18	10	P di Resta	1m50.611s	27	10	K Räikkönen	1m49.008s	17	10	S Vettel	2m01.863s	10	L Hamilton	1m49.067s
11	F Massa	1m56.863s	10	11	A Sutil	1m50.629s	30	11	D Ricciardo	1m49.035s	15	11	J Bianchi	2m02.110s	11	N Hulkenberg	1m49.088s
12	P Maldonado	1m57.081s	14	12	L Hamilton	1m50.751s	27	12	L Hamilton	1m49.046s	17	12	P di Resta	2m02.338s	12	A Sutil	1m49.103s
13	J-E Vergne	1m57.084s	17	13	N Hulkenberg	1m50.972s	33	13	A Sutil	1m49.122s	15	13	S Perez	2m02.425s	13	S Perez	1m49.304s
14	J Button	1m57.281s	14	14	P Maldonado	1m50.991s	28	14	V Bottas	1m49.177s	15	14	R Grosjean	2m02.476s	14	G van der Garde	1m52.036s
15	L Hamilton	1m57.358s	10	15	J Button	1m51.195s	28	15	P di Resta	1m49.226s	14	15	A Sutil	2m02.749s	15	J Bianchi	1m52.563s
16	H Kovalainen	1m57.821s	16	16	D Ricciardo	1m51.447s	26	16	S Perez	1m49.417s	14	16	M Chilton	2m02.948s	16	M Chilton	1m52.762s
17	G van der Garde	1m57.887s	16	17	V Bottas	1m51.568s	28	17	N Hulkenberg	1m49.478s	19	17	P Maldonado	2m03.072s			
18	M Chilton	1m58.600s	14	18	E Gutierrez	1m51.644s	26	18	P Maldonado	1m50.418s	14	18	J-E Vergne	2m03.300s			
19	M Webber	1m58.929s	12	19	G van der Garde	1m53.157s	21	19	C Pic	1m51.416s	15	19	D Ricciardo	2m03.317s			
20	J Button	1m59.209s	12	20	C Pic	1m53.251s	29	20	G van der Garde	1m51.800s	18	20	V Bottas	2m03.432s			
21	K Räikkönen	1m59.441s	11	21	J Bianchi	1m53.482s	28	21	J Bianchi	1m52.221s	17	21	E Gutierrez	2m04.324s			
22	R Grosjean	2m03.176s	15	22	M Chilton	1m54.418s	12	22	M Chilton	1m53.507s	18	22	C Pic	2m07.384s			

Best sectors – Practice			Speed trap – Practice			Best sectors – Qualifying			Speed trap – Qualifying		
Sec 1	J Button	31.555s	1	S Vettel	189.953mph	Sec 1	A Sutil	31.743s	1	M Webber	188.089mph
Sec 2	M Webber	47.048s	2	M Webber	188.462mph	Sec 2	K Räikkönen	46.661s	2	P di Resta	188.089mph
Sec 3	F Alonso	29.500s	3	P di Resta	188.213mph	Sec 3	P di Resta	29.314s	3	S Vettel	186.100mph

 Sebastian Vettel
"It wasn't clear if the rain was going to come at the end, so I kept pushing, but the gap I had by that stage meant we were able to control the race from there."

Fernando Alonso
"The result shows that qualifying bears little relation to the race result, although I think even if I'd started from pole I would still have finished in second place."

Jenson Button
"I was trying for a one-stopper, then adapted that to a two-stopper. We gave it a go, but our pace still wasn't quite as good as that of the cars in front of us."

Kimi Räikkönen
"I had brake failure so there was no point in continuing. There was not enough space into the first corner where I went over the kerb, but after that I pushed on."

 **Nico Rosberg**
"Fourth was okay. I had a great start but couldn't go as long as planned on the second stint and had to cover Felipe. In the end, it was nice to keep Mark back."

Nico Hulkenberg
"I was able to improve a couple of positions at the start. I had a good first lap, but the pace was missing from the beginning and the car was difficult to drive."

 Mark Webber
"I lost a couple of rows off the line, then had to clear people on track, which was difficult, as we had set up the top gear to race in clean air, rather than to pass."

Felipe Massa
"After making a good move at the start, I lost five places as I avoided a collision with Grosjean. Things got complicated owing to a KERS problem for a few laps."

Sergio Perez
"I made up a couple of places at the start, then a few more in the first 10 laps. Then came the drive-through. After that it was always going to be tricky to score."

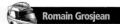 **Romain Grosjean**
"I had a difficult first lap, then lost a few more places in the incident with Sergio. We opted for a one-stopper. And if it had rained, we'd have been well-placed."

 **Lewis Hamilton**
"I wasn't as quick as Sebastian and Fernando. I made a nice start and it felt like the exit of Turn 1 was good, but Seb just caught me on the run out of Eau Rouge."

 **Esteban Gutierrez**
"From where I started I had to be clever about how much to push. I respect the FIA's decision to penalise me for passing Pastor, but don't agree with the penalty."

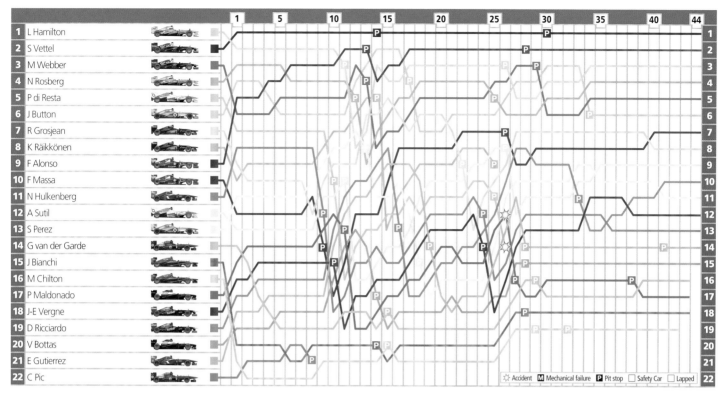

			1	5	10	15	20	25	30	35	40	44	
1	L Hamilton												1
2	S Vettel												2
3	M Webber												3
4	N Rosberg												4
5	P di Resta												5
6	J Button												6
7	R Grosjean												7
8	K Räikkönen												8
9	F Alonso												9
10	F Massa												10
11	N Hulkenberg												11
12	A Sutil												12
13	S Perez												13
14	G van der Garde												14
15	J Bianchi												15
16	M Chilton												16
17	P Maldonado												17
18	J-E Vergne												18
19	D Ricciardo												19
20	V Bottas												20
21	E Gutierrez												21
22	C Pic												22

☼ Accident M Mechanical failure P Pit stop ☐ Safety Car ☐ Lapped

QUALIFYING 3

	Driver	Time
1	L Hamilton	2m01.012s
2	S Vettel	2m01.200s
3	M Webber	2m01.325s
4	N Rosberg	2m02.251s
5	P di Resta	2m02.332s
6	J Button	2m03.075s
7	R Grosjean	2m03.081s
8	K Räikkönen	2m03.390s
9	F Alonso	2m03.482s
10	F Massa	2m04.059s

GRID

	Driver	Time
1	L Hamilton	2m01.012s
2	S Vettel	2m01.200s
3	M Webber	2m01.325s
4	N Rosberg	2m02.251s
5	P di Resta	2m02.332s
6	J Button	2m03.075s
7	R Grosjean	2m03.081s
8	K Räikkönen	2m03.390s
9	F Alonso	2m03.482s
10	F Massa	2m04.059s
11	N Hulkenberg	1m49.088s
12	A Sutil	1m49.103s
13	S Perez	1m49.304s
14	G van der Garde	1m52.036s
15	J Bianchi	1m52.563s
16	M Chilton	1m52.762s
17	P Maldonado	2m03.072s
18	J-E Vergne	2m03.300s
19	D Ricciardo	2m03.317s
20	V Bottas	2m03.432s
21	E Gutierrez	2m04.324s
22	C Pic	2m07.384s

RACE

	Driver	Car	Laps	Time	Avg. mph	Fastest	Stops
1	S Vettel	Red Bull-Renault RB9	44	1h23m42.196s	137.209	1m50.756s	2
2	F Alonso	Ferrari F138	44	1h23m59.065s	136.749	1m51.383s	2
3	L Hamilton	Mercedes F1 W04	44	1h24m09.930s	136.455	1m51.596s	2
4	N Rosberg	Mercedes F1 W04	44	1h24m12.068s	136.398	1m51.582s	2
5	M Webber	Red Bull-Renault RB9	44	1h24m16.041s	136.291	1m51.397s	2
6	J Button	McLaren-Mercedes MP4-298	44	1h24m22.990s	136.103	1m50.823s	2
7	F Massa	Ferrari F138	44	1h24m36.118s	135.751	1m52.182s	2
8	R Grosjean	Lotus-Renault E21	44	1h24m38.042s	135.700	1m52.497s	1
9	A Sutil	Force India-Mercedes VJM06	44	1h24m51.743s	135.335	1m52.226s	2
10	D Ricciardo	Toro Rosso-Ferrari STR8	44	1h24m55.666s	135.231	1m50.967s	2
11	S Perez	McLaren-Mercedes MP4-28	44	1h25m04.132s	135.006	1m53.472s	1
12	J-E Vergne	Toro Rosso-Ferrari STR8	44	1h25m08.936s	134.880	1m53.065s	2
13	N Hulkenberg	Sauber-Ferrari C32	44	1h25m10.454s	134.839	1m53.110s	2
14	E Gutierrez	Sauber-Ferrari C32	44	1h25m22.632s	134.519	1m51.849s	2
15	V Bottas	Williams-Renault FW35	44	1h25m29.652s	134.335	1m52.688s	2
16	G van der Garde	Caterham-Renault CT03	43	1h24m21.583s	133.046	1m53.995s	2
17	P Maldonado	Williams-Renault FW35	43	1h24m23.736s	132.989	1m52.579s	2
18	J Bianchi	Marussia-Cosworth MR-02	43	1h25m13.451s	131.696	1m54.894s	2
19	M Chilton	Marussia-Cosworth MR-02	42	1h23m50.036s	130.765	1m54.924s	2
R	P di Resta	Force India-Mercedes VJM06	26	Collision	-	1m54.757s	2
R	K Räikkönen	Lotus-Renault E21	25	Brakes	-	1m53.688s	1
R	C Pic	Caterham-Renault CT03	8	Oil leak	-	1m57.330s	0

CHAMPIONSHIP

	Driver	Pts
1	S Vettel	197
2	F Alonso	151
3	L Hamilton	139
4	K Räikkönen	134
5	M Webber	115
6	N Rosberg	96
7	F Massa	67
8	R Grosjean	53
9	J Button	47
10	P di Resta	36
11	A Sutil	25
12	S Perez	18
13	J-E Vergne	13
14	D Ricciardo	12
15	N Hulkenberg	7
16	P Maldonado	1

Grid penalties
None

Fastest lap	Fastest speed trap		Fastest pit stop	
S Vettel 1m50.756s	F Massa	190.885mph	1 F Alonso	22.444s
(141.466mph) on lap 40	Slowest speed trap		2 J Button	22.465s
	C Pic	181.689mph	3 S Perez	22.597s

	Constructor	Pts
1	Red Bull-Renault	312
2	Mercedes	235
3	Ferrari	218
4	Lotus-Renault	187
5	McLaren-Mercedes	65
6	Force India-Mercedes	61
7	Toro Rosso-Ferrari	25
8	Sauber-Ferrari	7
9	Williams-Renault	1

Paul di Resta

"There were four cars battling into the final chicane. Pastor missed the apex so I tried to get the cut-back but he decided to try and enter the pits and hit me."

Pastor Maldonado

"I gained a few places, but struggled for pace in the second stint, then collided with di Resta in the final corner when our lines crossed as I entered the pits."

Jean-Eric Vergne

"My pace was good until the last stint when I had a slow puncture. I managed to pass Hulkenberg, but couldn't catch Perez. Then Daniel, on new tyres, caught me."

Charles Pic

"I started on Options and passed Chilton and Bianchi. By lap 8, I was catching Giedo but then was told to pit as I had an oil leak, so stopped to avoid any damage."

Jules Bianchi

"It was a tough race, made more difficult by the fact that I had a radio problem from the start. Our pace wasn't as good as we had hoped for, which was a shame."

Adrian Sutil

"I lost a few places at the start, but settled into the race and was able to move into the top 10. I enjoy driving at Spa and had some exciting passing moves."

Valtteri Bottas

"We were struggling for pace in sector two and so built a good base to get close to cars in front and once I had been overtaken it was very difficult to regain the place."

Daniel Ricciardo

"I ran a long first stint on the Hards and so built a good base to have a strong pace in the final stints on the Option, and that's when my race really started."

Giedo van der Garde

"My start was good and I held 14th place until midway through lap 2, but then it wasn't possible to hold off some of the cars who had started behind us."

Max Chilton

"It felt like a long race as the dry conditions made it uneventful. The threat of rain meant we'd prepared for anything, so could capitalise on any opportunity."

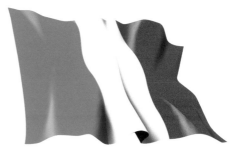

FORMULA 1 GRAN PREMIO D'ITALIA 2013

6-8 SEPTEMBER
AUTODROMO DI MONZA
MONZA

VETTEL WINS, RIVALS FLAG

Sebastian Vettel continued his relentless march towards a fourth consecutive title by dominating the Italian GP weekend. With Fernando Alonso now 53 points adrift, even his rivals were on the verge of conceding defeat

Monza wasn't supposed to be the best venue for a car that has traditionally lacked straight-line speed relative to the others, and yet Vettel was quick all weekend. He even overcame the handicap of flatspotting a front tyre at the first chicane and, after warnings from the team, protected a potentially fragile gearbox in the latter stages.

Usually, Vettel makes a point of logging the race's fastest lap, but this time he was only 12th on the list, showing just how much he had in hand late in the race when the car was lighter.

Vettel may have got the job done, but it wasn't the first time he had been given a less than rapturous applause on the podium. "I think anybody beating a Ferrari, in Italy, is never going to be cheered," said Red Bull Racing Team Principal Christian Horner. "It was inevitable that there wasn't going to be a big reaction for Sebastian beating Fernando Alonso in front of the *tifosi* who have come to cheer their car and team. I don't think the reaction surprised any of us. If anything, it fuels Sebastian's determination just to go out there and continue to improve."

Vettel dominated practice and qualifying, topping all three sessions to secure the 40th pole of his

career, and the 50th for Red Bull Racing. His main competition came from team-mate Mark Webber, who was second, just 0.2s slower.

But there were some big surprises in the second qualifying session as two championship contenders failed to make it through. After looking good in practice, Kimi Räikkönen couldn't do better than 11th for Lotus, while his team-mate, Romain Grosjean, was 13th. They were split by Lewis Hamilton after a disastrous session for the Mercedes driver in which he damaged his floor on a trip across the kerbs.

So, third in qualifying was a major surprise as it went to the Sauber of Nico Hulkenberg, as the

German driver and the Swiss team got everything right on the day. Felipe Massa bagged fourth spot for Ferrari, ahead of his team-mate Alonso.

Nico Rosberg ended up sixth on the grid after a scrappy day for the Mercedes driver saw him do very little running in the morning. Toro Rosso had looked good throughout qualifying, and Daniel Ricciardo ended up seventh fastest. McLaren got both cars into Q3, Sergio Perez ending up eighth, one ahead of Jenson Button. Having run wide at Parabolica on his hot lap, Jean-Eric Vergne took tenth.

Between qualifying and the race, Red Bull Racing changed the fifth, sixth and seventh gear ratios in both its cars, under FIA supervision, owing to reliability issues. That did at least give rivals some hope that the RB9s might have a weakness.

"We had a bit of damage to a couple of dog rings on both cars," said Horner after the race. "After applying to the FIA when the dog rings were damaged, we were allowed to replace them in parc ferme. We weren't sure why the damage had happened because we hadn't seen that before, and it's never happened on the Caterham gearbox that we supply. So, of course, when that's hanging over you, you get concerned."

At the start, Vettel got to the first corner safely in front, only to lock up his right front wheel into the chicane in a cloud of smoke. That left him with a flatspotted tyre, which created a vibration throughout the first stint.

In the middle of the pack, Räikkönen hit the back of Perez's McLaren, breaking his Lotus's front wing and forcing himself to make an immediate pit stop.

Then, at the second chicane, Paul di Resta ran hard into Grosjean. That put the Force India driver out of the race on the spot, but Grosjean was at least able to continue.

Massa enjoyed better luck and jumped up to

INSIDE LINE
FERNANDO ALONSO
FERRARI DRIVER

"Being on the podium here at Monza again is a fantastic feeling. It's the fourth year that I've driven for Ferrari here and four times I've been on the podium. Every time it's something amazing, the most spectacular podium of the year for sure, and hopefully next year we can come back in the top place.

"I think we did the maximum and had nearly a perfect weekend. It was difficult obviously, but the car was okay and I overtook Nico Hülkenberg then Mark Webber and Felipe Massa later on. With Sebastian, we weren't able to close the gap, so I was fighting with Mark until the end of the race, and second place was good.

"The overtaking move with Mark was very close. Obviously, we had to take the risk to get past, but we are second in the championship and there is nothing to lose for us now. I tried to pass him the lap before but wasn't close enough in Turn 4, the second chicane, but we were very close out of the first chicane on the next lap. Mark had a slightly slower exit, so I used all of my KERS on that straight hoping that, with the slipstream as well, it would be enough to pass. But

it wasn't and so we arrived at Turn 4 side-by-side.

"At one point I thought, 'Well, I'll miss the second chicane and give the place back,' but at the last moment I found the grip that I needed. We were very close to contact but, again, we come back to the point that it's certainly not the same fighting with an experienced and respectful driver like Mark compared to some others with whom you'd never try that move.

"I think we took the maximum from the car this weekend. Practice was alright and we learned some good information on Friday. Saturday was very good too, with both cars qualifying in the top five. The last time that happened was in the second race of the year, in Malaysia, so we were very, very happy.

"I always say the same thing – a big thanks to the team for everything and the huge support from the fans from all over Italy. Concerning qualifying, it's the third or fourth consecutive race that some people have tried to create tension between the team and drivers. We explain everything, but obviously this doesn't sell so many newspapers – that's normal.

"Every time I leave an airport, at the hotel, everywhere – there's huge support. We saw that today on the podium too. Maybe not many of them read the newspapers in the morning, luckily..."

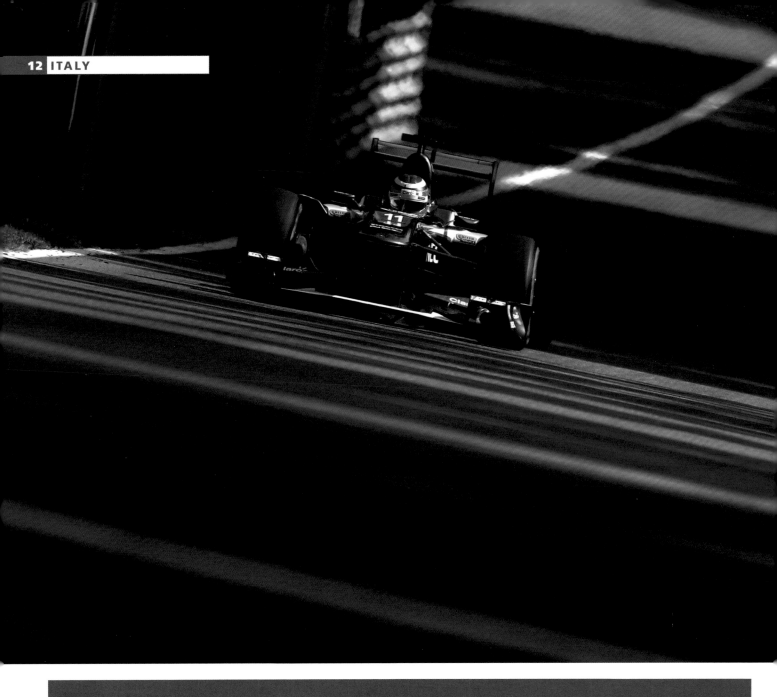

TALKING POINT
TENSION AT FERRARI

Ferrari has never been good at taking criticism from its drivers, and it hadn't been the best few months for Fernando Alonso. It had been two months since he'd won at home in Spain and he was left contemplating a fourth place at the Nürburgring and then a fifth at the Hungaroring.

There was frustration after Hungary, in particular, when the Ferrari hadn't worked in a high-downforce configuration and Alonso could see Mercedes coming increasingly into the frame. His comment that he needed a 'different car' had been milked by the Italian media and, in response, Luca di Montezemolo had admonished him.

Fuelling stories of a breakdown in the relationship was the news that Fernando's manager had been sounding out Christian Horner, and that Kimi Räikkönen, overlooked by Red Bull in favour of Daniel Ricciardo for 2014, was set to return to Ferrari. That much was confirmed in the aftermath of the Italian GP.

There was more controversy post-qualifying at Monza. Despite practice runs, the plan for Massa to tow Alonso onto the front row went awry as the Ferraris qualified fourth and fifth, Felipe finishing the quicker by 0.01s. The fastest Ferrari-engined car on the grid was Nico Hulkenberg's Sauber, which also embarrassed Ferrari – at Monza of all places.

Over the radio, Alonso said what sounded like 'scemi' (idiots) – but might have been 'geni' (geniuses) – in reaction to a badly timed release from the pits which caused Webber's Red Bull to get between them. Fernando's observation was either harshly critical or sarcastic.

Alonso played it down at his post-qualifying media sessions and after the race (see Inside Line, p189) but the damage had been done. With di Montezemolo in the Ferrari pit on Saturday, the double champion's timing was as badly out as Hulkenberg's was perfect.

The incident and the Räikkönen return sparked suggestions that the love affair between Ferrari and Alonso was over. Parallels were drawn with Alain Prost's criticism of car and team in 1991, which led to his dismissal, even if the political landscape was more complex then. With the other top seats taken, Prost ended up on a sabbatical in 1992.

In Italy, there were stories that Alonso's rumoured purchase of a professional cycling team may even lead to him taking a voluntary sabbatical too, particularly if he isn't convinced by Ferrari's progress relative to the major rule changes for 2014. "That's not an option," Alonso said at Monza, adding that he reckoned he had five years left in F1. But if he sees that future at Ferrari, perhaps he needs to be careful...

"In the end, we finished the race so it wasn't a disaster," said Vettel. "I think the heartbeat was a bit higher in the car and also on the pit wall, because we didn't know what was going on. Fortunately, we didn't have any big issues until the last 10 or 15 laps when I tried to pace myself a bit more and control the gaps. Obviously it was good to have 10s in hand, so I didn't have to push that much and also I didn't have to squeeze it all out of the tyres, even though I stopped a couple of laps earlier than Fernando.

"I don't know what they saw on the pit wall in terms of data, whether the problem got worse and worse or stabilised, but obviously I tried to save the car, engine and gearbox as much as I could. In the end, I still had to go full power on the straights but basically try to short shift and save the car a little bit."

There were still seven races to go after Monza, and therefore a theoretical 175 points to be picked up, but what made Vettel's day was the fact that none of his main opponents were able to maintain a consistent challenge. The *tifosi* didn't like this and even booed him when he reached the podium.

That said, Alonso seemed happy enough with his charge to second place on Ferrari's home ground, although he was well aware that his drivers' title hopes were slipping away once again. "We took the maximum from the car this weekend," the Spaniard said. "Practice was all right then, on Saturday, we qualified both cars in the top five for the first time in a very, very long time. Today, being on the podium again, it's a fantastic feeling here in Monza. Every year is something amazing, something unique, to be there in that moment."

Webber got ahead of Massa during the pit stops to claim third place. Despite his own gearbox worries and damaged wing, he was able to stay in Alonso's wheeltracks for the duration and so claim the final podium spot.

LEFT Nico Hulkenberg qualified his Sauber third, then impressed by racing to fifth place after being passed by the Ferrari pair

BELOW Mark Webber's Red Bull kicks up the dust on his way to third place, just behind Fernando Alonso

second place behind Vettel and ahead of Webber, Alonso and Hulkenberg. On lap 3, Alonso squeezed past Webber at the second chicane to claim third place, leaving the Australian with a broken front wing endplate. Five laps later, Massa offered no resistance as Alonso moved past him into second.

At that point, Vettel was already more than 4s clear, and the gap grew to as much as 6.6s on lap 18 before dropping back down to 5.3s. It appeared that Alonso was still in the game as he piled the pressure on Vettel.

Vettel came in for his sole pit stop a little earlier than planned on lap 23. Yet, rather than respond, Alonso stayed out for four further laps. Ferrari wanted to shorten his second and final stint and so give him extra tyre life for the end of the race but, by the time he emerged from his stop on lap 27, the gap had grown to more than 10s.

A gearbox oil pressure issue on Webber's car caused Red Bull Racing to tell both drivers to short shift to protect their equipment, but the advantage Vettel had over Alonso allowed him to stay safely clear of the Spaniard's Ferrari, and his advantage was still more than 5s at the chequered flag.

ABOVE Red Bull Racing celebrates as Vettel completes a drive that left the *tifosi* in a frustrated mood

BELOW Sergio Perez survived being hit by Kimi Räikkönen's Lotus on the opening lap; he also battled for much of the race with his McLaren team-mate, Jenson Button

"I wasn't super happy on the hard tyre," said the Australian, "but anyway that's the way it was. Fernando was into his rhythm a bit quicker. We had a good little battle in the second chicane and after that I just tried to manage the pace of the rear tyres to when we were going to stop, to try to pass Felipe.

"We executed that as a team effort: driver, pit crew and got the job done against Felipe. Then, actually, it was a good battle with Fernando on the other tyre. We had to nurse the gearbox a bit, but in the end, second was the maximum we could have done. I finished third but pushed Fernando all the way. It's always a good battle racing Fernando, as

you have to be very accurate. We pushed as hard as we could, and I'm satisfied with today's result."

Massa finished a solid fourth to claim his best result since his third in the Spanish Grand Prix. Hulkenberg dropped from third to fifth on the opening lap, but thereafter did a good job to retain the position all the way to the flag despite intense pressure from the Mercedes of fellow-countryman Rosberg. Ricciardo finished where he started, in seventh place, while Grosjean advanced to eighth.

Hamilton started on the hard tyre, but was hampered by a radio failure. He had the fastest car on the track for much of the race, and set fastest lap, but a slow puncture led to an early pit visit, which forced him to switch to a two-stop strategy. A late charge helped him climb to ninth place, and he finished ahead of his former team-mate Button.

The McLarens had run together for a while, but a slow pit stop for Perez led to them swapping positions and the pair spent much of the race sitting behind Ricciardo, who was faster on the straights. In the closing stages, Hamilton passed them both.

Räikkönen, like Hamilton, set a string of fastest laps, but his first-lap pit stop for a new nose after he hit Perez's tail at the first chicane left him fighting to recover. The Finn could only manage 11th place, 1s ahead of the Mexican, and with Esteban Gutierrez another 1s back in the second Sauber. It was Räikkönen's second non-score in a row and, in effect, signalled the end of his 2013 title hopes.

However, Räikkönen was still the man in the news as the weekend came to a close, and it became increasingly clear in the days after the race that he would be returning to Ferrari in 2014, four years after he had been paid to relinquish his drive and so make way for Alonso's arrival. This meant that Massa was finally on his way out of Ferrari. Räikkönen and Alonso in the same team? That'll be interesting...

SNAPSHOT FROM
ITALY

CLOCKWISE FROM RIGHT

Lewis Hamilton takes a history lesson with a walk on the old banked section of the circuit; Kimi Räikkönen seemed in a happy mood, but not after qualifying; a Lotus heads out into the light to practice; 50th anniversary headgear as modelled by McLaren's mechanics; Ferrari's 1964 champion, John Surtees, advises Fernando Alonso how to survive and thrive at Maranello; the *tifosi* have eyes only for the red cars; Mark Webber's straight and candid views are always worth hearing; Pastor Maldonado brings his Williams to a halt on the grid; McLaren put on a special celebration to mark the 50 years since Bruce McLaren formed the team; is Sergio Perez asking Christian Horner about a drive for Red Bull?

ITALY
MONZA
ROUND 12

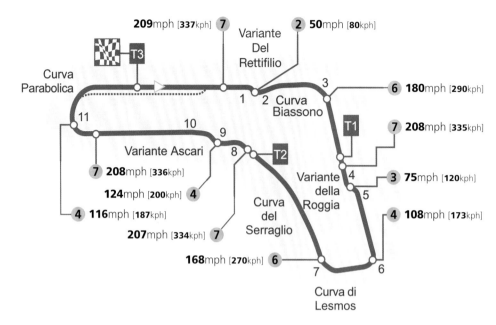

209mph [**337**kph] 7 — Variante Del Rettifilio — 2 **50**mph [**80**kph]

6 **180**mph [**290**kph]

7 **208**mph [**335**kph]

Curva Parabolica

Curva Biassono

T3

T1

T2

3 **75**mph [**120**kph]

4 **108**mph [**173**kph]

Variante Ascari

7 **208**mph [**336**kph]

124mph [**200**kph] 4

116mph [**187**kph] 4

Variante della Roggia

Curva del Serraglio

207mph [**334**kph] 7

168mph [**270**kph] 6

Curva di Lesmos

RACE RESULTS

RACE DATE 8 September 2013
CIRCUIT LENGTH 3.600 miles
NO. OF LAPS 53
RACE DISTANCE 190.800 miles
WEATHER Light rain before start, 26°C
TRACK TEMP 31°C
LAP RECORD Rubens Barrichello,
1m21.046s, 159.909mph, 2004

PRACTICE 1

	Driver	Time	Laps
1	L Hamilton	1m25.565s	24
2	F Alonso	1m25.600s	25
3	N Rosberg	1m25.704s	25
4	S Vettel	1m25.753s	26
5	K Räikkönen	1m25.941s	22
6	S Perez	1m26.007s	24
7	J Button	1m26.035s	23
8	M Webber	1m26.103s	27
9	P Maldonado	1m26.149s	21
10	J-E Vergne	1m26.155s	25
11	E Gutierrez	1m26.194s	25
12	R Grosjean	1m26.295s	23
13	D Ricciardo	1m26.387s	21
14	F Massa	1m26.449s	16
15	P di Resta	1m26.594s	13
16	V Bottas	1m26.802s	21
17	J Calado	1m27.041s	24
18	N Hulkenberg	1m27.224s	16
19	C Pic	1m27.818s	24
20	M Chilton	1m27.869s	20
21	H Kovalainen	1m28.192s	21
22	R Gonzalez	1m29.526s	26

PRACTICE 2

	Driver	Time	Laps
1	S Vettel	1m24.453s	39
2	M Webber	1m25.076s	39
3	K Räikkönen	1m25.116s	36
4	R Grosjean	1m25.116s	40
5	F Alonso	1m25.330s	38
6	L Hamilton	1m25.340s	39
7	N Rosberg	1m25.367s	42
8	F Massa	1m25.519s	29
9	J Button	1m25.532s	42
10	S Perez	1m25.627s	39
11	P di Resta	1m25.830s	40
12	E Gutierrez	1m25.888s	40
13	A Sutil	1m26.028s	37
14	P Maldonado	1m26.138s	36
15	J-E Vergne	1m26.224s	32
16	N Hulkenberg	1m26.385s	43
17	D Ricciardo	1m26.599s	39
18	V Bottas	1m27.198s	44
19	M Chilton	1m27.548s	30
20	C Pic	1m27.696s	37
21	G van der Garde	1m27.771s	38
22	J Bianchi	1m28.057s	32

PRACTICE 3

	Driver	Time	Laps
1	S Vettel	1m24.360s	18
2	F Alonso	1m24.643s	13
3	M Webber	1m24.677s	22
4	L Hamilton	1m24.712s	17
5	S Perez	1m24.864s	19
6	D Ricciardo	1m24.865s	19
7	F Massa	1m24.995s	14
8	J Button	1m25.103s	15
9	P Maldonado	1m25.116s	20
10	K Räikkönen	1m25.120s	18
11	J-E Vergne	1m25.136s	16
12	N Hulkenberg	1m25.273s	21
13	E Gutierrez	1m25.324s	22
14	R Grosjean	1m25.499s	17
15	V Bottas	1m25.660s	21
16	A Sutil	1m25.702s	19
17	P di Resta	1m26.120s	11
18	C Pic	1m26.607s	21
19	G van der Garde	1m27.172s	20
20	J Bianchi	1m27.605s	18
21	M Chilton	1m27.665s	18
22	N Rosberg	1m27.822s	5

QUALIFYING 1

	Driver	Time
1	S Vettel	1m24.319s
2	N Rosberg	1m24.527s
3	L Hamilton	1m24.589s
4	J-E Vergne	1m24.630s
5	S Perez	1m24.635s
6	D Ricciardo	1m24.655s
7	F Alonso	1m24.661s
8	R Grosjean	1m24.737s
9	J Button	1m24.739s
10	N Hulkenberg	1m24.776s
11	K Räikkönen	1m24.819s
12	P Maldonado	1m24.905s
13	M Webber	1m24.923s
14	F Massa	1m24.950s
15	P di Resta	1m25.009s
16	A Sutil	1m25.030s
17	E Gutierrez	1m25.226s
18	V Bottas	1m25.291s
19	G van der Garde	1m26.406s
20	C Pic	1m26.563s
21	J Bianchi	1m27.085s
22	M Chilton	1m27.840s

QUALIFYING 2

	Driver	Time
1	S Vettel	1m23.977s
2	F Alonso	1m24.227s
3	M Webber	1m24.263s
4	D Ricciardo	1m24.290s
5	N Hulkenberg	1m24.305s
6	N Rosberg	1m24.393s
7	F Massa	1m24.479s
8	J Button	1m24.563s
9	J-E Vergne	1m24.575s
10	S Perez	1m24.592s
11	K Räikkönen	1m24.610s
12	L Hamilton	1m24.803s
13	R Grosjean	1m24.848s
14	A Sutil	1m24.932s
15	P Maldonado	1m25.011s
16	P di Resta	1m25.077s

Best sectors – Practice

Sec 1	S Vettel	27.364s
Sec 2	S Vettel	28.585s
Sec 3	S Vettel	28.067s

Speed trap – Practice

1	D Ricciardo	211.328mph
2	J Calado	210.955mph
3	J-E Vergne	210.707mph

Best sectors – Qualifying

Sec 1	S Vettel	27.373s
Sec 2	S Vettel	28.278s
Sec 3	S Vettel	27.916s

Speed trap – Qualifying

1	D Ricciardo	211.514mph
2	E Gutierrez	211.266mph
3	J-E Vergne	211.142mph

Sebastian Vettel
"I locked the front right at Turn 1 and got a flat spot. I wasn't sure if it would last, but had a strong first stint. I then had a gearbox issue so had to short shift."

Fernando Alonso
"Stepping onto the podium is special, as it's the only one where you can feel the love that the fans have for Ferrari. It's the best prize after a near perfect weekend."

Jenson Button
"I lost a few places at the start. Then, once I got stuck behind Daniel, I couldn't get past as we didn't get the gear ratios right and were hitting our limiters."

Kimi Räikkönen
"When I lost the front wing I had to pit for a new one, meaning an extra pit stop we hadn't planned and then having to work my way through the field afterwards."

Nico Rosberg
"It's a real shame as the car's pace looked really good, but I wasn't able to take advantage because of problems when I lost time in the third practice."

Nico Hulkenberg
"Despite starting third, it was clear that keeping the Ferrari and Red Bulls back was unrealistic. I lost two places at the start, but was able to catch up again."

Mark Webber
"I had a good battle with Alonso, fair play to him on that, and then afterwards I settled in to getting my head down. We got Felipe on the pit stop, which was great."

Felipe Massa
"My race went really well thanks to a nice start that moved me up two places. I ran consistently and so it was a shame that I lost the place to Webber at the pit stop."

Sergio Perez
"I deserved more than that. I got hit from behind into Turn 1 and had to cut the chicane. Then, throughout the race, I was held up by Ricciardo's Toro Rosso."

Romain Grosjean
"It isn't easy to follow another car with the aero configurations that we had, but I did the best I could from 13th. Unfortunately, I had a poor pit stop as well."

Lewis Hamilton
"That was a difficult weekend for me, but these things happen. I gave it my all, but unfortunately I paid the price for not qualifying far enough up the field."

Esteban Gutierrez
"My start was alright. I gained a place, but the first corner was tricky. It was important to keep the car together and I was able to settle down in the early laps."

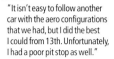

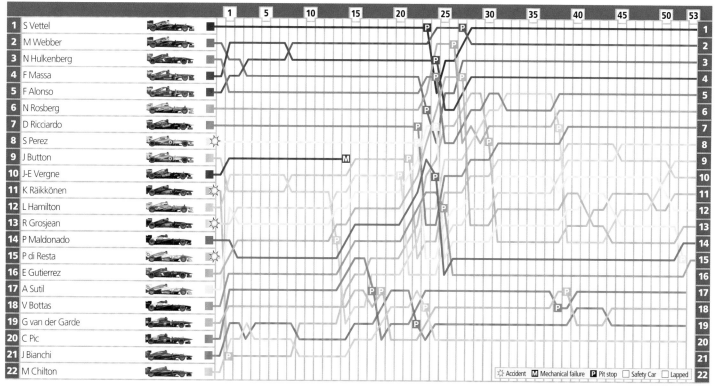

	Driver		
1	S Vettel		1
2	M Webber		2
3	N Hulkenberg		3
4	F Massa		4
5	F Alonso		5
6	N Rosberg		6
7	D Ricciardo		7
8	S Perez		8
9	J Button		9
10	J-E Vergne		10
11	K Räikkönen		11
12	L Hamilton		12
13	R Grosjean		13
14	P Maldonado		14
15	P di Resta		15
16	E Gutierrez		16
17	A Sutil		17
18	V Bottas		18
19	G van der Garde		19
20	C Pic		20
21	J Bianchi		21
22	M Chilton		22

☆ Accident ▉ Mechanical failure ▣ Pit stop ☐ Safety Car ☐ Lapped

QUALIFYING 3

	Driver	Time
1	S Vettel	1m23.755s
2	M Webber	1m23.968s
3	N Hulkenberg	1m24.065s
4	F Massa	1m24.132s
5	F Alonso	1m24.142s
6	N Rosberg	1m24.192s
7	D Ricciardo	1m24.209s
8	S Perez	1m24.502s
9	J Button	1m24.515s
10	J-E Vergne	1m28.050s

GRID

	Driver	Time
1	S Vettel	1m23.755s
2	M Webber	1m23.968s
3	N Hulkenberg	1m24.065s
4	F Massa	1m24.132s
5	F Alonso	1m24.142s
6	N Rosberg	1m24.192s
7	D Ricciardo	1m24.209s
8	S Perez	1m24.502s
9	J Button	1m24.515s
10	J-E Vergne	1m28.050s
11	K Räikkönen	1m24.610s
12	L Hamilton	1m24.803s
13	R Grosjean	1m24.848s
14	P Maldonado	1m25.011s
15	P di Resta	1m25.077s
16	E Gutierrez	1m25.226s
17	A Sutil	1m24.932s
18	V Bottas	1m25.291s
19	G van der Garde	1m26.406s
20	C Pic	1m26.563s
21	J Bianchi	1m27.085s
22	M Chilton	1m27.840s

RACE

	Driver	Car	Laps	Time	Avg. mph	Fastest	Stops
1	S Vettel	Red Bull-Renault RB9	53	1h18m33.352s	145.567	1m27.190s	1
2	F Alonso	Ferrari F138X	53	1h18m38.819s	145.399	1m26.797s	1
3	M Webber	Red Bull-Renault RB9	53	1h18m39.702s	145.371	1m26.690s	1
4	F Massa	Ferrari F138	53	1h18m42.713s	145.279	1m27.095s	1
5	N Hulkenberg	Sauber-Ferrari C32	53	1h18m43.707s	145.248	1m26.716s	1
6	N Rosberg	Mercedes F1 W04	53	1h18m44.351s	145.228	1m26.500s	1
7	D Ricciardo	Toro Rosso-Ferrari STR8	53	1h19m05.681s	144.576	1m27.294s	1
8	R Grosjean	Lotus-Renault E21	53	1h19m06.482s	144.551	1m27.043s	1
9	L Hamilton	Mercedes F1 W04	53	1h19m06.879s	144.539	1m25.849s	2
10	J Button	McLaren-Mercedes MP4-28	53	1h19m11.679s	144.393	1m27.830s	1
11	K Räikkönen	Lotus-Renault E21	53	1h19m12.047s	144.382	1m26.948s	2
12	S Perez	McLaren-Mercedes MP4-28	53	1h19m13.117s	144.349	1m27.607s	1
13	E Gutierrez	Sauber-Ferrari C32	53	1h19m14.232s	144.316	1m27.092s	1
14	P Maldonado	Williams-Renault FW35	53	1h19m22.437s	144.067	1m26.981s	1
15	V Bottas	Williams-Renault FW35	53	1h19m30.179s	143.833	1m27.166s	1
16	A Sutil	Force India-Mercedes VJM06	52	Brakes	-	1m27.418s	1
17	C Pic	Caterham-Renault CT03	52	1h19m17.871s	141.482	1m28.620s	2
18	G van der Garde	Caterham-Renault CT03	52	1h19m32.969s	141.034	1m28.663s	2
19	J Bianchi	Marussia-Cosworth MR-02	52	1h19m40.301s	140.818	1m29.595s	1
20	M Chilton	Marussia-Cosworth MR-02	52	1h19m52.527s	140.459	1m29.491s	1
R	J-E Vergne	Toro Rosso-Ferrari STR8	14	Transmission	-	1m29.710s	0
R	P di Resta	Force India-Mercedes VJM06	0	Collision	-	-	0

CHAMPIONSHIP

	Driver	Pts
1	S Vettel	222
2	F Alonso	169
3	L Hamilton	141
4	K Räikkönen	134
5	M Webber	130
6	N Rosberg	104
7	F Massa	79
8	R Grosjean	57
9	J Button	48
10	P di Resta	36
11	A Sutil	25
12	S Perez	18
13	D Ricciardo	18
14	N Hulkenberg	17
15	J-E Vergne	13
16	P Maldonado	1

Grid penalties

A Sutil Three-place grid penalty for impeding Lewis Hamilton

Fastest lap
L Hamilton 1m25.849s
(150.946mph) on lap 51

Fastest speed trap
E Gutierrez 211.949mph
Slowest speed trap
P di Resta 140.989mph

Fastest pit stop
1 N Rosberg 24.079s
2 M Webber 24.205s
3 F Alonso 24.208s

	Constructor	Pts
1	Red Bull-Renault	352
2	Ferrari	248
3	Mercedes	245
4	Lotus-Renault	191
5	McLaren-Mercedes	66
6	Force India-Mercedes	61
7	Toro Rosso-Ferrari	31
8	Sauber-Ferrari	17
9	Williams-Renault	1

Paul di Resta

"It's been a weekend to forget, with brake failure yesterday then early retirement. I got caught out into the second chicane as the cars ahead of me got backed up."

Pastor Maldonado

"It was a poor race as I lost two places at the start which were hard to recover. The car had little pace, but whatever we did wasn't enough to regain the lost places."

Jean-Eric Vergne

"I was conserving my tyres and controlling Button. Then I felt something was wrong and stopped by the track with some sort of transmission problem."

Charles Pic

"I held position into Turn 1 and was up with Bottas. Up to the first stop I was just about keeping up, but in the second stint I just didn't have the pace to fight with him."

Jules Bianchi

"I got ahead of the Caterhams into Turn 1, but they regained position by the end of lap 1. We began to catch them but after the pit stop the balance wasn't there."

Adrian Sutil

"A tough race and I had to retire due to braking issues. I tried my best and don't think I could have delivered any more as I was on the limit throughout the race."

Valtteri Bottas

"I maintained my position at the start but, from the first few laps, I couldn't really challenge any of the cars ahead of me as we just didn't have the race pace."

Daniel Ricciardo

"I'm delighted! After qualifying well, I got the most out of the car, managing to keep the guys behind me. The low downforce set-up helped on the straights."

Giedo van der Garde

"I was running a two-stop race and made my second pit stop when I was called, but there was a communication mistake and the guys weren't ready for me."

Max Chilton

"Another tough race and one that underlined our balance problems, but I was encouraged by my pace versus Jules as there was nothing between us for the first 25 laps."

2013 FORMULA 1 SINGTEL SINGAPORE GRAND PRIX

**20-22 SEPTEMBER
MARINA BAY STREET CIRCUIT
SINGAPORE**

IN A CLASS OF HIS OWN

Sebastian Vettel's impressive victory in Singapore not only further extended his lead in the championship table, it also dealt a crushing blow to any rivals who still harboured thoughts of beating him to the 2013 title

It wasn't just that Sebastian Vettel logged his third straight win when others were still hoping to find a chink in Red Bull Racing's armour, it was the way he did it. His dominance was such that after the race even those who had previously tried to stay upbeat about their title chances came close to admitting that it would now be impossible to catch him.

Since Pirelli reverted to its 2012 tyre constructions, everything seemed to go Red Bull Racing's way, and it was clear that the RB9 was happier on the revised tyres. Yet, just as important, the team had continued to develop its car successfully, finding marginal aero gains here and there that added up to a greater performance improvement than rivals had been able to achieve. Impressively, this had been done against the background of all teams making the gradual but inevitable switch of their R&D focus to 2014.

It was no great surprise to see Vettel take pole position after he dominated practice and the first part of qualifying. However, the way he secured it was unusual to say the least, in that he was standing in the garage watching the competition trying in vain to beat his time. He was so confident that his first run in Q3 would be quick enough that he stepped out of the car,

removed his helmet and let the others get on with it. They got closer than he perhaps expected, but he still ended up in pole position.

Only Vettel, his team-mate Mark Webber and Romain Grosjean made it out of Q1 without using the supersoft tyres. By saving a set, all three were well placed for the rest of the session, and the same trio also got through Q2 making only one run on new tyres.

Come Q3, Vettel set a 1m42.841s best on his first run and, given that he was as much as 0.8s clear of the rest in Q2, he felt that was enough. In the end, Nico Rosberg came closest, the Mercedes driver stopping the clock only 0.091s off Vettel's pace, while in third place, Grosjean was 0.217s shy of pole, both men having looked very good over the middle sector of the lap. Webber set the quickest first sector of the session, but faded over the rest of the lap, so he too missed out.

"It was a strange feeling at the end of Q3," said Vettel. "It's already strange when you stand in the garage with only two minutes left in the session, but much worse when you see the others making their final attempt and there's nothing you can do… I was watching the sector times closely, of Romain, Nico and Mark in particular."

RIGHT Felipe Massa ended up running all on his own after losing ground at the start, finishing sixth

BELOW Romain Grosjean blasts across the harbour bridge before his drive ended with engine failure

OPPOSITE Lewis Hamilton started and finished fifth and, towards the end of the race, overtook several cars including the fading McLarens

INSIDE LINE
CHRISTIAN HORNER
RED BULL RACING TEAM PRINCIPAL

"Sebastian's pace was outstanding. After the start, it was about making the duration of that soft-tyre stint last long enough, so it was about managing tyres and managing the situation. Sebastian is so good at that, as we've seen so many times.

"The safety car came at arguably the worst possible time for us because we weren't in a window where we could go to the end of the race. We'd recently changed tyres and, of course, track position is crucial here.

"We gave Sebastian a target and basically said, 'You've got 15 laps, do what you can.' His pace during that period of the race, building up what turned out to be a 30s advantage over Fernando that gave him a clear stop, was absolutely remarkable.

"The way the race panned out, it opened up reasonably okay for us and Sebastian had devastating speed and was at times 2s a lap quicker than anyone else. Grosjean was in a good position to maybe go to the end, but he would have needed to pass Alonso and Rosberg's Mercedes to be a threat. So, at no point did Sebastian seem to be under any undue pressure.

"I really don't understand anyone not being a Sebastian fan. The guy drove an absolutely unbelievable race today. What we all saw, I think, was one of the best drives that I've seen him produce in terms of raw pace and what he's been able to deliver. I just don't think it's right to see a driver who's put in a performance like that not getting the reception he deserves.

"He says it doesn't affect him and he doesn't feel it, but he's a human being at the end of the day and when you've driven your heart out, to me it's not fair if he doesn't get the reception he deserves. He's got broad shoulders but, like anyone, has feelings.

"I don't know why there's a problem, to be honest. For sure the Malaysian GP didn't help, but that's well gone, and an awful lot's been written about it. There were circumstances involved in that which Sebastian felt justified his drive.

"There's also the point about the guy winning all the time. When people watched Muhammad Ali, they wanted to see who was going to beat him, and I think that's the case a little bit at the moment with Sebastian. So, when he keeps winning, maybe it's not always the most popular result.

"But he's a great kid: he's got a sense of humour and a big heart, but he's a competitor, too, and loves winning. I just hope the criticism stops."

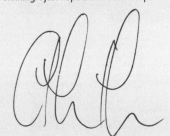

Behind Rosberg, Grosjean and Webber, fifth spot went to a disappointed Lewis Hamilton, as the British driver struggled to get pace out of his Mercedes. Felipe Massa outran Ferrari team-mate Fernando Alonso as the pair qualified sixth and seventh, while Jenson Button, Daniel Ricciardo and Esteban Gutierrez completed the top ten. Gutierrez was an impressive seventh in Q2, as he finally showed some good form during a difficult rookie season with Sauber.

Kimi Räikkönen had been suffering from a back problem, and that clearly didn't help the Finn as he lacked pace all day relative to team-mate Grosjean. He qualified only 13th as his title hopes continued to fade.

At the start of the race, Vettel nearly lost out to Rosberg, but the Mercedes driver ran wide at the first corner, and the title favourite was able to muscle back into the lead. Behind them, Hamilton had to give a place back to Massa for running off-road, although he would regain it at the first round of pit stops.

Vettel began to open up an advantage at an incredible rate. He was 1.9s ahead after the opening lap, and that rose to 4.1s on the second lap and 5.6s on the third as he left everyone trailing in his wake. The gap then stabilised at around 7-8s.

TALKING POINT
IS DI RESTA ON A SLIDE?

For the first half of 2013, Paul di Resta and Force India were punching well above their weight. As far as the British GP, the Scot had scored at every race bar Malaysia. He put 36 points on the board and the team was running ahead of McLaren in the constructors' championship, on perhaps a quarter of its budget.

Without the resources to be at the forefront of exhaust-blowing technology, Andrew Green and his Force India technical team had set up a tyre strategy group to concentrate on getting the most out of Pirelli's rubber. The move certainly seemed to stand them in good stead and, often, Force India's race strategy involved one fewer visit to the pits than rival teams.

Post-Silverstone, however, the return to 2012-spec Pirelli tyres hit Force India hard. There was a dramatic turnaround in fortune and, heading for Singapore five races on, Paul hadn't added to his pre-British GP points haul.

In 2012, the Scot qualified sixth at Marina Bay and finished fourth, just 19s behind Sebastian Vettel's Red Bull for his best F1 result.

This time, unable to generate enough heat in the rubber over one lap (team-mate Adrian Sutil is a little more aggressive), Paul failed to make it out of Q1.

Undeterred, he drove a marathon first stint on the supersoft tyre and was heading for sixth place (and possibly fourth but for the safety car interruption) until he went straight on into the tyre barrier at Turn 7 with seven laps to go.

"I didn't approach the corner any differently," he said, "and have no idea why that happened."

The timing wasn't great. It was the second successive race at which Paul, who has never had a reputation as a crasher, had finished his race with an on-track incident. And, with a contract option on the team's side for 2014

and talk of the new regulations legislating against heavier, taller drivers like him, some alarm bells were starting to ring.

Initially, Nico Hulkenberg's move from Force India to Sauber had seemed a bad call. But, since the Hungarian GP, Sauber – which had compromised an efficient 2012 exhaust-blowing layout – had re-engineered the exhausts, pods and floor area and was a competitive proposition once more.

Just as contract time approached, it looked as though things might all be heading in the wrong direction for Paul, the one saving grace perhaps being that Hulkenberg's size offered Force India no more options in the packaging department if they were considering re-signing the German.

After the first round of pit stops, Vettel was 10s ahead when, on lap 25, Ricciardo crashed at Turn 18 and triggered a safety car period that annulled his advantage. Vettel and Rosberg chose to stay out, as did Webber in fourth and Hamilton in sixth, but everybody else opted to pit for new tyres, led in by Alonso from third. As the safety car queue formed, it was therefore Vettel ahead of Rosberg, Webber and Hamilton, followed by Alonso and the others who had pitted. The question now was would everyone who had pitted be able to make it to the end of the race without another stop?

When the pace car was deployed, wrecking Vettel's pre-race plans, the team informed him that he really needed to fly for the next 15 laps, building up enough of a cushion so that he would be able to pit without interference. Coming back out behind a rival is particularly troublesome at a track like Marina Bay where overtaking is so difficult. Vettel duly delivered, and he was never under threat of losing the lead, despite losing his hard-won advantage. Aware that he would definitely have to pit again, he began to open up a gap at an astonishing rate from the restart on lap 30, helped by the fact that his initial pursuer, Rosberg, struggled in that stint.

Webber, Rosberg and Hamilton all duly pitted under green, and Vettel finally came in on lap 44 after an astonishing demonstration that saw him threading his RB9 between the narrow concrete walls. By then, he was more than 30s ahead of Alonso, and was easily able to pit without sacrificing his lead. After that, he continued to pull away until the chequered flag, leaving Red Bull Racing Team Principal Christian Horner to describe his drive as "remarkable". Indeed, it had been.

Behind him, Alonso showed no sign of pitting again and, by managing his tyres brilliantly, he was able to hang onto second place. He was followed

home by Räikkönen, who had gained some ground with an early first pit stop then, like the Ferrari driver, was able to get to the flag after pitting under the safety car, finishing 11s behind him.

"We had a plan and we know that at what stage of the race, if the safety car comes, we try to go until the end," said Räikkönen. "So, I knew what could happen and luckily some other teams couldn't do it and had to pit. I was kind of stuck behind Jenson for most of the race, but then I tried to give him some pressure and keep him pushing, so I noticed that he started running out of his tyres and I could start to get in closer and closer. In the end, I decided to try to overtake him and

OPPOSITE Sebastian Vettel was in control until the safety car came out, and then had to race hard again

ABOVE Toro Rosso's Daniel Ricciardo, who crashed out on lap 24, harries Adrian Sutil's Force India

BELOW Nico Rosberg started second, led to the first corner, and wasn't helped by the timing of the safety car period and only a late-race recovery brought him back to fourth

managed to get past, because there were people who had stopped for the fresh tyres who were catching very quickly. Luckily, once I got past, I could push a bit more and keep the gap big enough to finish in third place. After the weekend we had, with some problems for myself and a less than ideal set-up, I don't think we could have asked much more than to finish third."

Others who tried to make it to the end on older tyres weren't so lucky and were gradually picked off by Webber, Rosberg and Hamilton. However, right at the end, Webber was forced to slow as his engine lost its water through what was later determined to be a faulty radiator weld. He eventually stopped, amid a cloud of smoke, on the very last lap. Webber then walked onto the track to catch a lift back to the pits from Alonso and landed himself a third reprimand of the season, which duly triggered a somewhat controversial 10-place grid penalty for the Korean GP.

With Webber out, Rosberg claimed fourth place ahead of his Mercedes team-mate, Hamilton. Massa made a third pit stop and thus had good pace towards the end, which helped him to climb to sixth place.

Button was running eighth and Perez tenth when both McLaren drivers pitted under the safety car; they each lost a place to Paul di Resta, who didn't stop. After that, both men tried to get to the flag without another stop. They climbed as high as third and fifth respectively as others pitted, before their tyres faded and they dropped back to seventh and eighth.

Nico Hulkenberg got ahead of Sauber team-mate Gutierrez at the start, moving up to ninth while the Mexican fell back to 11th. Both pitted under the safety car and joined the group who tried to run to the flag without another pit stop. They were running sixth and seventh, but were gradually picked off by those on new rubber. Hulkenberg hung onto ninth place while Gutierrez fell to 12th, the Saubers split by Adrian Sutil in 10th and Pastor Maldonado in 11th.

Both Force India drivers opted for unusual strategies in the race, Sutil being the only driver to start on mediums and di Resta going for an ultra-late first stop on lap 20, after rising to third. He was a genuine seventh after the safety car, and that put the Scot well in contention for points until he crashed on lap 55.

Aside from Webber, the other key retirement was that of Grosjean, who could have beaten his Lotus team-mate to third. However, he dropped a couple of places to fifth on lap 1, was the second highest driver not to pit under the safety car, but soon after that had a long stop to replenish his engine's air system, prior to retirement on lap 37.

**ABOVE LEFT Mark Webber
was out of luck again, his engine
failing on the final lap when he was
fourth. The way he climbed aboard
Fernando Alonso's Ferrari for a lift to
the pits would earn him a penalty**

**LEFT The thrill of winning never
fades for Sebastian Vettel**

SNAPSHOT FROM
SINGAPORE

CLOCKWISE FROM RIGHT

Singapore's Marina Bay circuit at night provides a backdrop like no other; yet more celebrations for Red Bull Racing; like all the other drivers, Pastor Maldonado prepares to go out into the dark; Singapore daily life goes on as Romain Grosjean passes underneath; Valtteri Bottas and his Williams crew do their track walk in the evening to get accustomed to the dark; a McLaren all wrapped up for the night after another tough day at the office; the McLaren crew go to work on Jenson Button's MP4-28; everything is in its place in the Caterham garage; F1 supremo Bernie Ecclestone chats to former England football ace David Beckham; the speed of an F1 car is even more of a blur at night

SINGAPORE
MARINA BAY
ROUND 13

RACE RESULTS

RACE DATE 22 September 2013
CIRCUIT LENGTH 3.152 miles
NO. OF LAPS 61
RACE DISTANCE 192.272 miles
WEATHER Humid but dry, 29°C
TRACK TEMP 32°C
LAP RECORD Kimi Räikkönen,
1m45.599s, 107.358mph, 2008

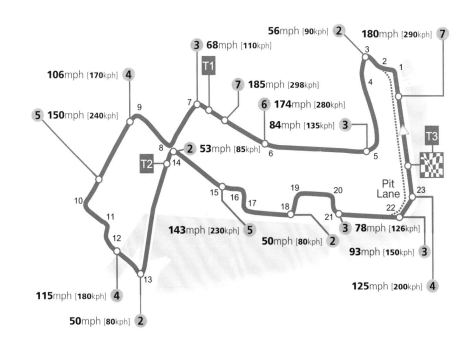

PRACTICE 1				PRACTICE 2				PRACTICE 3				QUALIFYING 1			QUALIFYING 2	
	Driver	Time	Laps		Driver	Time	Laps		Driver	Time	Laps		Driver	Time		Driver	Time
1	L Hamilton	1m47.055s	20	1	S Vettel	1m44.249s	34	1	S Vettel	1m44.173s	15	1	L Hamilton	1m44.196s	1	S Vettel	1m42.905s
2	M Webber	1m47.420s	20	2	M Webber	1m44.853s	30	2	R Grosjean	1m44.364s	16	2	J Button	1m45.009s	2	M Webber	1m43.727s
3	S Vettel	1m47.885s	19	3	N Rosberg	1m45.258s	34	3	N Rosberg	1m44.741s	18	3	F Alonso	1m45.115s	3	N Rosberg	1m43.892s
4	N Rosberg	1m48.239s	23	4	L Hamilton	1m45.368s	33	4	M Webber	1m44.906s	14	4	S Perez	1m45.164s	4	L Hamilton	1m43.920s
5	K Räikkönen	1m48.354s	18	5	R Grosjean	1m45.411s	18	5	L Hamilton	1m44.921s	14	5	N Rosberg	1m45.208s	5	R Grosjean	1m43.957s
6	R Grosjean	1m48.355s	12	6	F Alonso	1m45.691s	32	6	F Alonso	1m45.257s	13	6	M Webber	1m45.271s	6	F Alonso	1m44.153s
7	F Alonso	1m48.362s	21	7	J Button	1m45.754s	30	7	S Perez	1m45.500s	12	7	S Vettel	1m45.376s	7	E Gutierrez	1m44.245s
8	S Perez	1m49.267s	20	8	K Räikkönen	1m45.778s	32	8	N Hulkenberg	1m45.876s	19	8	D Ricciardo	1m45.379s	8	F Massa	1m44.376s
9	J-E Vergne	1m49.348s	23	9	A Sutil	1m46.002s	27	9	J Button	1m45.890s	13	9	N Hulkenberg	1m45.381s	9	D Ricciardo	1m44.407s
10	E Gutierrez	1m49.355s	21	10	S Perez	1m46.025s	31	10	F Massa	1m45.935s	13	10	E Gutierrez	1m45.483s	10	J Button	1m44.497s
11	P Maldonado	1m49.481s	20	11	D Ricciardo	1m46.406s	34	11	J-E Vergne	1m46.084s	15	11	K Räikkönen	1m45.522s	11	N Hulkenberg	1m44.555s
12	F Massa	1m49.493s	16	12	J-E Vergne	1m46.429s	33	12	K Räikkönen	1m46.147s	13	12	J-E Vergne	1m45.657s	12	J-E Vergne	1m44.588s
13	V Bottas	1m49.510s	21	13	P di Resta	1m46.606s	33	13	P Maldonado	1m46.338s	17	13	F Massa	1m45.658s	13	K Räikkönen	1m44.658s
14	J Button	1m49.608s	20	14	N Hulkenberg	1m46.808s	36	14	D Ricciardo	1m46.358s	16	14	R Grosjean	1m45.851s	14	S Perez	1m44.752s
15	P di Resta	1m49.887s	18	15	F Massa	1m46.870s	33	15	V Bottas	1m46.660s	17	15	A Sutil	1m45.960s	15	A Sutil	1m45.185s
16	A Sutil	1m50.092s	20	16	E Gutierrez	1m47.287s	29	16	P di Resta	1m46.879s	16	16	V Bottas	1m45.982s	16	V Bottas	1m45.388s
17	N Hulkenberg	1m50.222s	17	17	V Bottas	1m47.434s	33	17	E Gutierrez	1m46.893s	13	17	P di Resta	1m46.121s			
18	D Ricciardo	1m50.757s	16	18	P Maldonado	1m47.761s	25	18	A Sutil	1m47.249s	19	18	P Maldonado	1m46.619s			
19	J Bianchi	1m52.359s	16	19	G van der Garde	1m49.434s	34	19	G van der Garde	1m48.931s	17	19	C Pic	1m48.111s			
20	M Chilton	1m52.673s	15	20	C Pic	1m49.526s	34	20	C Pic	1m49.037s	18	20	G van der Garde	1m48.321s			
21	G Van der Garde	1m52.920s	24	21	M Chilton	1m49.619s	33	21	J Bianchi	1m49.182s	21	21	J Bianchi	1m48.830s			
22	C Pic	1m53.647s	23	22	J Bianchi	1m49.731s	30	22	M Chilton	1m49.982s	20	22	M Chilton	1m48.930s			

Best sectors – Practice		Speed trap – Practice		Best sectors – Qualifying		Speed trap – Qualifying	
Sec 1 S Vettel	28.030s	1 J Button	181.378mph	Sec 1 M Webber	27.881s	1 J Button	182.372mph
Sec 2 R Grosjean	39.787s	2 S Perez	181.254mph	Sec 2 S Vettel	39.430s	2 D Ricciardo	182.248mph
Sec 3 M Webber	36.043s	3 P di Resta	181.067mph	Sec 3 N Rosberg	35.438s	3 A Sutil	181.999mph

Sebastian Vettel
"The start was close, but I had strong pace, especially when the safety car came in, and pushed hard to build a gap. The last 10 laps seemed to go on for ever."

Fernando Alonso
"The keys were the start and the strategy. I passed four cars straight away but couldn't pass Rosberg. The decision to pit when the safety car came out paid off."

Jenson Button
"We expected to spend most of the race on the Option. The Prime didn't work so well for me, and having to hold Kimi off for so long destroyed my rear tyres."

Kimi Räikkönen
"It's been a difficult weekend, so to reach the podium is good. The car felt good and it could have been even better if I'd been able to do more work in practice."

Nico Rosberg
"The timing of the safety car was unfortunate for us and perhaps it wasn't the best decision to stay out, but we weren't sure if our tyres would last the distance."

Nico Hulkenberg
"I had a racing situation with Sergio. I had to give back the place and I didn't agree with that. Late on, it was a fight for survival, as the tyres were gone."

Mark Webber
"Six laps from the end, I had to short shift, but then, unlike at Monza, began to lose power. I was just trying to get home but, on the last lap, the car caught fire."

Felipe Massa
"After a fantastic start, I got stuck inside the cars that braked early. I was then always stuck behind others and we all know how hard it is to overtake at this track."

Sergio Perez
"The safety car came at the wrong time for us, so we had to take a risk by choosing to drive to the finish with two stops. It was hard to keep out of the barriers."

Romain Grosjean
"The race was going well and second or third was realistic. We had a good strategy pitting under the safety car, but unluckily my engine had other ideas today."

Lewis Hamilton
"I paid for poor qualifying. I went wide to avoid Mark at Turn 1. From there, it was difficult to follow the race and the timing of the safety car didn't help us."

Esteban Gutierrez
"I expected better. My race pace wasn't great, especially at the beginning. At times I pushed a bit too much, had a lot of oversteer and the tyres were degrading."

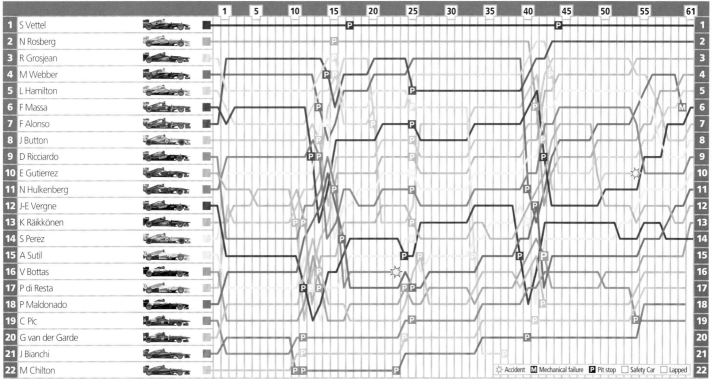

	Driver															
1	S Vettel															
2	N Rosberg															
3	R Grosjean															
4	M Webber															
5	L Hamilton															
6	F Massa															
7	F Alonso															
8	J Button															
9	D Ricciardo															
10	E Gutierrez															
11	N Hulkenberg															
12	J-E Vergne															
13	K Räikkönen															
14	S Perez															
15	A Sutil															
16	V Bottas															
17	P di Resta															
18	P Maldonado															
19	C Pic															
20	G van der Garde															
21	J Bianchi															
22	M Chilton															

☆ Accident   ▣ Mechanical failure   ℗ Pit stop   ☐ Safety Car   ☐ Lapped

QUALIFYING 3

	Driver	Time
1	S Vettel	1m42.841s
2	N Rosberg	1m42.932s
3	R Grosjean	1m43.058s
4	M Webber	1m43.152s
5	L Hamilton	1m43.254s
6	F Massa	1m43.890s
7	F Alonso	1m43.938s
8	J Button	1m44.282s
9	D Ricciardo	1m44.439s
10	E Gutierrez	No time

GRID

	Driver	Time
1	S Vettel	1m42.841s
2	N Rosberg	1m42.932s
3	R Grosjean	1m43.058s
4	M Webber	1m43.152s
5	L Hamilton	1m43.254s
6	F Massa	1m43.890s
7	F Alonso	1m43.938s
8	J Button	1m44.282s
9	D Ricciardo	1m44.439s
10	E Gutierrez	No time
11	N Hulkenberg	1m44.555s
12	J-E Vergne	1m44.588s
13	K Räikkönen	1m44.658s
14	S Perez	1m44.752s
15	A Sutil	1m45.185s
16	V Bottas	1m45.388s
17	P di Resta	1m46.121s
18	P Maldonado	1m46.619s
19	C Pic	1m48.111s
20	G van der Garde	1m48.321s
21	J Bianchi	1m48.830s
22	M Chilton	1m48.930s

RACE

	Driver	Car	Laps	Time	Avg. mph	Fastest	Stops
1	S Vettel	Red Bull-Renault RB9	61	1h59m13.132s	96.576	1m48.574s	2
2	F Alonso	Ferrari F138	61	1h59m45.759s	96.138	1m51.082s	2
3	K Räikkönen	Lotus-Renault E21	61	1h59m57.052s	95.987	1m51.140s	2
4	N Rosberg	Mercedes F1 W04	61	2h00m04.287s	95.891	1m50.353s	2
5	L Hamilton	Mercedes F1 W04	61	2h00m06.291s	95.864	1m49.916s	2
6	F Massa	Ferrari F138	61	2h00m17.009s	95.722	1m50.509s	3
7	J Button	McLaren-Mercedes MP4-28	61	2h00m36.486s	95.464	1m51.740s	2
8	S Perez	McLaren-Mercedes MP4-28	61	2h00m36.952s	95.458	1m51.926s	2
9	N Hulkenberg	Sauber-Ferrari C32	61	2h00m37.393s	95.452	1m52.186s	2
10	A Sutil	Force India-Mercedes VJM06X	61	2h00m37.800s	95.447	1m49.656s	3
11	P Maldonado	Williams-Renault FW35	61	2h00m41.611s	95.396	1m50.708s	3
12	E Gutierrez	Sauber-Ferrari C32	61	2h00m51.026s	95.273	1m52.007s	2
13	V Bottas	Williams-Renault FW32	61	2h00m58.293s	95.177	1m51.706s	3
14	J-E Vergne	Toro Rosso-Ferrari STR8	61	2h01m06.644s	95.068	1m50.328s	3
15	M Webber	Red Bull-Renault RB9	60	Engine	-	1m49.783s	2
16	G van der Garde	Caterham-Renault CT03	60	1h59m34.235s	94.713	1m52.472s	3
17	M Chilton	Marussia-Cosworth MR-02	60	1h59m41.391s	94.619	1m53.041s	3
18	J Bianchi	Marussia-Cosworth MR-02	60	1h59m48.515s	94.525	1m52.898s	4
19	C Pic	Caterham-Renault CT03	60	1h59m48.663s	94.523	1m50.990s	3
20	P di Resta	Force India-Mercedes VJM06	54	Accident	-	1m50.739s	2
R	R Grosjean	Lotus-Renault E21	37	Engine	-	1m51.097s	3
R	D Ricciardo	Toro Rosso-Ferrari STR8	23	Accident	-	1m53.052s	1

CHAMPIONSHIP

	Driver	Pts
1	S Vettel	247
2	F Alonso	187
3	L Hamilton	151
4	K Räikkönen	149
5	M Webber	130
6	N Rosberg	116
7	F Massa	87
8	R Grosjean	57
9	J Button	54
10	P di Resta	36
11	A Sutil	26
12	S Perez	22
13	N Hulkenberg	19
14	D Ricciardo	18
15	J-E Vergne	13
16	P Maldonado	1

Grid penalties
None

Fastest lap
S Vettel 1m48.574s
(104.353mph) on lap 46

Fastest speed trap
N Rosberg 184.795mph
Slowest speed trap
D Ricciardo 170.193mph

Fastest pit stop

1	S Perez	28.709s
2	S Vettel	28.787s
3	M Webber	28.909s

	Constructor	Pts
1	Red Bull-Renault	377
2	Ferrari	274
3	Mercedes	267
4	Lotus-Renault	206
5	McLaren-Mercedes	76
6	Force India-Mercedes	62
7	Toro Rosso-Ferrari	31
8	Sauber-Ferrari	19
9	Williams-Renault	1

Paul di Resta
"It's a shame to come away with nothing. I was looking to push the cars ahead of me in the final laps. Then I had the crash at Turn 7 where the car went straight on."

Pastor Maldonado
"I gained two places at the start and after two laps was pushing towards the cars in front while trying to manage the rear tyres, but I just missed out on points."

Jean-Eric Vergne
"My start wasn't great and so we switched to a three-stop strategy. It could have got me back into the points, but I then had trouble just keeping the car on track."

Charles Pic
"I got stuck behind Bianchi at the start. I came out clear of him and chased Giedo. When he pitted, I switched to two stops, but with six laps left had to pit again."

Jules Bianchi
"I lost gears when I pitted and was worried it was mechanical, but I pitted again to change the steering wheel. Then the safety car helped me to catch up."

Adrian Sutil
"I was catching Perez, Button and Hulkenberg late on. I thought I had a chance to pass at least one of them but, as soon as I caught them, my tyres went off."

Valtteri Bottas
"It was one of the most difficult races of 2013 for me. I had a clutch problem at the start. After the safety car, I then had trouble with debris on my front wing."

Daniel Ricciardo
"At the start, my car just sat there and I dropped to 14th. I was on the back foot from then and was trying to make up time when I went off at Turn 18. My fault."

Giedo van der Garde
"I passed Pic, Bianchi and Bottas on lap 1. The car was great on the supersofts. I pitted for mediums and spent many laps fighting Bottas, but he passed me again."

Max Chilton
"Degradation was quite high and it was a challenge to manage the tyres and push for opportunities with Caterham which came along when Pic stopped late in the race."

2013 FORMULA 1 KOREAN GRAND PRIX

4-6 OCTOBER
KOREA INTERNATIONAL CIRCUIT, YEONGAM

BATTLE FOR YEONGAM

Korea provided a fourth victory in a row for Sebastian Vettel, but it was a race packed with incident and entertainment. The three-time champion may have been ahead all the way, but he had to work incredibly hard for it

Sebastian Vettel truly earned his 25 points for the win as he certainly didn't enjoy the advantage that he'd had at the Singapore GP. Behind him, there were all sorts of dramas, with two safety car periods livening things up as the field closed, and with the emergence of good action down the order over the last part of the race. Inevitably, tyres also played their part as everyone struggled to keep them alive.

On display was yet another faultless performance by Vettel. But it was telling that afterwards, both Lewis Hamilton and Fernando Alonso – who finished in fifth and sixth places – were in a downbeat mood as they reflected on their tough afternoon which had brought them little reward. Red Bull Racing were in a different league.

Vettel was fastest in Q2 and did a good first lap in Q3. He was the last driver out for the second and final run and, when nobody managed to beat his time, he had the luxury of aborting the lap and cruising into the pits, saving a little mileage on his tyres. Hamilton came closest to beating his time. Second after the first runs, the Mercedes driver improved marginally on his second run, but it wasn't quite enough.

ABOVE Sebastian Vettel makes a clean start to lead away from pole position, followed by Lewis Hamilton, Romain Grosjean, Nico Rosberg and Fernando Alonso

OPPOSITE Both Saubers qualified in the top 10, but Esteban Gutierrez lost ground avoiding Felipe Massa's first lap spin and would finish just outside the points

Mark Webber made a mistake on his second run and also aborted it, but his time was still good enough for third. However, he carried a 10-place grid penalty from Singapore so tumbled to 13th, leaving third to Romain Grosjean, with his Lotus looking strong in race configuration.

Nico Rosberg struggled to get his set-up right, and qualified fourth, ahead of Alonso. Felipe Massa took sixth in the other Ferrari, while Sauber did well to get both cars into the top 10, with Nico Hulkenberg and Esteban Gutierrez qualifying seventh and eighth. Kimi Räikkönen made a mistake on his only run in Q3 and so finished bottom of the session, although he at least inherited a place from Webber's penalty. Sergio Perez was the quickest driver not to make Q3, the Mexican outpacing McLaren team-mate Jenson Button by just 0.003s.

Hamilton knew that his big chance to make life difficult for Vettel was to get ahead on the opening lap, but Vettel didn't leave him any opportunity and held on in front. Instead, Hamilton suddenly found he had his hands full with Grosjean, who dived down the inside to claim second at Turn 3.

There was drama right behind, too, as Massa tried to come down the inside into Turn 3 and spun in an attempt to avoid Rosberg, very nearly collecting Alonso in the process. As everyone backed up, Button hit Hulkenberg and was forced to make a pit stop for a new front wing. So was Adrian Sutil who damaged his Force India's wing by going across the inside kerbs to avoid contact.

"It's always tricky here," said Vettel, "because the run to the first corner is quite short, but then you have two big straights. To be the first car is the worst, as you have no tow. I had a good start and could focus on the first corner. I then had a very good exit from there and was able to put a couple of metres between myself and Lewis, and then I think Lewis was in more trouble with Romain from behind into Turn 3.

"I obviously benefited from that, and had a little bit of a cushion and again for the next straight, and then kept the lead which was crucial. After that, I tried to build a gap and keep it quite consistent."

As had become a familiar sight in the later races of the season, Vettel opened a gap on the pursuing Grosjean, with the gap going out from 2.1s to 2.6s

INSIDE LINE
TOM McCULLOUGH
SAUBER
HEAD OF TRACK ENGINEERING

"Nico Hulkenberg has been driving well all year but, when we were uncompetitive at the start of the season, nobody noticed. Fundamentally, the Sauber C32 had some problems at the rear: downforce, stability, the wing, quite a few issues. The low-speed corners in particular were really hurting us.

"For the Hungarian GP onwards, we totally revised the exhaust and rear bodywork down to the tyre seal area, and designed in the undercut like the Red Bull RB9s were doing. We also brought forward some parts that we had planned for the Indian GP at the end of October.

"Nico was a bit fortunate with the safety car on his way to fourth place at Yeongam, but he wasn't alone. And, having taken the place, he was able to defend it brilliantly from the likes of Lewis Hamilton and Fernando Alonso. His performance there wasn't simply all about the car's strong straightline speed, either.

"There was a disbelieving radio message from Hamilton about our traction out of Turn 1 onto the long straight. There were a few elements in play there, not least Nico himself.

"Our low wing level meant that he didn't need too much KERS between Turns 3 and 4, so most of it could be deployed to defend on that long run down to Turn 3. Even with no DRS against Hamilton and Alonso with DRS, we were using only half our KERS to defend.

"The decisions on wing and downforce levels were part of that, sure, but you still need to be able to race and to defend. The line that Nico was using at Turn 1 was textbook stuff as far as being slow enough in, but getting a flat, straight exit was special. I engineered him at Williams and it reminded me of Brazil 2010 when he qualified on pole in changeable conditions with a car that wasn't good.

"Points were important for us that day and we'd discussed how Interlagos's last corner was the only one that you had to get out of perfectly. In the last stint we had Kubica behind, in a much quicker car, and Nico was able to save enough rear tyre for that one corner and bang, he was gone.

"This weekend it was the same. He was managing his pace. Yes, we were looking after the right front tyre as you must here, but also the rears, so that out of Turn 1 he was like a bullet every time.

"What's impressed me this year is his consistency in qualifying well and his race craft in making the best of what he's got. The car didn't deserve fourth position today – we weren't actually that quick."

after two laps. Then it stabilised as he tried to save his supersoft tyres. Hamilton was able to stay in touch with Grosjean, although he was unable to do anything about getting ahead of the Lotus driver.

Immediately after the first round of pit stops, Vettel had a lead of 2.7s, but on the medium tyres he began to pull away from Grosjean, who was in turn able to extend his advantage over Hamilton. The real action was further down the order, as sixth-placed Hulkenberg held off a busy group that included Alonso, Räikkönen and Webber, who had advanced from 13th on the grid.

Through those second stints more and more drivers complained about their tyres as they hit graining problems. Hamilton was particularly vocal as his lap times increased dramatically. One by one, those trailing in Vettel's wake had to come in for their second pit stops, as Grosjean alone stayed out with the leader.

The complexion of the race changed when Perez suffered a front tyre delamination on lap 30, the result of a severe locking-up moment. With the tyre tread and pieces of bodywork on the back straight, the safety car came out. Vettel and

In the brief period of racing in the middle of all that, Räikkönen managed to jump Grosjean, who made a mistake, to claim second place. Thus, at the restart, it was Vettel-Räikkönen-Grosjean-Hulkenberg-Hamilton-Alonso in what had become a 15-lap sprint race to the flag, albeit with Vettel and Grosjean best placed in terms of the age of their tyres.

Frustrated that the first safety car had cost him a lead of over 5s, Vettel did what he did post safety car in Singapore and drove flat out, posting a succession of fastest laps. This time he didn't build up such a spectacular lead, but he was soon 5s clear once again. Not surprisingly, Vettel's engineer then got on the radio to remind him to take it easy.

"Obviously, the cars get lighter towards the end," said Vettel. "Fortunately, we didn't have to take the absolute maximum out of the tyres, as I think the Lotuses were probably a little bit better in terms of endurance. So, I think the speed was there and in the end I tried to build up a little bit of a gap to Kimi and keep it quite consistent."

While the German was edging clear, Grosjean was reminded by his team that he was free to race Räikkönen, and was told that Kimi wouldn't be asked to move over for him. However, despite his slight tyre advantage, the French racer couldn't find a way past, and the Lotuses crossed the line together in second and third.

"It's not ideal to start so far back," said Räikkönen. "It was quite similar to the last race really, but the car was a bit better in the race. Still, it wasn't ideal as I had a bit too much understeer and lost one or two places at the start and then got them back in Turn 3. I was then able to pass people before getting stuck behind them again after the pit stop. I had more speed but just couldn't get past, and then we decided to pit a bit earlier. When

ABOVE Hamilton had a torrid time, slipping from third down to fifth as he suffered with a lack of grip

OPPOSITE Massa spun on at Turn 3 on lap 1, almost hitting team-mate Alonso, and ended the day in ninth

BELOW Nico Hulkenberg produced an impressive defensive drive to hold onto fourth place despite pressure from Hamilton and Alonso

Grosjean both pitted, as did several drivers further back, while those who'd made a recent stop stayed out. An unlucky Webber was forced to make an extra stop after picking up a puncture from Perez's debris, so his earlier charge was undone.

After nine laps under yellows, the field was released again. However, the safety car was out again almost immediately after Sutil spun under braking for Turn 3 and collected Webber. The Australian had to pull off with his car on fire, and initially very little attention was given to it by the marshals. When a tardy local course vehicle entered the track and headed off to help, the safety car was sent out again.

TALKING POINT
COMPETITIVE MIDFIELD

Nico Hulkenberg's fourth place in Korea was the combination of a fine opportunistic, defensive drive and the progress now being made with Sauber's C32.

In a tough economic climate, a team's position in the constructors' championship and hence the money it receives from Formula One

Management (FOM) has never been more crucial. After the British GP at the end of June, Force India sat fifth in the table with 59 points to McLaren's 37. At this point in the season, Sauber had scored just six points.

Two things then happened that hurt Force India. First, the tyre problems at the British GP prompted a return to the 2012-spec Kevlar-belted Pirelli tyres, which run cooler and gave the Silverstone-based team a problem generating enough heat, especially in qualifying.

Almost simultaneously, as Sauber's Tom McCullough explained (see Inside Line, p 209), a design direction on the C32 that had hurt the team's strong exhaust-blowing effect, was rectified, and the team started to look more like the one

that often punched above its weight in the 2012 season, to the extent that Sergio Perez was able to put himself on McLaren's radar.

The contrast with the first half of the season was stark. Hulkenberg was suddenly a fixture in the top ten qualifiers and followed up his fifth at low-downforce Monza with fourth place at Yeongam.

McLaren, meanwhile, after non-scores at the Canadian and British GPs, had taken 12 points in Germany, its best haul of the season and hadn't failed to score since – even if, for the first time in more than 30 years, it was contemplating a year without a podium finish.

Martin Whitmarsh's troops had thus moved 19 points clear of Force India into fifth place in the constructors' championship while

Vijay Mallya's squad were looking anxiously over their shoulder at fast-closing Sauber. Leaving Korea for Japan, the score was 62:31 but, since Silverstone, Sauber had scored 24 points, Force India just three.

The other consideration was that the widespread rule changes coming for 2014 mean that Force India doesn't have the staffing structure to develop its 2013 car at the same time as preparing for 2014. The same was largely true of Sauber, but the prospect of finishing the season with what they had and five races still to go, appeared to be playing into the hands of the Swiss squad.

With customer 2014 powertrains from Mercedes and Ferrari to be paid for by Force India and Sauber respectively, a few extra million was a target well worth chasing!

ABOVE Williams's hunt for more points continued, but Pastor Maldonado could work his way forward only to 13th, one place behind team-mate Valtteri Bottas

BELOW Vettel led every lap of the race, also setting fastest lap along the way for good measure; and his eighth win of the season moved him 77 points clear of Alonso

the safety car came out for five laps or something, it helped me to close the gap in the front again.

"Romain made a mistake and I managed to pass him, but just didn't have enough speed at the end and not enough tyres were left compared to the others. It was good fun, but I'd rather start in the front and finish in the front."

For many people, the hero of the race was Hulkenberg. After starting seventh, he quickly rose to fifth and from there grabbed the opportunity to show the world what he can do. Helped by good traction and superior straightline speed, he kept ahead of an increasingly frustrated Hamilton.

"I started seventh but, if anything, was looking more to defend than attack in the race," said Hulkenberg. "I think it was an almost perfect race for us. We put everything together and we grabbed the opportunities. It was tough, really tough, and long and demanding. I couldn't really afford any kind of mistake. It was one of those days where we weren't expecting that much from the race but, when the opportunity came, we grabbed it."

Hamilton was disappointed with the way his race unfolded. "It's strange, you know," he said, "with me and Fernando fifth and sixth at the end, and having our own little race. We are of a higher calibre than that, we should be further ahead and fighting with the champions at the front, up with Sebastian. I guess that just shows where the sport is today.

"Of course, there was plenty of action, but going backwards and having to defend isn't much fun. When I was behind Grosjean at the start, that was it, there was no way to get past. Those guys up ahead of us just had too much traction, which is where I was losing out to everyone."

Alonso had to settle for sixth, chased across the line by Rosberg who'd been delayed early on by a front-wing mounting failure. Button's McLaren was also right with them as this little group provided great entertainment, with Massa and Perez completing the top ten.

Afterwards, eight of the top drivers took private flights to Japan – unreachable on Sunday night by scheduled airlines – and six of the biggest names in the sport ended up partying until the early hours in a Tokyo shot bar, in virtual anonymity. It was a rare night of pure fun for guys who are usually so much in the spotlight, and who could begrudge them that...?

SNAPSHOT FROM
KOREA

CLOCKWISE FROM RIGHT

The Korea International Circuit is built
on reclaimed land, with landmarks
provided by structures such as this
bridge over the start/finish straight;
Sebastian Vettel, Kimi Räikkönen and
Lewis Hamilton find something to laugh
about; the enormous logistical challenge
of moving the F1 show around the globe
is clear to see in the paddock;
the charred remains of Mark Webber's
RB9; a relaxed mood on the grid
between Red Bull Racing's Christian
Horner, Webber and his engineer
Simon Rennie; a rare break for a Ferrari
mechanic; Giedo van der Garde hones
his reflexes; Sergio Perez locking up in
a determined charge that yields a single
point for 10th place; even the tyres are
expected to shine in the paddock

KOREA
YEONGAM
ROUND 14

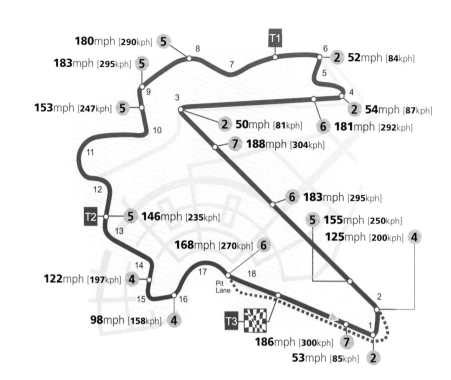

180mph [290kph] 5 — 8 — T1
183mph [295kph] 5 — 9 — 7 — 6 2 52mph [84kph]
153mph [247kph] 5 — 9 — 3 — 5
10 — 4
2 50mph [81kph] 2 — 54mph [87kph]
7 188mph [304kph] 6 181mph [292kph]
11
12
6 183mph [295kph]
T2 5 146mph [235kph] 5 155mph [250kph]
13 — 125mph [200kph] 4
168mph [270kph] 6
14 — 17 — 18
122mph [197kph] 4 — Pit Lane — 2
15 — 16 — 1
98mph [158kph] 4 — T3 🏁
186mph [300kph] 7
53mph [85kph] 2

RACE RESULTS

RACE DATE 6 October 2013
CIRCUIT LENGTH 3.492 miles
NO. OF LAPS 55
RACE DISTANCE 192.060 miles
WEATHER Overcast but dry, 27°C
TRACK TEMP 29°C
LAP RECORD Sebastian Vettel, 1m39.605s, 126.101mph, 2011

PRACTICE 1

	Driver	Time	Laps
1	L Hamilton	1m39.630s	20
2	S Vettel	1m39.667s	20
3	M Webber	1m39.816s	19
4	N Rosberg	1m40.117s	20
5	J Button	1m40.215s	22
6	F Alonso	1m40.374s	18
7	R Grosjean	1m40.396s	19
8	K Räikkönen	1m40.677s	15
9	S Perez	1m40.860s	20
10	F Massa	1m40.880s	13
11	N Hulkenberg	1m40.899s	20
12	A Sutil	1m41.432s	18
13	P Maldonado	1m41.482s	22
14	E Gutierrez	1m41.626s	21
15	J-E Vergne	1m41.924s	19
16	V Bottas	1m42.002s	20
17	D Ricciardo	1m42.043s	18
18	J Calado	1m43.008s	21
19	C Pic	1m43.660s	20
20	G van der Garde	1m43.883s	19
21	M Chilton	1m44.100s	14
22	R Gonzalez	1m46.810s	10

PRACTICE 2

	Driver	Time	Laps
1	L Hamilton	1m38.673s	31
2	S Vettel	1m38.781s	30
3	N Rosberg	1m38.797s	32
4	M Webber	1m38.844s	35
5	F Massa	1m39.114s	30
6	R Grosjean	1m39.226s	34
7	F Alonso	1m39.444s	31
8	K Räikkönen	1m39.757s	33
9	J Button	1m39.774s	29
10	A Sutil	1m40.006s	34
11	P di Resta	1m40.007s	34
12	S Perez	1m40.152s	31
13	E Gutierrez	1m40.186s	33
14	N Hulkenberg	1m40.210s	34
15	J-E Vergne	1m40.446s	30
16	D Ricciardo	1m40.552s	26
17	P Maldonado	1m41.117s	35
18	V Bottas	1m41.289s	34
19	G van der Garde	1m42.461s	36
20	C Pic	1m42.798s	35
21	J Bianchi	1m43.108s	31
22	M Chilton	1m43.441s	29

PRACTICE 3

	Driver	Time	Laps
1	S Vettel	1m37.881s	17
2	M Webber	1m38.018s	17
3	N Rosberg	1m38.318s	16
4	L Hamilton	1m38.332s	15
5	F Alonso	1m38.486s	13
6	R Grosjean	1m38.701s	19
7	F Massa	1m38.816s	14
8	K Räikkönen	1m38.857s	17
9	N Hulkenberg	1m38.961s	16
10	J Button	1m39.114s	14
11	E Gutierrez	1m39.128s	15
12	P Maldonado	1m39.196s	16
13	A Sutil	1m39.204s	17
14	S Perez	1m39.274s	15
15	D Ricciardo	1m39.327s	17
16	P di Resta	1m39.371s	19
17	J-E Vergne	1m39.665s	15
18	V Bottas	1m40.128s	17
19	C Pic	1m41.360s	19
20	G van der Garde	1m41.614s	20
21	J Bianchi	1m41.646s	14
22	M Chilton	1m42.267s	17

QUALIFYING 1

	Driver	Time
1	K Räikkönen	1m38.341s
2	N Rosberg	1m38.418s
3	N Hulkenberg	1m38.427s
4	F Alonso	1m38.520s
5	D Ricciardo	1m38.525s
6	L Hamilton	1m38.574s
7	S Vettel	1m38.683s
8	E Gutierrez	1m38.725s
9	J Button	1m38.882s
10	F Massa	1m38.884s
11	A Sutil	1m38.988s
12	S Perez	1m39.049s
13	R Grosjean	1m39.065s
14	J-E Vergne	1m39.075s
15	M Webber	1m39.138s
16	P di Resta	1m39.185s
17	V Bottas	1m39.470s
18	P Maldonado	1m39.987s
19	C Pic	1m40.864s
20	G van der Garde	1m40.871s
21	J Bianchi	1m41.169s
22	M Chilton	1m41.322s

QUALIFYING 2

	Driver	Time
1	S Vettel	1m37.569s
2	L Hamilton	1m37.824s
3	M Webber	1m37.840s
4	N Hulkenberg	1m37.913s
5	F Alonso	1m37.978s
6	N Rosberg	1m38.031s
7	R Grosjean	1m38.076s
8	K Räikkönen	1m38.181s
9	F Massa	1m38.295s
10	E Gutierrez	1m38.327s
11	S Perez	1m38.362s
12	J Button	1m38.365s
13	D Ricciardo	1m38.417s
14	A Sutil	1m38.431s
15	P di Resta	1m38.718s
16	J-E Vergne	1m38.781s

Best sectors – Practice
Sec 1	M Webber	34.538s
Sec 2	S Vettel	43.003s
Sec 3	M Webber	20.194s

Speed trap – Practice
1	D Ricciardo	199.460mph
2	M Webber	199.149mph
3	F Massa	198.838mph

Best sectors – Qualifying
Sec 1	N Hulkenberg	34.382s
Sec 2	L Hamilton	42.599s
Sec 3	S Vettel	20.005s

Speed trap – Qualifying
1	F Alonso	198.838mph
2	F Massa	198.466mph
3	M Webber	198.217mph

Sebastian Vettel
"I got off the line well and had a strong exit out of Turn 1 and controlled the race from there. Mercedes had more range than us, but we were able to win."

Fernando Alonso
"The results confirmed our concerns about tyres. At the start, I couldn't keep Hulkenberg back and that meant I had a very stressful race in tyre terms."

Jenson Button
"A car got hit at Turn 3, went wide and damaged an endplate, so I had to pit. Later, there was a fault with my pit-release lights, so eighth wasn't a bad result."

Kimi Räikkönen
"Qualifying was awful, but it's hard to say whether a better grid position would have made any difference as Vettel was faster than us and his tyres fresher."

Nico Rosberg
"I was on course for a podium after passing Lewis when the front wing broke. It was scary, but the engineers told me I could carry some speed to the pits."

Nico Hulkenberg
"I drove one of the best races of my career. I've had cars in the mirrors before, but today there were a lot and Lewis really put the pressure on at the end."

Mark Webber
"At Turn 3 on the restart, cars backed up and I was looking for a big exit to use some KERS on Daniel and the Williams. Then Sutil hit me from the inside."

Felipe Massa
"My chances evaporated on lap 1 when I found myself in the middle of a group, was forced right and spun. But my car was okay, and I scored some points."

Sergio Perez
"Felipe and I were racing hard. I thought he was going to leave me more space, then he turned in and we touched. On the second incident, I thought I had the turn."

Romain Grosjean
"At the restart I should have been in front of Kimi but I ran wide and that let him get a run on me. Then there were yellows into Turn 3 so I couldn't take the place back."

Lewis Hamilton
"After Grosjean got ahead of me, there was no way past. Our car was strong through the middle sector, but not quick enough on the straights to stay ahead."

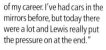

Esteban Gutierrez
"I had a good start, then I arrived at Turn 3, saw what was going on and my rears locked. That's why I lost a couple of places. To recover from that was a challenge."

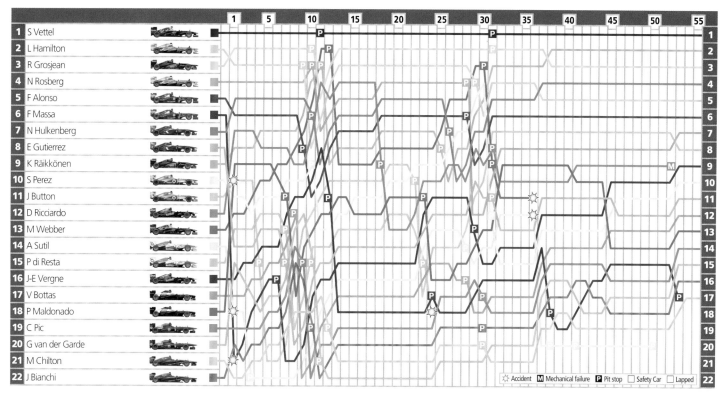

	Driver			1	5	10	15	20	25	30	35	40	45	50	55	
1	S Vettel															1
2	L Hamilton															2
3	R Grosjean															3
4	N Rosberg															4
5	F Alonso															5
6	F Massa															6
7	N Hulkenberg															7
8	E Gutierrez															8
9	K Räikkönen															9
10	S Perez															10
11	J Button															11
12	D Ricciardo															12
13	M Webber															13
14	A Sutil															14
15	P di Resta															15
16	J-E Vergne															16
17	V Bottas															17
18	P Maldonado															18
19	C Pic															19
20	G van der Garde															20
21	M Chilton															21
22	J Bianchi															22

☆ Accident ■ Mechanical failure P Pit stop □ Safety Car □ Lapped

QUALIFYING 3

	Driver	Time
1	S Vettel	1m37.202s
2	L Hamilton	1m37.420s
3	M Webber	1m37.464s
4	R Grosjean	1m37.531s
5	N Rosberg	1m37.679s
6	F Alonso	1m38.038s
7	F Massa	1m38.223s
8	N Hulkenberg	1m38.237s
9	E Gutierrez	1m38.405s
10	K Räikkönen	1m38.822s

GRID

	Driver	Time
1	S Vettel	1m37.202s
2	L Hamilton	1m37.420s
3	R Grosjean	1m37.531s
4	N Rosberg	1m37.679s
5	F Alonso	1m38.038s
6	F Massa	1m38.223s
7	N Hulkenberg	1m38.237s
8	E Gutierrez	1m38.405s
9	K Räikkönen	1m38.822s
10	S Perez	1m38.362s
11	J Button	1m38.365s
12	D Ricciardo	1m38.417s
13	M Webber	1m37.464s
14	A Sutil	1m38.431s
15	P di Resta	1m38.718s
16	J-E Vergne	1m38.781s
17	V Bottas	1m39.470s
18	P Maldonado	1m39.987s
19	C Pic	1m40.864s
20	G van der Garde	1m40.871s
21	M Chilton	1m41.322s
22	J Bianchi	1m41.169s

RACE

	Driver	Car	Laps	Time	Avg. mph	Fastest	Stops
1	S Vettel	Red Bull-Renault RB9	55	1h43m13.701s	111.465	1m41.380s	2
2	K Räikkönen	Lotus-Renault E21	55	1h43m17.925s	111.389	1m41.975s	2
3	R Grosjean	Lotus-Renault E21	55	1h43m18.628s	111.377	1m41.936s	2
4	N Hulkenberg	Sauber-Ferrari C32	55	1h43m37.815s	111.033	1m42.608s	2
5	L Hamilton	Mercedes F1 W04	55	1h43m38.956s	111.013	1m42.539s	2
6	F Alonso	Ferrari F138	55	1h43m39.890s	110.996	1m42.709s	2
7	N Rosberg	Mercedes F1 W04	55	1h43m40.399s	110.987	1m42.471s	2
8	J Button	McLaren-Mercedes MP4-28	55	1h43m45.963s	110.888	1m43.073s	2
9	F Massa	Ferrari F138	55	1h43m48.091s	110.850	1m42.954s	2
10	S Perez	McLaren-Mercedes MP4-28	55	1h43m48.856s	110.836	1m42.973s	2
11	E Gutierrez	Sauber-Ferrari C32	55	1h43m49.691s	110.821	1m42.744s	2
12	V Bottas	Williams-Renault FW35	55	1h44m00.750s	110.625	1m43.869s	2
13	P Maldonado	Williams-Renault FW35	55	1h44m03.714s	110.572	1m44.136s	2
14	C Pic	Caterham-Renault CT03	55	1h44m17.279s	110.333	1m44.477s	2
15	G van der Garde	Caterham-Renault CT03	55	1h44m18.202s	110.316	1m44.375s	2
16	J Bianchi	Marussia-Cosworth MR-02	55	1h44m21.671s	110.255	1m44.991s	2
17	M Chilton	Marussia-Cosworth MR-02	55	1h44m26.599s	110.168	1m45.408s	2
18	J-E Vergne	Toro Rosso-Ferrari STR8	53	Brakes	-	1m44.090s	3
19	D Ricciardo	Toro Rosso-Ferrari STR8	52	Brakes	-	1m42.947s	2
20	A Sutil	Force India-Mercedes VJM06	50	Accident damage	-	1m44.095s	3
R	M Webber	Red Bull-Renault RB9	36	Accident	-	1m43.863s	3
R	P di Resta	Force India-Mercedes VJM06	24	Accident	-	1m46.411s	2

CHAMPIONSHIP

	Driver	Pts
1	S Vettel	272
2	F Alonso	195
3	K Räikkönen	167
4	L Hamilton	161
5	M Webber	130
6	N Rosberg	122
7	F Massa	89
8	R Grosjean	72
9	J Button	58
10	P di Resta	36
11	N Hulkenberg	31
12	A Sutil	26
13	S Perez	23
14	D Ricciardo	18
15	J-E Vergne	13
16	P Maldonado	1

Grid penalties

M Webber Ten-place grid penalty for receiving three reprimands in the season

J Bianchi Three-place grid-penalty for impeding Paul di Resta

Fastest lap
S Vettel 1m41.380s
(123.894mph) on lap 53

Fastest speed trap
M Webber 198.901mph

Slowest speed trap
R Grosjean 192.687mph

Fastest pit stop
1	F Alonso	22.208s
2	L Hamilton	22.251s
3	L Hamilton	22.270s

Constructor

	Constructor	Pts
1	Red Bull-Renault	402
2	Ferrari	284
3	Mercedes	283
4	Lotus-Renault	239
5	McLaren-Mercedes	81
6	Force India-Mercedes	62
7	Sauber-Ferrari	31
8	Toro Rosso-Ferrari	31
9	Williams-Renault	1

Paul di Resta

"Maybe I took a bit too much kerb and that sent me off. The way we've set the car up means it's edgy and difficult to drive, and that's what caught me out."

Pastor Maldonado

"I moved to ninth on lap 1 after an incident at Turn 3. The safety car hindered me as those behind were able to close in and, after the second restart, pass me."

Jean-Eric Vergne

"We're not sure what happened: I felt the car pull to one side, so the team called me in to the pits. Starting from 16th, this was always going to be a tricky race."

Charles Pic

"I had a good start, but had to go off to avoid Massa who'd spun and lost two places. I was on plan when the safety car came out so made my second stop right away."

Jules Bianchi

"I was hoping to fight with the Caterhams and, despite my grid penalty, I was in a good position after the first few corners, but had to focus on tyre management."

Adrian Sutil

"After Massa spun, somebody hit the side of my wing. I had to pit for a new one. At the restart, I lost the rear of the car under braking for Turn 3 and hit Webber."

Valtteri Bottas

"I lost a place behind the incident on lap 1. I was in ninth place with the supersoft, but my pace improved on the mediums and the safety cars let me close on the top 10."

Daniel Ricciardo

"I tried to run as long as possible on the prime. I was in ninth place with a few laps to go. When I came to Turn 3, I braked and the car simply shot to the left."

Giedo van der Garde

"When everyone was moving to avoid Massa, I had to push out wide to avoid contact. I don't think I'd pushed any other cars out but was given a drive-through."

Max Chilton

"We were lacking a little in pace and the lap 1 mêlée set me back, but then I caught Jules. The stops were really slick and I think that we did everything we could."

2013 FORMULA 1
JAPANESE GRAND PRIX
11-13 OCTOBER
SUZUKA

SEB'S WHEEL OF FORTUNE

Sebastian Vettel's title hunt rolled on with a fifth consecutive win, following a surprise roll of the dice from Red Bull Racing. A change of strategy benefited the German, but ended the chances of his team-mate Mark Webber

While the trio of Sebastian Vettel, Mark Webber and Romain Grosjean fought for victory, using different race strategies in their attempts to finish on top, a fourth-place finish for Fernando Alonso kept the championship fight open as they left Suzuka – at least, in theory. Vettel would have to wait at least another fortnight for a chance to seal his fourth consecutive title.

Webber took his first pole position of 2013, but the Australian driver admitted that the achievement was a hollow one given that his Red Bull Racing team-mate, Vettel, was handicapped by a KERS problem. Vettel had already experienced trouble in the third practice session, which curtailed his run and left him going into qualifying with less certainty about his car than his rivals. In fact, he duly topped the second qualifying session, but when it mattered in the final session he had no KERS boost at all, which clearly cost him lap time.

Webber was ahead after the first runs and went marginally quicker on his second run to confirm his pole with 1m30.915s. Despite his handicap, Vettel came impressively close with a lap of 1m31.089s, securing himself second place on the grid.

"We decided to change the batteries on the car because we had an issue with KERS," said Vettel. "Unfortunately, we had the same problem in qualifying, so I think we now have a little bit more time to have a look and see whether there's something else broken or damaged. The whole team was pushing very hard. Obviously my car crew, but also Mark's crew, helped to fix the car in time and get it out for qualifying. So we tried everything. It worked sometimes and I'm sure we'll find the problem tonight and hopefully it will work tomorrow."

Behind the two Red Bull RB9s, there was intense competition for third place. In the end, the position went to Mercedes AMG Petronas's Lewis Hamilton, who beat Lotus's Romain Grosjean by 0.112s to claim the spot. Felipe Massa again beat team-mate Alonso to qualify fifth fastest, while Nico Rosberg earned sixth. Nico Hulkenberg put in another strong performance for Sauber to qualify seventh fastest, ahead of Alonso, Kimi Räikkönen and Jenson Button.

Sergio Perez was the quickest driver not to make it out of Q2, the Mexican qualifying 11th after McLaren built up the spare chassis overnight following the Mexican's heavy crash on Friday.

The grid line-up of Webber-Vettel-Hamilton-Grosjean meant little once the lights went out at the start. Both Red Bulls made poor getaways and Grosjean burst through to take the lead from Webber. Behind them, Vettel hit the rear wheel of Hamilton's Mercedes, giving the British driver a puncture and damaging his own front wing, while Räikkönen had a poor first lap and dropped to 11th.

At the rear of the field, Jules Bianchi and Giedo van der Garde tangled heading into the first corner and the Dutchman was lucky to escape without injury after a heavy impact with the tyre wall.

Hamilton had to pit at the end of the first lap, but the long tour back to the pits did too much damage

ABOVE Romain Grosjean is wheeled into position on the grid. His great start gave him an early lead

OPPOSITE TOP Nico Rosberg sweeps out of Turn 1 as team-mate Lewis Hamilton slows with a puncture after being hit by Vettel

OPPOSITE BOTTOM Hamilton's race was wrecked by a clash with Vettel on lap 1 that left him with a puncture that damaged his floor

INSIDE LINE
ROMAIN GROSJEAN
LOTUS DRIVER

"I thought this was the day that my first grand prix win would come! It felt a lot better in Suzuka this year than last when I collided with Mark on lap 1, for sure. It took a while, psychologically, to go from first lap nutcase in 2012 to being able to make decisive, aggressive moves again.

"This year I got a brilliant start to lead from fourth place on the grid. Terrific! When I dropped the clutch I thought: 'Whoa, whoa! That was a good one. Come on, go for it,' and I got into the lead.

"Then, from there, it was just a very, very good race. The car was fantastic on option tyres in the early stages of the race and I managed to pull away a little. When you're leading, it makes the first stint easier as the car uses the tyres less and it felt very driveable.

"Then Mark pitted earlier than we thought he would and when we fitted the hard tyres the degradation wasn't the same any more and it was making the car more difficult to drive. The Prime tyre was less good for some reason, which is the opposite of how it was on Saturday. My pace

dropped off a bit and Sebastian was just too quick for us.

"I think I lost second place behind a Caterham in the middle stint when Mark caught me just before he pitted, and then in the last few laps there were a lot of cars in front of us. I know it isn't easy for anyone to let us by, but it can cost you a lot here.

"I think it would have been a good battle with Mark for second place all the way to the chequered flag, but we caught some slower lapped cars and they blocked me quite a lot, so I lost a position to Mark. I'm not sure if I would have held him off otherwise, but it did cost me. As my tyres were really on the edge, every small aero effect was costing me. I got a little bit too much wheelspin at the exit of the chicane and Mark was in a strong position to go for it.

"It was a bit of a shame to lose the second place to Mark. Okay, the Red Bulls did catch and overtake me but, with the work we've done, we were the only ones capable of following those guys.

"It was a home race for my engineer (Ayao Komatsu) and I think he's very happy with how it went. The fans are special at Suzuka and it's always great to race here and to score a podium finish at such a difficult track."

to the floor. He eventually retired after running around at the rear of the field for seven more laps.

Grosjean led strongly ahead of the Red Bulls through the first stint. Webber pitted from second on lap 11, and the Lotus followed a lap later. That put Vettel into the lead and, crucially, with better tyre mileage he was able to stay out until lap 14. After the stops, the status quo continued, but Vettel had those extra laps in his pocket, which would prove crucial.

Running less downforce, Webber was struggling to keep his tyres in good shape, and the team eventually switched him from a two-stop to a three-stop strategy. He came in for the second time on lap 26, while Grosjean pitted for the second and final time on lap 29. In contrast to Webber, he planned to run to the end of the race from there.

That put Vettel into the lead once more and he put in a long middle stint before eventually pitting on lap 37. The stop dropped him to third place behind Webber and Grosjean, but he now had fresher tyres and the momentum with which to pass the Frenchman, which he did at the start of lap 41.

Webber made his third pit stop on lap 42, giving himself a fresh set of the quicker medium tyres for the

sprint to the line. He was in better shape than Vettel – who was on the harder tyre – but he had to get past Grosjean before he could hunt down his team-mate. Alas, that wasn't on until the start of the penultimate lap, at which point Vettel was a long stretch up the road. Vettel duly crossed the line 7.1s ahead of Webber, who was 2s ahead of Grosjean.

Inevitably, there was much discussion about the contrasting strategies of the two Red Bulls, with Webber himself questioning whether the team had got it right, and the conspiracy theorists suggesting that the team had engineered things to ensure that Vettel won.

"Obviously, after the first pit stop, very early in the second stint, Mark decided to go for the three-stop, which wasn't far off," said Vettel. "Before the race, I think we tended to favour two stops, but the tyres weren't holding up as well as we probably expected. I really tried to manage the gaps in the beginning of the stint and then close the gap, which worked brilliantly, especially with Romain.

"At the end of the second stint, I was on Mark's tail when he pitted, and was able to stay out another couple of laps. So I had more or less fresh tyres when I

RIGHT Sebastian Vettel moves his Red Bull right onto the tail of Romain Grosjean's Lotus as they battle for the lead

BELOW Fernando Alonso rose from eighth to fourth for Ferrari to keep his title hopes alive after being delayed by Nico Hulkenberg's Sauber

was able to pass him. So, yeah, it was a great strategy. We didn't lose patience early on. Obviously, we tried to make the stints as long as possible to help us at the end of the race."

Webber was typically sanguine about how the race unfolded: "I didn't think the battle was going to be with Seb at the end to be honest, as I think that it was pretty much done when we didn't do enough damage with the three-stop strategy against Seb's pace on the two-stop. We tried to race Romain at the start and then in the end we switched to the three. I was a little surprised.

"In the end, Seb ran a good race, the strategy worked out and, yeah, the three-stop strategy wasn't absolutely ridiculous, although it was certainly a bit more high risk, we know, as obviously you've got to clear people." (See Talking Point, opposite page, for more of Webber's thoughts).

Although he'd slipped back to third place after leading the first part of the race, this was nevertheless a good day for Grosjean and, realistically, the Red Bulls were always going to be very hard to beat.

"We were very quick on the option tyres at the start of the race," said the Frenchman. "The car

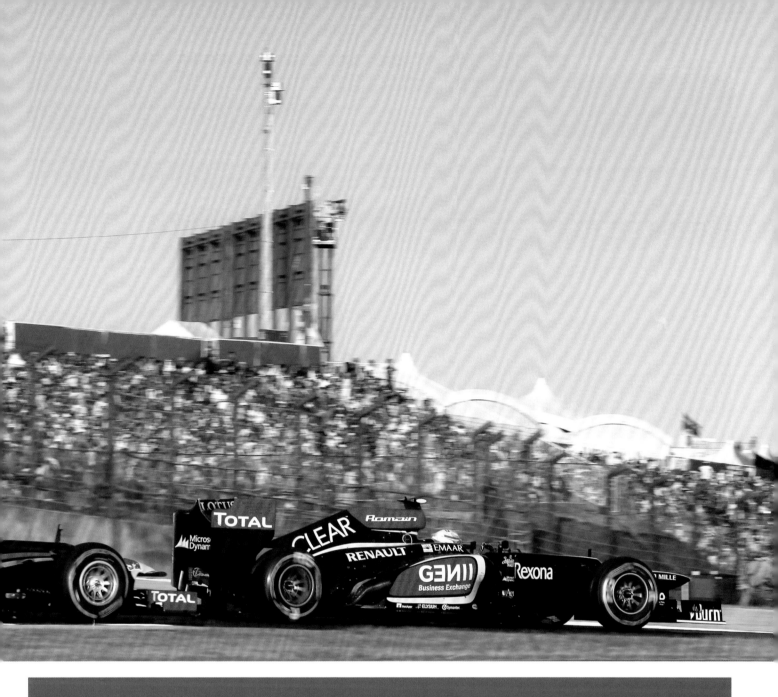

TALKING POINT
RED BULL STRATEGY

No sooner was the Japanese GP over than the conspiracy theorists were suggesting that Red Bull Racing switching Mark Webber from a two-stop strategy to a three-stop during the race had all been about ensuring the collection of a maximum points haul for his title-chasing team-mate, Sebastian Vettel.

Webber himself fuelled suspicions at the post-race press conference, when he said: "I was the meat in the sandwich, trying to beat Romain on a two-stop strategy and then all of a sudden we decided to do a three-stop.

"I was a little surprised. I asked if it was the right thing to do because I felt we could get to the lap that we were looking to get to. Of course, Seb was out a few laps longer but, in terms of getting to the target lap that we looked to get to for the two-stop strategy, I thought that was achievable.

"In the end," the Australian continued, "we got back to where we were in terms of position, but Seb jumped both of us..."

That admission was somewhat at odds with Red Bull Racing Team Principal Christian Horner, who said that Webber was pitted and put onto a three-stop strategy simply because his tyres had gone.

The Red Bull RB9s, having monopolised the front row of the grid, were unexpectedly on the back foot when they made bad starts and were beaten away by Grosjean's Lotus but, whether he was on a two-stop or three-stop strategy, Webber faced an uphill struggle to win.

His best chance was if Grosjean, when caught by Vettel, had been able to go defensive and keep Vettel behind him for a time. At the point that Vettel caught the Lotus, Webber was 15.5s in front of both and still edging away from Grosjean slightly on tyres that were three laps older. Webber needed a 22s window to make the extra stop and still emerge in the lead. So, if Grosjean had suddenly lost 1s or more a lap defending from Vettel successfully for a few laps, Webber might just have opened a window for the stop.

Yet, as soon as Vettel overtook Grosjean, on lap 41, that possibility went out of the window as Vettel was appreciably quicker on his new five-lap-old tyres.

Thus Red Bull switched Webber's strategy. Across the line on lap 41, Webber led Vettel by 14.5s with 12 laps to go with Seb having 1m35.3s pace to Webber's 1m36.3s. It might have been close if they'd left Mark out, but Webber would have needed a 27-lap stint on those Primes. Opposing strategists estimated the life of the hard tyre at 22 laps and Webber, we know, is tough on them. It would have been a long shot.

ABOVE The McLarens kept each
other company mid-race, before
Jenson Button raced on to ninth
and Sergio Perez fell back to 15th

BELOW Vettel's trademark victory
celebration could just as easily
signify 'one race to go' as he
stretched his lead to 90 points

was less hard on its tyres and I could open the gap.
Unfortunately, it was less good on the Prime tyre
today for some reason, rather than yesterday when it
was the opposite, so the pace dropped a little and Seb
was really too quick for us."

Any hopes of at least beating Webber were then
scuppered when he was encountered traffic and was
obstructed by the slower cars as he tried to overtake.
Grosjean was more than a little frustrated by this
(see Inside Line, p218), believing that it denied him
a chance to at least be the meat in a Red Bull Racing
sandwich. With no other challengers, though, he
was at least able to concentrate on throwing

everything that he had into attempting to pass
Webber for second place.

Indeed, the rest were miles behind, the group
having at one point lost a lot of time behind Daniel
Ricciardo, who started on the hard tyre and got ahead
by making a late first pit stop. Hulkenberg lost a place
to Alonso at the start but did a good job to jump
both Ferraris at the first pit stops. He ran fourth for
much of the race, often under pressure from Alonso.
However, his tyres gave up in the closing laps and he
lost out both to the Spaniard and to Räikkönen, the
latter doing a good job to salvage some points after
his poor opening lap.

Hulkenberg, who had now finished in fifth, ninth,
fourth and sixth places in four races, said he wasn't
too upset to lose places so close to the finish: "We
shouldn't be too disappointed," he said. "I think
we did everything we could, and my tyres were just
giving up a little bit. We were fighting all through the
race. Just after the pit stop, I was surprised that I was
able to pull away a bit from Fernando, but he was also
trying to save his tyres for the end of the race."

Hulkenberg's Sauber team-mate Esteban Gutierrez
moved into ninth place on the opening lap and drove
a strong race to seventh at the flag to score his first
points in F1. Rosberg's race was spoiled by a drive-
through penalty for an unsafe pit stop release, and he
eventually finished eighth.

Perez had a good first lap and jumped up to eighth
place, while Button ran tenth in the first stint, but lost
time in the pits when he picked up a puncture after
contact with Rosberg, dropping him back to 15th.
After flatspotting his tyres to avoid a first lap incident,
Button had to pit earlier than planned, which meant
switching to a three-stop strategy. He advanced to
ninth by the end, beating Massa to the finish line by a
matter of inches, the Brazilian having earlier picked up
a drive-through penalty for speeding in the pit lane.

SNAPSHOT FROM
JAPAN

CLOCKWISE FROM RIGHT

Things are about to get serious for Romain Grosjean as he's pushed to the grid in Suzuka; Jenson Button waits to show off his Japanese Sumo wrestling-themed helmet; Romain Grosjean enjoys the calm before the storm; one team, two drivers and three trophies – it's smiles all round as Red Bull celebrate yet another successful day this season; Lotus Team Principal Eric Boullier patrols the grid; Valtteri Bottas is an oasis of tranquility amid a blur of activity in the Williams garage; Sebastian Vettel deep in thought; 'Ice Man' Räikkönen watches and waits in second qualifying; fabrication on site will always be a feature of F1 life; ...especially if your car has been involved in an incident like Caterham's Giedo van der Garde

JAPAN
SUZUKA
ROUND 15

RACE RESULTS

RACE DATE 13 October 2013
CIRCUIT LENGTH 3.608 miles
NO. OF LAPS 53
RACE DISTANCE 191.224 miles
WEATHER Dry and bright, 24°C
TRACK TEMP 35°C
LAP RECORD Kimi Räikkönen,
1m31.540s, 141.904mph, 2005

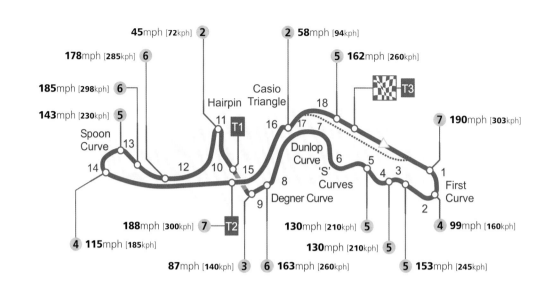

Circuit map labels:
45mph [72kph] 2 — 2 58mph [94kph]
178mph [285kph] 6 — 5 162mph [260kph]
185mph [298kph] 6
143mph [230kph] 5
Casio Triangle — Hairpin — 18 — 7 190mph [303kph]
Spoon Curve — 11 T1 16 17 — Dunlop Curve
13 — 12 10 15 — 'S' Curves — First Curve
14 — 8 Degner Curve — 6 5 4 3 1
9 — 2
188mph [300kph] 7 T2 — 130mph [210kph] 5 — 4 99mph [160kph]
4 115mph [185kph] — 130mph [210kph] 5
87mph [140kph] 3 — 6 163mph [260kph] — 5 153mph [245kph]
T3

PRACTICE 1				PRACTICE 2				PRACTICE 3				QUALIFYING 1			QUALIFYING 2	
	Driver	Time	Laps		Driver	Time	Laps		Driver	Time	Laps		Driver	Time		Driver	Time
1	L Hamilton	1m34.157s	19	1	S Vettel	1m33.852s	35	1	M Webber	1m32.053s	17	1	R Grosjean	1m31.824s	1	S Vettel	1m31.290s
2	N Rosberg	1m34.487s	19	2	M Webber	1m34.020s	35	2	L Hamilton	1m32.187s	18	2	F Massa	1m31.994s	2	M Webber	1m31.513s
3	S Vettel	1m34.768s	24	3	N Rosberg	1m34.114s	36	3	N Rosberg	1m32.355s	18	3	N Rosberg	1m32.244s	3	R Grosjean	1m31.565s
4	M Webber	1m34.787s	20	4	K Räikkönen	1m34.202s	17	4	R Grosjean	1m32.707s	26	4	M Webber	1m32.271s	4	L Hamilton	1m31.636s
5	F Massa	1m35.126s	14	5	R Grosjean	1m34.411s	30	5	F Alonso	1m32.800s	14	5	P di Resta	1m32.286s	5	K Räikkönen	1m31.662s
6	F Alonso	1m35.154s	16	6	L Hamilton	1m34.442s	36	6	F Massa	1m32.815s	14	6	L Hamilton	1m32.340s	6	F Massa	1m31.668s
7	R Grosjean	1m35.179s	15	7	D Ricciardo	1m34.473s	30	7	J Button	1m32.869s	17	7	F Alonso	1m32.371s	7	N Rosberg	1m31.764s
8	K Räikkönen	1m35.364s	17	8	F Massa	1m34.698s	35	8	K Räikkönen	1m32.946s	25	8	K Räikkönen	1m32.377s	8	F Alonso	1m31.828s
9	S Perez	1m35.450s	27	9	J Button	1m34.912s	34	9	S Vettel	1m33.036s	8	9	S Vettel	1m32.397s	9	J Button	1m31.838s
10	D Ricciardo	1m35.635s	19	10	F Alonso	1m35.087s	32	10	N Hulkenberg	1m33.076s	12	10	N Hulkenberg	1m32.465s	10	N Hulkenberg	1m31.848s
11	J Button	1m35.868s	22	11	E Gutierrez	1m35.089s	36	11	S Perez	1m33.158s	15	11	J Button	1m32.606s	11	S Perez	1m31.989s
12	N Hulkenberg	1m35.900s	18	12	J-E Vergne	1m35.109s	34	12	J-E Vergne	1m33.260s	15	12	V Bottas	1m32.613s	12	P di Resta	1m31.992s
13	J-E Vergne	1m36.066s	20	13	N Hulkenberg	1m35.182s	34	13	D Ricciardo	1m33.490s	16	13	E Gutierrez	1m32.673s	13	V Bottas	1m32.013s
14	A Sutil	1m36.165s	19	14	P di Resta	1m35.275s	35	14	P Maldonado	1m33.638s	17	14	S Perez	1m32.718s	14	E Gutierrez	1m32.063s
15	P Maldonado	1m36.178s	12	15	A Sutil	1m35.341s	25	15	P di Resta	1m33.660s	19	15	D Ricciardo	1m32.804s	15	P Maldonado	1m32.093s
16	V Bottas	1m36.340s	23	16	S Perez	1m35.709s	8	16	E Gutierrez	1m33.732s	15	16	P Maldonado	1m32.875s	16	D Ricciardo	1m32.485s
17	P di Resta	1m36.399s	18	17	V Bottas	1m36.136s	41	17	V Bottas	1m33.955s	18	17	A Sutil	1m32.890s			
18	E Gutierrez	1m36.760s	22	18	P Maldonado	1m36.722s	6	18	A Sutil	1m34.773s	8	18	J-E Vergne	1m33.357s			
19	H Kovalainen	1m37.595s	22	19	C Pic	1m37.630s	31	19	G van der Garde	1m35.473s	20	19	M Chilton	1m34.320s			
20	J Bianchi	1m37.629s	8	20	G van der Garde	1m37.905s	36	20	C Pic	1m35.518s	18	20	C Pic	1m34.556s			
21	G van der Garde	1m38.025s	15	21	M Chilton	1m38.121s	33	21	M Chilton	1m35.844s	16	21	G van der Garde	1m34.879s			
22	M Chilton	1m38.763s	18	22	J Bianchi	No time	0	22	J Bianchi	1m39.378s	20	22	J Bianchi	1m34.958s			

Best sectors – Practice			Speed trap – Practice			Best sectors – Qualifying			Speed trap – Qualifying	
Sec 1	L Hamilton	32.238s	1	M Webber	189.145mph	Sec 1	S Vettel	31.946s	1 M Webber	187.840mph
Sec 2	M Webber	41.508s	2	M Chilton	188.337mph	Sec 2	M Webber	41.123s	2 D Ricciardo	187.529mph
Sec 3	M Webber	18.048s	3	J-E Vergne	187.964mph	Sec 3	S Vettel	17.889s	3 M Chilton	187.032mph

 Sebastian Vettel

"It was a horrible start: I found myself third and tried to go longer in the first stint. I had great traction after I passed Romain, then the only threat was Mark."

Fernando Alonso

"Fourth place was the most that I could do, as the three ahead were really out of reach and so, given my starting position and how practice went, I'm happy."

 Jenson Button

"My first two stints were hard. For the third set, we added front wing, and the car was good to drive, so I made a great move outside Paul at the chicane."

 **Kimi Räikkönen**

"I lost a few places at the start, but got them back later on. After the final stop, the car worked much better. It's hard to pass here so it's good that I got points."

Nico Rosberg

"I was in a strong position until my first pit stop. I then had the incident as I left the pit box. So I switched to a three-stop and that worked out as well as it could."

Nico Hulkenberg

"I managed to keep both Ferraris behind me for a long time again, even if it wasn't enough as my tyres gave up a little towards the end of the race."

 **Mark Webber**

"We were on the back foot after Romain's great start. I wanted to pressure him for the win. Seb was on a different strategy and in the end it worked out pretty similar."

Felipe Massa

"The drive-through for speeding wiped out any chance of a good race. After the penalty, I was stuck in traffic and cars that had made a third stop then passed me."

 **Sergio Perez**

"Everything that could go wrong, did. I had an incident with Nico in the pits, some slow pit stops, and then another incident with Nico, which gave me a puncture."

 **Romain Grosjean**

"It was superb, passing the Red Bulls. It'll be one of my memories of 2013. The car was great on the first set of tyres and I pulled away, but the Red Bulls reeled me in."

Lewis Hamilton

"I got a great start. Mark moved right, so I had to move as well, which left Seb between me and Romain. Seb's front wing clipped my right rear and cut the tyre."

 **Esteban Gutierrez**

"Finally I can feel satisfaction. Over the past few races we've improved a lot and knowing that we can achieve something like this, you really go forward."

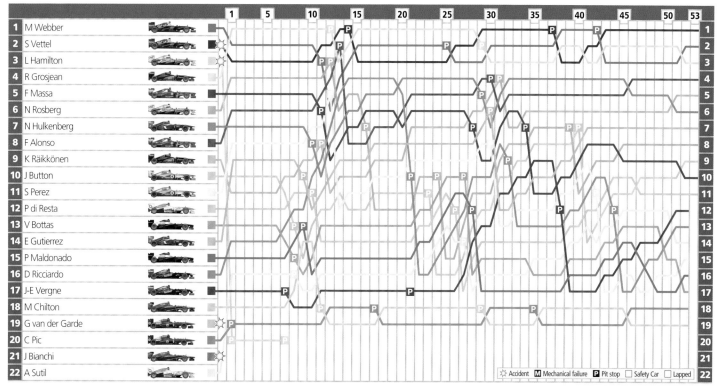

	Driver				
1	M Webber				1
2	S Vettel				2
3	L Hamilton				3
4	R Grosjean				4
5	F Massa				5
6	N Rosberg				6
7	N Hulkenberg				7
8	F Alonso				8
9	K Räikkönen				9
10	J Button				10
11	S Perez				11
12	P di Resta				12
13	V Bottas				13
14	E Gutierrez				14
15	P Maldonado				15
16	D Ricciardo				16
17	J-E Vergne				17
18	M Chilton				18
19	G van der Garde				19
20	C Pic				20
21	J Bianchi				21
22	A Sutil				22

☼ Accident ▣ Mechanical failure ▣ Pit stop ☐ Safety Car ☐ Lapped

QUALIFYING 3

	Driver	Time
1	M Webber	1m30.915s
2	S Vettel	1m31.089s
3	L Hamilton	1m31.253s
4	R Grosjean	1m31.365s
5	F Massa	1m31.378s
6	N Rosberg	1m31.397s
7	N Hulkenberg	1m31.644s
8	F Alonso	1m31.665s
9	K Räikkönen	1m31.684s
10	J Button	1m31.827s

GRID

	Driver	Time
1	M Webber	1m30.915s
2	S Vettel	1m31.089s
3	L Hamilton	1m31.253s
4	R Grosjean	1m31.365s
5	F Massa	1m31.378s
6	N Rosberg	1m31.397s
7	N Hulkenberg	1m31.644s
8	F Alonso	1m31.665s
9	K Räikkönen	1m31.684s
10	J Button	1m31.827s
11	S Perez	1m31.989s
12	P di Resta	1m31.992s
13	V Bottas	1m32.013s
14	E Gutierrez	1m32.063s
15	P Maldonado	1m32.093s
16	D Ricciardo	1m32.485s
17	J-E Vergne	1m33.357s
18	M Chilton	1m34.320s
19	G van der Garde	1m34.879s
20	C Pic	1m34.556s
21	J Bianchi	1m34.958s
22	A Sutil	1m32.890s

RACE

	Driver	Car	Laps	Time	Avg. mph	Fastest	Stops
1	S Vettel	Red Bull-Renault RB9	53	1h26m49.301s	132.031	1m35.317s	2
2	M Webber	Red Bull-Renault RB9	53	1h26m56.430s	131.851	1m34.587s	3
3	R Grosjean	Lotus-Renault E21	53	1h26m59.211s	131.780	1m35.991s	2
4	F Alonso	Ferrari F138	53	1h27m34.906s	130.885	1m35.877s	2
5	K Räikkönen	Lotus-Renault E21	53	1h27m36.626s	130.843	1m35.516s	2
6	N Hulkenberg	Sauber-Ferrari C32	53	1h27m40.916s	130.736	1m36.482s	2
7	E Gutierrez	Sauber-Ferrari C32	53	1h28m00.931s	130.240	1m36.499s	2
8	N Rosberg	Mercedes F1 W04	53	1h28m01.324s	130.230	1m34.650s	4
9	J Button	McLaren-Mercedes MP4-28	53	1h28m10.122s	130.014	1m35.549s	3
10	F Massa	Ferrari F138	53	1h28m18.564s	129.807	1m37.001s	3
11	P di Resta	Force India-Mercedes VJM06	53	1h28m27.873s	129.579	1m37.407s	2
12	J-E Vergne	Toro Rosso-Ferrari STR8	52	1h26m52.410s	129.461	1m35.895s	3
13	D Ricciardo	Toro Rosso-Ferrari STR8	52	1h26m54.598s	129.406	1m35.020s	3
14	A Sutil	Force India-Mercedes VJM06	52	1h27m06.344s	129.115	1m37.367s	2
15	S Perez	McLaren-Mercedes MP4-28	52	1h27m06.462s	129.112	1m35.845s	3
16	P Madonado	Williams-Renault FW35	52	1h27m08.671s	129.058	1m37.423s	3
17	V Bottas	Williams-Renault FW35	52	1h27m09.253s	129.043	1m37.856s	3
18	C Pic	Caterham-Renault CT03	52	1h28m09.524s	127.573	1m37.489s	3
19	M Chilton	Marussia-Cosworth MR-02	52	1h28m28.731s	127.111	1m38.713s	2
R	L Hamilton	Mercedes F1 W04	7	Collision damage	-	1m41.202s	1
R	G van der Garde	Caterham-Renault CT03	0	Collision	-	-	0
R	J Bianchi	Marussia-Cosworth MR-02	0	Collision	-	-	0

CHAMPIONSHIP

	Driver	Pts
1	S Vettel	297
2	F Alonso	207
3	K Räikkönen	177
4	L Hamilton	161
5	M Webber	148
6	N Rosberg	126
7	F Massa	90
8	R Grosjean	87
9	J Button	60
10	N Hulkenberg	39
11	P di Resta	36
12	A Sutil	26
13	S Perez	23
14	D Ricciardo	18
15	J-E Vergne	13
16	E Gutierrez	6
17	P Maldonado	1

Grid penalties
C Pic Five-place grid penalty for changing gearbox
J Bianchi Five-place grid penalty for changing gearbox
A Sutil Ten-place grid penalty

Fastest lap
M Webber 1m34.587s
(137.332mph) on lap 44

Fastest speed trap
M Webber 191.755mph

Slowest speed trap
L Hamilton 176.966mph

Fastest pit stop
1	N Rosberg	22.551s
2	F Alonso	22.645s
3	N Rosberg	22.771s

	Constructor	Pts
1	Red Bull-Renault	445
2	Ferrari	297
3	Mercedes	287
4	Lotus-Renault	264
5	McLaren-Mercedes	83
6	Force India-Mercedes	62
7	Sauber-Ferrari	45
8	Toro Rosso-Ferrari	31
9	Williams-Renault	1

Paul di Resta
"I didn't get a good launch and a few cars went by. Then I lost out to Bottas at the first stop, which is why I made an early second stop, to get track position."

Pastor Maldonado
"I was pleased to be able to make a move on the last lap to gain a position over Valtteri. I felt we got the strategy slightly wrong and so I struggled a bit for pace."

Jean-Eric Vergne
"I found myself in traffic, so the team called me in early for Primes, but the stop was slow and put me back in traffic. We then tried lengthening the next two stints."

Charles Pic
"We'd decided to serve the drive-through at the end of lap 1 so I then played catch up. My target was to pass Chilton and I did, finishing almost 20s clear."

Jules Bianchi
"This is a weekend that was destined not to come my way. Unfortunately, as I turned into Turn 1, van der Garde hit my rear wing which pushed me into the gravel."

Adrian Sutil
"Starting from the back made it hard to score. I finished 14th and had some good battles, but there was a lot of oversteer and it wasn't easy to be consistent."

Valtteri Bottas
"At the start of the race, I didn't look too bad and managed to keep some cars behind me but, from the end of the second stint, my pace seemed to drop off."

Daniel Ricciardo
"I started on the hard tyre and overtook Bottas. Later, I made a move outside Sutil at 130R but ran onto the grass and was hit with a drive-through penalty."

Giedo van der Garde
"Going into Turn 1, I was squeezed between the two Marussias, losing my front wing in contact with Bianchi. Then the car went into the wall."

Max Chilton
"I was happy with the way my race was going, but on the prime tyre in the final stint I struggled and ran wide onto the marbles, which caused me to go off."

2013 FORMULA 1 AIRTEL INDIAN GRAND PRIX

**25-27 OCTOBER
BUDDH INTERNATIONAL
CIRCUIT, NEW DELHI**

CHAMPION TAKES A BOW

Sebastian Vettel secured his fourth world title in a row with a dominant victory in India – and a few smoke-shrouded doughnuts at the finish. It was his sixth consecutive win of 2013 and his third win in only the third Indian GP

Sebastian Vettel celebrated clinching his fourth title by ignoring parc ferme and heading past the pit lane entry to return to the grid, where he performed a series of donuts in front of the grandstands before climbing out and bowing to his car in homage. It was a great piece of showmanship, but the FIA Stewards had to act, because he hadn't headed to the winner's correct parking slot. He duly earned a reprimand and a €25,000 fine for the team. But perhaps his ebullient high spirits were understandable in the circumstances.

The practice sessions showed that the option tyre was very fragile, especially when fitted to a Red Bull RB9, and thus strategies for both qualifying and the race were based on minimising its use and spending as much time as possible on the medium tyre. Indeed, there was speculation that some leading drivers would qualify and start on the medium, hoping that a long first stint would propel them up the order.

Vettel took the more orthodox route as he snagged his 43rd pole position with his first run in the final qualifying session. Once again he was able to abort his second run after nobody else went quicker. Mercedes proved the closest challenger, as Nico Rosberg and Lewis Hamilton claimed second and third on the grid.

A driver who did take the strategy gamble, though, was Vettel's team-mate Mark Webber. He was hoping to edge into the top six on the grid on the medium tyre, and did so, qualifying an impressive fourth, suggesting that he would be a threat to his team-mate. "We thought it was worth trying something a bit different with the strategy, so that's why we ran the Primes in Q3," said the Australian. "We thought that we'd probably be a bit further back than the second row, so it turned out to be a good session for us."

Like Red Bull Racing, Ferrari also decided to split its strategies. Felipe Massa went for softs and qualified fifth, while Fernando Alonso joined Webber in using the medium tyre and was eighth fastest. The Italian cars were separated by Kimi Räikkönen's Lotus and Nico Hulkenberg's Sauber. Both McLaren drivers made it through to the third qualifying session and decided to go with the mediums, Sergio Perez edging out Jenson Button as the pair qualified ninth and tenth.

The big story of Saturday was a bad call by Lotus for Romain Grosjean in the opening part of qualifying. A little too confident, the team stuck to the medium tyre as most others ran on softs. While Vettel did the same and made it through in tenth, the Frenchman

had a somewhat scrappy lap and ended up 17th and was therefore unable to progress. Until then, he'd been seen as a serious contender for the first couple of rows.

All eyes were on how much progress medium runners Webber and Alonso could make at the start, given that those around them potentially had grippier tyres. Ironically, they managed to collide at the first corner as Webber hit the back of Räikkönen's Lotus and everyone backed up. The Australian dropped to seventh, wasting his good qualifying performance, while Alonso suffered front wing damage. Further around the lap, Alonso also clashed with Button.

Vettel duly made his escape and was 2.4s ahead of the fast-starting Massa at the end of the first lap, as the Mercedes drivers dropped to third and fourth. That proved crucial as they'd lose valuable time behind the Brazilian's Ferrari and thus any slim chance they had of challenging for victory.

We knew we might see some oddball strategies, and at the end of lap 1 both Paul di Resta and Jean-Eric Vergne pitted to off-load their soft tyres so that they could run the rest of the race on mediums.

Vettel had a similar plan, and came in on lap 2 to swap his softs for mediums, dropping to 17th. At the same time, Alonso had to pit for a new front wing, and the Spaniard's race was, in effect, ruined as he lost the advantage of starting on mediums, so the tiny chance he had of keeping the title battle alive for one more weekend, should Vettel hit trouble, was over.

Massa assumed the lead, confidently heading the Mercedes pair. Then Rosberg relinquished second place when he pitted on lap 7, with Massa and Hamilton coming in a lap later.

Not planning to stop any time soon, Webber moved into the lead after those on softs had stopped, but after his bad first lap he never really had enough advantage to be in a position to beat his team-mate. Indeed, after dropping to 17th, Vettel made quick progress, gaining

BELOW Jenson Button's race was hampered when he was forced to pit on lap 1 after being hit by Alonso

BOTTOM Sebastian Vettel leads Mercedes duo Lewis Hamilton (right) and Nico Rosberg towards Turn 1

OPPOSITE Felipe Massa accelerates past the pits early in the race when he took over the lead from Mark Webber as his rivals pitted early to get rid of their softs

INSIDE LINE
CHRISTIAN HORNER
RED BULL RACING TEAM PRINCIPAL

"That was a phenomenal drive by Sebastian. It was a great way to win a fourth championship. We weren't reacting to Fernando Alonso's problem, as we had always planned to bring Seb in at the end of the second lap. He knew that he would come out at the back of the field and would have to go through the traffic from there and be decisive and quick in the way he did it.

"Seb knew that he needed to keep the gap to the lead car at less than 22 seconds and his passing and execution to manage that was fabulous. He actually gained on the race leader while going through traffic, which was quite remarkable. Then, as the strategy started to unfold, he got himself back into the lead and managed the race exceptionally well from there.

"Putting Mark on the option tyres for the middle stint of the race rather than the last stint was no conspiracy as we'd looked at it before the race. We'd managed to have the window of a free stop and the exposure, on Mark's strategy, was to a safety car. Let's say it had come out with 15 laps to go, he then couldn't have changed tyres and got to the end on the Options, so it was

the most risk-free way of running his race. So we gave him a few hard laps on new Options in clean air and then went back onto the Prime tyre.

"After the sudden failure on Mark's car, there was no reason to think that it couldn't happen on the other one, so we immediately tried to reduce the amount of draw on the alternator as much as possible, which even included turning off the KERS. A problem with a sensor on the alternator then gave us some more heart-in-mouth moments, and in the meantime Seb was lighting up the timing screens with purple sectors. That caused a bit of tension too!

"Seb has raised the bar continually, and he's still only 26 years old. He hasn't achieved these results by accident. He has done it by having an enormous amount of natural ability, commitment and a fantastic work ethic. There

has also been tremendous passion, determination and dedication within the whole team.

"Seb got his knuckles rapped for doing the donuts, but to win a world championship and then show a bit of exuberance in front of a crowd like that is surely great for F1, and great for the show, on TV as well as the stands.

"We've still got three races to go and we'll treat them like three FA Cup Finals and leave the proper celebrations until then."

TALKING POINT
DOWN TO EARTH

Sebastian Vettel's victory in India meant that he joined Juan Manuel Fangio, Michael Schumacher and Alain Prost in an exclusive club of four-time world champions.

Rather than celebrating this achievement into the small hours, though, the Red Bull man joined his team-mates back at the garage, helping to pack up equipment. That says a lot about Vettel, who may be intensely competitive but, behind the scenes, also has a great sense of humour and a likeable personality.

Adrian Newey, who has given Vettel the sharpest of tools, believes the German driver undoubtedly deserves to be considered a great.

"In measuring great drivers, numbers are only part of it," says Newey. "Stirling Moss is probably the exception, but I think you need to have won two championships to be considered a great.

"After that, it's how you achieved them and how you conduct yourself. For me, Sebastian thoroughly deserves to be considered one of the all-time greats because he's also very humble – the success and the fame he's achieved would go to the head of many, but it hasn't with Seb."

through pit stops on those ahead and also with some decisive overtaking. By lap 21, he was up to second and only about 10s behind Webber, and it was clear that he'd have the upper hand as the strategy played out.

Webber pitted for the first time on lap 28, handing the lead to Vettel. The latter then made his second and final pit stop on lap 31. On lap 32, Webber made his own second stop to go back to the mediums, after just four laps with the softs. Vettel was left with a 12s lead over Webber, with both men set to run to the flag.

However, Webber slowed on lap 40 and retired with an alternator failure, logging his second retirement in three races. He had a wry smile on his face as he walked back as, yet again, he'd suffered bad luck with a part that could have been fitted to either car.

After that, the remaining 20 laps became a demonstration run for Vettel, although inevitably the team were concerned about a repeat alternator failure, even asking him not to use his drinks bottle to avoid draining power. "Thankfully, the car got to the end, and Seb did what he needed to," said Red Bull Racing Team Principal Christian Horner. "It was tremendously cruel luck not to have Mark up there as well."

Vettel ultimately came home 29s clear of Rosberg. It might have looked easy, but his donut display on the grid showed how relieved he was as the tension was released, while the team enjoyed the bonus of securing its fourth constructors' title.

"It was a difficult emotion to cross the line and to feel happy all of a sudden," said Vettel, "as you're in a rhythm, you know what you're doing, you have a certain routine. Yes, I was very nervous before the race but I am all the time. I'm nervous, usually the last hour of my sleep from Saturday to Sunday is quite poor, as I'm looking forward to the race, I'm seeing all sorts of scenarios in my head.

"It takes time to understand what happened, but I think it's also a special place to win at and, yeah,

LEFT Adrian Sutil headed Force India's intra-team battle until lap 44 when he was passed by Paul di Resta as they raced to eighth and ninth

BELOW Kimi Räikkönen looked set for third place towards the end, but his Lotus was struggling for grip and he had to pit for new tyres with only two laps to go, falling to seventh

ABOVE The four-time champion risks the wrath of the stewards as he pays homage to his RB9, the tenth championship-winning car created by Adrian Newey

BELOW Vettel pats Newey on the head as he is held shoulder-high on the podium by Nico Rosberg and Romain Grosjean

when my engineer called for the usual procedure – parc ferme, park the car – I said to myself I don't care, I go there, the crowd was great in the main grandstand and I'll have some fun which I enjoyed a lot..."

Having pitted on lap 7, Räikkönen tried to run a marathon stint to the flag on the mediums, and after Webber retired he ran second until his tyres began to give up a few laps from home. Rosberg was thus able to claim the place after a solid performance.

"The start was a bit difficult, dropping behind Massa," he said. "He was definitely a lot slower. I gave it a go on one lap, but I couldn't make it happen and he passed me back on the exit. Then the team did a

fantastic strategy. I managed to get by Kimi like that for second place and I'm pleased with that."

Räikkönen's tumble down the order continued when his team-mate Grosjean came up behind him with five laps to go. They nearly touched as the Frenchman tried to find a way past the struggling Finn, which led to an expletive-filled "get out of the way" radio message from the pit wall. Grosjean had proved to be the star of the race. Starting from 17th on the grid on new softs, he rose to fifth before pitting for mediums on lap 13. From there, he completed a huge 47-lap stint to the flag. Third place was a just reward.

After running second in the early laps, Massa finished in fourth place, but it was still a good effort by the Brazilian. Behind him, Perez enjoyed a great race, running a long opening stint on the medium tyre and holding second behind Webber before pitting. Later, a great double pass on the battling Räikkönen and Hamilton helped the Mexican into an encouraging fifth place. Not for the first time in 2013, Hamilton faded with his tyres, so had to settle for sixth.

Räikkönen's attempt to run to the chequered flag failed and, after dropping to seventh, Lotus finally called him in for a second pit stop with just two laps to go, knowing that it wouldn't cost him another place. Inevitably, he then set a fired-up fastest lap. In the light of the near clash between the team-mates and the colourful radio traffic, there was probably a fair bit of tension in the Lotus camp afterwards.

Tyre strategy worked well for Force India, with di Resta taking eighth place after stopping on the first lap and again at half distance, and Adrian Sutil finishing in ninth place after a 41-lap opening stint on the medium tyre. Scuderia Toro Rosso's Daniel Ricciardo completed the top 10, while Alonso – hampered by a handling problem after his clashes on the opening lap – was left in a frustrated 11th. It certainly wasn't a great way for his title challenge to end.

SNAPSHOT FROM
INDIA

CLOCKWISE FROM RIGHT

Hazy sunlight casts a glow over Buddh International Circuit; it's all over and Sebastian Vettel can celebrate being crowned champion for the fourth time; Felipe Massa is a picture of relaxation; Sebastian Vettel and Red Bull Racing Team Manager Jonathan Wheatley continue the team's title celebrations; tyre choice was easier if you were a Ferrari mechanic, choosing which one to sit on being about as complex as it got; the rubber laid down in the pit lane; instructions are issued in the Caterham F1 Team pit; Paddy Lowe takes in the action at the Mercedes AMG Petronas pit wall; Nicolas Hamilton was in India to check on big brother Lewis's progress; life in downtown Delhi was considerably less high-tech than at the circuit...

INDIA
NEW DELHI
ROUND 16

Official Results © [2013]
Formula One World Championship Limited,
6 Princes Gate, London, SW7 1QJ.
No reproduction without permission.
All copyright and database rights reserved.

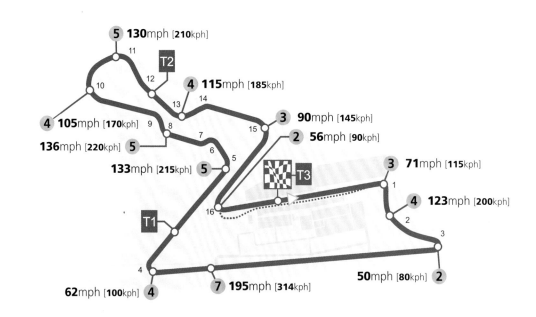

5 **130**mph [**210**kph]

T2

4 **115**mph [**185**kph]

4 **105**mph [**170**kph]

3 **90**mph [**145**kph]

136mph [**220**kph] 5

2 **56**mph [**90**kph]

133mph [**215**kph] 5

3 **71**mph [**115**kph]

4 **123**mph [**200**kph]

T3

T1

50mph [**80**kph] 2

62mph [**100**kph] 4

7 **195**mph [**314**kph]

RACE RESULTS

RACE DATE 27 October 2013
CIRCUIT LENGTH 3.185 miles
NO. OF LAPS 60
RACE DISTANCE 191.100 miles
WEATHER Overcast & hazy, 29°C
TRACK TEMP 31°C
LAP RECORD Sebastian Vettel,
1m27.249s, 131.397mph, 2011

PRACTICE 1		
Driver	**Time**	**Laps**
1 S Vettel	1m26.683s	24
2 M Webber	1m26.871s	17
3 N Rosberg	1m26.899s	23
4 R Grosjean	1m26.990s	20
5 L Hamilton	1m27.227s	21
6 J Button	1m27.335s	23
7 S Perez	1m27.416s	23
8 F Massa	1m27.692s	21
9 N Hulkenberg	1m27.770s	19
10 V Bottas	1m27.800s	23
11 J-E Vergne	1m28.035s	25
12 F Alonso	1m28.214s	6
13 D Ricciardo	1m28.336s	18
14 P Maldonado	1m28.342s	21
15 A Sutil	1m28.468s	20
16 E Gutierrez	1m28.538s	18
17 K Räikkönen	1m28.730s	18
18 J Calado	1m29.197s	22
19 G van der Garde	1m29.413s	24
20 J Bianchi	1m29.560s	20
21 C Pic	1m30.026s	23
22 M Chilton	1m30.471s	17

PRACTICE 2		
Driver	**Time**	**Laps**
1 S Vettel	1m25.722s	35
2 M Webber	1m26.011s	38
3 R Grosjean	1m26.220s	36
4 L Hamilton	1m26.399s	36
5 F Alonso	1m26.430s	39
6 N Rosberg	1m26.582s	40
7 F Massa	1m26.601s	41
8 K Räikkönen	1m26.632s	32
9 S Perez	1m26.857s	40
10 J Button	1m26.972s	39
11 D Ricciardo	1m27.304s	17
12 A Sutil	1m27.375s	36
13 V Bottas	1m27.429s	31
14 N Hulkenberg	1m27.491s	40
15 P di Resta	1m27.608s	38
16 P Maldonado	1m27.720s	23
17 E Gutierrez	1m27.949s	34
18 J-E Vergne	1m28.431s	30
19 G van der Garde	1m28.692s	39
20 J Bianchi	1m28.799s	32
21 C Pic	1m29.366s	37
22 M Chilton	1m30.164s	27

PRACTICE 3		
Driver	**Time**	**Laps**
1 S Vettel	1m25.332s	16
2 M Webber	1m25.892s	14
3 F Alonso	1m26.105s	19
4 N Hulkenberg	1m26.306s	17
5 R Grosjean	1m26.350s	16
6 F Massa	1m26.435s	20
7 P di Resta	1m26.438s	15
8 N Rosberg	1m26.441s	19
9 J Button	1m26.489s	15
10 L Hamilton	1m26.557s	17
11 K Räikkönen	1m26.635s	14
12 P Maldonado	1m26.641s	13
13 S Perez	1m26.737s	13
14 A Sutil	1m26.847s	17
15 J-E Vergne	1m26.876s	17
16 V Bottas	1m26.883s	15
17 D Ricciardo	1m27.259s	18
18 C Pic	1m27.941s	18
19 E Gutierrez	1m28.019s	15
20 G van der Garde	1m28.498s	16
21 M Chilton	1m29.094s	11
22 J Bianchi	1m29.169s	13

QUALIFYING 1	
Driver	**Time**
1 J Button	1m25.574s
2 M Webber	1m25.665s
3 D Ricciardo	1m25.673s
4 F Massa	1m25.793s
5 L Hamilton	1m25.802s
6 K Räikkönen	1m25.819s
7 N Rosberg	1m25.833
8 N Hulkenberg	1m25.883s
9 P di Resta	1m25.908s
10 F Alonso	1m25.934s
11 S Vettel	1m25.943s
12 E Gutierrez	1m26.057s
13 S Perez	1m26.107s
14 J-E Vergne	1m26.155s
15 A Sutil	1m26.164s
16 V Bottas	1m26.178s
17 R Grosjean	1m26.577s
18 P Maldonado	1m26.842s
19 J Bianchi	1m26.970s
20 G van der Garde	1m27.105s
21 C Pic	1m27.487s
22 M Chilton	1m28.138s

QUALIFYING 2	
Driver	**Time**
1 S Vettel	1m24.568s
2 F Alonso	1m24.885s
3 M Webber	1m25.097s
4 K Räikkönen	1m25.191s
5 L Hamilton	1m25.259s
6 N Rosberg	1m25.304s
7 N Hulkenberg	1m25.339s
8 S Perez	1m25.365s
9 F Massa	1m25.389s
10 J Button	1m25.458s
11 D Ricciardo	1m25.519s
12 P di Resta	1m25.711s
13 A Sutil	1m25.740s
14 J-E Vergne	1m25.798s
15 V Bottas	1m26.134s
16 E Gutierrez	1m26.336s

Best sectors – Practice			Speed trap – Practice			Best sectors – Qualifying			Speed trap – Qualifying		
Sec 1	S Vettel	41.885s	1	J Button	199.895mph	Sec 1	S Vettel	41.418s	1	N Hulkenberg	199.460mph
Sec 2	S Vettel	22.216s	2	A Sutil	198.963mph	Sec 2	S Vettel	21.875s	2	E Gutierrez	198.776mph
Sec 3	S Vettel	21.170s	3	N Hulkenberg	198.776mph	Sec 3	S Vettel	20.826s	3	P di Resta	198.217mph

 **Sebastian Vettel**

"I'd love to thank the crowds. It was an unbelievable reception and it's a shame we're not racing here next year. I'm speechless. I felt empty as I crossed the line."

Fernando Alonso

"The problem I had on lap 1 hurt my race, as we had to change the nose and with an extra stop, without any chance to overtake, it was all an uphill struggle."

Jenson Button

"This was just one of those days... Exiting Turn 4 on lap 1, I got hit hard on the right hand side by Alonso. That damaged the car and gave me a puncture."

Kimi Räikkönen

"I ran the first 20 laps with no brakes as they'd overheated, so when I got close to somebody I lost braking. Late in the race, my tyre performance fell away too."

 **Nico Rosberg**

"I had good pace and we nailed the set-up. The team did a great job on strategy and the only thing that didn't work was when I fell behind Felipe at the start."

Nico Hulkenberg

"I would have finished eighth, but braking into the last turn, something clicked and my brakes were gone. I pitted and went out again, but it wasn't okay."

 **Mark Webber**

"There's not much I can do, the alternator went wrong at short notice so I had to stop straight away. It's tough, as we did a lot of things right this weekend."

Felipe Massa

"I had good pace, even with the softs. I could have fought for the podium, but as the track evolved, Grosjean made just one stop, which made it impossible for us."

 **Sergio Perez**

"I was finally able to enjoy a race without any bad luck! Fifth is a great result. In the closing laps, it felt fantastic to get past Kimi and Lewis in a single move."

 **Romain Grosjean**

"When I was fourth ahead of Massa with 27 laps to go, I had to take care of my tyres, plus I had an engine issue. Then Kimi was struggling so I passed him"

Lewis Hamilton

"The car was okay this weekend, but the race was frustrating. I tried hard to get past Felipe, but it just wasn't possible and I destroyed my tyres by trying."

 **Esteban Gutierrez**

"Unfortunately, I made a mistake at the start and paid for that with a drive-through penalty. We had good pace and I had battles with Fernando and Romain."

POSITIONS LAP BY LAP

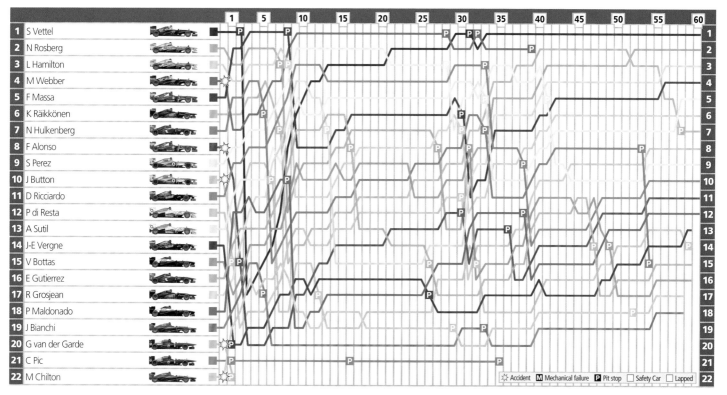

		Lap markers: 1, 5, 10, 15, 20, 25, 30, 35, 40, 45, 50, 55, 60
1	S Vettel	
2	N Rosberg	
3	L Hamilton	
4	M Webber	
5	F Massa	
6	K Räikkönen	
7	N Hulkenberg	
8	F Alonso	
9	S Perez	
10	J Button	
11	D Ricciardo	
12	P di Resta	
13	A Sutil	
14	J-E Vergne	
15	V Bottas	
16	E Gutierrez	
17	R Grosjean	
18	P Maldonado	
19	J Bianchi	
20	G van der Garde	
21	C Pic	
22	M Chilton	

Legend: ☼ Accident · M Mechanical failure · P Pit stop · Safety Car · Lapped

QUALIFYING 3

	Driver	Time
1	S Vettel	1m24.119s
2	N Rosberg	1m24.871s
3	L Hamilton	1m24.941s
4	M Webber	1m25.047s
5	F Massa	1m25.201s
6	K Räikkönen	1m25.248s
7	N Hulkenberg	1m25.334s
8	F Alonso	1m25.826s
9	S Perez	1m26.153s
10	J Button	1m26.487s

GRID

	Driver	Time
1	S Vettel	1m24.119s
2	N Rosberg	1m24.871s
3	L Hamilton	1m24.941s
4	M Webber	1m25.047s
5	F Massa	1m25.201s
6	K Räikkönen	1m25.248s
7	N Hulkenberg	1m25.334s
8	F Alonso	1m25.826s
9	S Perez	1m26.153s
10	J Button	1m26.487s
11	D Ricciardo	1m25.519s
12	P di Resta	1m25.711s
13	A Sutil	1m25.740s
14	J-E Vergne	1m25.798s
15	V Bottas	1m26.134s
16	E Gutierrez	1m26.336s
17	R Grosjean	1m26.577s
18	P Maldonado	1m26.842s
19	J Bianchi	1m26.970s
20	G van der Garde	1m27.105s
21	C Pic	1m27.487s
22	M Chilton	1m28.138s

Grid penalties
None

RACE

	Driver	Car	Laps	Time	Avg. mph	Fastest	Stops
1	S Vettel	Red Bull-Renault RB9	60	1h31m12.187s	125.598	1m28.116s	2
2	N Rosberg	Mercedes F1 W04	60	1h31m42.010s	124.916	1m28.816s	2
3	R Grosjean	Lotus-Renault E21	60	1h31m52.079s	124.688	1m28.796s	1
4	F Massa	Ferrari F138	60	1h31m53.879s	124.648	1m28.886s	2
5	S Perez	McLaren-Mercedes MP4-28	60	1h31m56.016s	124.600	1m28.503s	2
6	L Hamilton	Mercedes F1 W04	60	1h32m04.662s	124.404	1m29.052s	2
7	K Räikkönen	Lotus-Renault E21	60	1h32m20.175s	124.057	1m27.679s	2
8	P di Resta	Force India-Mercedes VJM06	60	1h32m25.055s	123.947	1m29.300s	2
9	A Sutil	Force India-Mercedes VJM06	60	1h32m26.921s	123.906	1m28.419s	1
10	D Ricciardo	Toro Rosso-Ferrari STR8	60	1h32m28.424s	123.872	1m28.831s	2
11	F Alonso	Ferrari F138	60	1h32m30.484s	123.826	1m28.709s	3
12	P Maldonado	Williams-Renault FW35	60	1h32m31.138s	123.811	1m29.012s	2
13	J-E Vergne	Toro Rosso-Ferrari STR8	59	1h31m15.708s	123.423	1m29.280s	2
14	J Button	McLaren-Mercedes MP4-28	59	1h31m15.816s	123.421	1m28.814s	3
15	E Gutierrez	Sauber-Ferrari C32	59	1h31m29.761s	123.107	1m28.682s	3
16	V Bottas	Williams-Renault FW35	59	1h31m30.288s	123.095	1m28.928s	2
17	M Chilton	Marussia-Cosworth MR-02	58	1h31m24.197s	121.142	1m30.335s	2
18	J Bianchi	Marussia-Cosworth MR-02	58	1h31m24.919s	121.126	1m30.171s	2
19	N Hulkenberg	Sauber-Ferrari C32	54	Brakes	-	1m28.947s	3
R	M Webber	Red Bull-Renault RB9	39	Alternator	-	1m29.500s	2
R	C Pic	Caterham-Renault CT03	35	Hydraulics	-	1m32.907s	2
R	G van der Garde	Caterham-Renault CT03	1	Crash damage	-	-	0

Fastest lap
K Räikkönen 1m27.679s (130.752mph) on lap 60

Fastest speed trap
E Gutierrez 199.957mph
Slowest speed trap
R Grosjean 193.432mph

Fastest pit stop
1	F Massa	23.332s
2	M Webber	23.459s
3	M Webber	23.487s

CHAMPIONSHIP

	Driver	Pts
1	S Vettel	322
2	F Alonso	207
3	K Räikkönen	183
4	L Hamilton	169
5	M Webber	148
6	N Rosberg	144
7	R Grosjean	102
8	F Massa	102
9	J Button	60
10	P di Resta	40
11	N Hulkenberg	39
12	S Perez	33
13	A Sutil	28
14	D Ricciardo	19
15	J-E Vergne	13
16	E Gutierrez	6
17	P Maldonado	1

	Constructor	Pts
1	Red Bull-Renault	470
2	Mercedes	313
3	Ferrari	309
4	Lotus-Renault	285
5	McLaren-Mercedes	93
6	Fore India-Mercedes	68
7	Sauber-Ferrari	45
8	Toro Rosso-Ferrari	32
9	Williams-Renault	1

Paul di Resta

"It's great to score in India. I pitted at the end of lap 1 to change from soft to medium tyres then pitted again for my second set of mediums on lap 30."

Pastor Maldonado

"The car showed better race pace this weekend. I made up a few places on lap 1 and was fighting hard to get into the top ten. I was unlucky not to quite make it."

Jean-Éric Vergne

"Our strategy was good, coming in very early to get rid of the soft tyre. It could have paid off to the extent of getting into the points, but we were just too slow."

Charles Pic

"Out of Turn 1, I was ahead of Chilton and Giedo didn't have anywhere to go and hit my right rear tyre. On lap 16, I had another puncture, then a hydraulics leak."

Jules Bianchi

"I'm happy we finished with both cars, but disappointed as my car was good and my strategy should have paid off had it not been for a problem at my first pit stop."

Adrian Sutil

"The target was to score, so eighth and ninth is a great result. My one-stop strategy was riskier and it was only during the race that we decided to go for it."

Valtteri Bottas

"The first lap was slippery for me and I lost ground, but my pace got better. I had radio failure that meant my first pit stop was later than planned and I lost position."

Daniel Ricciardo

"Out of Turn 1, Giedo didn't have anywhere to go and punctured my right rear tyre. On lap 16, I had another puncture. Then I had to retire with a hydraulics leak."

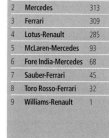

Giedo van der Garde

"I'm disappointed my race ended so early. I made a fair start but out of Turn 1, Chilton left me no room and we made contact, breaking my front wing and suspension."

Max Chilton

"I'm happy with my race. The start was great and, with the help of my engineers, we did a good job of driving around a problem that had looked as though it might stop me."

2013 FORMULA 1 ETIHAD AIRWAYS ABU DHABI GRAND PRIX

**1-3 NOVEMBER
YAS MARINA CIRCUIT
ABU DHABI**

SEVENTH HEAVEN

Having secured his fourth world title a week earlier, Sebastian Vettel made it seven wins in seven races with another dominant victory. This was another demonstration run, as the German disappeared off into the distance

Mark Webber may have been approaching the end of his F1 career, but he showed that he'd lost none of his speed by beating Sebastian Vettel to pole position. It was his second pole in three races although, in Suzuka, he had benefited from the German's struggles with a KERS failure. This time around, Webber simply got it right on the crucial final lap of a qualifying session that saw times tumble as darkness fell and temperatures dropped.

Vettel had set the benchmark early in the third qualifying session with a lap of 1m40.091s on used tyres, before Webber beat it with 1m39.957s on his last run. A mistake early in his final lap then cost Vettel, who improved only marginally to 1m40.075s.

Nico Rosberg did a good job to qualify third after Mercedes team-mate Lewis Hamilton spun off on his final run when a rear wishbone failed as he headed for a quick time. The Briton still hung on to fourth best time with his best lap from his first run.

A late arrival in Abu Dhabi due to a pay dispute with Lotus, Kimi Räikkönen was initially fifth fastest at the track where he'd won in 2012. However, after qualifying, his Lotus failed a floor deflection test, owing to a breakage over kerbs. Romain Grosjean

INSIDE LINE
MANSOOR IJAZ
QUANTUM INVESTMENTS CHIEF EXECUTIVE

On Sunday night in Abu Dhabi, Quantum Investments' Mansoor Ijaz, said that the deal to purchase 35 per cent of Lotus F1 had finally been approved: "This is a team whose results, technological base and fluidity – you go to Enstone and feel you're with a family – should have a much more sustainable financial backbone. So we're going to clear the debt and bring in high-quality sponsors, which will be seen very soon. They will give us the capacity and longevity to compete at the top end of the business for a long time.

"This is not our only investment. We're in the process of buying a piece of an NBA basketball team, we're also thinking of doing a European football team, and so this is part of a larger strategic design.

"I met Kimi Räikkönen's manager, Steve Robertson. My father taught me to admit when you're wrong and make sure people know you didn't purposely try to cause harm. I asked Steve to convey to Kimi (thus far unpaid, see Talking Point) that we have a great deal of regret about why this has taken so long.

"Genii probably made certain commitments on the basis of the deal that they were proposing to do and they knew that we were strong enough to close it as we proved our funds when we signed the deal. However, moving those funds became the complication. We intend to make sure that not only are Kimi and Steve made whole, and then some, but we intend also to compensate our employees and management team for taking it on the chin.

"Our deal is to buy 35 per cent in newly issued shares, so we're essentially diluting Genii Capital, and have options that allow us, in a fixed time, to take control. We're going to do that in a co-ordinated way with our partners at Genii. Without the support of Eric Lux and Eric Boullier, Patrick Louis and Gerard Lopez, we had no chance of finishing this deal. They believed in what we're trying to do, and fortunately understood the complications and had the wherewithal to keep the team alive and let us get the deal across the line.

"Whether we've signed a contract with Nico Hulkenberg is not for me to comment on, but it was prepared, ready to go and I know Nico was excited about it, so I think it's a matter of a very short period. As incoming shareholders, we've made it clear what our preference is. He's an up-and-coming driver with a long F1 lifespan, and there's no better Team Principal and Manager than Eric Boullier."

Boullier's own take? "I can't say what's been agreed, but it's all settled with Kimi. It hasn't been easy being distracted by so many different things. Any racing team needs stability."

had been given the benefit of the doubt in similar circumstances at the Hungarian GP, but this time the stewards excluded the car, forcing him to start from the back of the grid. All those behind moved up a place. Thus Nico Hulkenberg followed his run of three seventh place starts in the previous three races by landing the fifth grid spot for Sauber, lining up ahead of Grosjean, Felipe Massa, Sergio Perez and Daniel Ricciardo.

There was drama in the second qualifying session too, when Fernando Alonso failed to make it through. He made a mistake on his second run, so was forced to do another lap on the tyres, which left him 11th and excluded from Q3 for the first time in 2013.

Inevitably, Webber's chance of beating his team-mate rested on the start. Once again he didn't make a clean getaway, losing out not only to Vettel, but also to Rosberg. Further back, Jenson Button hit Paul di Resta, forcing the McLaren driver to stop for a new wing.

A lot of eyes were on Räikkönen, starting from the back of the grid on the medium tyre. Unfortunately, he clipped the back of Giedo van der Garde's Caterham at the first corner, and immediately retired from the race with front suspension breakage. That removed a degree of suspense from the afternoon.

At the front, Rosberg wasn't able to keep up with Vettel. Stuck behind the Mercedes, a frustrated Webber saw his chances of victory disappear quickly as he struggled for pace.

"I had no real feeling for those tyres when they're scrubbed, so I was very slow in the first stint," said the Australian. "I had very, very poor feeling at the rear, and that made it even worse. You have more and more slip and temperature control problems, and all of those types of things."

Vettel was more than 7s clear of Rosberg when Webber pitted from third place on lap 8. The rest of the leading group followed suit over the next few laps, but Vettel typically stayed out as long as he could to

ensure that when he did pit, he could do so without losing the lead, while also giving himself further strategic options for the remainder of the race.

He finally came in on lap 14, and resumed around 10s clear of the Ferraris of Massa and Alonso, neither of whom had pitted. After they did, fellow late stopper di Resta held second briefly, and when Force India's Scot finally came in on lap 20 we saw the real picture. Webber, who'd overtaken Rosberg for second place when the German got caught behind di Resta, was already 26s behind his team-mate.

After that, it was an untroubled run to the flag for Vettel, who as usual had to deal with messages from

OPPOSITE Nico Rosberg (left) goes past Mark Webber, while Sebastian Vettel and Lewis Hamilton pass on the other side on the dash to Turn 1

ABOVE Romain Grosjean raced to fourth place for Lotus, finishing right on the tail of Rosberg's Mercedes

BELOW The lights are switched on as day turns to dusk and Sergio Perez presses on towards a ninth-place finish for McLaren

ABOVE Webber rued his poor start, but acknowledged that there was nothing that he could have done about team-mate Vettel, so focused on getting back ahead of Rosberg, which he did, to take second place

OPPOSITE Pastor Maldonado presses on for Williams as the sun sets, advancing from 14th to 11th, just behind Adrian Sutil's Force India

the team urging him to slow. He pitted for a second time on lap 37, and eventually came home 30s clear of Webber after 55 laps. It could have been a lot more if he'd really been pushing.

"I realised that I was pulling away from Nico and Mark," he said of his pace. "Obviously you make use of it, as you don't know what may happen later on in the race. We had a very, very strong pace on the Option. We could even have stayed out a little longer. I was busy, for sure, I was pushing as I felt that I can take the lap time, I can take a couple of seconds out of the guys behind, so I was pushing but I was also trying to look after the tyres to be flexible on strategy and help the guys on the pit wall to make the call. Also, I could then afford to take it a little easier in the pit lane which I think is one of the trickiest all year with its slippery entry and a very narrow exit. It just all came together. I think it was a perfect day for us."

Webber was clearly disappointed that, as in Japan, he hadn't been able to convert his pole position into victory, but the margin to Vettel indicated that he'd have had a tough time staying in front even if he had made a better start, and he agreed: "I don't think the start was decisive. Seb was in another category today.

So this was probably the maximum result, even if I had got away in front. He was quick and very, very strong. It was then obviously a recovery job against Nico, who got a better start than both of us. Obviously, it's a short run to Turn 1. If it had been a longer run, he would probably have got both of us."

Rosberg had a steady race to third, logging valuable points for Mercedes in the battle for second in the constructors' championship. For the second race in a row, he led the chase of Red Bull. "Third place is good," said Rosberg. "The aim for the weekend was to be best of the rest behind the Red Bulls and that's worked out, even though second place would have been possible in a perfect world. Mark just got me with di Resta. That was a little bit disappointing, but otherwise I'm very happy. The main thing was that I got my balance wrong in the car for that second stint, and that's why I just wasn't as quick as I was hoping."

Grosjean jumped from sixth to fourth at the start. Lotus usually runs long stints and tries to stop once, but this time he came in early, on lap 8, as the team were forced to react to what others were doing. Nevertheless, he enjoyed another solid, trouble-free race and held fourth place all the way to the flag.

TALKING POINT
TRIALS AND TRIBULATIONS

On Thursday in Abu Dhabi, there was no sign of Kimi Räikkönen.

Following the Indian GP, Lotus wasn't a happy camp. In the closing stages of the race, Räikkönen's tyres were shot, Kimi having tried to eke 52 laps out of a set of Pirelli's mediums. Team-mate Romain Grosjean was bearing down on him, his own tyres also well-used but still in good shape. Closing down on both of them was Felipe Massa, as Lotus battled Ferrari and Mercedes for second place in the constructors' championship.

On top of that, Romain's air bottle was all but empty and Renault were suggesting he might not finish the race. When Romain tried to go around the outside of Kimi at Turn 4, Kimi ran him out wide, to the point where all four wheels were over the line and Romain had to give the place back, allowing Felipe to catch the pair of them.

Trackside operations chief Alan Permane got agitated. "Get out of the ****ing way!" he instructed Kimi in no uncertain terms.

"Don't shout!" Kimi shot back.

In the following week, Team Principal Eric Boullier made a public apology to his driver. What we didn't know was that Kimi hadn't been paid all year. Earlier, it was understood he'd been paid his basic salary, said to be €8 million, but hadn't received his €50,000 per point bonus money. In Abu Dhabi, though, Kimi said he hadn't been paid "a single euro".

It's one thing being shouted at for millions, quite another to be shouted at for nothing! Permane's heat-of-the-moment instruction was understandable enough but, in the circumstances, so was Kimi's reaction. The pair agreed to differ on it and Kimi flew back to Europe. He needed a little ego-massaging to be persuaded to fly back to Abu Dhabi three days later.

Thursday, media day, was certainly not on Kimi's agenda, but he got down to business as usual in a short wheelbase chassis on Friday. He qualified fifth, and then the 'tea tray' front section of the floor failed the FIA's flexibility test, putting him to the back...

"I'm unhappy with the rationale behind the decision," said Boullier. "Nothing was intended. In first qualifying, Kimi went wide, jumped a kerb and destroyed the tea tray. You can see in the data, he went off and there was a spike of 21g. Because everything was destroyed, the deflection was much freer."

So why wasn't the explanation accepted? "I've no idea..."

After Kimi crashed on lap 1, he didn't hang around long either.

ABOVE More donuts from Vettel as he celebrates his seventh win in a row. This time, there was no punishment for his antics

BELOW Nico Rosberg lets rip with the spray from the podium and Webber prepares to follow suit, but most of the accolades went to Vettel

From tenth on the grid, Alonso had another charging race to fifth, although an attempt to get away with just one stop had to be abandoned. He stopped for soft tyres with 11 laps to go, and coming out of that stop, ran off the road as Jean-Eric Vergne's Toro Rosso came alongside, the Ferrari taking off as he bumped over a kerb in the process.

The soft tyres gave Alonso the pace he needed to make up a few places as he set a string of fastest laps. He then had to face a post-race investigation for exceeding the track limits but, after the stewards accepted that Vergne hadn't given him enough room, he escaped without penalty. Of more concern was a

sore back from the kerb-jumping incident, which led to a hospital visit and a check-up. "I still have all my teeth after the bump," he joked after the race, "and my back is obviously in a bit of pain right now. It was a big hit. After a minimum of g-forces, there's this alarm on the chassis for big crashes, like on the medical car. And this alarm was going off in parc ferme, so for sure it was a big hit. But hopefully I'll be okay for Austin and Brazil."

The last car Alonso passed in his late charge was di Resta's, the Scot making his one-stop strategy work, as he ran 35 laps to the flag on the medium tyre. He was unable to do anything about the Ferrari, but still managed to hold off Hamilton for sixth place, the Mercedes driver suffering a low-key race that often saw him stuck behind other cars. At the end, the downbeat British driver blamed himself for not doing as good a job as team-mate Rosberg.

Massa had run ahead of Alonso for much of the race, but ultimately lost out because he was given medium rather than soft tyres at his final stop, and thus didn't have the speed he could have enjoyed over the final 17 laps. Perez dropped back to ninth place on the opening lap, but struggled to overtake and finished in the same place. Sutil did the same as di Resta in reverse, starting on the medium and stopping once on lap 28 on his way to tenth.

Pastor Maldonado gained three spots on lap 1 and was on the edge of scoring points for Williams for much of the race, but eventually finished 11th. And after his unplanned stop for a new nose, Button worked his way back to finish in his grid position, 12th, having run a 44-lap final stint on Primes.

From his promising fifth grid spot, Hulkenberg lost out to Grosjean at the start and, having briefly got ahead of Hamilton, was quickly re-passed. He didn't have the pace to hang on to sixth, then a drive-through for an unsafe release in front of Perez's McLaren on lap 27 ruined his race.

SNAPSHOT FROM
ABU DHABI

CLOCKWISE FROM RIGHT

Yas Marina provides a backdrop like no other, especially at night; Bernie Ecclestone offers Sebastian Vettel some pre-race encouragement; yet more trophies for Christian Horner, Mark Webber, Adrian Newey and Vettel; Jenson Button's McLaren is dwarfed by the Yas Viceroy hotel walkway, one of the few times all year that the cars are made to look small; Vettel's Red Bull RB9 is wheeled back into its garage; Button gathers his thoughts as his mechanics prepare his MP4-28 for another run; looking out for bumps, Pastor Maldonado does his reconnaissance walk; Lewis Hamilton and Fernando Alonso seem in good spirits before the driver parade; Romain Grosjean's office, seen from above

ABU DHABI
YAS MARINA
ROUND 17

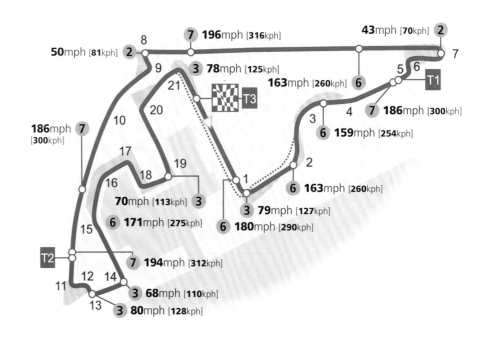

RACE RESULTS

RACE DATE 3 November 2013
CIRCUIT LENGTH 3.451 miles
NO. OF LAPS 56
RACE DISTANCE 189.805 miles
WEATHER Sunny and dry, 33°C
TRACK TEMP 39°C
LAP RECORD Sebastian Vettel,
1m40.279s, 131.387mph, 2009

PRACTICE 1				**PRACTICE 2**				**PRACTICE 3**				**QUALIFYING 1**			**QUALIFYING 2**	
	Driver	Time	Laps		Driver	Time	Laps		Driver	Time	Laps		Driver	Time		Driver	Time
1	R Grosjean	1m44.241s	21	1	S Vettel	1m41.335s	35	1	S Vettel	1m41.349s	19	1	L Hamilton	1m40.693s	1	N Rosberg	1m40.473s
2	L Hamilton	1m44.433s	23	2	M Webber	1m41.490s	32	2	M Webber	1m41.571s	17	2	F Massa	1m41.254s	2	L Hamilton	1m40.477s
3	S Vettel	1m44.499s	18	3	L Hamilton	1m41.690s	37	3	L Hamilton	1m41.580s	18	3	K Räikkönen	1m41.276s	3	M Webber	1m40.575s
4	M Webber	1m44.712s	20	4	K Räikkönen	1m41.726s	42	4	N Rosberg	1m41.721s	19	4	P Maldonado	1m41.365s	4	S Vettel	1m40.781s
5	N Rosberg	1m44.741s	24	5	N Rosberg	1m41.758s	41	5	R Grosjean	1m41.832s	19	5	F Alonso	1m41.397s	5	S Perez	1m40.812s
6	K Räikkönen	1m44.929s	23	6	S Perez	1m42.006s	36	6	J Button	1m41.956s	19	6	N Rosberg	1m41.420s	6	D Ricciardo	1m40.852s
7	P di Resta	1m45.040s	20	7	J Button	1m42.010s	31	7	N Hulkenberg	1m42.055s	19	7	R Grosjean	1m41.447s	7	N Hulkenberg	1m40.931s
8	J Button	1m45.099s	20	8	F Alonso	1m42.171s	31	8	E Gutierrez	1m42.282s	19	8	M Webber	1m41.568s	8	R Grosjean	1m40.948s
9	P Maldonado	1m45.150s	24	9	H Nulkenberg	1m42.324s	41	9	K Räikkönen	1m42.387s	18	9	N Hulkenberg	1m41.631s	9	K Räikkönen	1m40.971s
10	S Perez	1m45.331s	20	10	F Massa	1m42.440s	36	10	J-E Vergne	1m42.457s	21	10	P di Resta	1m41.676s	10	F Massa	1m40.989s
11	N Hulkenberg	1m45.378s	23	11	E Gutierrez	1m42.509s	39	11	F Alonso	1m42.516s	15	11	S Vettel	1m41.683s	11	F Alonso	1m41.093s
12	F Alonso	1m45.440s	18	12	R Grosjean	1m42.607s	18	12	P di Resta	1m42.681s	23	12	S Perez	1m41.687s	12	P di Resta	1m41.133s
13	V Bottas	1m45.823s	22	13	P di Resta	1m42.806s	27	13	V Bottas	1m42.698s	19	13	J-E Vergne	1m41.692s	13	J Button	1m41.200s
14	J Calado	1m45.924s	20	14	P Maldonado	1m42.952s	36	14	F Massa	1m42.702s	16	14	J Button	1m41.817s	14	J-E Vergne	1m41.279s
15	E Gutierrez	1m46.068s	18	15	A Sutil	1m42.998s	27	15	D Ricciardo	1m42.727s	18	15	V Bottas	1m41.862s	15	P Maldonado	1m41.395s
16	J-E Vergne	1m46.114s	22	16	D Ricciardo	1m43.152s	29	16	P Maldonado	1m42.798s	18	16	D Ricciardo	1m41.884s	16	V Bottas	1m41.447s
17	F Massa	1m46.124s	18	17	J-E Vergne	1m43.271s	36	17	A Sutil	1m42.989s	22	17	E Gutierrez	1m41.999s			
18	D Ricciardo	1m46.126s	21	18	V Bottas	1m43.565s	36	18	S Perez	1m43.142s	15	18	A Sutil	1m42.051s			
19	C Pic	1m47.600s	22	19	G van der Garde	1m44.138s	35	19	G van der Garde	1m44.472s	20	19	G van der Garde	1m43.252s			
20	H Kovalainen	1m47.670s	22	20	J Bianchi	1m44.459s	35	20	C Pic	1m44.728s	21	20	J Bianchi	1m43.398s			
21	J Bianchi	1m47.723s	23	21	C Pic	1m44.525s	38	21	M Chilton	1m45.621s	20	21	C Pic	1m43.528s			
22	R Gonzalez	1m49.565s	22	22	M Chilton	1m45.565s	27	22	J Bianchi	1m47.506s	15	22	M Chilton	1m44.198s			

Best sectors – Practice			**Speed trap – Practice**			**Best sectors – Qualifying**			**Speed trap – Qualifying**		
Sec 1	M Webber	17.829s	1	F Massa	198.590mph	Sec 1	M Webber	17.675s	1	F Massa	198.776mph
Sec 2	N Hulkenberg	42.810s	2	J Button	198.155mph	Sec 2	M Webber	42.339s	2	J Button	197.596mph
Sec 3	S Vettel	40.408s	3	D Ricciardo	197.906mph	Sec 3	N Rosberg	39.804s	3	S Perez	197.596mph

 Sebastian Vettel

"Today was incredible; the pace we had was scary at some stages. I felt very, very good. There aren't that many races when you're in such complete control of the car."

Fernando Alonso

"When we saw that I was always behind another car, we scrapped our one-stop plan. As the mediums were holding up well, we decided to use the softs for a short stint."

 **Jenson Button**

"There was argy-bargy into Turn 1. I locked up both my front tyres, couldn't slow the car enough and drove into the back of Paul, which broke my front-wing endplate."

Kimi Räikkönen

"There was contact in front of me through the first corner so I stuck to the inside but, unluckily, one of the Caterhams touched my front wheel and broke the track rod."

Nico Rosberg

"I was able to catch Mark off the line and then push on the option tyres, but the second stint wasn't as good as the car had oversteer on the Primes and Mark got by."

Nico Hulkenberg

"I had felt comfortable with the car all weekend but, from lap 1 I struggled with it. Then came the unsafe release from my second stop resulting in a drive-through."

 Mark Webber

"Seb was on another planet and very, very strong in the first stint. He was super quick and his tyres didn't wear, which spelled disaster for the rest of us."

Felipe Massa

"Our strategy was based on a single stop but, when we realised the pace was too quick for the rear tyres and the wear too high, we decided to make a second."

 **Sergio Perez**

"We'd opted to run with minimal downforce. Despite that, I found it hard to pass, and the fact that I spent a lot of the race stuck in traffic made things very tricky."

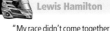 **Romain Grosjean**

"I made up two places on lap 1, but then lost time behind Sutil. I could pass him with DRS, but he had better top speed and could get by on the next straight."

Lewis Hamilton

"My race didn't come together and I'm not sure why as I gave it my all. I had problems with grip and, of course, it's so difficult to pass here when you're in traffic."

 **Esteban Gutierrez**

"We were looking for a better result, so we can't be happy. The pace is there, but qualifying yesterday affected the race today. Our strategy wasn't ideal either."

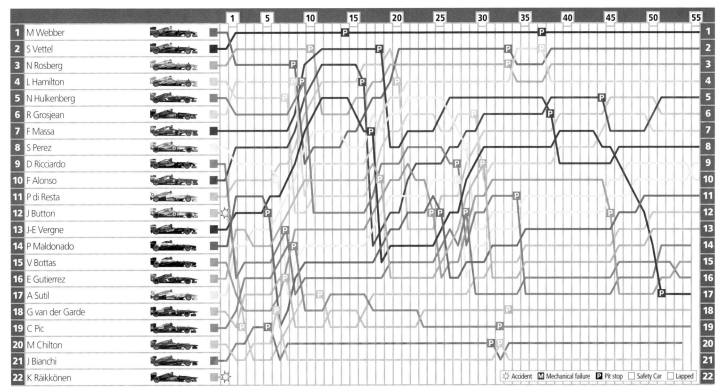

	Driver		1	5	10	15	20	25	30	35	40	45	50	55	
1	M Webber						P			P					1
2	S Vettel				P										2
3	N Rosberg														3
4	L Hamilton														4
5	N Hulkenberg												P		5
6	R Grosjean									P					6
7	F Massa							P							7
8	S Perez														8
9	D Ricciardo														9
10	F Alonso														10
11	P di Resta														11
12	J Button				P					P P					12
13	J-E Vergne					P									13
14	P Maldonado														14
15	V Bottas														15
16	E Gutierrez														16
17	A Sutil												P		17
18	G van der Garde										P				18
19	C Pic				P										19
20	M Chilton									P P					20
21	J Bianchi														21
22	K Räikkönen														22

☆ Accident M Mechanical failure P Pit stop ☐ Safety Car ☐ Lapped

QUALIFYING 3

	Driver	Time
1	M Webber	1m39.957s
2	S Vettel	1m40.075s
3	N Rosberg	1m40.419s
4	L Hamilton	1m40.501s
5	K Räikkönen	1m40.542s
6	N Hulkenberg	1m40.576s
7	R Grosjean	1m40.997s
8	F Massa	1m41.015s
9	S Perez	1m41.068s
10	D Ricciardo	1m41.111s

GRID

	Driver	Time
1	M Webber	1m39.957s
2	S Vettel	1m40.075s
3	N Rosberg	1m40.419s
4	L Hamilton	1m40.501s
5	N Hulkenberg	1m40.576s
6	R Grosjean	1m40.997s
7	F Massa	1m41.015s
8	S Perez	1m41.068s
9	D Ricciardo	1m41.111s
10	F Alonso	1m41.093s
11	P di Resta	1m41.133s
12	J Button	1m41.200s
13	J-E Vergne	1m41.279s
14	P Maldonado	1m41.395s
15	V Bottas	1m41.447s
16	E Gutierrez	1m41.999s
17	A Sutil	1m42.051s
18	G van der Garde	1m43.252s
19	C Pic	1m43.528s
20	M Chilton	1m44.198s
21	J Bianchi	1m43.398s
22	K Räikkönen	1m40.542s

RACE

	Driver	Car	Laps	Time	Avg. mph	Fastest	Stops
1	S Vettel	Red Bull-Renault RB9	55	1h38m06.106s	116.046	1m43.893s	2
2	M Webber	Red Bull-Renault RB9	55	1h38m36.935s	115.441	1m44.364s	2
3	N Rosberg	Mercedes F1 W04	55	1h38m39.756s	115.386	1m44.458s	2
4	R Grosjean	Lotus-Renault E21	55	1h38m40.908s	115.364	1m44.301s	2
5	F Alonso	Ferrari F138	55	1h39m13.287s	114.736	1m43.434s	2
6	P di Resta	Force India-Mercedes VJM06	55	1h39m24.280s	114.525	1m45.786s	1
7	L Hamilton	Mercedes F1 W04	55	1h39m25.373s	114.504	1m45.463s	2
8	F Alonso	Ferrari F138	55	1h39m28.992s	114.434	1m45.447s	2
9	S Perez	McLaren-Mercedes MP4-28	55	1h39m37.304s	114.275	1m45.435s	2
10	A Sutil	Force India-Mercedes VJM06	55	1h39m39.363s	114.236	1m45.609s	1
11	P Maldonado	Williams-Renault FW35	55	1h39m42.095s	114.184	1m45.530s	2
12	J Button	McLaren-Mercedes MP4-28	55	1h39m49.873s	114.035	1m46.336s	2
13	E Gutierrez	Sauber-Ferrari C32	55	1h39m50.401s	114.025	1m45.974s	2
14	N Hulkenberg	Sauber-Ferrari C32	54	1h38m06.670s	113.924	1m45.570s	3
15	V Bottas	Williams-Renault FW35	54	1h38m07.113s	113.915	1m44.351s	2
16	D Ricciardo	Toro Rosso-Ferrari STR8	54	1h38m11.436s	113.813	1m46.042s	2
17	J-E Vergne	Toro Rosso-Ferrari STR8	54	1h38m43.418s	113.217	1m44.517s	2
18	G van der Garde	Caterham-Renault CT03	54	1h39m07.945s	112.750	1m46.592s	2
19	C Pic	Caterham-Renault CT03	54	1h39m19.054s	112.540	1m46.432s	2
20	J Bianchi	Marussia-Cosworth MR-02	53	1h38m29.356s	111.384	1m47.619s	2
21	M Chilton	Marussia-Cosworth MR-02	53	1h39m34.241s	111.292	1m47.707s	2
R	K Räikkönen	Lotus-Renault E21	0	Collision	-	-	0

CHAMPIONSHIP

	Driver	Pts
1	S Vettel	347
2	F Alonso	217
3	K Räikkönen	183
4	L Hamilton	175
5	M Webber	166
6	N Rosberg	159
7	R Grosjean	114
8	F Massa	106
9	J Button	60
10	P di Resta	48
11	N Hulkenberg	39
12	S Perez	35
13	A Sutil	29
14	D Ricciardo	19
15	J-E Vergne	13
16	E Gutierrez	6
17	P Maldonado	1

Grid penalties
J Bianchi Five-place penalty for gearbox change
K Räikkönen Excluded for a technical infringement

Fastest lap
F Alonso 1m43.434s
(120.114mph) on lap 55

Fastest speed trap
F Massa 199.087mph
Slowest speed trap
S Vettel 192.314mph

Fastest pit stop
1	M Webber	21.175s
2	S Vettel	21.298s
3	S Perez	21.370s

	Constructor	Pts
1	Red Bull-Renault	513
2	Mercedes	334
3	Ferrari	323
4	Lotus-Renault	297
5	McLaren-Mercedes	95
6	Force India-Mercedes	77
7	Sauber-Ferrari	45
8	Toro Rosso-Ferrari	32
9	Williams-Renault	1

 Paul di Resta

"It's great to make a one-stop strategy work. I was fighting Fernando and Lewis, but it was impossible to keep Fernando back as he was on fresher tyres."

 **Pastor Maldonado**

"This was a really tough race for managing the tyres, but I coped pretty well as the car's pace and consistency have improved with the new aero package."

Jean-Eric Vergne

"Going for a one-stop strategy was the right decision, but we made the change from soft to medium too early, so there was no life in the tyres near the end."

 Charles Pic

"I passed Chilton and Bottas by lap 2 and pulled away until the first stop. In the second stint, the car didn't have any balance and the team told me to let Giedo by."

 Jules Bianchi

"We're surprised by our pace after we had seemed to find an improvement in qualifying. The balance wasn't as expected and I had to push hard to keep up."

Adrian Sutil

"Considering that I started 17th, I'm happy. The strategy was right. I was ninth from Perez until the last lap, but I'd done 27 laps on softs and it was hard to defend."

Valtteri Bottas

"P15 didn't reflect the pace we had. My race was compromised when I was jumped by the Caterhams who started on the Option tyres and had more grip."

Daniel Ricciardo

"If the start doesn't go well, it's hard to recover. There was chaos at Turn 1 and I ran wide to avoid some accidents and from then on my race was pretty much over."

Giedo van der Garde

"That was one of my best races. Räikkönen hit my left rear in Turn 1 and I nearly spun. I was behind Charles after the pit stops but had more pace and he let me by."

Max Chilton

"We made progress this weekend but for some reason we were unable to show that. The start was good but the balance was difficult and we were battling for pace."

2013 FORMULA 1
UNITED STATES GRAND PRIX
15-17 NOVEMBER
CIRCUIT OF THE AMERICAS
AUSTIN

STRAIGHT EIGHT

Now it's eight in a row, breaking the record for a single-season string of victories. Rivals are left to console themselves with thoughts of a possible new pecking order in 2014, when the rules will be comprehensively changed

For this second event at the fabulous Circuit of The Americas facility, a healthy crowd watched Vettel undertake another demonstration run from the front. At least there was some engaging action behind him – overtaking up and down the field – but overall there was an end-of-term feeling to proceedings, despite the major stakes being played for in the continuing battle for second, third and fourth places in the constructors' championship.

When Vettel took yet another pole position few observers were surprised. However, tricky conditions made it a far more interesting qualifying session than the familiar looking front row might suggest.

"It was a very unusual day," said a bewildered Nico Rosberg, one of several high-profile 'victims'. "Very hard tyres, very cold conditions and very smooth asphalt. The combination of all three meant that the tyres weren't gripping properly and weren't working properly, and that's why there were surprises. If the car works the tyre properly, even if it's a fundamentally slower car, you get so much more grip from the tyre itself, and that's why you are able to go quickly."

With just one more race of his F1 career to come, Mark Webber looked set to beat his team-mate to

pole. The Australian was fastest on the first runs in Q3 before setting an even quicker time for the German to challenge, but it wasn't quick enough, owing to a small mistake at the end of the lap. Vettel was off-target, too, in the first two sectors of the lap and looked as though he'd have to settle for second, but in that critical third sector he clawed back the missing time to snatch pole by just over 0.1s.

Behind the Red Bulls, five different teams filled the next five places, highlighting just how hard it was to get the tyres into the right performance window. Romain Grosjean continued his good form to qualify third for Lotus, then Nico Hulkenberg impressed by going fourth fastest for Sauber. Mercedes had been the closest challenger to Red Bull Racing on the Friday, but Lewis Hamilton could manage only fifth. Ferrari had looked set for a bad afternoon as the red cars initially struggled for pace, but Fernando Alonso dismissed his Abu Dhabi neck injury to find some speed when it mattered to qualify sixth.

Dropped by McLaren just days earlier, Sergio Perez put his frustration behind him to claim seventh, ahead of Heikki Kovalainen, the Finn standing in at Lotus for his countryman Kimi Räikkönen, who had

opted to pass on the last two races, in favour of back surgery in France. But the real star of qualifying was Valtteri Bottas, who did an amazing job for Williams by being fastest in Q1 and fourth in Q2 – in fact, the Finn was ultimately disappointed not to do better than ninth. Rather less happy were Jenson Button (13th), Rosberg (14th) and Felipe Massa (15th) all of whom failed to qualify for Q3. The downcast Button was further hampered by a grid penalty for a red flag offence in first practice.

With everyone aiming for just one stop – and all cars bar Jean-Eric Vergne starting on the medium Option tyre – there was never much chance of

strategy surprises providing much excitement, although with on-track conditions running much hotter than they did in qualifying, drivers were forced to take care with their tyres.

From pole, Vettel stayed safely in front from the start and, as expected, those on the dirty inside line got away badly. Webber was squeezed down to fourth as third and fifth qualifiers, Grosjean and Hamilton, both got past on his outside.

Further around the lap, Adrian Sutil and Pastor Maldonado made contact on the straight, the Force India spinning hard into the barriers, to bring out a safety car. Maldonado carried on unharmed while

OPPOSITE TOP Vettel gets the jump from pole at the start, as usual, leaving Webber to drop back to fourth

OPPOSITE BOTTOM Bottas in battling mood, working his tyres hard as he protects his eighth place

ABOVE Sergio Perez has experienced the ups and downs of life at McLaren this season

INSIDE LINE
VALTTERI BOTTAS
WILLIAMS DRIVER

"I should have been happy with qualifying ninth after my first dry Q3, but there were a few more tenths of a second to be had there, and one extra position but for a gust of wind.

"I was confident in the car here from the start with the current package (minus the Coanda effect

exhaust that we took off in Abu Dhabi). We tried to develop the Coanda for too long, but that's easy to say now. We also got the option tyres to work in the right window with the temperatures and pressures, which was key.

"The FW35 is now more stable off-throttle from entry to mid-corner, more consistent without aerodynamic losses from the floor and we also gained straight-line speed, so can now perhaps carry more downforce and have more grip. For the past five or six grands prix, my starts have been poor, sometimes with some clutch problems, but this was good…

"I also enjoyed the pass on Esteban Gutierrez. We'd had some battles on the lap before and there were only two or three laps in the

whole stint that I was allowed to push hard because of the tyres, so I decided to use those laps at that moment. He was on the inside of Turn 1 and I got a good exit. It was close but fair and I was committed, so there was no way of backing off.

"In my Prime tyre stint, there was quite a lot of tyre management and I've never done such a long stint, so that was an unknown. I still had some tyres left when Nico Rosberg was closing, so I could lift the pace a bit. The team were also giving me good information.

"It was a big relief to score points and better late than never. We went in the right direction with the car set-up all weekend and when it came to Sunday we still performed really well. I'm very happy for us as a team. The race certainly felt as

though it went the quickest of the whole season because running in the top 10 brings a bit of extra focus.

"This circuit was pretty good for our car, but looking at Abu Dhabi and this race, we were much stronger than any races before, so I'm hopeful. We were good on the straight all weekend and our sector one was strong, which protected us against DRS on the back straight. I'm happy with eighth and it's very nice now to have scored more points than Pastor.

McLaren's decision to drop Sergio Perez dominated talk in the Austin paddock. Perez was shocked by the team's choice of Kevin Magnussen, son of former F1 star Jan, for the seat in 2014, having only been informed the previous Friday.

McLaren didn't do Sergio too many favours by pitching him back into a crowded driver market in mid-November, and the Mexican faced a barrage of media questions, yet he handled himself admirably at a difficult time.

Many were sceptical about McLaren's decision to sign him a year ago, when Lewis Hamilton's defection to Mercedes was confirmed. Sergio had scored a number of good results for Sauber, but many of them reflected prudent tyre usage rather than the stunning pace that McLaren lost when Hamilton moved on.

While Sergio is deserving of a place in F1, there were many who questioned whether he had therefore earned a place at McLaren. They assumed that the signing had been more about his backing from Telmex, owned by Carlos Slim, the world's richest man, at a time when Vodafone's title sponsorship of McLaren was about to end. But that evidently wasn't the case.

There was also the question of whether Perez, at 23, was ready for the step-up in pressure that came from a team that always expects to be competing for wins and championships. The great irony was that he scored many more points in 2012 for Sauber than he did at McLaren in 2013, the team having gone all year without a podium either from him or Jenson Button.

A slightly uncomfortable element for McLaren was that the decision not to retain Sergio came on the back of Abu Dhabi where he'd comfortably out-qualified and out-raced Button, something he did again at Austin. In fact, their personal qualifying battle was 9-9 post-Austin, with just Interlagos to come. Button, once again, couldn't switch the tyres on in qualifying and, unlike Perez, didn't even reach Q3. That impacted heavily on a race in which he spent much of the first stint trapped behind Felipe Massa's Ferrari and finished more than half a minute behind his dropped team-mate…

Ultimately, though, McLaren has Honda in the wings for 2015 and will require a top-drawer driver when the Japanese company returns to F1. Sergio may not fit that bill and the team has nothing to lose by putting in one of its young hot shots. Indeed, McLaren think that both Magnussen and Belgian youngster Stoffel Vandoorne are pretty special talents. Perez, though, must look elsewhere.

of relieving the Frenchman of second place. At one stage, it looked as though he might do it but, after dropping back before making a second, final charge over the closing laps, he couldn't quite manage it.

"I think the strategy was pretty clear," Grosjean said of his efforts to stay ahead. "We were copying what Mark was doing. When he was pitting for hard tyres, we pitted for hard tyres, if he was pitting for Prime or Option. Then in the race I was just trying to build up as much gap as I could before the DRS zone. Turns 8 and 9 are pretty hard to follow in another car.

"We had a pretty good balance around there, and then used all the power we could on the back straight, trying to avoid the DRS, and then I know that by Turns 17,18 and 19 it was very difficult to follow me. So he was very close every time into Turn 1, but never had a go. I think the closest he got into Turn 12 was probably 10 metres. He pushed me wide once because I outbraked myself, but as long as he didn't seem to be too big in the mirror, that was fine."

Vettel had paced himself and let his lead fall into the 7s range, although inevitably he took the chance to bang in the fastest lap right at the end, much to the consternation of his engineer. Vettel ended his afternoon with another display of victory doughnuts on the run-off area, this time achieved with an impressive symmetrical perfection. A relieved Christian Horner pointed out that the RB9 gearbox, abused in India, Abu Dhabi and now Austin, had now reached the end of its FIA-mandated life. The champion would have a new one to play with in Brazil…

"I think it's one of those records [eight consecutive wins in one season] that you never expect to achieve, so it's very difficult to find the right words," said Vettel of his latest achievement. "I didn't really answer the questions in the last couple of days because what makes me jump into the car is not a certain number. But, today, when you realise you've done it, it makes

Esteban Gutierrez also suffered first lap contact with Sutil and had to pit with a puncture.

After four laps under yellow, the field were released and, unsurprisingly, Vettel soon began to build his lead. He was 2.4s ahead of Grosjean after two laps, after which, as usual, he kept an eye on his tyres as he continued to edge slowly away, opening up an advantage of 3.8s by the 10th lap, and then 8.3s by the 20th.

It was around that time that drivers further down the order began to make their first and only pit stops, but those at the front preferred to stretch things out. Hamilton had run third initially before losing out to Webber on lap 13, and he was the first of the top group to pit, coming in on lap 25. Unusually, Vettel didn't wait for all his immediate pursuers to stop, and the leader came in on lap 27. Webber followed a lap later, and Grosjean – after leading briefly – came in a lap after that.

When it all shook out, Vettel had a slightly extended 10s lead over Grosjean, while Webber – who had a record pit stop time – was 2s down on Grosjean. The main excitement over the latter half of the race centred on Webber and his prospects

ABOVE Hamilton had a satisfying drive to fourth. It may have been a lonely race but the car ran well

BELOW A new record of eight consecutive race wins by Vettel

you very proud and, yeah, I think it's very difficult for all of us to realise what it actually means. If you look back at those names of who had similar records or outstanding performances in the past, I think it's impossible to understand."

Crossing the finish line 6s behind him, Grosjean enjoyed a faultless race to second, surviving the pressure from Webber in impressive style and logging yet another good podium finish. The opportunity to take up the team leader role, in the absence of Kimi Räikkönen, is clearly one he relishes.

"Romain drove a very good race," said Webber. "He was very strong in the last part of the first sector

which you need to be to get out of there. It's super, super difficult to stay close. I did what I could for most of the time but the tyres are screaming for lap after lap and you have to drop back, give them a breather, then go again. So, I did a pretty clean race. I think the performance and pace were very strong from my side, but victory was made easier for Seb yesterday."

Behind them, Hamilton had a relatively lonely run to fourth, but the Mercedes driver was happy enough with the result and felt that at least he'd been able to push hard all day without a dramatic drop-off in tyre performance. He had Alonso in his mirrors in the closing laps, too, and was happy just to stay safely in front of his old rival.

Having lost a place to Perez off the line, Alonso jumped the Mexican for sixth with a later pit stop, and finally he passed Nico Hulkenberg to claim fifth. The Sauber driver fought back in the closing laps, briefly getting ahead, but the wily Alonso managed to reclaim the position. Nevertheless, sixth was another great result for Hulkenberg and an eloquent sales pitch for his impressive talent.

Perez shrugged off his obvious frustration and did well to claim seventh place, while Bottas was one of the stars of the race for Williams, turning his ninth on the grid into eighth at the flag with a feisty performance. From 12th, Rosberg had a tough race which saw him recover only to ninth, while Button claimed the final point after passing Daniel Ricciardo right at the end. But the former champion was very much overshadowed by his team-mate.

Heikki Kovalainen's return to the sport after almost a year out was spoiled by a bad start in his Lotus. He then had to make an extra pit stop after a problem with his front wing, which wasn't the result of contact. Later, he was hampered further by a KERS failure on his way to 14th.

SNAPSHOT FROM
USA

CLOCKWISE FROM RIGHT
Vettel holds off the challenge
of Romain Grosjean at the first
corner; Pastor Maldonado was
at odds with his Williams team
all weekend; only in America –
actually, Texas; the Red Bull trophy
haul for 2013 is beginning to look
embarrassing; Heikki Kovalainen
checks everything is in place as he
returns to F1 after a year away;
Max Chilton had a frustrating
weekend, a drive-through penalty
hampering his race; Alonso relaxes
with the fans as his points tally
secures second place; the Stars
and Stripes for ever; Hamilton and
Button wonder where the season
went; here's one Red Bull that
could be caught in Austin

UNITED STATES
CIRCUIT OF THE AMERICAS
ROUND 18

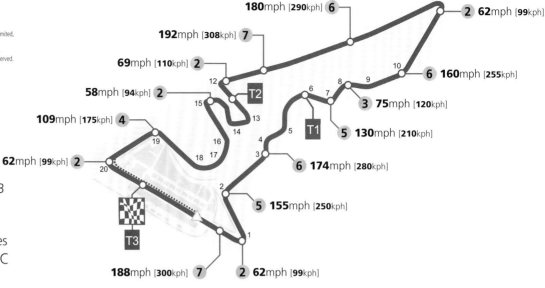

180mph [290kph] 6
192mph [308kph] 7
69mph [110kph] 2
58mph [94kph] 2
109mph [175kph] 4
62mph [99kph] 2
2 62mph [99kph]
6 160mph [255kph]
3 75mph [120kph]
5 130mph [210kph]
6 174mph [280kph]
5 155mph [250kph]
188mph [300kph] 7
2 62mph [99kph]

RACE RESULTS

RACE DATE 17 November 2013
CIRCUIT LENGTH 3.427 miles
NO. OF LAPS 56
RACE DISTANCE 191.912 miles
WEATHER Sunny & bright, 30°C
TRACK TEMP 35°C
LAP RECORD Sebastian Vettel,
1m39.347s, 124.132mph, 2012

PRACTICE 1

	Driver	Time	Laps
1	F Alonso	1m38.343s	16
2	J Button	1m38.371s	25
3	V Bottas	1m38.388s	17
4	E Gutierrez	1m38.532s	18
5	N Rosberg	1m38.657s	21
6	L Hamilton	1m38.979s	21
7	F Massa	1m39.005s	17
8	M Webber	1m39.083s	17
9	N Hulkenberg	1m39.158s	17
10	P Maldonado	1m39.200s	15
11	R Grosjean	1m39.238s	13
12	S Perez	1m39.256s	17
13	H Kovalainen	1m39.487s	18
14	A Sutil	1m39.699s	15
15	P di Resta	1m39.836s	15
16	D Ricciardo	1m39.863s	19
17	D Kvyat	1m40.065s	20
18	S Vettel	1m40.662s	21
19	A Rossi	1m41.399s	21
20	M Chilton	1m41.605s	19
21	C Pic	1m42.054s	19
22	R Gonzalez	1m43.716s	17

PRACTICE 2

	Driver	Time	Laps
1	S Vettel	1m37.305s	35
2	M Webber	1m37.420s	37
3	N Rosberg	1m37.785s	38
4	L Hamilton	1m37.958s	38
5	H Kovalainen	1m38.073s	41
6	E Gutierrez	1m38.229s	40
7	N Hulkenberg	1m38.254s	40
8	R Grosjean	1m38.255s	33
9	J Button	1m38.269s	34
10	F Alonso	1m38.461s	33
11	A Sutil	1m38.719s	31
12	F Massa	1m38.938s	37
13	S Perez	1m38.941s	31
14	D Ricciardo	1m39.246s	38
15	P di Resta	1m39.410s	34
16	V Bottas	1m39.512s	37
17	J-E Vergne	1m39.579s	36
18	P Maldonado	1m39.784s	33
19	C Pic	1m40.376s	39
20	G van der Garde	1m40.563s	35
21	M Chilton	1m46.226s	31
22	J Bianchi	1m47.009s	20

PRACTICE 3

	Driver	Time	Laps
1	S Vettel	1m36.733s	14
2	M Webber	1m36.936s	20
3	L Hamilton	1m37.064s	22
4	N Hulkenberg	1m37.272s	20
5	R Grosjean	1m37.345s	20
6	J Button	1m37.534s	18
7	N Rosberg	1m37.578s	24
8	S Perez	1m37.583s	19
9	V Bottas	1m37.747s	17
10	A Sutil	1m37.748s	21
11	F Alonso	1m37.763s	16
12	E Gutierrez	1m37.774s	18
13	H Kovalainen	1m37.879s	21
14	P Maldonado	1m38.022s	16
15	D Ricciardo	1m38.109s	23
16	P di Resta	1m38.275s	22
17	F Massa	1m38.408s	17
18	J-E Vergne	1m38.636s	21
19	C Pic	1m39.578s	19
20	G van der Garde	1m40.056s	21
21	J Bianchi	1m40.825s	21
22	M Chilton	1m41.293s	18

QUALIFYING 1

	Driver	Time
1	V Bottas	1m37.821s
2	L Hamilton	1m37.959s
3	E Gutierrez	1m38.082s
4	M Webber	1m38.161s
5	N Hulkenberg	1m38.339s
6	S Perez	1m38.367s
7	H Kovalainen	1m38.375s
8	S Vettel	1m38.516s
9	J Button	1m38.588s
10	R Grosjean	1m38.676s
11	N Rosberg	1m38.743s
12	J-E Vergne	1m38.880s
13	D Ricciardo	1m38.882s
14	P di Resta	1m38.894s
15	F Alonso	1m38.929s
16	F Massa	1m39.094s
17	A Sutil	1m39.250s
18	P Maldonado	1m39.351s
19	G van der Garde	1m40.491s
20	J Bianchi	1m40.528s
21	C Pic	1m40.596s
22	M Chilton	1m41.401s

QUALIFYING 2

	Driver	Time
1	S Vettel	1m37.065s
2	M Webber	1m37.312s
3	F Alonso	1m37.368s
4	V Bottas	1m37.439s
5	R Grosjean	1m37.523s
6	N Hulkenberg	1m37.828s
7	L Hamilton	1m37.854s
8	E Gutierrez	1m38.031s
9	S Perez	1m38.040s
10	H Kovalainen	1m38.078s
11	D Ricciardo	1m38.131s
12	P di Resta	1m38.139s
13	J Button	1m38.217s
14	N Rosberg	1m38.364s
15	F Massa	1m38.592s
16	J-E Vergne	1m38.696s

Best sectors – Practice

Sec 1	S Perez	26.206s
Sec 2	S Vettel	38.788s
Sec 3	M Webber	31.521s

Speed trap – Practice

1	P di Resta	195.421s
2	A Sutil	195.172s
3	J Button	194.862s

Best sectors – Qualifying

Sec 1	M Webber	26.091s
Sec 2	M Webber	38.507s
Sec 3	S Vettel	31.524s

Speed trap – Qualifying

1	P di Resta	195.297s
2	A Sutil	194.240s
3	J Button	194.116s

 Sebastian Vettel

"I'm not sure what we've done since the break, but it's worked. I kept saying there's no guarantee for the next race! You never know what's coming."

 Fernando Alonso

"We weren't quick and decided to save the tyres, then attack around the pit stop. I was more competitive on the hard tyres, got by Perez and chased Nico."

 Jenson Button

"I made contact with another car on lap 1 and that broke a front-wing endplate. We considered changing the nose, but instead added extra front wing."

 **Heikki Kovalainen**

"My start wasn't great, then I had problems after the first stop, including downforce issues, so we changed the front wing. There was a KERS issue too."

 Nico Rosberg

"I didn't have a great weekend. In qualifying, I struggled to get temperature into the tyres and starting from 12th place made our race difficult."

 **Nico Hulkenberg**

"It would've been the eighth points finish in a row but for brake-disc failure in India and a drive-through in Abu Dhabi. That is a pretty impressive statistic."

  Mark Webber

"I got boxed in at Turn 1, but then it was a strong race. Our pace was good, but you have to manage the tyres. Qualifying was where the race was won."

Felipe Massa

"I got into a poor situation, so risked a second pit stop for medium tyres. If anything had happened ahead of us, I might have profited from this tactic."

Sergio Perez

"I was expecting more. I got past Alonso on lap 1. From lap 10-15, though, the tyre deg kicked in, and I struggled relative to the others around us."

Romain Grosjean

"I had to have one of my best drives to keep Mark back and it's a great feeling to have tamed at least one of the Bulls in Texas as they clearly had the fastest car."

Lewis Hamilton

"I'm happy with fourth. It was nice to have a race where I could fight for position. The car felt better so the change in chassis made a difference."

 **Esteban Gutierrez**

"It was tough starting from 20th. I did a good first lap and when the safety car was deployed, we went on a different strategy to my rivals."

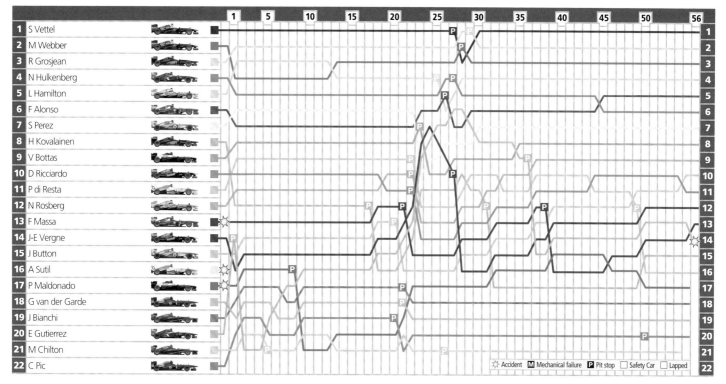

	Driver		1	5	10	15	20	25	30	35	40	45	50	56
1	S Vettel													1
2	M Webber													2
3	R Grosjean													3
4	N Hulkenberg													4
5	L Hamilton													5
6	F Alonso													6
7	S Perez													7
8	H Kovalainen													8
9	V Bottas													9
10	D Ricciardo													10
11	P di Resta													11
12	N Rosberg													12
13	F Massa													13
14	J-E Vergne													14
15	J Button													15
16	A Sutil													16
17	P Maldonado													17
18	G van der Garde													18
19	J Bianchi													19
20	E Gutierrez													20
21	M Chilton													21
22	C Pic													22

☆ Accident M Mechanical failure P Pit stop ☐ Safety Car ☐ Lapped

QUALIFYING 3

	Driver	Time
1	S Vettel	1m36.338s
2	M Webber	1m36.441s
3	R Grosjean	1m37.155s
4	N Hulkenberg	1m37.296s
5	L Hamilton	1m37.345s
6	F Alonso	1m37.376s
7	S Perez	1m37.452s
8	H Kovalainen	1m37.715s
9	V Bottas	1m37.836s
10	E Gutierrez	1m38.034s

GRID

	Driver	Time
1	S Vettel	1m36.338s
2	M Webber	1m36.441s
3	R Grosjean	1m37.155s
4	N Hulkenberg	1m37.296s
5	L Hamilton	1m37.345s
6	F Alonso	1m37.376s
7	S Perez	1m37.452s
8	H Kovalainen	1m37.715s
9	V Bottas	1m37.836s
10	D Ricciardo	1m38.131s
11	P di Resta	1m38.139s
12	N Rosberg	1m38.364s
13	F Massa	1m38.592s
14	J-E Vergne	1m38.696s
15	J Button	1m38.217s
16	A Sutil	1m39.250s
17	P Maldonado	1m39.351s
18	G van der Garde	1m40.491s
19	J Bianchi	1m40.528s
20	E Gutierrez	1m38.034s
21	M Chilton	1m41.401s
22	C Pic	1m40.590s

Grid penalties
J Button Three-place grid penalty for overtaking under red flags
J Button Ten-place grid penalty for impeding Pastor Maldonado
C Pic Five-place grid penalty for changing the gearbox

RACE

	Driver	Car	Laps	Time	Avg. mph	Fastest	Stops
1	S Vettel	Red Bull-Renault RB9	56	1h39m17.148s	115.807	1m39.856s	1
2	R Grosjean	Lotus-Renault E21	56	1h39m23.432s	115.685	1m40.445s	1
3	M Webber	Red Bull-Renault RB9	56	1h39m25.544s	115.644	1m40.591s	1
4	L Hamilton	Mercedes F1 W04	56	1h39m44.506s	115.278	1m40.818s	1
5	F Alonso	Ferrari F138	56	1h39m46.740s	115.234	1m41.186s	1
6	N Hulkenberg	Sauber- Ferrari C32	56	1h39m47.548s	115.219	1m40.952s	1
7	S Perez	McLaren-Mercedes MP4-28	56	1h40m03.840s	114.906	1m41.830s	1
8	V Bottas	Williams-Renault FW35	56	1h40m11.657s	114.757	1m40.492s	1
9	N Rosberg	Mercedes F1 W04	56	1h40m16.289s	114.668	1m41.133s	1
10	J Button	McLaren-Mercedes MP4-28	56	1h40m34.426s	114.324	1m41.285s	1
11	D Ricciardo	Toro Rosso-Ferrari STR8	56	1h40m38.152s	114.253	1m42.119s	1
12	F Massa	Ferrari F138	56	1h40m44.062s	114.141	1m41.209s	2
13	E Gutierrez	Sauber-Ferrari C32	56	1h40m48.855s	114.051	1m41.401s	2
14	H Kovalainen	Lotus-Renault E21	56	1h40m52.211s	113.988	1m41.028s	2
15	P di Resta	Force India-Mercedes VJM06	56	1h40m54.001s	113.954	1m41.148s	2
16	J-E Vergne	Toro Rosso-Ferrari STR8	56	1h41m01.722s*	114.186	1m41.320s	1
17	P Maldonado	Williams-Renault FW35	55	1h39m34.305s	113.410	1m43.058s	1
18	J Bianchi	Marussia-Cosworth MR-02	55	1h40m13.681s	112.667	1m43.419s	1
19	G van der Garde	Caterham-Renault CT03	55	1h40m15.632s	112.631	1m43.933s	1
20	C Pic	Caterham-Renault CT03	55	1h40m45.887s	112.067	1m43.968s	2
21	M Chilton	Marussia-Cosworth MR-02	54	1h39m35.785s	111.318	1m43.775s	2
R	A Sutil	Force India-Mercedes VJM06	0	Accident	-	-	0

*20s penalty for colliding with Esteban Gutierrez

Fastest lap	Fastest speed trap		Fastest pit stop	
S Vettel 1m39.856s	**J Button**	195.669	1 **M Webber**	23.537s
(123.500mph) on lap 54	**Slowest speed trap**		2 **N Rosberg**	23.806s
	L Hamilton	185.355	3 **S Perez**	23.808s

CHAMPIONSHIP

	Driver	Pts
1	S Vettel	372
2	F Alonso	227
3	L Hamilton	187
4	K Räikkönen	183
5	M Webber	181
6	N Rosberg	161
7	R Grosjean	132
8	F Massa	106
9	J Button	61
10	P di Resta	48
11	N Hulkenberg	47
12	S Perez	41
13	A Sutil	29
14	D Ricciardo	19
15	J-E Vergne	13
16	E Gutierrez	6
17	V Bottas	4
18	P Maldonado	1

	Constructor	Pts
1	Red Bull-Renault	553
2	Mercedes	348
3	Ferrari	333
4	Lotus-Renault	315
5	McLaren-Mercedes	102
6	Force India-Mercedes	77
7	Sauber-Ferrari	53
8	Toro Rosso-Ferrari	32
9	Williams-Renault	5

Paul di Resta
"I was struggling for pace and not in the zone with the tyres. The wear was higher than expected and I ran out of tyres with nine laps to go."

Pastor Maldonado
"It was a hard race as the Sutil incident compromised my strategy. We managed to get 40 laps out of the Primes which was pleasing on a track like this."

Jean-Eric Vergne
I tried to pass Daniel at Turn 1 on the last lap and we ran wide. I then used my KERS to try to pass him, but Gutierrez clipped my rear wheel at Turn 12."

Charles Pic
"I passed Chilton off the line and was right with Giedo and Bianchi at the end of lap 1. But the balance wasn't there, which meant I couldn't push at all."

Jules Bianchi
"This was the toughest race of the year. With one stop, switching to the hard, it was a really long race with so much of my focus just on looking after the tyres."

Adrian Sutil
"I gained a few places at the start and was ahead of Maldonado on the back straight. He hit my left rear wheel and I lost control and crashed."

Valtteri Bottas
"I'm very happy to get my first F1 points. We managed the tyres well. We did have pressure from Rosberg, but I was able to keep pushing and hold the position."

Daniel Ricciardo
"It looked like I was going to finish tenth, but in the last five laps I lost almost all the grip. I tried to hold them off but didn't have enough left in the tyres."

Giedo van der Garde
"I fell behind Bianchi on lap 1. From there, it wasn't possible to pass him as, even though I had a quicker car around the lap, his straight-line speed was better."

Max Chilton
"Heading into this race with the drive-through to serve, I knew I'd hit the blue flag phase much earlier and so pay a hefty price in the second half of the race."

FORMULA 1 GRANDE PRÊMIO PETROBRAS DO BRASIL 2013

22-24 NOVEMBER
AUTODROMO JOSE CARLOS PACE, SÃO PAULO

NINE IN A LINE

Not even the threat of rain could knock Sebastian Vettel from his path as he raced to a record ninth straight victory. It rounded off a remarkable season for Red Bull in the last race for normally-aspirated engines

Sebastian Vettel logged his ninth win in a row with another well-judged victory at Interlagos. His win at the Circuit of The Americas the previous weekend had equalled the record for most consecutive wins in one season, this ninth in Brazil meant that he matched Alberto Ascari's streak that spanned the 1952 and 1953 seasons. He can now target beating that record outright if he wins the first race of 2014 in Melbourne in March.

However, it wasn't the most straightforward win of a triumphant season for Vettel. He lost the lead briefly at the start, wasted valuable time with a pit stop mix-up and was then kept on his toes by team-mate Mark Webber. He also had to keep a wary eye on the sky, as the threat of rain hung in the air almost from the start.

In the end, it all fell into place and a typically emotional Vettel celebrated with yet more doughnuts in front of the main grandstand. Meanwhile, Webber finished second in his final F1 start, and marked the occasion by driving back to the pits with the wind in his hair. It was another sight unlikely to impress the FIA but, at that stage, the Aussie clearly didn't give a hoot.

Friday and Saturday practice sessions were both marked by rain and the bad weather extended into qualifying. It looked as if things might be a lottery,

OPPOSITE For once, Sebastian Vettel was slow off the line, allowing Nico Rosberg to take the lead into the first corner

ABOVE Lewis Hamilton was given a drive-through penalty for his clash with Williams' Valtteri Bottas

but in the end the big guns were all at the front, indicating that there was no substitute for having a good car.

In his final race for McLaren, Sergio Perez had a heavy crash at the end of Q2, showing just how difficult it was getting. With standing water on the track, the FIA postponed the start of Q3 until 47 minutes after the last track action.

There was an air of inevitability about the way Vettel secured pole, beating nearest challenger Nico Rosberg by over 0.6s as the action ramped up in the closing minutes. It was a good effort by the Mercedes driver to secure second place, while Fernando Alonso matched his best qualifying result of 2013 with third.

Webber didn't quite get things right and had to settle for fourth, but at least that gave him a good shot at a podium. Lewis Hamilton was rather less happy with fifth, a man who usually thrives in the wet finding things a struggle with the W04. Romain Grosjean had been top early in Q3 after being the first driver to make the switch from wets to intermediates, but slipped to an eventual sixth. Daniel Ricciardo, Jean-Eric Vergne, Felipe Massa and Nico Hulkenberg were the other drivers to make it through to the final session.

It was another disappointing day for McLaren, with Perez qualifying in 14th after his shunt, and later to be demoted to 19th following a gearbox change. The only bright side of that was that at least it handed a spot to team-mate Jenson Button, who had finished the session only 15th.

After two days of rain, Sunday dawned dry and, despite a few clouds, the rain held off as the start drew near. With nobody having any data for dry running, the race was predicted to be something of a shot in the dark. Everybody started on mediums, bar Button and Gutierrez in 17th, who went for

the harder primes. Also, of course, everyone had a complete set of new tyres to play with.

Vettel got away badly while, from second, Rosberg made a great start. Unlike in Korea, the Mercedes driver made it stick and managed to emerge from the first corner in front. "The start was quite bad for me," said Vettel. "I had lots of wheel-slip, and didn't get the launch off the line as good as I was hoping for. Nico passed me straight away, Fernando was closing in and I was lucky that as soon as I got on the KERS I could recover a bit, and then it's not a long way to Turn 1, which helped."

It looked all set for an exciting race for the lead, but at the end of the first lap, Vettel ducked past and reclaimed top spot. Alonso followed in third, ahead of Hamilton, who got ahead of Webber at the start. There was then drama on lap 2, when eighth-placed Grosjean suffered a spectacular engine failure.

Vettel soon began to edge away from Rosberg. The man on the move in the early laps was Webber, who passed Hamilton on lap 2 and then began chasing Alonso. The Spaniard in turn got ahead of the troubled Rosberg on lap 4, before the German dropped another place to Webber who then began

INSIDE LINE
LEWIS HAMILTON
MERCEDES DRIVER

"I'm happy that we secured second place in the constructors' championship. That was the main target this weekend.

"The car was set up for the wet, we didn't have all the diff settings right and so it took some laps to get that spot on. We had to make some adjustments, but everyone was in the same boat. I was the quickest at one point and it's just unfortunate I had the collision with Valtteri Bottas.

"In the first couple of laps, Mark Webber was much quicker than me and there was only a certain amount of risk that I was willing to take. I was being sensible…

"For some reason this year the Lotus, Red Bull and Ferraris have been very quick on the opening laps, particularly the Ferraris. That's a team thing, because Nico struggles with it as well.

"With Valtteri, I guess it was a racing incident. I saw him catching me and I moved over. I didn't think he was going to make it in time because we were in the braking zone, so I started creeping back across to turn in, but he dived down the outside and braked quite a lot later. I didn't think he was going to go there. It was last minute and we touched just as I was turning.

"It was all a bit unfortunate and I don't think he could have gone around the outside. Plus, he was a lap down. I was trying to catch Fernando Alonso and thinking that if he went past I was going to lose time. In hindsight, perhaps I should have just let him past because it would have avoided the incident. He was quick at that point because he had much newer tyres than me. It doesn't matter too much what I think about the penalty – I took it…

"The only real positive is the team's performance this year. Obviously, nobody expected that and I couldn't have hoped for better, but I feel like I should have done more. There are lots of areas to work on next year. It's been an average year in terms of my performance, so I'm looking forward to working hard and getting myself to the point that I feel I can be. I'm going to have a winter a bit like 2006-07.

"I don't care about losing third place in the championship to Mark. He should be there because his car has been much faster all year. If I'd stayed in my position we'd have been equal, but I'd have been ahead because of my win. But no big deal."

TALKING POINT
WEBBER'S LAST

Going out on the podium was a fitting end to Mark Webber's F1 career, his second place in Brazil ensuring that he finished the season third overall, behind world champion Sebastian Vettel and second-placed Fernando Alonso.

Less comfortable for him will be a season in a Red Bull RB9 passing him by without a win, while Vettel was first past the chequered flag a record-equalling 13 times.

Mark has never been anything less than 100 per cent honest, a quality that has made him one of the most highly respected figures in the paddock. On Sunday night, reflecting on what he will miss about F1, he said: "Places like Suzuka, Spa, Monte Carlo, Silverstone, and here to a degree, with a car on the edge, particularly in qualifying.

"But, you want to make sure that you are getting the best out of yourself in those situations. If you think you're a little bit off, then it's not as rewarding as once it was..."

At 37, Mark is 11 years older than his team-mate Vettel and you wonder how they might have compared on a high-speed place like Sepang in a Jaguar with sticky Michelins a decade ago.

There have been some great memories: the debut win at Nürburgring despite a drive-through penalty; the dominant victory from pole at Monaco 2010; "Not bad for a No2 driver" later that year after winning at Silverstone; the stunning pass of Alonso at Eau Rouge; "Multi 21" this year in Malaysia, since when Webber and Vettel have spoken barely a dozen words.

Yet, after five years in a winning Adrian Newey car, Webber knows he has had a fair crack. He's happy with his nine wins and 42 podiums as he heads for a Porsche WEC drive and pastures new.

What won't he miss? He wants to pull back the travel and spend more time with his nearest and dearest. It's time, he says, to get a bit more life balance and a little less intensity in his personal and professional life. But that doesn't mean he won't be trying just as hard in a Porsche next year...

"I'm going to have a few weeks out doing nothing," he admitted. "I love chopping some wood, putting the fire on at home, maybe a bit of red wine and a chill out with some chocolate." Given his size and the weight-limit demands of F1, there hasn't been much of that these past 12 years...

A class act is gone and F1, to a man, wished him well.

On lap 46, there was drama when Hamilton tangled with Valtteri Bottas, who had just been lapped. The Williams was left stuck close to the edge of the track and, fearing a safety car, Red Bull called Vettel in at the last moment. The risk was that he would pass the pits, the yellow would come out, and everyone else would pit.

The mechanics were waiting for Webber's scheduled stop, so some 10s were lost while the German's tyres were found. In turn, Webber lost a bit of time stacked behind him but, with Alonso making the same pit stop call, the top three positions remained unchanged.

"We were afraid of a safety car at that stage," said Vettel. "I came in, hoping everybody was ready. I think I had three wheels on the car but I was waiting for the front right. For some reason, last year and this year, there seemed to be a problem with the front right, so they let me wait for a bit. I saw that Mark was queuing behind me, and I wanted to go. That caused a bit of chaos in the pitlane, but it was fine to get the right tyres in the end, get out again and still have a bit of a gap."

There would be no safety car deployment, but Hamilton received a drive-through penalty for causing a collision, which subsequently ruined his afternoon. "I don't know what happened exactly with Valtteri and I will have to have a look at the replay," said Hamilton. "I thought that I'd moved to the left, he outbraked me and then we touched, but it happened so quickly and it was judged that I did something wrong. I was having a good race until that point in fourth and a podium might have been possible as I was closing in on Fernando."

The pit stop drama had allowed Webber to get to within 6.3s of Vettel. The gap first shrank, then remained stable at a little over 5s before Vettel began to edge away again, despite a few spots of

LEFT Mark Webber feels the wind in his hair as he completes the final race of an illustrious F1 career

BELOW Felipe Massa marked his final race for Ferrari with a few doughnuts, though he'll be back next season in a Williams

to pressure Alonso, finally getting by at the end of lap 12. This was all typical Interlagos action, and reflective somewhat of how the grid didn't entirely reflect dry weather potential.

"Both Seb and I had tough starts. I was happy that I only lost out to Lewis, actually," said Webber. "I had a good scrap on the first lap: Fernando and Lewis were having a battle and then we settled into it. It looked like the Mercedes were struggling to hold the tempo of Fernando, myself and Seb, so we had to clear them as best we could. Then I was coming up to Fernando, so I managed to pass him too."

Alonso and Hamilton were the first frontrunners to pit, both coming in on lap 21, followed by Rosberg on lap 22 and Webber on lap 23. A left rear wheelgun problem meant Webber was stationary for 5.1s, dropping him to third behind Alonso.

Typically, Vettel waited until everyone else had stopped before pitting on lap 24. Fired up by the bad stop, Webber was on a charge and soon regained second by passing Alonso for the second time. At that point, the gap to Vettel was around 10s and over the next 20 laps it expanded by only 2.3s.

rain giving the drivers something to think about. With a historic ninth win up for grabs, there was never any question of Vettel deliberately slowing down to hand Webber a farewell victory – not that the Australian would have wanted to inherit the victory in that manner anyway – so the positions remained unchanged.

So, despite Vettel's record-breaking win, all eyes were on Webber after the finish, as he toured around without his helmet. "It's not easy to get the HANS device system away from the helmet, so I spent half a lap trying to get the left hand side off. I finally managed to get it off, but the cars are bloody noisy with no helmet on, with all the vibrations. You can hear lots of things that you don't want to be hearing with the helmet on, that's for sure..."

Alonso finished third, while arguably the best performance of the day came from Jenson Button, who put in a storming drive from 14th place on the grid, to fourth at the end, to at least finish McLaren's disastrous season on a high. Button's departing team-mate Perez was equally impressive as he rose from 19th to sixth.

The two McLarens were split by Rosberg, who recovered from his frustrating first stint to hold on to

fifth. Together with ninth for the penalised Hamilton, it was enough to secure second in the constructors' championship for Mercedes, leaving a frustrated Ferrari in third. It might have been different had Felipe Massa not been given a drive-through penalty for crossing the white line on the pit entry, which left him fuming and gesticulating wildly at the race control centre as he passed along the pit lane. That penalty dropped Massa down to seventh in his final Ferrari start, but with the FIA having issued a "don't do this" warning before the race, the drivers cannot claim they hadn't known about it.

Behind Massa, Hulkenberg, Hamilton and Ricciardo completed the top 10. Further down the order, Marussia beat Caterham to 10th in the championship, the latter failing to earn the 13th place it needed. This was a great result for the smallest and friendliest team on the grid.

With Webber saying farewell to F1 and Massa to Ferrari, and many other drivers leaving their teams, it was a day of some emotions. It was farewell too to the V8 engine. The team members dashing to Sao Paulo airport on Sunday night knew only too well that they wouldn't be getting much time off in the coming months...

SNAPSHOT FROM
BRAZIL

CLOCKWISE FROM RIGHT
Romain Grosjean's engine gives up
in spectacular style; Ross Brawn
meets Brazilian former world
champion Emerson Fittipaldi; Bernie
Ecclestone presents Mark Webber
with a signed flag to mark his
final race; Jean-Eric Vergne looks
forward to a break after a long,
hard season; a bird's eye view; this
season has been one of torture
for Sergio Perez and McLaren; the
Toro Rosso drivers share an end-
of-term joke; Toro Rosso's Daniil
Kvyat gets an early taste of F1;
Race director Charlie Whiting and
assistant Herbie Blash assess the
track conditions; Fernando Alonso
congratulates Sebastian Vettel on
extending his record breaking run

BRAZIL
INTERLAGOS
ROUND 19

Official Results © [2013]
Formula One World Championship Limited,
6 Princes Gate, London, SW7 1QJ.
No reproduction without permission.
All copyright and database rights reserved.

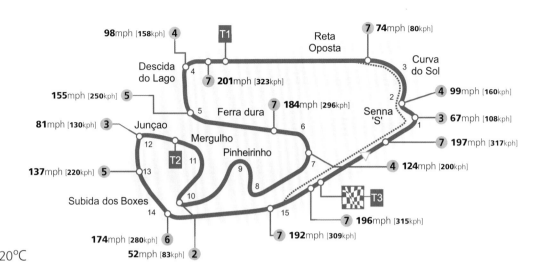

Track map labels:
98mph [158kph] 4 — T1 — Reta Oposta — 7 74mph [80kph]
Descida do Lago — 7 201mph [323kph] — Curva do Sol
155mph [250kph] 5 — Ferra dura — 7 184mph [296kph] — Senna 'S' — 4 99mph [160kph]
81mph [130kph] 3 — Junçao — Mergulho — 3 67mph [108kph]
T2 — Pinheirinho — 7 197mph [317kph]
137mph [220kph] 5 — 4 124mph [200kph]
Subida dos Boxes — T3 — 7 196mph [315kph]
174mph [280kph] 6 — 7 192mph [309kph]
52mph [83kph] 2

RACE RESULTS

RACE DATE 24 November 2013
CIRCUIT LENGTH 2.667 miles
NO. OF LAPS 71
RACE DISTANCE 190.067 miles
WEATHER Overcast then light rain, 20°C
TRACK TEMP 25°C
LAP RECORD Juan Pablo Montoya,
1m11.473, 134.837mph, 2004

PRACTICE 1

	Driver	Time	Laps
1	N Rosberg	1m24.781s	14
2	L Hamilton	1m25.230s	13
3	S Vettel	1m25.387s	17
4	J Button	1m25.391s	25
5	F Alonso	1m25.593s	13
6	M Webber	1m25.797s	17
7	S Perez	1m25.946s	15
8	D Kvyat	1m26.064s	17
9	H Kovalainen	1m26.133s	31
10	N Hulkenberg	1m26.232s	17
11	F Massa	1m26.248s	15
12	E Gutierrez	1m26.326s	28
13	R Grosjean	1m26.570s	28
14	J-E Vergne	1m26.593s	22
15	A Sutil	1m27.115s	25
16	V Bottas	1m27.269s	23
17	P Maldonado	1m27.358s	23
18	J Calado	1m27.436s	9
19	G van der Garde	1m28.107s	18
20	C Pic	1m28.199s	17
21	J Bianchi	1m30.004s	24
22	R Gonzalez	1m32.646s	19

PRACTICE 2

	Driver	Time	Laps
1	N Rosberg	1m27.306s	12
2	S Vettel	1m27.531s	10
3	M Webber	1m27.592s	18
4	H Kovalainen	1m28.129s	13
5	L Hamilton	1m28.147s	9
6	J-E Vergne	1m28.405s	11
7	F Massa	1m28.540s	9
8	N Hulkenberg	1m28.560s	20
9	D Ricciardo	1m28.739s	20
10	R Grosjean	1m28.891s	12
11	F Alonso	1m28.928s	10
12	E Gutierrez	1m29.049s	17
13	P di Resta	1m29.174s	11
14	P Maldonado	1m29.717s	13
15	A Sutil	1m29.783s	7
16	V Bottas	1m30.425s	15
17	S Perez	1m30.748s	8
18	J Bianchi	1m31.061s	18
19	G van der Garde	1m31.118s	16
20	C Pic	1m31.165s	15
21	M Chilton	1m31.211s	19
22	J Button	1m31.770s	6

PRACTICE 3

	Driver	Time	Laps
1	M Webber	1m27.891s	5
2	R Grosjean	1m28.195s	5
3	H Kovalainen	1m28.595s	6
4	V Bottas	1m28.600s	12
5	N Hulkenberg	1m28.830s	15
6	J-E Vergne	1m28.921s	5
7	E Gutierrez	1m29.215s	21
8	P Maldonado	1m29.686s	10
9	P di Resta	1m29.736s	6
10	A Sutil	1m29.913s	8
11	L Hamilton	1m29.980s	8
12	D Ricciardo	1m29.988s	9
13	J Bianchi	1m30.635s	9
14	C Pic	1m30.837s	14
15	M Chilton	1m30.972s	10
16	G van der Garde	1m31.154s	14
17	S Vettel	1m31.857s	4
18	S Perez	1m32.731s	4
19	N Rosberg	No time	4
20	F Alonso	No time	2
21	F Massa	No time	2
22	J Button	No time	1

QUALIFYING 1

	Driver	Time
1	L Hamilton	1m25.342s
2	S Vettel	1m25.381s
3	N Rosberg	1m25.556s
4	N Hulkenberg	1m26.071s
5	H Kovalainen	1m26.266s
6	P di Resta	1m26.275s
7	J Button	1m26.398s
8	R Grosjean	1m26.453s
9	F Alonso	1m26.656s
10	M Webber	1m26.689s
11	S Perez	1m26.741s
12	V Bottas	1m26.790s
13	F Massa	1m26.817s
14	A Sutil	1m26.874s
15	J-E Vergne	1m27.124s
16	D Ricciardo	1m27.209s
17	P Maldonado	1m27.367s
18	E Gutierrez	1m27.445s
19	C Pic	1m27.843s
20	G van der Garde	1m28.320s
21	J Bianchi	1m28.366s
22	M Chilton	1m28.950s

QUALIFYING 2

	Driver	Time
1	R Grosjean	1m26.161s
2	S Vettel	1m26.420s
3	F Alonso	1m26.590s
4	N Rosberg	1m26.626s
5	L Hamilton	1m26.698s
6	M Webber	1m26.963s
7	F Massa	1m27.049s
8	D Ricciardo	1m27.078s
9	J-E Vergne	1m27.363s
10	N Hulkenberg	1m27.441s
11	H Kovalainen	1m27.456s
12	P di Resta	1m27.798s
13	V Bottas	1m27.954s
14	S Perez	1m28.269s
15	J Button	1m28.308s
16	A Sutil	1m28.586s

Best sectors – Practice
Sec 1	N Rosberg	21.251s
Sec 2	N Rosberg	44.156s
Sec 3	J Button	19.030s

Speed trap – Practice
1	F Alonso	181.564mph
2	P Maldonado	180.197mph
3	J Button	178.271mph

Best sectors – Qualifying
Sec 1	L Hamilton	21.266s
Sec 2	L Hamilton	44.177s
Sec 3	F Alonso	19.261s

Speed trap – Qualifying
1	A Sutil	184.360mph
2	F Alonso	181.999mph
3	R Grosjean	181.564mph

Sebastian Vettel
"My start wasn't so good, but I got past Rosberg. When I came in for the second pit stop, it was a late call and I had to wait for my tyres, but I managed to recover"

Fernando Alonso
"A podium is the best way to end this long season. It's a shame the much awaited rain didn't arrive because we could definitely been more competitive in the wet"

Jenson Button
"For Checo, myself and the whole team, today was an incredible day. I'm pleased to have finished fourth: it's almost the podium position that I came here aiming for"

Heikki Kovalainen
"Like at Austin, my start was really poor, due to procedural issues. That was disappointing as it's such a big part of the race and it's difficult to recover positions"

Nico Rosberg
"I had a perfect start but then struggled a lot with my rear tyres. I could have cleared Jenson in the pits but it was better to focus on our battle with Ferrari"

Nico Hulkenberg
"I had a good start and nice battles early on. Then I was by myself for most of the race and my main problem was understeer which ruined by front tyres"

Mark Webber
"The difficult part for me today was getting in to the car for the final time as I was overcome with the strongest emotion that I had all day to be honest"

Felipe Massa
"I was having a great race up until the moment I was given a penalty for crossing the white line. I'm disappointed as I could have finished fourth or third"

Sergio Perez
"I was praying for heavier rain at the end so that I could have a go at making up some more places. Unfortunately, I had to save fuel and couldn't really attack Nico"

Romain Grosjean
"Everyone needs a holiday, but my engine decided to go on vacation early… But it's been a fantastic season and we can be proud of what we've achieved"

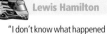

Lewis Hamilton
"I don't know what happened with Valtteri. I thought that I had moved left, he outbraked me and then we touched. I was having a good race until that point"

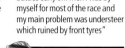

Esteban Gutierrez
"I had a good first lap, overtaking a few cars. I was struggling a bit with the hard tyres, but managed to recover some time with the mediums in the next two stints"

POSITIONS LAP BY LAP

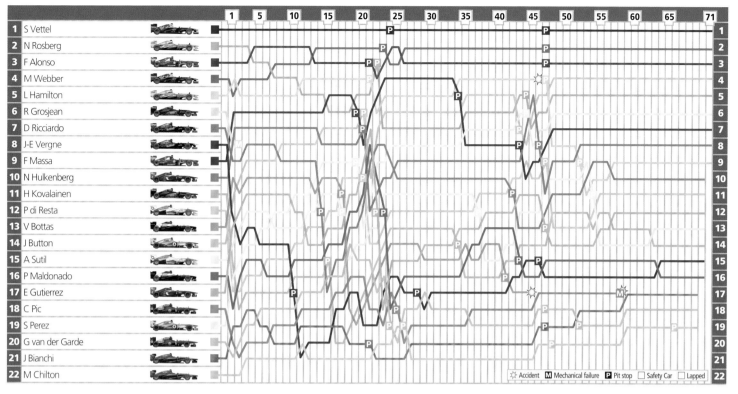

	Driver		1	5	10	15	20	25	30	35	40	45	50	55	60	65	71	
1	S Vettel																	1
2	N Rosberg																	2
3	F Alonso																	3
4	M Webber																	4
5	L Hamilton																	5
6	R Grosjean																	6
7	D Ricciardo																	7
8	J-E Vergne																	8
9	F Massa																	9
10	N Hulkenberg																	10
11	H Kovalainen																	11
12	P di Resta																	12
13	V Bottas																	13
14	J Button																	14
15	A Sutil																	15
16	P Maldonado																	16
17	E Gutierrez																	17
18	C Pic																	18
19	S Perez																	19
20	G van der Garde																	20
21	J Bianchi																	21
22	M Chilton																	22

☆ Accident　Ⓜ Mechanical failure　Ⓟ Pit stop　☐ Safety Car　☐ Lapped

QUALIFYING 3

	Driver	Time
1	S Vettel	1m26.479s
2	N Rosberg	1m27.102s
3	F Alonso	1m27.539s
4	M Webber	1m27.572s
5	L Hamilton	1m27.677s
6	R Grosjean	1m27.737s
7	D Ricciardo	1m28.052s
8	J-E Vergne	1m28.081s
9	F Massa	1m28.109s
10	N Hulkenberg	1m29.582s

GRID

	Driver	Time
1	S Vettel	1m26.479s
2	N Rosberg	1m27.102s
3	F Alonso	1m27.539s
4	M Webber	1m27.572s
5	L Hamilton	1m27.677s
6	R Grosjean	1m27.737s
7	D Ricciardo	1m28.052s
8	J-E Vergne	1m28.081s
9	F Massa	1m28.109s
10	N Hulkenberg	1m29.582s
11	H Kovalainen	1m27.456s
12	P di Resta	1m27.798s
13	V Bottas	1m27.954s
14	J Button	1m28.308s
15	A Sutil	1m28.586s
16	P Maldonado	1m27.367s
17	E Gutierrez	1m27.445s
18	C Pic	1m27.843s
19	S Perez	1m28.269s
20	G van der Garde	1m28.320s
21	J Bianchi	1m28.366s
22	M Chilton	1m28.950s

RACE

	Driver	Car	Laps	Time	Avg. mph	Fastest	Stops
1	S Vettel	Red Bull-Renault RB9	71	1h32m36.300s	123.157	1m15.624s	2
2	M Webber	Red Bull-Renault RB9	71	1h32m46.752s	122.926	1m15.436s	2
3	F Alonso	Ferrari F138	71	1h32m55.213s	122.739	1m15.496s	2
4	J Button	McLaren-Mercedes MP4-28	71	1h33m13.660s	122.334	1m16.450s	2
5	N Rosberg	Mercedes F1 W04	71	1h33m15.348s	122.297	1m16.442s	2
6	S Perez	McLaren-Mercedes MP4-28	71	1h33m20.351s	122.188	1m16.246s	2
7	F Massa	Ferrari F138	71	1h33m25.410s	122.077	1m16.470s	3
8	N Hulkenberg	Sauber-Ferrari C32	71	1h33m40.552s	121.749	1m16.802s	2
9	L Hamilton	Mercedes F1 W04	71	1h33m49.203s	121.562	1m16.692s	3
10	D Ricciardo	Toro Rosso-Ferrari STR8	70	1h32m39.709s	121.347	1m16.974s	2
11	P di Resta	Force India-Mercedes VJM06	70	1h32m41.354s	121.311	1m16.855s	2
12	E Gutierrez	Sauber-Ferrari C32	70	1h32m41.884s	121.300	1m16.528s	2
13	A Sutil	Force India-Mercedes VJM06	70	1h32m42.243s	121.292	1m16.049s	3
14	H Kovalainen	Lotus-Renault E21	70	1h32m52.825s	121.062	1m17.249s	2
15	J-E Vergne	Toro Rosso-Ferrari STR8	70	1h33m07.908s	120.735	1m16.790s	3
16	P Maldonado	Williams-Renault FW35	70	1h33m22.743s	120.415	1m17.554s	2
17	J Bianchi	Marussia-Cosworth MR-02	69	1h32m56.221s	119.260	1m17.717s	2
18	G van der Garde	Caterham-Renault CT03	69	1h33m06.035s	119.050	1m17.590s	3
19	M Chilton	Marussia-Cosworth MR-02	69	1h33m51.624s	118.086	1m17.281s	3
R	C Pic	Caterham-Renault CT03	58	Suspension	-	1m18.434s	1
R	V Bottas	Williams-Renault FW35	45	Collision	-	1m16.840s	2
R	R Grosjean	Lotus-Renault E21	2	Engine	-	1m20.898s	0

CHAMPIONSHIP

	Driver	Pts
1	S Vettel	397
2	F Alonso	242
3	M Webber	199
4	L Hamilton	189
5	K Räikkönen	183
6	N Rosberg	171
7	R Grosjean	132
8	F Massa	112
9	J Button	73
10	N Hulkenberg	51
11	S Perez	49
12	P di Resta	48
13	A Sutil	29
14	D Ricciardo	20
15	J-E Vergne	13
16	E Gutierrez	6
17	V Bottas	4
18	P Maldonado	1

Grid penalties
S Perez Five-place grid penalty for changing gearbox

Fastest lap
M Webber 1m15.436s
(127.776mph) on lap 51

Fastest speed trap
S Perez	194.178mph
Slowest speed trap	
R Grosjean	177.650mph

Fastest pit stop
1	F Massa	22.342s
2	S Perez	22.397s
3	S Vettel	22.510s

	Constructor	Pts
1	Red Bull-Renault	595
2	Mercedes	360
3	Ferrari	354
4	Lotus-Renault	315
5	McLaren-Mercedes	122
6	Force India-Mercedes	77
7	Sauber-Ferrari	57
8	Toro Rosso-Ferrari	33
9	Williams-Renault	5

Paul di Resta
"Losing six places off the line with too much wheelspin was a key moment and really put me on the back foot, but I wasn't able to challenge Ricciardo for tenth"

Pastor Maldonado
"I was fighting with the cars around me, but the pace wasn't in the car to challenge for the top ten. I lost time in the pit stops and couldn't recover the places"

Jean-Eric Vergne
"Catastrophic starts for both of us and, after that, I had a car that was difficult to drive. My balance improved in the second and third stints but it was a struggle"

Charles Pic
"I put in a long first stint on the mediums with one eye on rain to come and came out clear of Bianchi after my pit stop. On lap 58, I had a suspension problem"

Jules Bianchi
"I got fantastic start but, a few laps in, struggled with graining, but I knew it was about the long game and knew that the balance would be better on the prime"

Adrian Sutil
"It was drizzling for most of the race but I felt sure that the tack was going to stay mostly dry. The main issue for me was tyre wear and I had to stop three times"

Valtteri Bottas
"I struggled with the prime tyre, but it was better on the option. In the incident with Hamilton, I tried to keep my line overtaking on the outside and we touched"

Daniel Ricciardo
"We weren't quick at the start and I struggled with cold graining on the front right. We struggled in terms of pure pace, so I'm happy to come away with a point"

Giedo van der Garde
"I passed Bianchi early on and pushed on after Kovalainen. My second set of tyres weren't as good and I was asked to let Pic by. Then I had to had a drive-through"

Max Chilton
"In the last stint, I struggled with a vibration on my front left tyre, which cost me time and was why I pitted for an unscheduled third stop. I'm proud of my 19 finishes"

DRIVER RESULTS

				ROUND 1 March 17 AUSTRALIAN GP	ROUND 2 March 24 MALAYSIAN GP	ROUND 3 April 14 CHINESE GP	ROUND 4 April 21 BAHRAIN GP	ROUND 5 May 12 SPANISH GP	ROUND 6 May 26 MONACO GP	ROUND 7 June 9 CANADIAN GP
1	Sebastian Vettel	German	Red Bull-Renault RB9	3P	1P	4F	1F	4	2F	1P
2	Fernando Alonso	Spanish	Ferrari F138	2	R	1	8	1	7	2
3	Mark Webber	Australian	Red Bull-Renault RB9	6	2	R	7	5	3	4F
4	Lewis Hamilton	British	Mercedes F1 W04	5	3	3P	5	12	4	3
5	Kimi Räikkönen	Finnish	Lotus-Renault E21	1F	7	2	2	2	10	9
6	Nico Rosberg	German	Mercedes F1 WO4	R	4	R	9P	6P	1P	5
7	Romain Grosjean	French	Lotus-Renault E21	10	6	9	3	R	R	13
8	Felipe Massa	Brazilian	Ferrari F138	4	5	6	15	3	R	8
9	Jenson Button	British	McLaren-Mercedes MP4-28	9	17	5	10	8	6	12
10	Nico Hulkenberg	German	Sauber-Ferrari C32	NS	8	10	12	15	11	R
11	Sergio Perez	Mexican	McLaren-Mercedes MP4-28	11	9F	11	6	9	16	11
12	Paul di Resta	British	Force India-Mercedes VJM06	8	R	8	4	7	9	7
13	Adrian Sutil	German	Force India-Mercedes VJM06	7	R	R	13	13	5	10
14	Daniel Ricciardo	Australian	Toro Rosso-Ferrari STR8	R	18	7	16	10	R	15
15	Jean-Eric Vergne	French	Toro Rosso-Ferrari STR8	12	10	12	R	R	8	6
16	Esteban Gutierrez	Mexican	Sauber-Ferrari C32	13	12	R	18	11F	13	20
17	Valtteri Bottas	Finnish	Williams-Renault FW35	14	11	13	14	16	12	14
18	Pastor Maldonado	Venezuelan	Williams-Renault FW35	R	R	14	11	14	R	16
19	Jules Bianchi	French	Marussia-Cosworth MR-02	15	13	15	19	18	R	17
20	Charles Pic	French	Caterham-Renault CT03	16	14	16	17	17	R	18
21	Giedo van der Garde	Dutch	Caterham-Renault CT03	18	15	18	21	R	15	R
22	Max Chilton	British	Marussia-Cosworth MR-02	17	16	17	20	19	14	19
23	Heikki Kovalainen	Finnish	Lotus-Renault E21	-	-	-	-	-	-	-

RACE SCORING

1st	25	POINTS
2nd	18	POINTS
3rd	15	POINTS
4th	12	POINTS
5th	10	POINTS
6th	8	POINTS
7th	6	POINTS
8th	4	POINTS
9th	2	POINTS
10th	1	POINT

DATA KEY

D	DISQUALIFIED
F	FASTEST LAP
NC	NON-CLASSIFIED
NS	NON-STARTER
NQ	NON-QUALIFIER
P	POLE POSITION
R	RETIRED
W	WITHDRAWN

Race results for both drivers; ie, first and second listed as 1/2 with team's best result listed first.

CONSTRUCTOR RESULTS

1	Red Bull-Renault
2	Mercedes
3	Ferrari
4	Lotus-Renault
5	McLaren-Mercedes
6	Force India-Mercedes
7	Sauber-Ferrari
8	Toro Rosso-Ferrari
9	Williams-Renault
10	Marussia-Cosworth
11	Caterham-Renault

	ROUND 8 June 30 BRITISH GP	ROUND 9 July 7 GERMAN GP	ROUND 10 July 28 HUNGARIAN GP	ROUND 11 August 25 BELGIAN GP	ROUND 12 September 8 ITALIAN GP	ROUND 13 September 22 SINGAPORE GP	ROUND 14 October 6 KOREAN GP	ROUND 15 October 13 JAPANESE GP	ROUND 16 October 27 INDIAN GP	ROUND 17 November 3 ABU DHABI GP	ROUND 18 November 17 UNITED STATES GP	ROUND 19 November 24 BRAZILIAN GP	TOTAL POINTS
	R	1	3	1F	1P	1PF	1PF	1	1P	1	1PF	1P	397
	3	4F	5	2	2	2	6	4	11	5F	5	3	242
	2F	7	4F	5	3	15	R	2PF	R	2P	3	2F	199
	4P	5P	1P	3P	9F	5	5	R	6	7	4	9	189
	5	2	2	R	11	3	2	5	7F	R	-	-	183
	1	9	19	4	6	4	7	8	2	3	9	5	171
	19	3	6	8	8	R	3	3	3	4	2	R	132
	6	R	8	7	4	6	9	10	4	8	13	7	112
	13	6	7	6	10	7	8	9	14	12	10	4	73
	10	10	11	13	5	9	4	6	11	14	6	8	51
	20	8	9	11	12	8	10	15	5	9	7	6	49
	9	11	18	R	R	20	R	11	8	6	16	11	48
	7	13	R	9	16	10	R	14	9	10	R	13	29
	8	12	13	10	7	R	R	13	10	16	11	10	20
	R	R	12	12	R	14	R	12	13	17	12	15	13
	14	14	R	14	13	12	11	7	15	13	14	12	6
	12	16	R	15	15	13	12	17	16	15	8	R	4
	11	15	10	17	14	11	13	16	12	11	17	16	1
	16	R	16	18	19	18	16	R	18	20	18	17	0
	15	17	15	R	17	19	14	18	R	19	20	R	0
	18	18	14	16	18	16	15	R	R	18	19	18	0
	17	19	17	19	20	17	17	19	17	21	21	19	0
	-	-	-	-	-	-	-	-	-	-	14	14	0

ROUND 1 AUSTRALIAN GP March 17	ROUND 2 MALAYSIAN GP March 24	ROUND 3 CHINESE GP April 14	ROUND 4 BAHRAIN GP April 21	ROUND 5 SPANISH GP May 12	ROUND 6 MONACO GP May 26	ROUND 7 CANADIAN GP June 9	ROUND 8 BRITISH GP June 30	ROUND 9 GERMAN GP July 7	ROUND 10 HUNGARIAN GP July 28	ROUND 11 BELGIAN GP August 25	ROUND 12 ITALIAN GP September 8	ROUND 13 SINGAPORE GP September 22	ROUND 14 KOREAN GP October 6	ROUND 15 JAPANESE GP October 13	ROUND 16 INDIAN GP October 27	ROUND 17 ABU DHABI GP November 3	ROUND 18 UNITED STATES GP November 17	ROUND 19 BRAZILIAN GP November 24	TOTAL POINTS
3/6	1/2	4/R	1/7	4/5	2/3	1/4	2/R	1/7	3/4	1/5	1/3	1/15	1/R	1/2	1/R	1/2	1/3	1/2	596
5/R	3/4	3/R	5/9	6/12	1/4	3/5	1/4	5/9	1/19	3/4	6/9	4/5	5/7	8/R	2/6	3/7	4/9	5/9	360
2/4	5/R	1/6	8/15	1/3	7/R	2/8	3/6	4/R	5/8	2/7	2/4	2/6	6/9	4/10	4/11	5/8	5/13	3/7	354
1/10	6/7	2/9	2/3	2/R	10/R	9/13	15/19	2/3	2/6	8/R	8/11	3/R	2/3	3/5	3/7	4/R	2/15	14/R	315
9/11	9/17	5/11	6/10	8/9	6/16	11/12	13/20	6/8	7/9	6/11	10/12	7/8	8/10	9/15	5/14	9/12	7/10	4/7	122
7/8	R/R	8/R	4/13	7/13	5/9	7/10	7/9	11/13	18/R	9/R	16/R	10/20	R/R	11/14	8/9	6/10	16/R	11/13	77
13/NS	8/12	10/R	12/18	11/15	11/13	20/R	10/14	10/14	11/R	13/14	5/13	9/12	4/11	6/7	11/15	13/14	6/14	8/12	57
12/R	10/18	7/12	16/R	10/R	8/R	6/15	8/R	12/R	12/13	10/12	7/R	14/R	R/R	12/13	10/13	16/17	11/12	10/15	33
14/R	11/R	13/14	11/14	14/16	12/R	14/16	11/12	15/16	10/R	15/17	14/15	11/13	12/13	16/17	12/16	11/15	8/17	16/R	5
15/17	13/16	15/17	19/20	18/19	14/R	17/19	16/17	19/R	16/17	18/19	19/20	17/18	16/17	19/R	17/18	20/21	18/21	17/19	0
16/18	14/15	16/18	17/21	17/R	15/R	18/R	15/18	17/18	14/15	16/R	17/18	16/19	14/15	18/R	R/R	18/19	19/20	18/R	0

2013 FASTEST SPEED TRAP FIGURES

Figures from races, not qualifying

MONZA	Esteban Gutierrez	211.949mph
BUDDH INTERNATIONAL	Esteban Gutierrez	199.957mph
MONTREAL	Nico Hulkenberg	199.833mph
SHANGHAI	Daniel Ricciardo	199.398mph
YAS MARINA	Felipe Massa	199.087mph
YEONGAM	Mark Webber	198.901mph
BARCELONA	Fernando Alonso	198.093mph
CIRCUIT OF THE AMERICAS	Jenson Button	195.669mph
SAKHIR	Felipe Massa	195.234mph
INTERLAGOS	Sergio Perez	194.178mph
SILVERSTONE	Felipe Massa	193.495mph
MELBOURNE	Jean-Eric Vergne	193.060mph
SUZUKA	Mark Webber	191.755mph
NURBURGRING	Nico Rosberg	191.568mph
SEPANG	Esteban Gutierrez	191.444mph
SPA-FRANCORCHAMPS	Felipe Massa	190.885mph
HUNGARORING	Nico Rosberg	189.580mph
MARINA BAY	Nico Rosberg	184.795mph
MONACO	Jenson Button	179.576mph

184.795mph
Nico Rosberg (Marina Bay)

2013 QUALIFYING HEAD-TO-HEAD

RED BULL-RENAULT
Vettel–Webber **17–2**

FERRARI
Alonso–Massa **11–8**

MERCEDES
Hamilton–Rosberg **11–8**

LOTUS-RENAULT
Räikkönen–Grosjean **10–7**

LOTUS-RENAULT
Grosjean–Kovalainen **2–0**

MCLAREN-MERCEDES
Perez–Button **10–9**

F1 HISTORY: MOST STARTS

325	Rubens Barrichello		Kimi Räikkönen	120	Sebastian Vettel		Valtteri Bottas
308	Michael Schumacher	192	Felipe Massa	119	Pierluigi Martini		Max Chilton
256	Riccardo Patrese	187	Nigel Mansell	116	Damon Hill		Esteban Gutierrez
	Jarno Trulli	185	Nick Heidfeld		Jacky Ickx		Giedo van der Garde
247	Jenson Button	180	Ralf Schumacher		Alan Jones		
	David Coulthard	176	Graham Hill	114	Keke Rosberg		**CONSTRUCTORS**
230	Giancarlo Fisichella	175	Jacques Laffite		Patrick Tambay	870	Ferrari
217	Fernando Alonso	171	Niki Lauda	112	Denny Hulme	743	McLaren
216	Mark Webber	165	Jacques Villeneuve		Jody Scheckter	662	Williams
210	Gerhard Berger	163	Thierry Boutsen	111	John Surtees	534	Lotus* *(Toleman, Benetton, Renault II)*
208	Andrea de Cesaris	162	Mika Hakkinen		Heikki Kovalainen	492	Lotus
204	Nelson Piquet		Johnny Herbert	109	Philippe Alliot	488	Toro Rosso *(Minardi)*
201	Jean Alesi	161	Ayrton Senna		Mika Salo	418	Tyrrell
199	Alain Prost	159	Heinz-Harald Frentzen		Adrian Sutil	409	Prost *(Ligier)*
194	Michele Alboreto	158	Martin Brundle	108	Elio de Angelis	397	Force India
			Olivier Panis	106	Jos Verstappen		*(Jordan, Midland, Spyker)*
		152	John Watson	104	Jo Bonnier	394	Brabham
		149	Rene Arnoux		Pedro de la Rosa	383	Arrows
		147	Eddie Irvine		Jochen Mass	364	Sauber *(including BMW Sauber)*
			Nico Rosberg	100	Bruce McLaren	317	Benetton
			Derek Warwick		*(to current drivers)*	300	Red Bull *(Stewart, Jaguar Racing)*
247 starts		146	Carlos Reutemann	58	Paul di Resta	230	March
Jenson Button		144	Emerson Fittipaldi		Nico Hulkenberg	227	Mercedes GP
		135	Jean-Pierre Jarier		Pastor Maldonado		*(BAR, Honda Racing, Brawn GP)*
		132	Eddie Cheever	56	Sergio Perez	197	BRM
			Clay Regazzoni	50	Daniel Ricciardo	132	Osella
		129	Lewis Hamilton	45	Romain Grosjean	123	Renault
		128	Mario Andretti	39	Charles Pic		*(to current drivers)*
		126	Jack Brabham		Jean-Eric Vergne	77	Caterham
		123	Ronnie Peterson	19	Jules Bianchi		Marussia

247 starts
Jenson Button

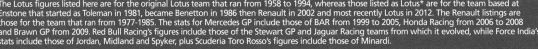

The Lotus figures listed here are for the original Lotus team that ran from 1958 to 1994, whereas those listed as Lotus* are for the team based at Enstone that started as Toleman in 1981, became Benetton in 1986 then Renault in 2002 and most recently Lotus in 2012. The Renault listings are those for the team that ran from 1977-1985. The stats for Mercedes GP include those of BAR from 1999 to 2005, Honda Racing from 2006 to 2008 and Brawn GP from 2009. Red Bull Racing's figures include those of the Stewart GP and Jaguar Racing teams from which it evolved, while Force India's stats include those of Jordan, Midland and Spyker, plus Scuderia Toro Rosso's figures include those of Minardi.

2013 LAPS COVERED

Figures include all laps from practice, qualifying and race

2808	Nico Rosberg	2386	Kimi Räikkönen	5168	Lotus*
2771	Lewis Hamilton	2383	Max Chilton	5075	Ferrari
2743	Nico Hulkenberg	2326	Giedo van der Garde	4899	Force India
2703	Jenson Button	2241	Jules Bianchi	4737	Caterham
2681	Sebastian Vettel	160	Rodolfo Gonzalez	4660	Marussia
2678	Mark Webber	413	Heikki Kovalainen		
2674	Esteban Gutierrez	96	James Calado		
2669	Valtteri Bottas	41	Alexander Rossi		
2640	Daniel Ricciardo	37	Daniil Kvyat		
2618	Sergio Perez	20	Ma Qing Hua		
2577	Fernando Alonso				
2557	Jean-Eric Vergne	**CONSTRUCTORS**			
2525	Pastor Maldonado	5579	Mercedes		
2498	Felipe Massa	5417	Sauber		
2484	Romain Grosjean	5359	Red Bull		
2450	Adrian Sutil	5321	McLaren		
2440	Paul di Resta	5234	Toro Rosso		
2390	Charles Pic	5194	Williams		

2386 laps
Kimi Räikkönen

SAUBER-FERRARI
Hulkenberg–Gutierrez **18–1**

FORCE INDIA-MERCEDES
Di Resta–Sutil **12–7**

TORO ROSSO-FERRARI
Ricciardo–Vergne **15–4**

WILLIAMS-RENAULT
Bottas–Maldonado **11–8**

MARUSSIA-COSWORTH
Bianchi–Chilton **17–2**

CATERHAM-RENAULT
Pic– Van der Garde **11–8**

MOST USED CIRCUITS

63	**Monza**
60	Monaco
47	**Silverstone**
46	Spa-Francorchamps
40	**Nurburgring**
34	Montreal
33	**Hockenheim**
31	Interlagos
30	**Zandvoort**
26	Imola

MOST WINS AT A CIRCUIT

18	**Ferrari**	Monza
15	**McLaren**	Monaco
14	**Ferrari**	Nurburgring
13	**Ferrari**	Silverstone
12	**Ferrari**	Spa-Francorchamps
	McLaren	Silverstone
11	**Ferrari**	Hockenheim
	McLaren	Hungaroring
10	**Ferrari**	Montreal
9	**Williams**	Hockenheim

F1 HISTORY: MOST WINS IN A SEASON

13	Michael Schumacher	2004
	Sebastian Vettel	2013
11	Michael Schumacher	2002
	Sebastian Vettel	2011
9	Nigel Mansell	1992
	Michael Schumacher	1995
	Michael Schumacher	2000
	Michael Schumacher	2001
8	Mika Hakkinen	1998
	Damon Hill	1996
	Michael Schumacher	1994
	Ayrton Senna	1988
7	Fernando Alonso	2005
	Fernando Alonso	2006
	Jim Clark	1963
	Alain Prost	1984
	Alain Prost	1988
	Alain Prost	1993
	Kimi Räikkönen	2005
	Ayrton Senna	1991
	Jacques Villeneuve	1997
6	Mario Andretti	1978
	Alberto Ascari	1952
	Jim Clark	1965
	Juan Manuel Fangio	1954
	Damon Hill	1994
	James Hunt	1976
	Nigel Mansell	1987
	Kimi Räikkönen	2007
	Michael Schumacher	1998
	Michael Schumacher	2003
	Michael Schumacher	2006
	Ayrton Senna	1989
	Ayrton Senna	1990

CONSTRUCTORS

15	Ferrari	2002		Lotus	1973
	Ferrari	2004		McLaren	1999
	McLaren	1988		McLaren	2000
13	Red Bull	2013		McLaren	2012
12	McLaren	1984		Red Bull	2012
	Red Bull	2011		Tyrrell	1971
	Williams	1996		Williams	1991
11	Benetton	1995		Williams	1994
10	Ferrari	2000			
	McLaren	2005			
	McLaren	1989			
	Williams	1992			
	Williams	1993			
9	Ferrari	2001			
	Ferrari	2006			
	Ferrari	2007			
	McLaren	1998			
	Red Bull	2010			
	Williams	1986			
	Williams	1987			
8	Benetton	1994			
	Brawn GP	2009			
	Ferrari	2003			
	Lotus	1978			
	McLaren	1991			
	McLaren	2007			
	Renault	2005			
	Renault	2006			
	Williams	1997			
7	Ferrari	1952			
	Ferrari	1953			
	Ferrari	2008			
	Lotus	1963			

13 wins
Sebastian Vettel

F1 HISTORY: MOST WINS

91 Michael Schumacher		Jacques Villeneuve		*(Toleman, Benetton, Renault II)*
51 Alain Prost	**10** Gerhard Berger	**48** Red Bull *(including Stewart)*
41 Ayrton Senna	James Hunt	**35** Brabham
39 Sebastian Vettel	Ronnie Peterson	**27** Benetton
32 Fernando Alonso	Jody Scheckter	**23** Tyrrell
31 Nigel Mansell	**9** Mark Webber	**17** BRM
27 Jackie Stewart	**8** Denny Hulme	**16** Cooper
25 Jim Clark	Jacky Ickx	**15** Renault
Niki Lauda	**7** Rene Arnoux	**14** Mercedes GP
24 Juan Manuel Fangio	Juan Pablo Montoya	*(including Honda Racing and Brawn GP)*
23 Nelson Piquet	**6** Tony Brooks	**10** Alfa Romeo
22 Lewis Hamilton	Jacques Laffite	**9** Ligier
Damon Hill	Riccardo Patrese	Maserati
20 Mika Hakkinen	Jochen Rindt	Matra
Kimi Räikkönen	Ralf Schumacher	Mercedes
16 Stirling Moss	John Surtees	Vanwall
15 Jenson Button	Gilles Villeneuve	**4** Jordan
14 Jack Brabham	*(to current drivers)*	**3** March
Emerson Fittipaldi	**3** Nico Rosberg	Wolf
Graham Hill	**1** Pastor Maldonado	**2** Honda
13 Alberto Ascari		**1** BMW Sauber
David Coulthard	**CONSTRUCTORS**	Eagle
12 Mario Andretti	**221** Ferrari	Hesketh
Alan Jones	**181** McLaren	Penske
Carlos Reutemann	**114** Williams	Porsche
11 Rubens Barrichello	**79** Lotus	Shadow
Felipe Massa	**49** Lotus*	Stewart
		Toro Rosso

CIRCUITS WITH FASTEST LAP RECORDS

Monza	**159.909mph**
Silverstone	153.053mph
Spa-Francorchamps	**152.049mph**
Osterreichring	150.509mph
Hockenheim	**150.059mph**
Avus	149.129mph
Suzuka	**141.904mph**
A1-Ring	141.606mph
Reims	**141.424mph**
Melbourne	141.009mph

MOST RACES BEFORE BECOMING WORLD CHAMPION

180	**Nigel Mansell**
170	Jenson Button
121	**Kimi Räikkönen**
112	Mika Hakkinen
97	**Jody Scheckter**
87	Alain Prost
80	**Mario Andretti**
	Ian Jones
77	**Ayrton Senna**
67	Fernando Alonso
	Damon Hill

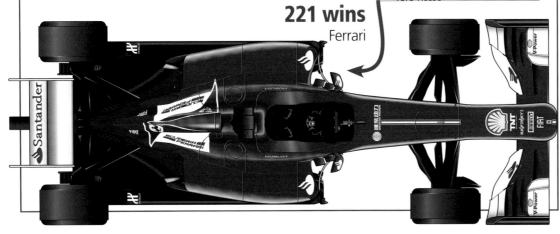

221 wins
Ferrari

RACES LED

142 Michael Schumacher
86 Ayrton Senna
84 Alain Prost
82 Fernando Alonso
65 Sebastian Vettel
62 David Coulthard
Kimi Räikkönen
58 Nelson Piquet
55 Nigel Mansell
53 Lewis Hamilton

CONSTRUCTORS

408 Ferrari
321 McLaren
220 Williams
150 Lotus
111 Lotus*
91 Brabham
77 Red Bull
40 BRM
38 Tyrrell
36 Renault

LAPS LED

5111 Michael Schumacher
2987 Ayrton Senna
2684 Alain Prost
2437 Sebastian Vettel
2089 Nigel Mansell
1943 Jim Clark
1921 Jackie Stewart
1735 Fernando Alonso
1600 Nelson Piquet
1592 Niki Lauda

CONSTRUCTORS

13640 Ferrari
10577 McLaren
7534 Williams
5498 Lotus
3001 Lotus*
2995 Red Bull
2717 Brabham
1493 Tyrrell
1347 BRM
1183 Renault

TYRE MANUFACTURER WITH MOST WINS

368 Goodyear
175 Bridgestone
102 Michelin
Pirelli
83 Dunlop
38 Firestone
10 Continental
8 Englebert

DRIVERS WITH MOST WINS WITHOUT A WORLD TITLE

16 Stirling Moss
13 David Coulthard
12 Carlos Reutemann
11 Rubens Barrichello
Felipe Massa
10 Gerhard Berger
Ronnie Peterson
9 Mark Webber
8 Jacky Ickx
7 Rene Arnoux

COUNTRIES WITH MOST WINS

227 Great Britain
145 Germany
101 Brazil
79 France
46 Finland
43 Italy
41 Austria
38 Argentina
35 Australia
32 Spain

F1 HISTORY: MOST POLE POSITIONS

Figures include all laps from practice, qualifying and race

68	Michael Schumacher		Mark Webber	**8**	Mercedes
65	Ayrton Senna	**12**	Gerhard Berger	**7**	Vanwall
45	Sebastian Vettel		David Coulthard	**5**	March
33	Jim Clark	**10**	Jochen Rindt	**4**	Matra
	Alain Prost	*(to current drivers)*		**3**	Force India *(including Jordan)*
32	Nigel Mansell	**8**	Jenson Button		Shadow
31	Lewis Hamilton	**4**	Nico Rosberg		Toyota
29	Juan Manuel Fangio	**1**	Nico Hulkenberg	**2**	Lancia
26	Mika Hakkinen		Pastor Maldonado	**1**	Sauber
24	Niki Lauda				Toro Rosso
	Nelson Piquet	**CONSTRUCTORS**			
22	Fernando Alonso	**207**	Ferrari		
20	Damon Hill	**154**	McLaren		
18	Mario Andretti	**127**	Williams		
	Rene Arnoux	**107**	Lotus		
17	Jackie Stewart	**58**	Red Bull		
16	Stirling Moss	**39**	Brabham		
	Kimi Räikkönen	**34**	Lotus*		
15	Felipe Massa		*(Toleman, Benetton, Renault II)*		
14	Alberto Ascari	**31**	Renault		
	Rubens Barrichello	**17**	Mercedes GP		
	James Hunt		*(including Brawn GP, Honda Racing, BAR)*		
	Ronnie Peterson	**14**	Tyrrell		
13	Jack Brabham	**12**	Alfa Romeo		
	Graham Hill	**11**	BRM		
	Jacky Ickx		Cooper		
	Juan Pablo Montoya	**10**	Maserati		
	Jacques Villeneuve	**9**	Ligier		

31 poles
Lewis Hamilton

F1 HISTORY: MOST FASTEST LAPS

76	Michael Schumacher		Lewis Hamilton	**40**	Brabham
41	Alain Prost		Alan Jones	**22**	Tyrrell
39	Kimi Räikkönen		Riccardo Patrese	**18**	Renault
30	Nigel Mansell	**12**	Rene Arnoux	**15**	BRM
28	Jim Clark		Jack Brabham		Maserati
25	Mika Hakkinen		Juan Pablo Montoya	**14**	Alfa Romeo
24	Niki Lauda	**11**	John Surtees	**13**	Cooper
23	Juan Manuel Fangio	*(to current drivers)*		**12**	Matra
	Nelson Piquet	**8**	Jenson Button		Mercedes GP
22	Sebastian Vettel	**4**	Nico Rosberg		*(Brawn GP, BAR, Honda Racing)*
21	Fernando Alonso	**2**	Sergio Perez		Prost *(including Ligier)*
	Gerhard Berger	**1**	Romain Grosjean	**9**	Mercedes
19	Damon Hill		Esteban Gutierrez	**7**	March
	Stirling Moss		Nico Hulkenberg	**6**	Vanwall
	Ayrton Senna			**5**	Sauber
	Mark Webber	**CONSTRUCTORS**			
18	David Coulthard	**228**	Ferrari		
17	Rubens Barrichello	**152**	McLaren		
15	Felipe Massa	**131**	Williams		
	Clay Regazzoni	**71**	Lotus		
	Jackie Stewart	**54**	Lotus*		
14	Jacky Ickx		*(Toleman, Benetton, Renault II)*		
13	Alberto Ascari	**41**	Red Bull		

19 fastest laps
Mark Webber

F1 HISTORY: MOST POINTS

(this figure is gross tally, ie. including scores that were later dropped)

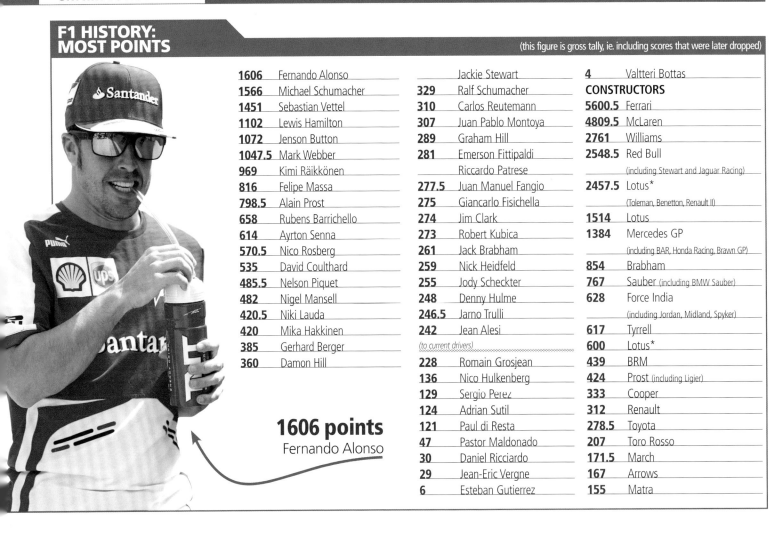

1606	Fernando Alonso
1566	Michael Schumacher
1451	Sebastian Vettel
1102	Lewis Hamilton
1072	Jenson Button
1047.5	Mark Webber
969	Kimi Räikkönen
816	Felipe Massa
798.5	Alain Prost
658	Rubens Barrichello
614	Ayrton Senna
570.5	Nico Rosberg
535	David Coulthard
485.5	Nelson Piquet
482	Nigel Mansell
420.5	Niki Lauda
420	Mika Hakkinen
385	Gerhard Berger
360	Damon Hill

1606 points
Fernando Alonso

	Jackie Stewart
329	Ralf Schumacher
310	Carlos Reutemann
307	Juan Pablo Montoya
289	Graham Hill
281	Emerson Fittipaldi
	Riccardo Patrese
277.5	Juan Manuel Fangio
275	Giancarlo Fisichella
274	Jim Clark
273	Robert Kubica
261	Jack Brabham
259	Nick Heidfeld
255	Jody Scheckter
248	Denny Hulme
246.5	Jarno Trulli
242	Jean Alesi

(to current drivers)

228	Romain Grosjean
136	Nico Hulkenberg
129	Sergio Perez
124	Adrian Sutil
121	Paul di Resta
47	Pastor Maldonado
30	Daniel Ricciardo
29	Jean-Eric Vergne
6	Esteban Gutierrez

4	Valtteri Bottas

CONSTRUCTORS

5600.5	Ferrari
4809.5	McLaren
2761	Williams
2548.5	Red Bull
	(including Stewart and Jaguar Racing)
2457.5	Lotus*
	(Toleman, Benetton, Renault II)
1514	Lotus
1384	Mercedes GP
	(including BAR, Honda Racing, Brawn GP)
854	Brabham
767	Sauber *(including BMW Sauber)*
628	Force India
	(including Jordan, Midland, Spyker)
617	Tyrrell
600	Lotus*
439	BRM
424	Prost *(including Ligier)*
333	Cooper
312	Renault
278.5	Toyota
207	Toro Rosso
171.5	March
167	Arrows
155	Matra

F1 HISTORY: DRIVERS' TITLES

7	Michael Schumacher
5	Juan Manuel Fangio
4	Alain Prost
	Sebastian Vettel
3	Jack Brabham
	Niki Lauda
	Nelson Piquet
	Ayrton Senna
	Jackie Stewart
2	Fernando Alonso
	Alberto Ascari
	Jim Clark
	Emerson Fittipaldi
	Mika Hakkinen
	Graham Hill
1	Mario Andretti
	Jenson Button
	Giuseppe Farina
	Lewis Hamilton
	Mike Hawthorn
	Damon Hill
	Phil Hill
	Denis Hulme

James Hunt
Alan Jones
Nigel Mansell
Kimi Räikkönen
Jochen Rindt
Keke Rosberg
Jody Scheckter
John Surtees
Jacques Villeneuve

CONSTRUCTORS' TITLES

16	Ferrari
9	Williams
8	McLaren
7	Lotus
4	Red Bull
3	Lotus*
2	Brabham
	Cooper
1	Brawn
	BRM
	Matra
	Tyrrell
	Vanwall

8 titles
McLaren

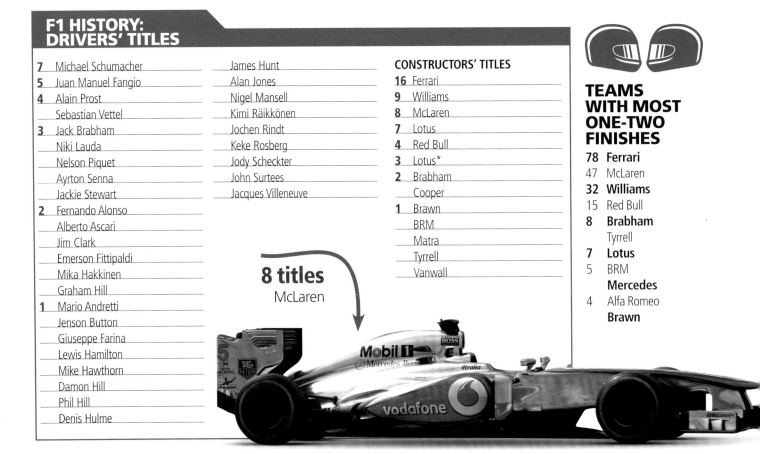

TEAMS WITH MOST ONE-TWO FINISHES

78	Ferrari
47	McLaren
32	Williams
15	Red Bull
8	Brabham
	Tyrrell
7	Lotus
5	BRM
	Mercedes
4	Alfa Romeo
	Brawn